Platform

Edited by
Jennifer Bonne
with
Michelle Benoit
and Patrick Herron

Still Life

Published by the Harvard University Graduate School of Design and Actar D.

Printed in Germany

ISBN 978-1-945150-17-3

Copyright 2016. President & Fellows of Harvard College.

All rights reserved. No part of this book may be reproduced in any form without prior written permission from the Harvard University Graduate School of Design.

The Harvard University Graduate School of Design is a leading center for education, information, and technical expertise on the built environment. Its Departments of Architecture, Landscape Architecture, Urban Planning and Design, Design Studies, and Design Engineering, offer master and doctoral degree programs, and provide the foundation for the school's Advanced Studies and Executive Education Programs.

Actar D
355 Lexington Avenue
8th Floor
New York, NY 10017
actar-d.com

Harvard University
Graduate School of Design
48 Quincy Street
Cambridge, MA 02138
gsd.harvard.edu

PLATFORM:
STILL LIFE
EDITORIAL TEAM

Jennifer Bonner
Faculty Editor

Michelle Benoit
Student Editor

Patrick Herron
Student Editor

GSD PUBLICATIONS TEAM

Jennifer Sigler
Editor in Chief

Claire Barliant
Managing Editor

Meghan Sandberg
Publications Coordinator

Travis Dagenais
Editorial Support

BOOK DESIGN

Neil Donnelly
Designer

Sean Yendrys
Production Assistant

STILL LIFE
PHOTOGRAPHY

Adam DeTour
Photographer

OTHER
PHOTOGRAPHY

Anita Kan
Photographer

Raymond Vincent Coffey
Assistant Photographer

Maggie Janik
Photographer

Yusuke Suzuki
Photographer

Zara Tzanev
Photographer

SPECIAL THANKS

The editors would like to thank Jennifer Sigler for the many in-depth discussions around the conceptual framework of the book. Without her expertise and enthusiasm, the process would not have been as rigorous. We would like to acknowledge the steady hand and professionalism of the GSD publications team, especially Claire Barliant and Travis Dagenais. It was an absolute pleasure to work with Neil Donnelly, whose idea for three graphic treatments and insistence on conceptual clarity brought a small idea about "Still Life" to life. Many thanks must also go to Adam DeTour, who braved a photography assignment with infectious curiosity and technical precision. Lastly, we would like to thank the many folks at the GSD who offered exhaustive support for the project, including many last-minute requests: Mohsen Mostafavi, K. Michael Hays, Iñaki Ábalos, Diane E. Davis, Mariana Ibañez, Silvia Benedito, Ed Eigen, Andrew Holder, Ann Baird Whiteside, Alastair Gordon, Hal Gould, Anita Kan, Raymond Vincent Coffey, David Zimmerman-Stuart, Dan Borelli, Meghan Sandberg, Shantel Blakely, Kevin Lau, Janina Mueller, Ryan Jacob, Erica George, Tom Childs, and Ben Halpern. The faculty editor would also like to thank a group of strong editors before her who took the time to pass along insightful information: Mariana Ibañez, Rosetta Elkin, Leire Asensio Villoria, and Zaneta Hong.

4
Letter from
the Dean:
Mohsen
Mostafavi

7
Letter from
the Editor:
Jennifer
Bonner

10
All Things Infinite

34
Salon

58
Glam Craft

72
Form Ruckus

94
Sample Samples

108
Out of Bounds

130
Locations

150
Sectional

177
Appendix

234
Lightness

246
On(e) Point

266
Heavy Matter

288
Variations on the Display

316
Hold the Color

330
Double-Takes

346
Lather, Rinse, Repeat

362
Drawing Props

Letter from the Dean

The ninth edition of *Platform*, like its predecessors, is a record of the work and other activities carried out at the Harvard University Graduate School of Design over the past academic year. And, like its predecessors, *Platform: Still Life* frames this work within the particular viewpoint of its editorial team, composed of a faculty member working in close collaboration with two students. The last edition of *Platform* adopted the rubric of the index—an index that provided a sense of the intellectual milieu of the school through the diversity of words used to describe and discuss the work. This time, the editors have chosen the conceptual parameters of the still life as a visual device for reconfiguring the work of the school. The projects of the students are in a sense remade as they are presented and literally re-presented within new compositional groupings. Through these relational techniques and arrangements, new potentials emerge.

As a device, the still life invariably produces an interruption as it decouples the project from its original context and juxtaposes it with a number of equally distinct projects. Here, unlike traditional paintings, the scalar difference of architectural, landscape, and urban projects defines their relational conditions as well as their role as part of a single still life. We are required to view each project in three separate states of becoming—the presumed original, its new relational condition as part of the still life, and then the overarching coherence of the still life itself. Despite its emphasis on the speed of visual interpretation, the documentation of the work requires a slow, methodical study of each element to comprehend the possible consequences of the whole. The method of the still life provides a rich and complex means of rereading projects that were never simple to begin with. What the editors of the book ask of us is to view the work of the school as multiple projects, at once singular and part of a collective.

    Regardless of the valuable and provocative artifice of the still life as a relational device, I would like to think this is what we do with our projects constantly—that is to say, we consider our architectural, landscape, and urban projects as instigators of multiple representations. Each project designed at the GSD bears the responsibility to consider and respond to a multiplicity of factors. From site to program, from construction to use, each project is an attempt at discovery—learning—and a potential contribution—gift—to a virtual or particular user. This framing of our students' projects also conveys that the work of the school is in a constant state of negotiation between creativity and social impact, between aesthetic pleasure and useful outcomes.

Mohsen Mostafavi
Dean and Alexander and Victoria Wiley
Professor of Design, Harvard University
Graduate School of Design

Letter from the Editor

Platform: Still Life begins with a list:
Infill, Big Box, Inverted, Las Vegas, Live
Work, Perimeter Plan, Pink Foam, Ruin,
and Pop-out.

   This is not your ordinary grocery list.
As editors, we assigned lists of words to
the student work selected for this book. We
based these words on design typologies,
course descriptions, first impressions, and
close readings that hint at what inspired and
nurtured the work shown here. Other kinds
of organizing systems and lists—floating
words, paint-by-number diagrams, and
still-life photographs—further reinterpret,
redact, and recombine the typical roll
call of student names and projects. With
blatant disregard for disciplinary silos, these
"lists" provide multiple readings of the
work produced at the Harvard University
Graduate School of Design over the 2015–
2016 academic year.

   How to present projects from academic
programs including architecture, landscape
architecture, urban planning and design,
design studies, and doctoral degrees, and
reveal the relationships among them rather

than confine them to their respective disciplines? How to take hundreds of white and brown chipboard models— the starting point for projects including mixed-use mid-rise towers, modest passive-housing typologies, and outlandish formal experiments—and make each look like the singular and fabulous object it is?

As curators, we chose to challenge conventional ways of viewing work by adopting the model of the still life. We invited photographer Adam DeTour to Piper Auditorium (GSD's beloved intellectual black box, where events, lectures, and studio crits take place) and turned it into a makeshift photo studio oozing colorful lighting and other special effects. To stage our still lifes, we borrowed freely from 16th-century oil paintings as well as food photography— a contemporary cultural obsession. We referenced advertisements in high-fashion magazines, Caravaggio's *Basket of Fruit* (1595), Giorgio Morandi's obsessive tracings, and Umberto Eco's *The Infinity of Lists* (2009). Most radically, perhaps, we experimented with color gels, partly in homage to the artist Barbara Kasten, whose influence we gratefully acknowledge, and partly to nudge our peers to take more liberties in the spectrums they choose, even during the earliest stages of making work. Students and faculty of these disciplines mingle all the time in the studios and review spaces and lobby of Gund Hall, debating and absorbing and playing with new ideas and disciplinary positions. Our goal was to reflect these overlaps, as well as the exuberance of production and enthusiasm for experimentation.

Lastly, I would like to draw the reader's attention to the Appendix, placed smack in the middle of the book, represented here in a list format akin to that of a telephone book. A record of lectures, exhibitions, courses, people, and more, it provides a respite from our raucous visuals with an assortment of factual information.

It is an intellectual exercise to make sense of the ways that Pink Foam, the Ruin, a Big Box, and Las Vegas are intertwined. We do it once—and then 15 more times.

Jennifer Bonner
Assistant Professor of Architecture;
Editor of *Platform: Still Life*

Infinite perpendicular lines help us understand our placement and relation to one another, other places, and other objects, through coordinate points, latitude, and longitude. Lines bring order, proportion, and regularity. Warped by perspective, lines project depth onto flat surfaces. Lines provide frames of reference. The work assembled here wrestles with the infinite condition of the grid, yet is also content with breaking away from it.

    Infinite grids become the thermal wrap for a police station in Gifu, Japan. Other projects recall the nine-square and mat typology. Projects in Boston, Las Vegas, and Bahrain all utilize the grid, but also gain momentum with a particular set of sub-agendas such as collective space, thermal mass, and mass housing for a new nation, respectively. Elevations, envelopes, and structural bays love the grid, but the trick is to flip it as the editors have done here: Superstudio's Supersurface becomes wallpaper for this grouping of GSD work. Look closely to spot work from the Rotterdam study abroad studio titled Smart Countrysides, which hacks the image of the Supersurface in Central Park, and makes an even trade with Amazon's big-box storage facility.

All Things Infinite

12

ALL THINGS INFINITE

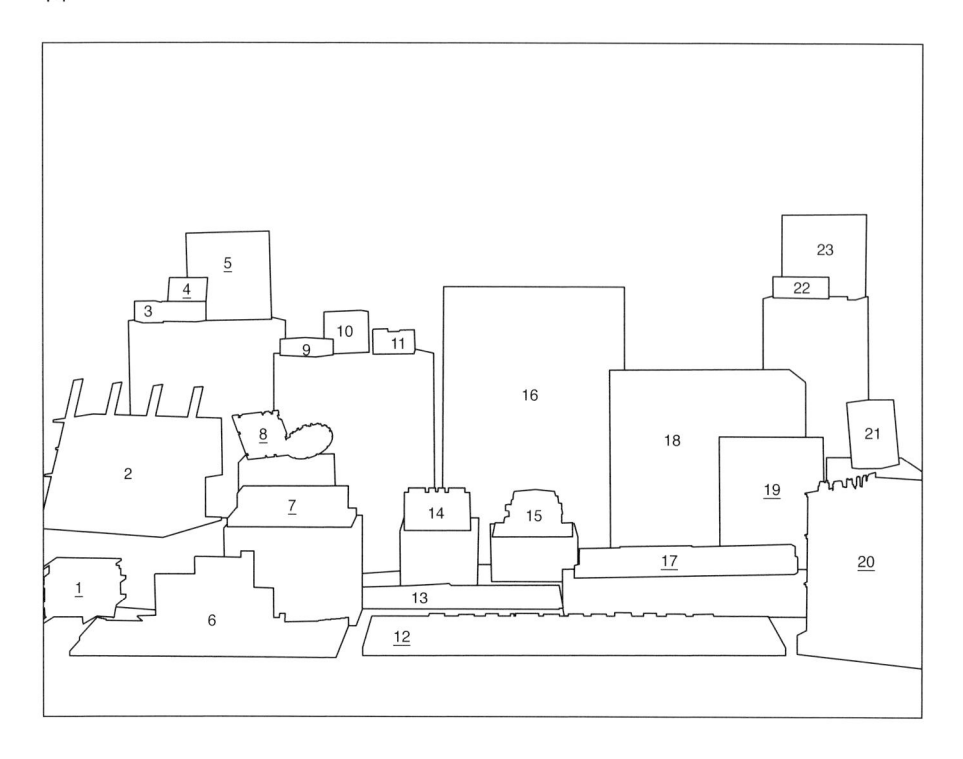

1 Infill
p. 16
Ruben Segovia
MArch II, 2017
Housing in Merida Yucatan:
  The Urban and the
  Territorial
Instructors: Jose Castillo,
  Diane E. Davis

2 Pocket
Xiaodi Yan
MLA II, 2016
Seoul Remade: Design of the
  "Kool" and the Everyday
Instructor: Niall Kirkland

3 Monumental Stair
Yu Kun Snoweria Zhang
MArch I, 2017
The Architectural Double in the
  Museum City
Instructors: Sharon
  Johnston, Mark Lee

4 Big Box
p. 18
Stephanie Conlan,
  Davis Owen, Sophia
  Panova, Jiayu Qiu
MArch I, 2017
Matthew Gindlesperger
MLA I AP, 2016
Bradley Kraushaar
MLA I, 2016
Christian Lavista
MArch II, 2016
Shiyao Liu
MAUD, 2016
Yuyangguang Mou
MArch II, 2017
Qun Pan, Xiaohan Wu
MAUD, 2017
Jennifer Saura
MLA I / MUP, 2016
David Zielnicki
MLA II, 2017
Smart Countrysides:
  Rotterdam Studio Abroad
Instructor: Rem Koolhaas

ALL THINGS INFINITE

5 Inverted
p. 20

Iman Fayyad
MArch I, 2016
Thesis: The Phantom Projective
Advisors: Preston Scott Cohen, Cameron Wu

6 Vertical

Yanchen Liu
MArch I, 2017
Alimentary Design: The Final Course
Instructors: Shohei Shigematsu, Christine Cheng

7 Las Vegas
p. 22

Hanguang Wu
MArch I, 2018
Architecture Core III: Integrate
Instructor: John May

8 Live Work
p. 24

Jyri Eskola
MArch I AP, 2016
Thesis: A Day in the Sun: A Toolkit for the New Productive Domestic
Advisor: Carles Muro

9 151,000 Sq. Ft.

Insu Kim
MArch I, 2017
The Architectural Double in the Museum City
Instructors: Sharon Johnston, Mark Lee

10 Sunken Court

Poap Panusittikorn
MArch II, 2017
The Architectural Double in the Museum City
Instructors: Sharon Johnston, Mark Lee

11 Nine Square

Justin Jiang
MArch I, 2017
The Architectural Double in the Museum City
Instructors: Sharon Johnston, Mark Lee

12 Bahrain
p. 26

Ali Karimi
MArch I, 2016
Thesis: Good Arab, ~~Bad City~~
Advisor: Christopher C. M. Lee

13 Endless

Gideon Finck
MLA I, 2018
Landscape Core I
Instructor: Luis Callejas

14 Rectangular

Ya Gao
MArch I, 2018
Architecture Core III: Integrate
Instructor: Elizabeth Whittaker

15 Structural Bay

Benjamin Bromberg Gaber
MArch I, 2019
Architecture Core II: Situate
Instructor: Max Kuo

16 Boston

Esther Bang, Haram Kim, Shaina Kim, Bryant Nguyen
MArch I, 2018
Architecture Core IV: Relate
Instructor: Luis Callejas

17 Perimeter Plan
p. 28

Suthata Jiranuntarat
MArch I, 2019
Architecture Core I: Project
Instructor: Cristina Parreno Alonso

18 Enclosed

Tamotsu Ito
MArch II, 2016
Dualisms: A House, a Palace
Instructor: Iñaki Ábalos

19 Pink Foam
p. 30

Joanne Cheung, Douglas Harsevoort, Steven Meyer, Jennifer Shen, Yiliu Shen-Burke
MArch I, 2018
Unbuilt, Design Miami
Advisors: Dan Borelli, Luis Callejas, K. Michael Hays, Hanif Kara, Benjamin Prosky

20 Ruin
p. 32

Juan Sala
MArch II, 2017
Territorio Guaraní III
Instructor: Jorge Silvetti

21 Pop-Out

Khorshid Naderi-Azad
MArch I, 2019
Architecture Core I: Project
Instructor: Mariana Ibañez

22 Mat

Jia Gu
MArch I, 2017
Ranjit Korah
MArch II, 2016
Work Environments 2: Glass Works
Instructor: Florian Idenburg

23 Envelope

Zahra Safaverdi
MArch II, 2017
Third Natures: London's Typological Imagination
Instructors: Cristina Díaz Moreno, Efrén García Grinda

Infill

Ruben Segovia
MArch II, 2017

Housing in Merida Yucatan: The Urban and the Territorial

Instructors
Jose Castillo,
Diane E. Davis

ALL THINGS INFINITE — Option Studio — 17

This is the third studio sponsored by Infonavit, the National Workers Housing Institute of Mexico. As in previous years, this studio sought to generate new ideas for fostering sustainable urbanism through housing, and addressed the spatial and social concerns related to sprawl through the lens of a comprehensive and critical planning and urban design studio.

Smart Countrysides: Rotterdam Studio Abroad

Instructor Rem Koolhaas

The countryside is where all faculties of our primitive origins were originally automated. Today, thanks to robotics and tablets, the burden of laboring on the land has successfully been lifted. The alternative to this "smart" countryside is the "neo-rustic": a refuge for our new, spiritual engagements, satisfying our hunger for darkness, isolation, and authenticity. This studio explored the countryside's political form and its potential as a new space for testing the implications of technological and data-driven innovation, and analyzed the effects of our increasing absence from off-the-radar developments. It simultaneously imagined spaces for mental release, forging social, neo-rural coalitions that could develop and counteract the effects of losing open space to the built environment.

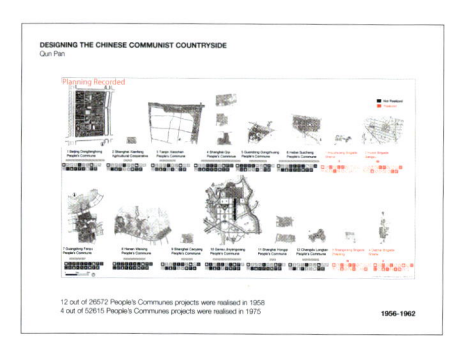

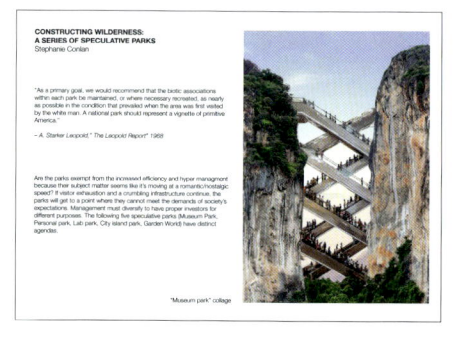

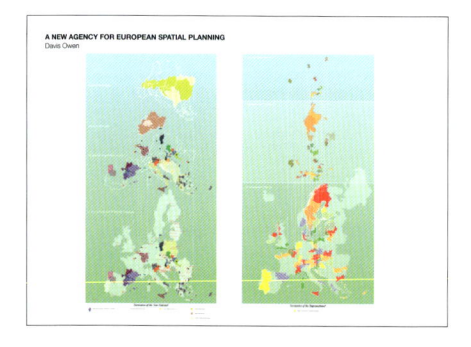

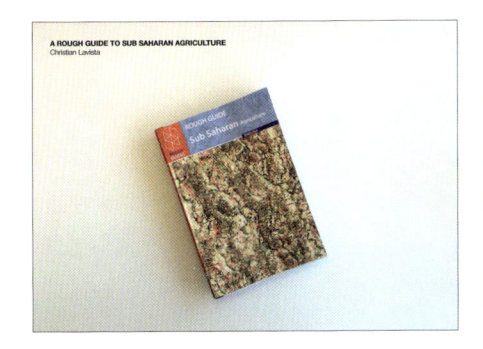

ALL THINGS INFINITE   Option Studio   19

A ROUGH GUIDE TO SUB SAHARAN AGRICULTURE
Christian Lavista

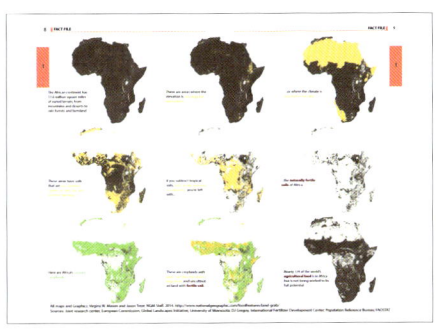

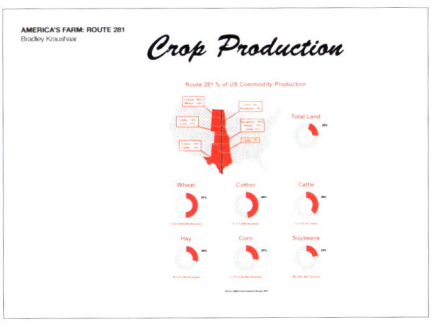

AMERICA'S FARM: ROUTE 281
Bradley Kraushaar

AMERICA'S FARM: ROUTE 281
Bradley Kraushaar

COUNTRYSIDE STANDARD X: THE MASS MIGRATION OF EXCEPTION
Sophia Panovska

PROFILING DATA CENTERS
Jennifer Saura

GRADATIM FEROCITER: GRADUALLY FIERCELY, THE ARCHITECTURE OF AMAZON
David Zielnicki

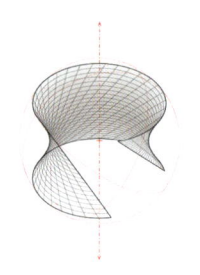

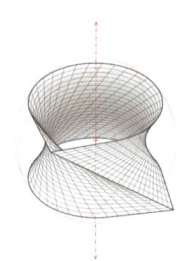

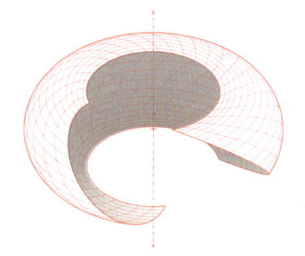

Inverted

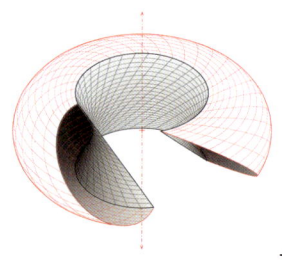

Iman Fayyad
MArch I, 2016

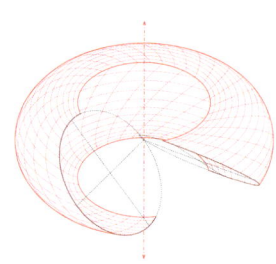

Thesis
The Phantom Projective

Advisors
Preston Scott Cohen,
Cameron Wu

This thesis is an investigation of the production of form—both real and illusory. Using variations of the mathematical principle of inversion, a "phantom" object is geometrically transformed to create a perceived reality that is, in fact, fictional.

ALL THINGS INFINITE / Thesis Project / 21

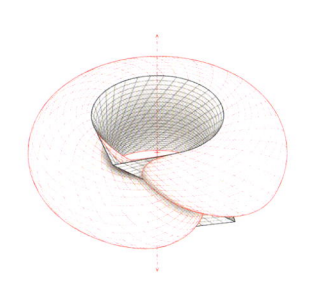

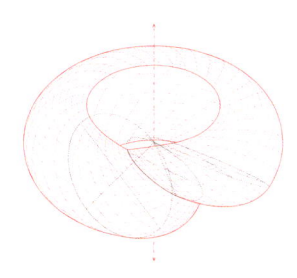

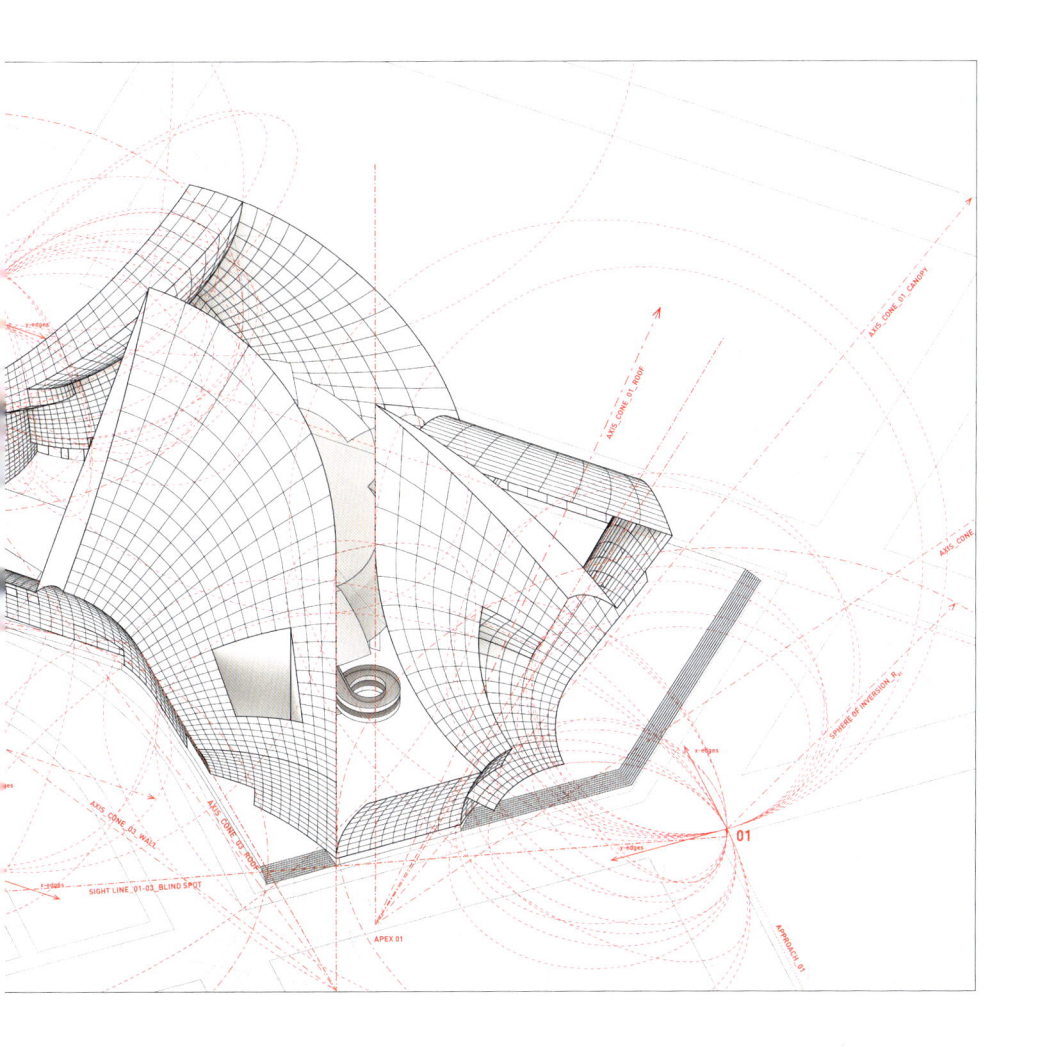

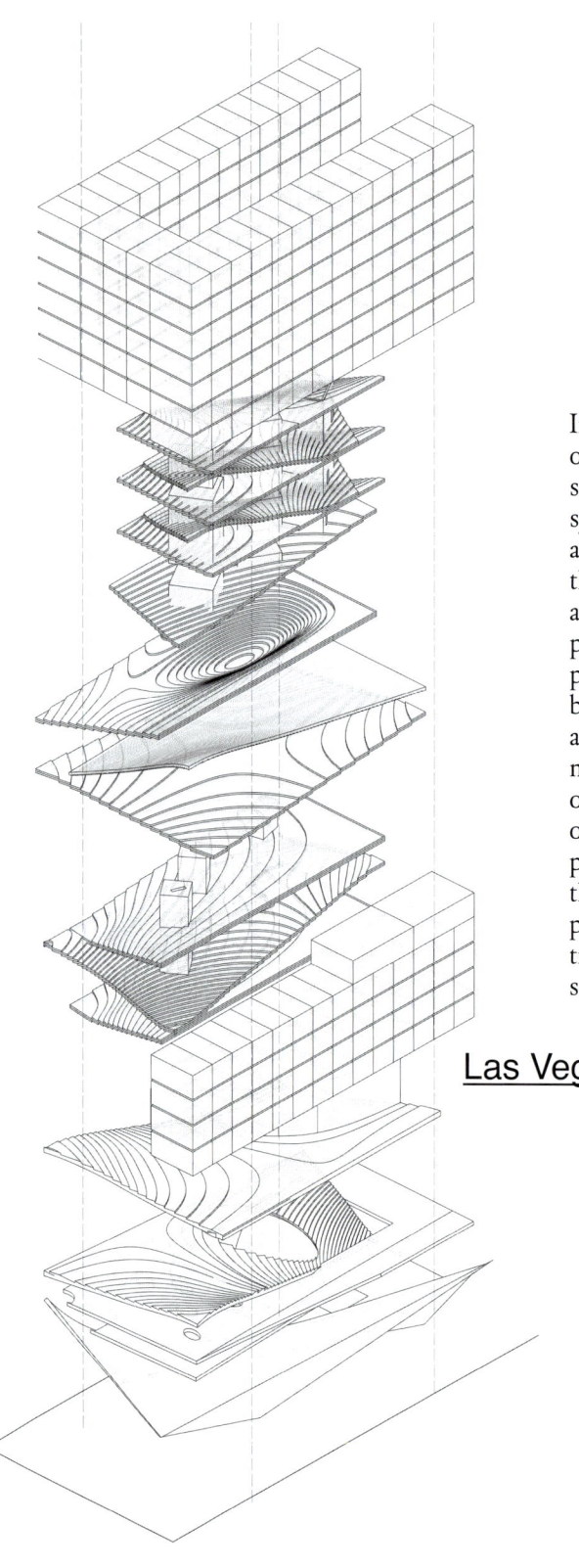

In the third semester of Architecture Core studio, structural systems, envelope design, and environmental and thermodynamic processes are addressed in a single project. The project pictured here is propelled by the idea of intermezzo, a musical interlude connecting movements in an opera. It is the condition of intermezzo that the project celebrates, through the alliance of programs and levels that traditionally remain separate.

Las Vegas

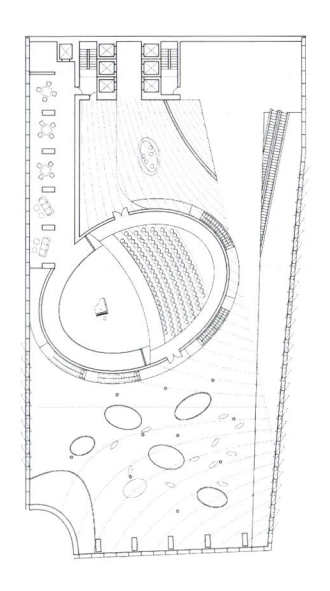

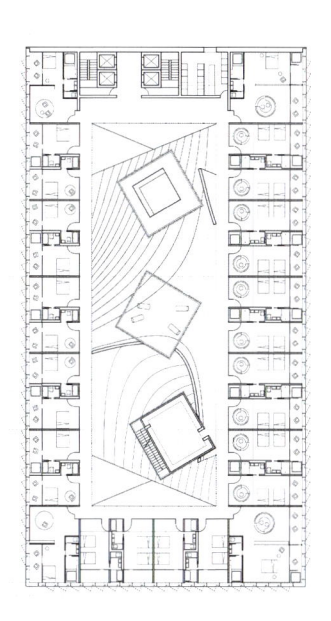

ALL THINGS INFINITE　　　　Core Studio　　　　23

Hanguang Wu
MArch I, 2018

Architecture Core
III: Integrate

Instructor
John May

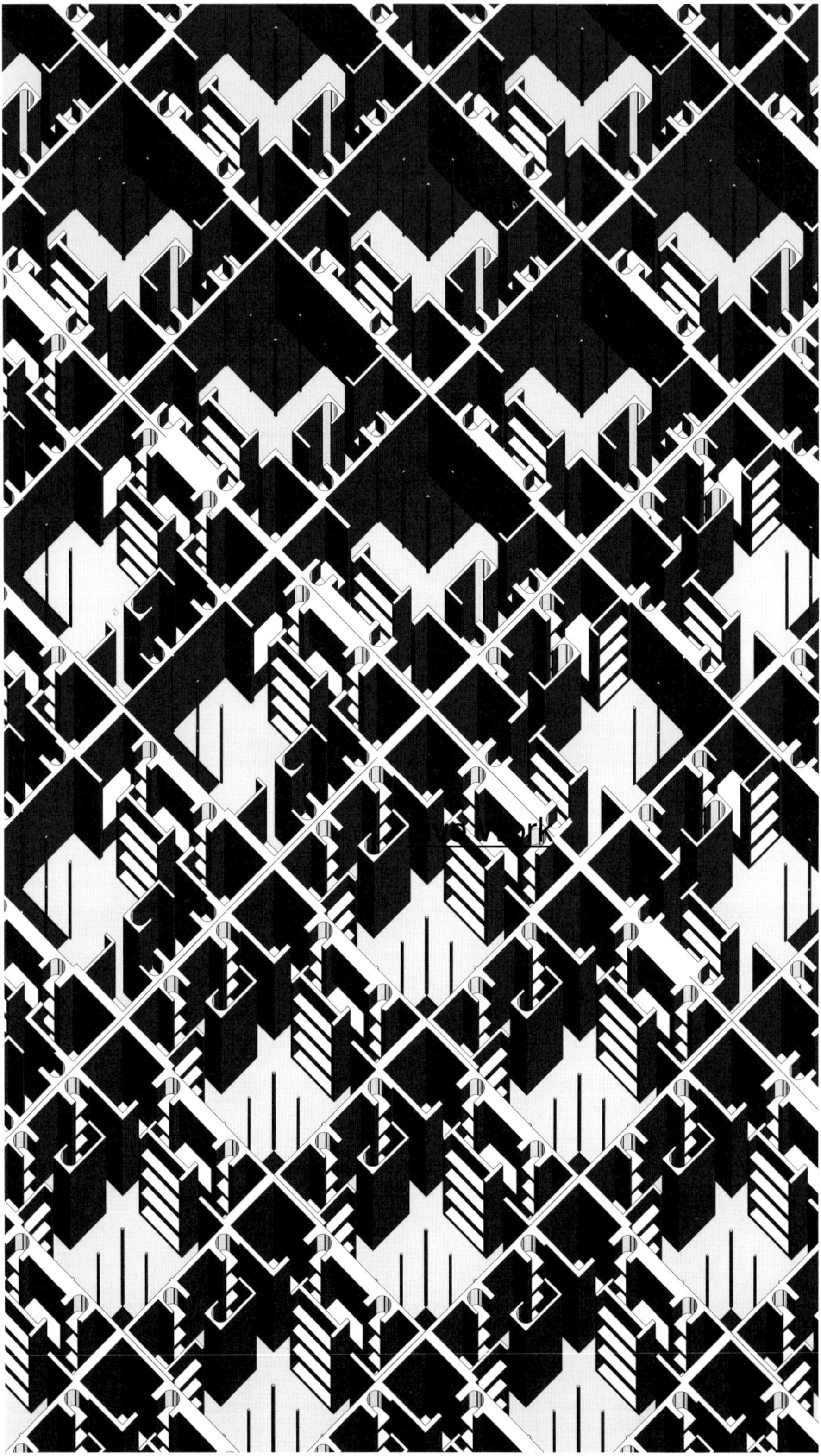

Jyri Eskola
MArch I AP, 2016

Thesis
A Day in the Sun: A Toolkit for the New Productive Domestic

Advisor
Carles Muro

This thesis proposes an architectural toolkit for the creation of residential prototypes receptive to future modes of production and living. The project objective is to shift housing and the domestic from minor players to key elements in the discussion of urban sociopolitical and economic conditions.

Government-built housing tells the story of the Arab city-state over the past century, marking the transitions from tribal protectorate to a modernizing nation to today's politically hostage rentier state. This thesis looks at government housing as a state tool for reinventing the citizen and the city, asking how housing can recuperate the national as a 21st-century project.

Ali Karimi
MArch I, 2016

Thesis
Good Arab, ~~Bad City~~

Advisor
Christopher C. M. Lee

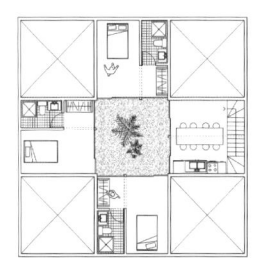

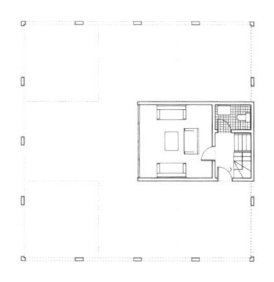

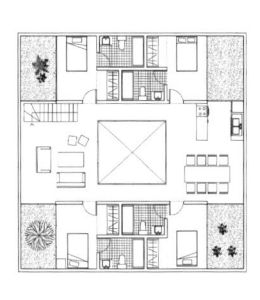

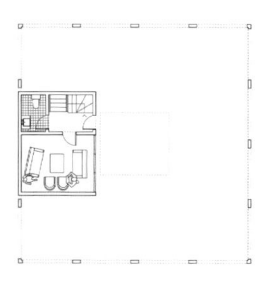

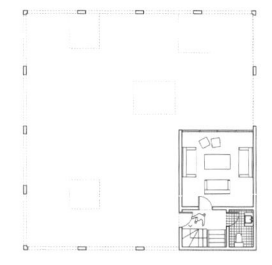

Bahrain

ALL THINGS INFINITE — Thesis Project — 27

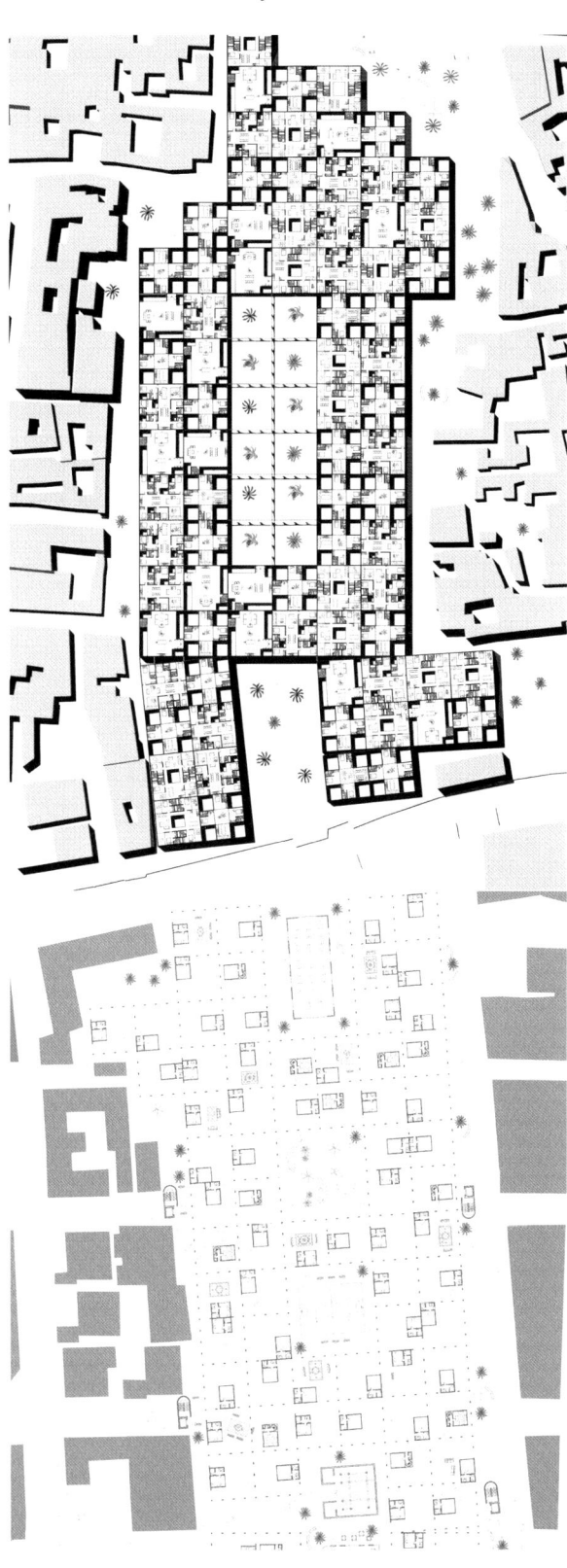

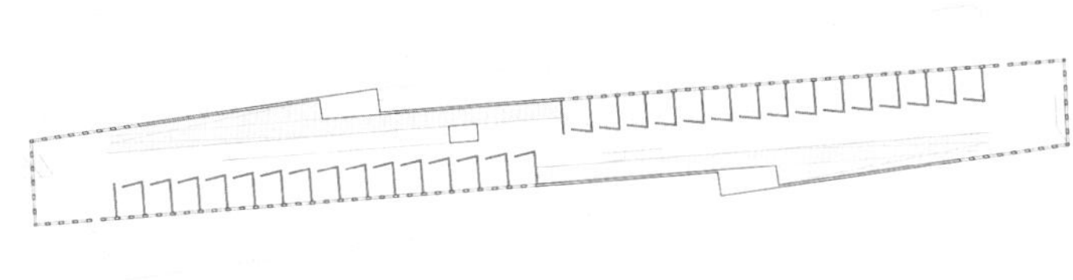

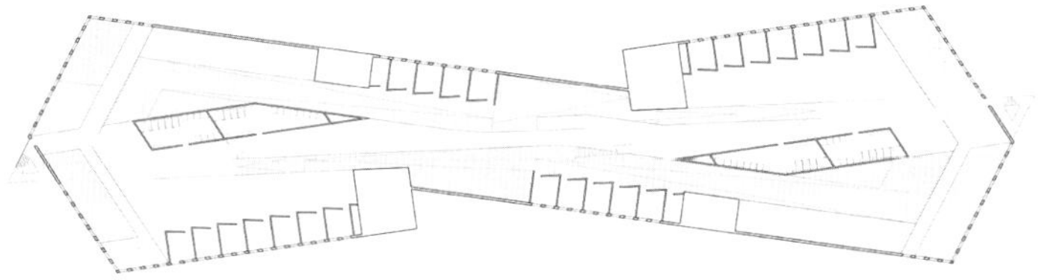

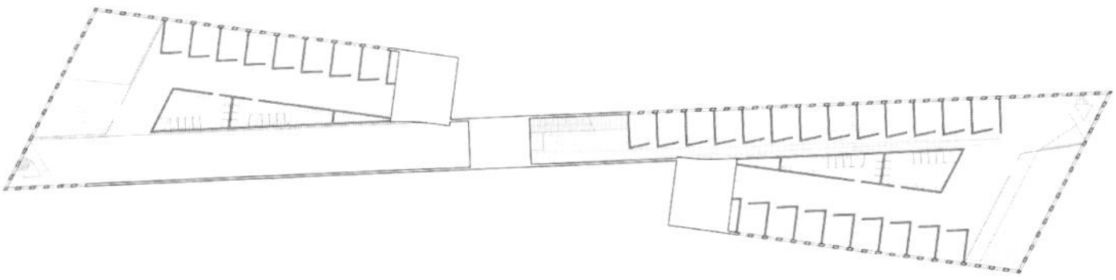

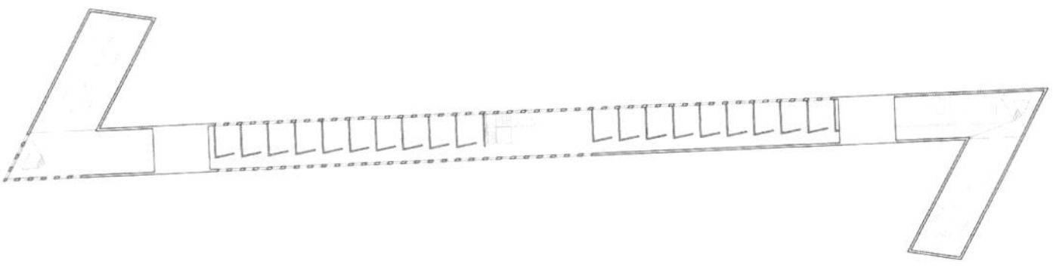

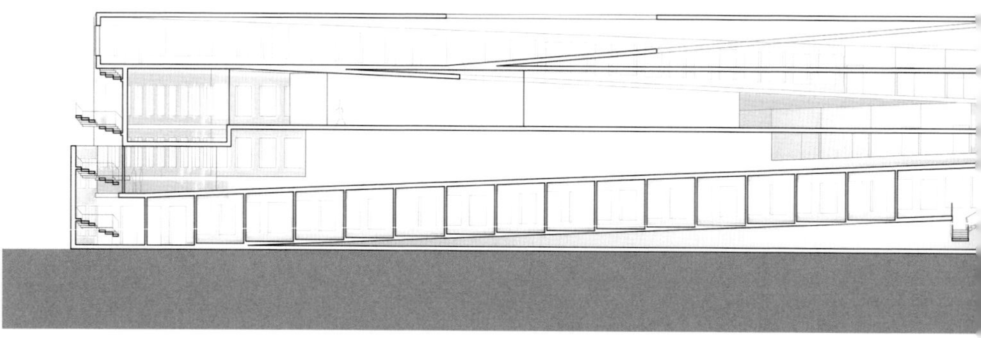

ALL THINGS INFINITE — Core Studio

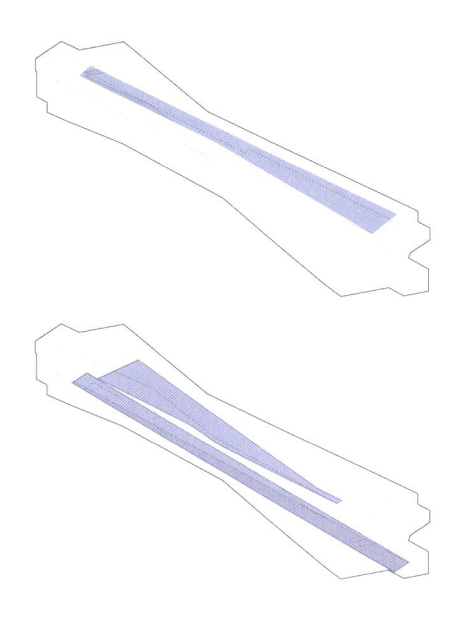

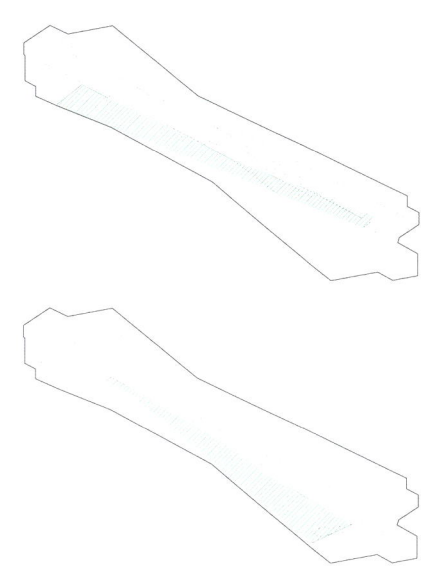

In the first semester of Architecture Core, students are given a series of design challenges that require them to question the role of innovation within architecture. Here, the "perimeter plan" assignment stretches the facade to its limits, forcing the levels of the building to cross and overlap.

Suthata Jiranuntarat
MArch I, 2019

Architecture Core I: Project

Instructor
Cristina Parreno Alonso

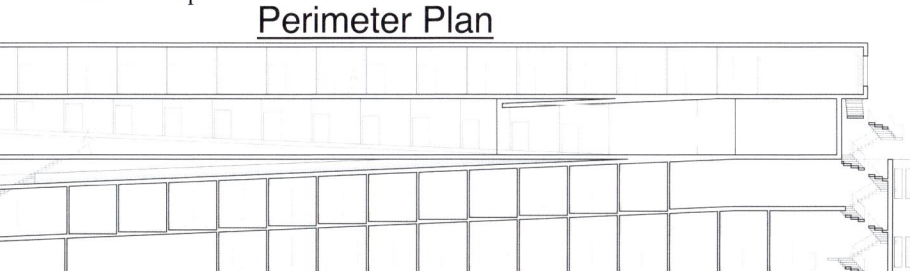

Perimeter Plan

Joanne Cheung, Douglas Harsevoort, Steven Meyer, Jennifer Shen, Yiliu Shen-Burke
MArch I, 2018

Unbuilt, Design Miami

Advisors
Dan Borelli,
Luis Callejas,
K. Michael Hays,
Hanif Kara,
Benjamin Prosky

For every building that exists, there is a prospective and invisible city that has yet to be built. In this sense, design is the production of knowledge not only for a singular structure but for an entire field of possibilities. The entrance pavilion for Design Miami 2015, Unbuilt, brings this invisible city to light. The pavilion is a canopy of 198 hand-crafted architectural models that showcases a range of experimental and speculative projects by students and faculty at the GSD. While these projects may never be built, the models manifest the skills, research, and imagination of their designers.

ALL THINGS INFINITE Competition 31

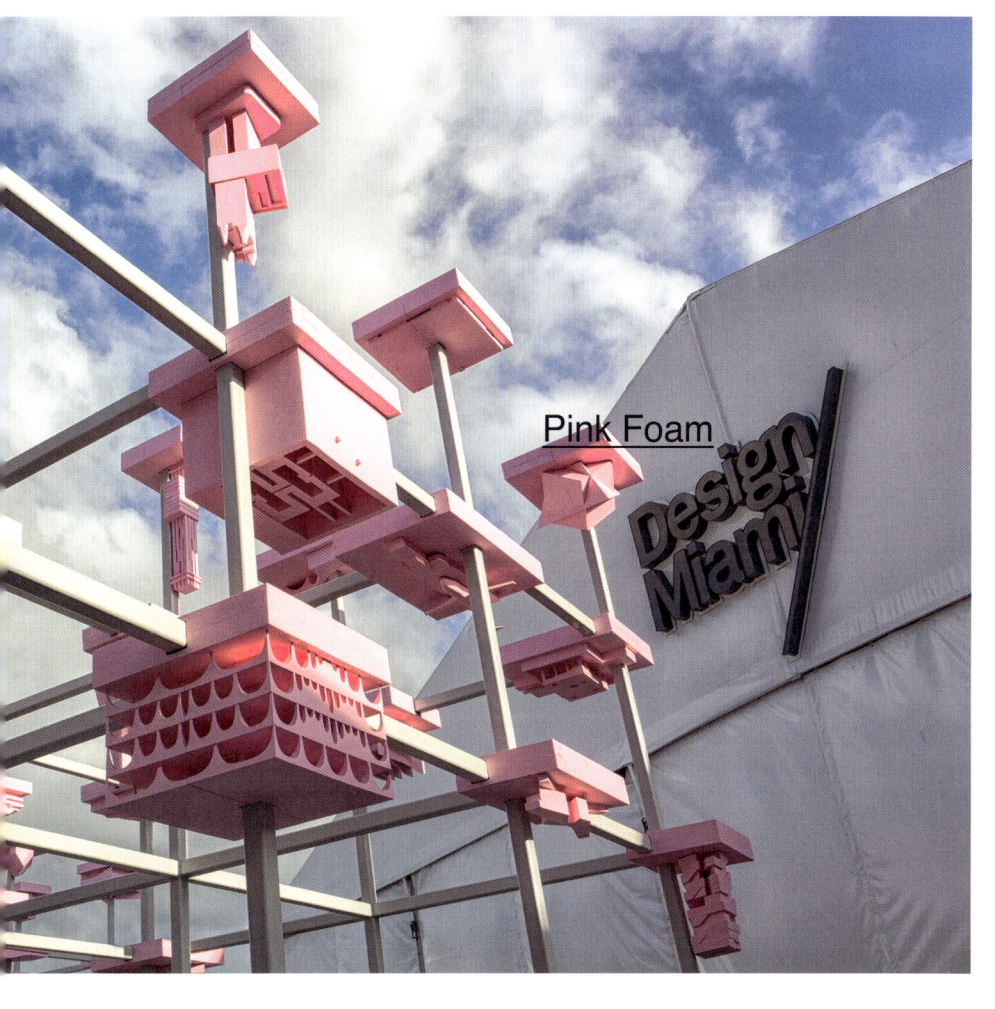

Pink Foam

This was the third consecutive studio to investigate architectural strategies and modes of intervention in the culturally and environmentally rich Territorio Guaraní, the South American region broadly defined by the Paraná River system and engaging adjacent large subtropical areas of Argentina, Brazil, Paraguay, and Uruguay.

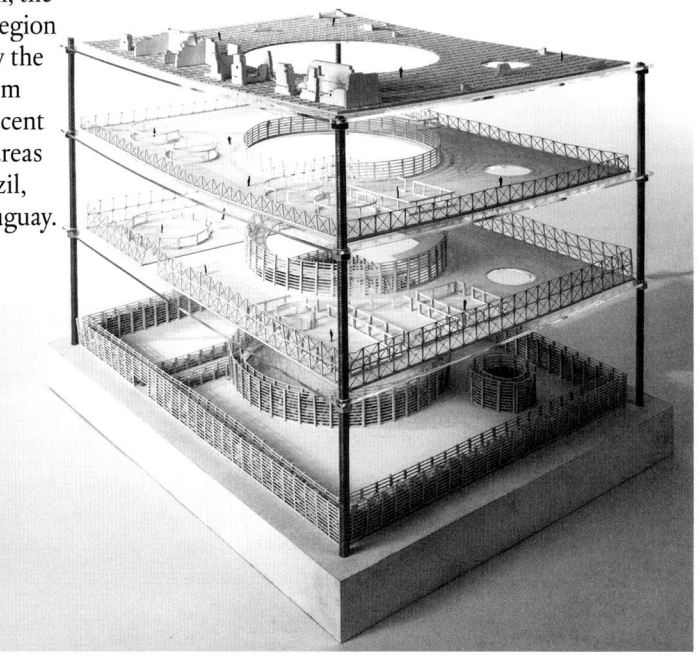

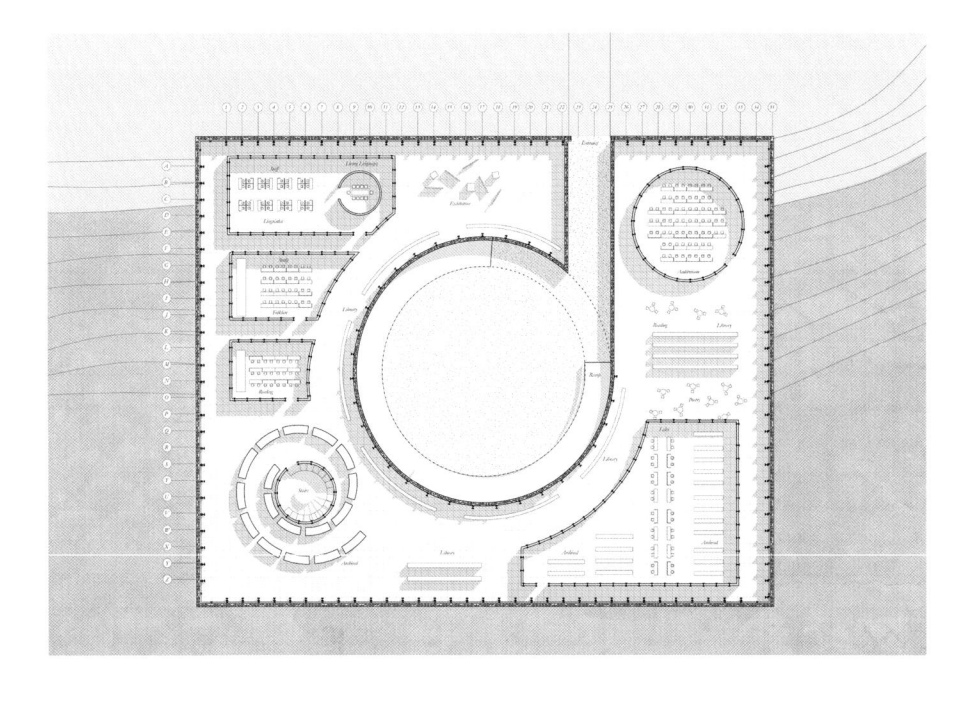

Juan Sala
MArch II, 2017

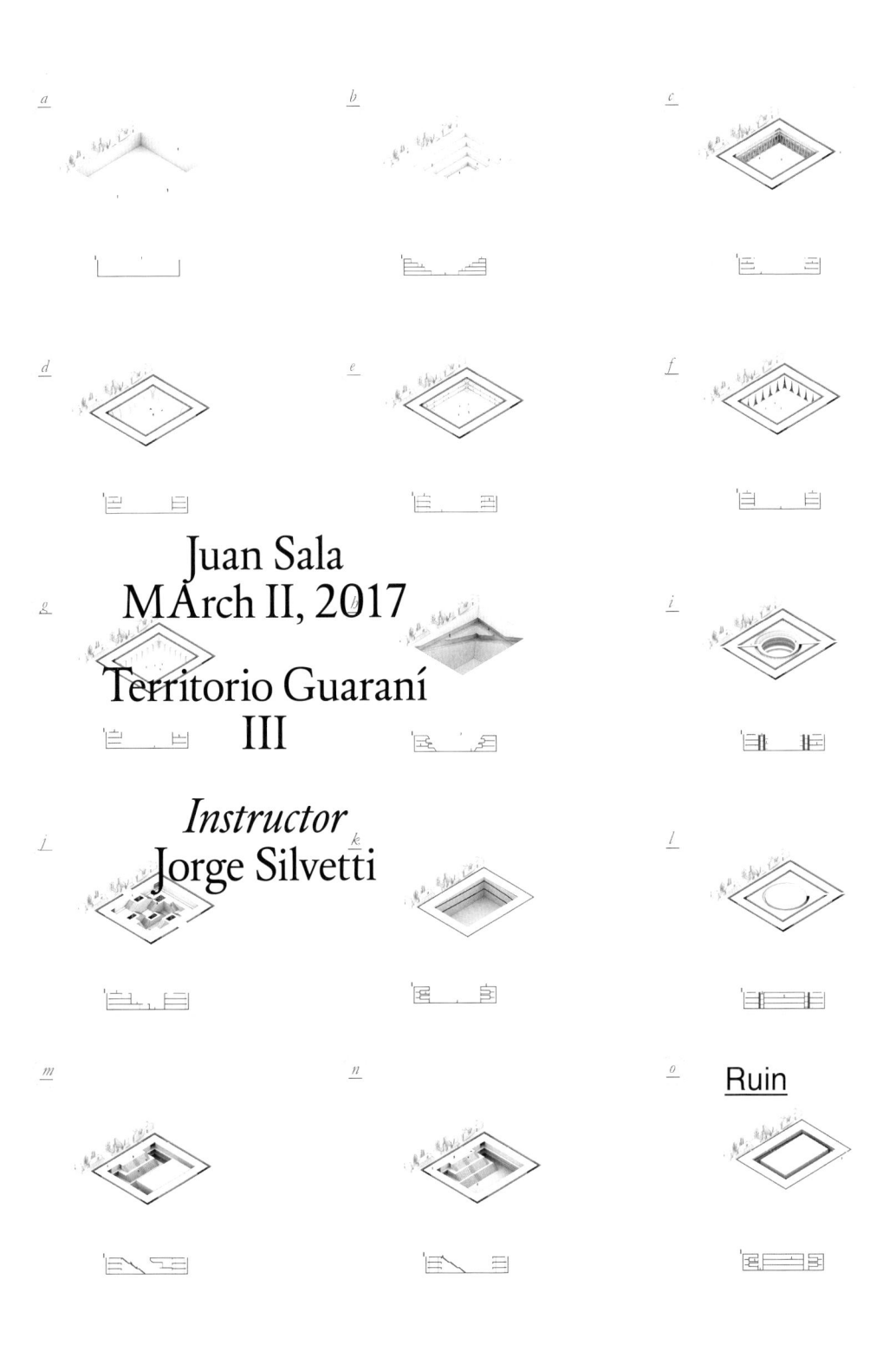

Territorio Guaraní
III

Instructor
Jorge Silvetti

Ruin

The Still, It Still Breathes

Still life? Is it not paradoxical to associate "still" with "life"? To associate something that evokes lifelessness with the organic and pulsating? When we breathe, we're not motionless. On the grand scale of time, and referring to Eadweard Muybridge's unpacking of motion, this image is indeed (a one-of-a-kind) "still" in the life of the GSD; a manifestation of desires and attitudes in a particular timeline of associated knowledge. This is one "still" of a *tempo* that is in constant mutation. More than lifeless, this image stands as an active witness—it proposes a moment of focus and captures an instance of the state of design(ing). This collage collapses past and future; it adds unfixed perceptions to the stillness of a moment and opens it up to discovery and imagining through design. So, voilà—the "still" breathes. And it's pink! Can't you heart it?

Silvia Benedito
Assistant Professor of
Landscape Architecture

This *Platform* still life plays off of traditional Parisian salons (or the informal chatter that unfolds inside a hair salon). The goal is to incite and encourage discourse by showcasing compositions that exemplify intentionality and mastery of content. Sixty-eight-inch-high images of experiential sequences, made for urban design and landscape architecture studios, confront complex urban sites by deploying connectivity, contemporary programs, and accessibility. Another landscape architecture studio takes on Moscow's severe traffic problems by imagining large-scale strategies within existing infrastructure, in the form of a giant concentric mountain. Yet another tackles the rising water levels threatening Miami Beach.

    This collection of work engages "real" design problems in a variety of global contexts, but it doesn't stop at superficial solutions. These projects dive deep, offering optimistic takes on the future with representational agendas to back them up.

Salon

38

SALON

39

40

SALON

1 Betula papyrifera

Mengfan Sha
MLA I, 2018
Landscape Core II
Instructor: Jill Desimini

2 Blueprint
p. 42

Shao Lun Lin, Marcus Mello
MArch I, 2018
Long Chuan Zhang
MArch I AP, 2018
Architecture Core IV: Relate
Instructor: Belinda Tato

3 Chongqing

Marios Botis
MAUD, 2017
"Regular City" in Chongqing: Searching for Domesticated Superstructures
Instructor: Joan Busquets

4 Jakarta
p. 44

Andrew Boyd
MLA I, 2016
Michael Keller
MAUD / MLA I AP, 2016
Jakarta: Models of Collective Space for the Extended Metropolis
Instructor: Felipe Correa

5 Chart
p. 46

Timothy Logan
MArch II, 2016
Meteorological Architecture
Instructor: Philippe Rahm

6 Retreat
p. 48

Bin Zhu
MAUD, 2016
Making Omishima the Best Island to Live on in Japan: Tokyo Studio Abroad
Instructor: Toyo Ito

7 FAR
p. 50

William Adams, Long Chuan Zhang
MArch I AP, 2018
Alice Armstrong
MArch I, 2018
Architecture Core IV: Relate
Instructor: Andrew Holder

8 Curiosity

Noel Fah
ETH Zurich Exchange Program, 2016
The Naked Eye: Medusae & Other Stories
Instructors: Eelco Hooftman, Bridget Baines

9 Block

Kyriaki Kasabalis
MAUD, 2016
Extreme Urbanism IV: Looking at Hyper Density— Dongri, Mumbai
Instructor: Rahul Mehrotra

10 Lagoon
p. 52

Alexander Cassini
MLA I, 2016
Lagoa das Furnas: A Dynamic Approach to a Landscape Project
Instructors: João Nunes, João Gomes da Silva

11 Traffic Jam
p. 54

Mengchen Xia
MAUD, 2016
Moscow's Future: Tied Up in Traffic
Instructor: Martha Schwartz

12 River

Thomas Nideroest
MLA II, 2016
Ruben Segovia
MArch II, 2017
Urban Blackholes: Development and Heritage in the Lima Metropolis
Instructor: Jean Pierre Crousse

13 Cocos nucifera
p. 56

Daniel Widis
MLA I, 2016
Miami Rise and Sink: Design for Urban Adaptation
Instructor: Rosetta Elkin

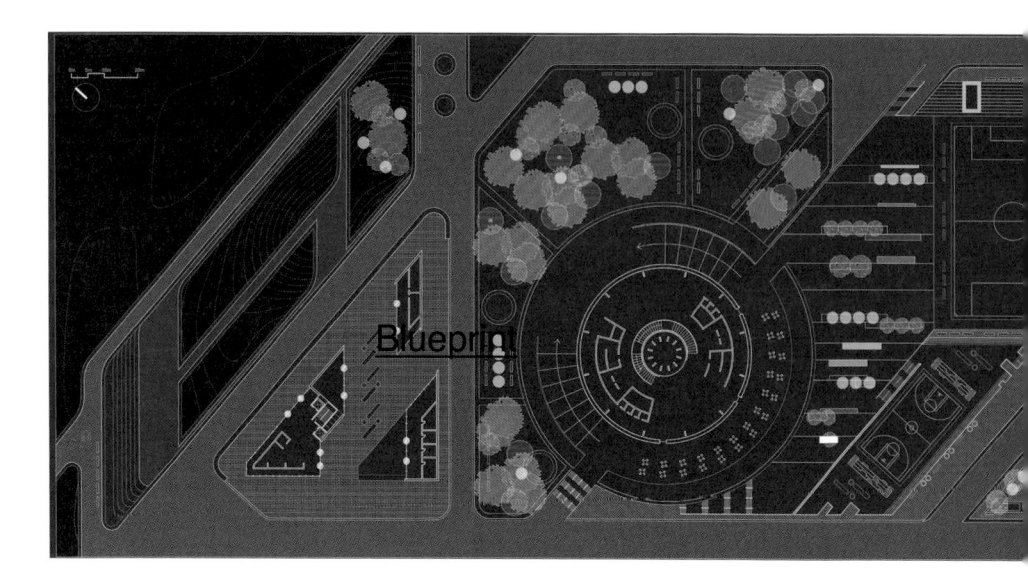

Shao Lun Lin,
Marcus Mello
MArch I, 2018

Long Chuan Zhang
MArch I AP, 2018

Architecture Core
IV: Relate

Instructor
Belinda Tato

The drawings pictured here were produced for the fourth Architecture Core studio, Relate, which explores the role of housing as a central component of the physical fabric of the city and as a fundamental site of negotiation between the individual and the collective in the search for new forms of inhabitation.

SALON — Core Studio — 43

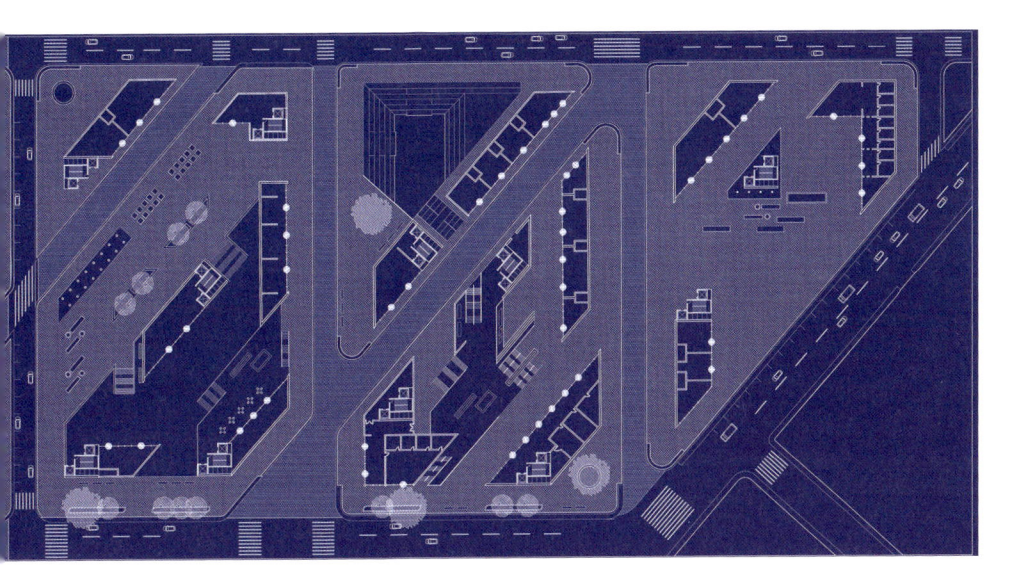

Andrew Boyd
MLA I, 2016

Michael Keller
MAUD / MLA I AP, 2016

Jakarta: Models of Collective Space for the Extended Metropolis

Instructor
Felipe Correa

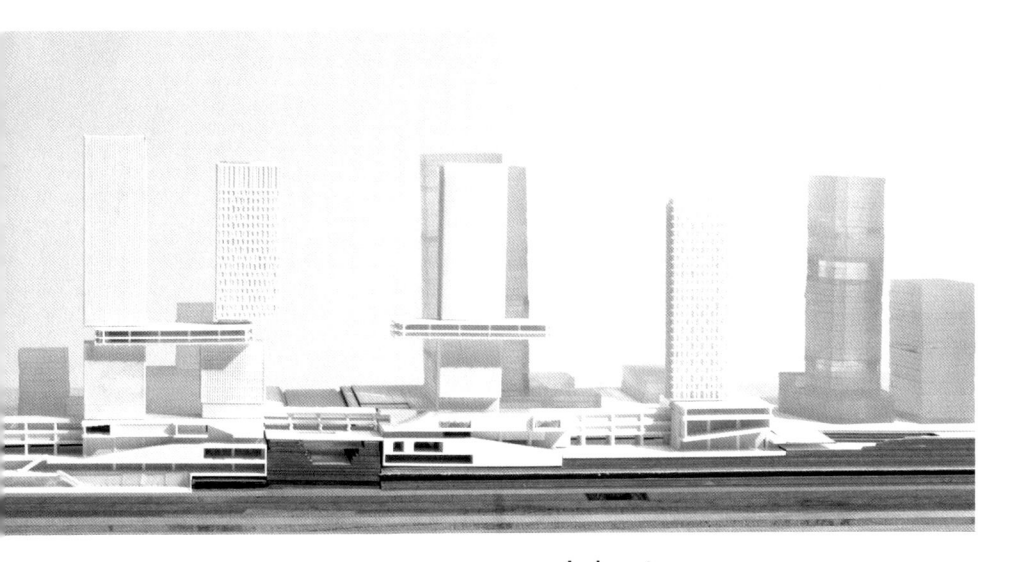

Jakarta

This studio examined the role of mass-transit infrastructure as a driver for new models of collective space, in a context of extreme rapid urbanization. As an alternative typology to the tower and plinth, this project proposes an urbanism of clustered towers, urban terraces, and suspended amenities.

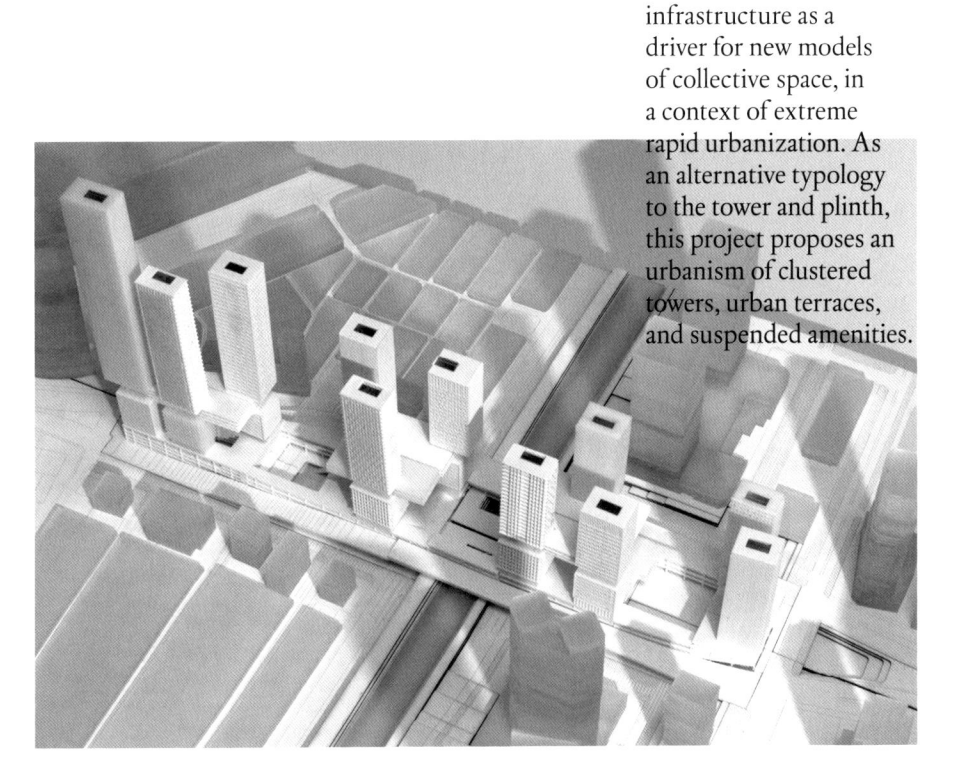

Timothy Logan
MArch II, 2016

Instructor
Philippe Rahm

Meteorological Architecture

PRESSURE
(research)

SCALE I: PLANETARY

$P = \dfrac{F}{A}$

SCALE II: ARCHITECTURAL

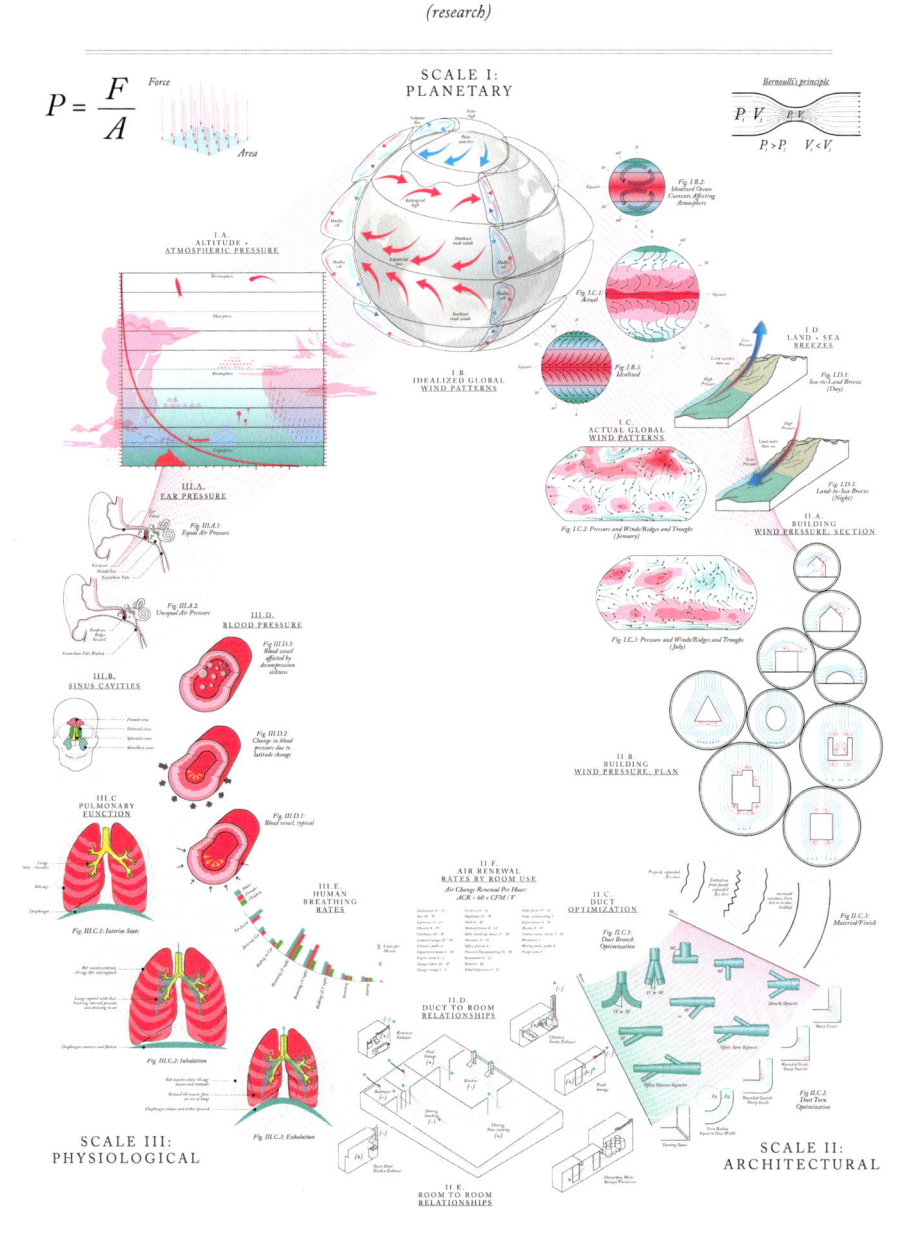

SCALE III: PHYSIOLOGICAL

SALON   Option Studio   47

Climate change is forcing us to rethink architecture and shift our approach from focusing solely on the visual and functional toward one that is more sensitive and attentive to the invisible, climate-related aspects of space. The task of this studio was not to build images and functions, but to open up climates and interpretations.

CLIMATIC FORCING
(climate research)

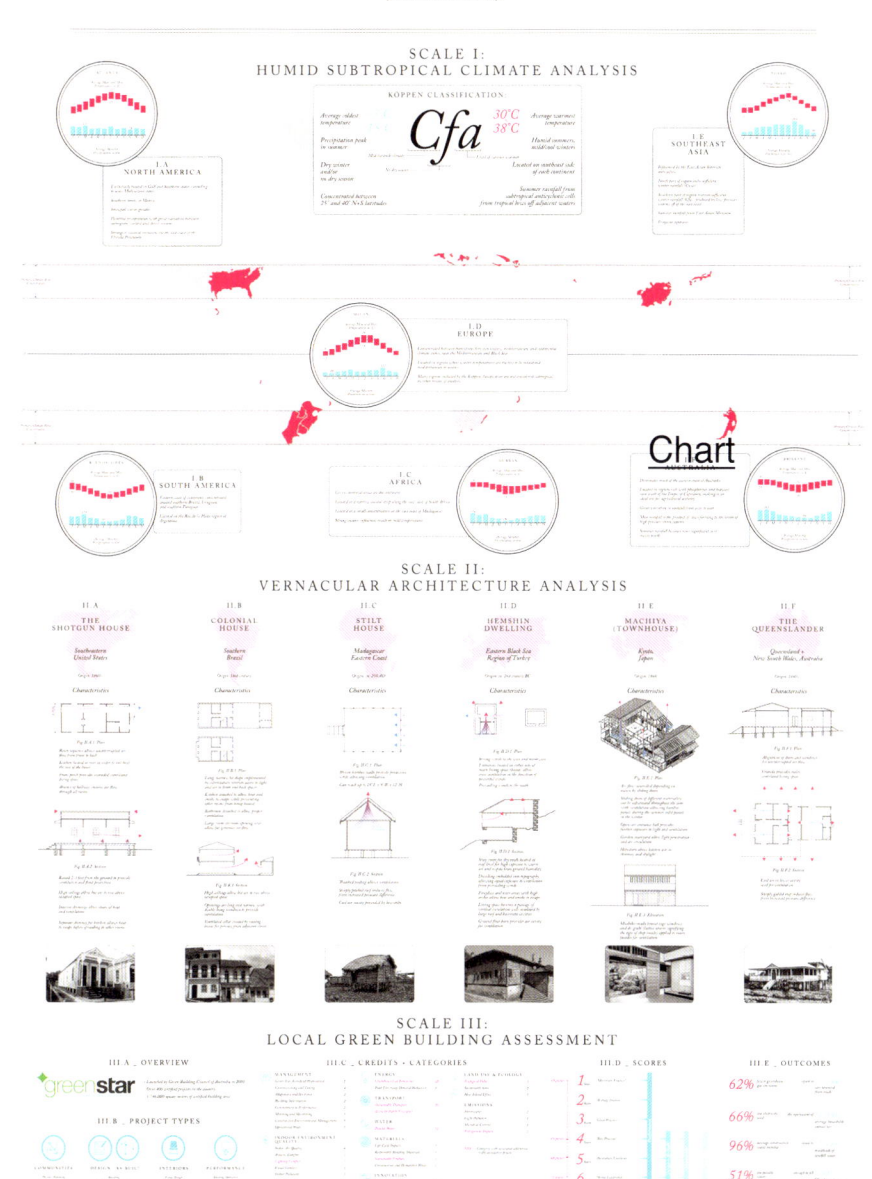

SCALE I:
HUMID SUBTROPICAL CLIMATE ANALYSIS

SCALE II:
VERNACULAR ARCHITECTURE ANALYSIS

SCALE III:
LOCAL GREEN BUILDING ASSESSMENT

Bin Zhu
MAUD, 2016

Making Omishima the Best Island to Live on in Japan: Tokyo Studio Abroad

Instructor
Toyo Ito

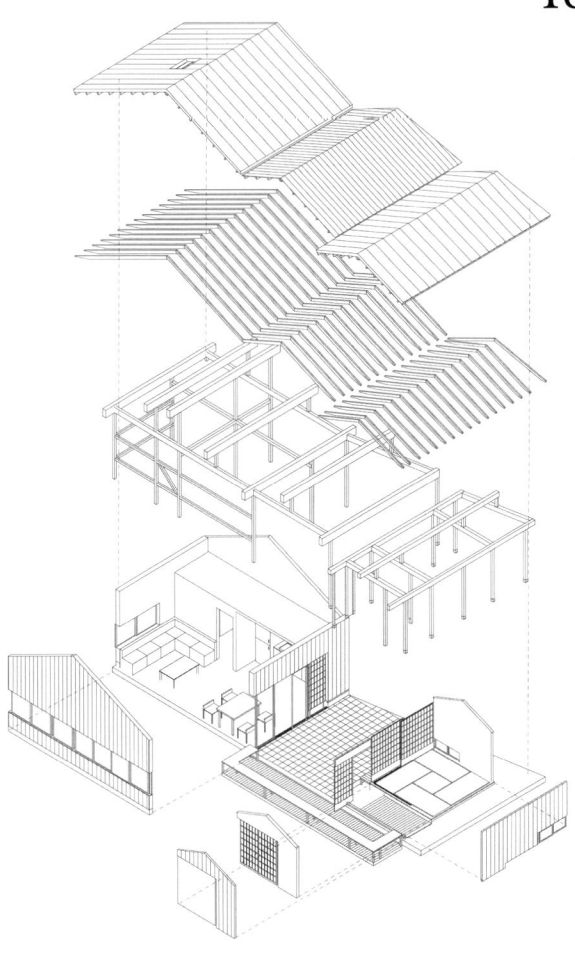

Omishima Island, in Imabari, Japan, has a population of about 6,400 and is located in the middle of the Seto Inland Sea. The serene hillside landscape, covered with mandarin orange orchards and home to the Oyamazumi Shrine, one of the oldest shrines in Japan, has yet to be extensively developed. This studio gathered the forces of local residents and students to carry out numerous small projects as part of a 10-year plan with the goal of "Making Omishima the Best Island to Live on in Japan."

SALON | Option Studio | 49

William Adams,
Long Chuan Zhang
MArch I AP, 2018

Alice Armstrong
MArch I, 2018

Architecture Core
IV: Relate

Instructor
Andrew Holder

This project, produced for the fourth Architecture Core studio, Relate, which explores the role of housing as a central component of the physical fabric of the city, utilizes vernacular forms to transform the reading of urban housing structures.

SALON   Core Studio   51

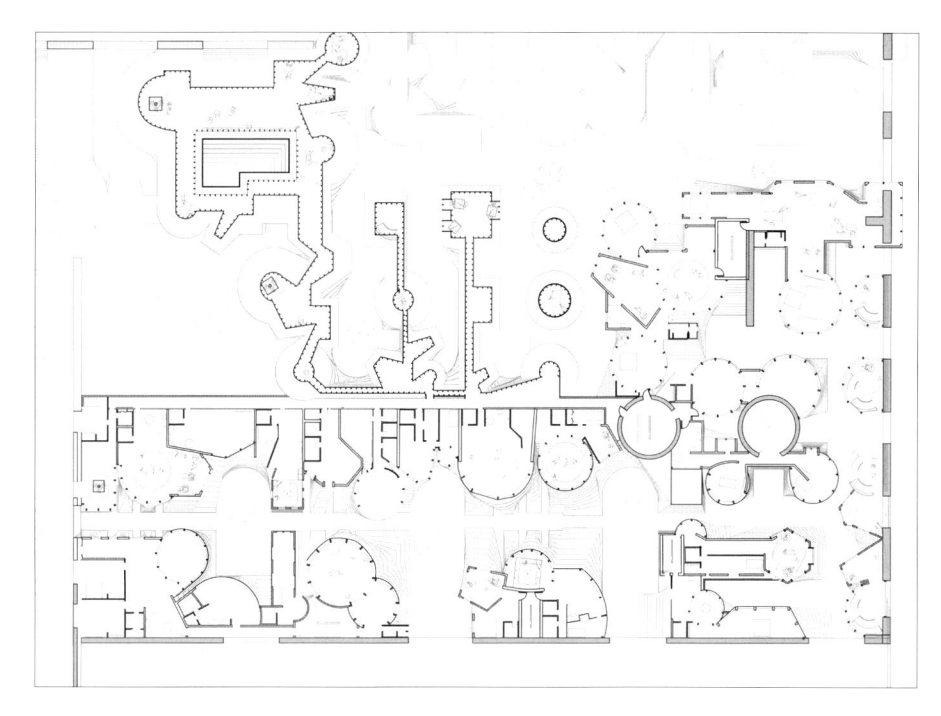

Lagoon

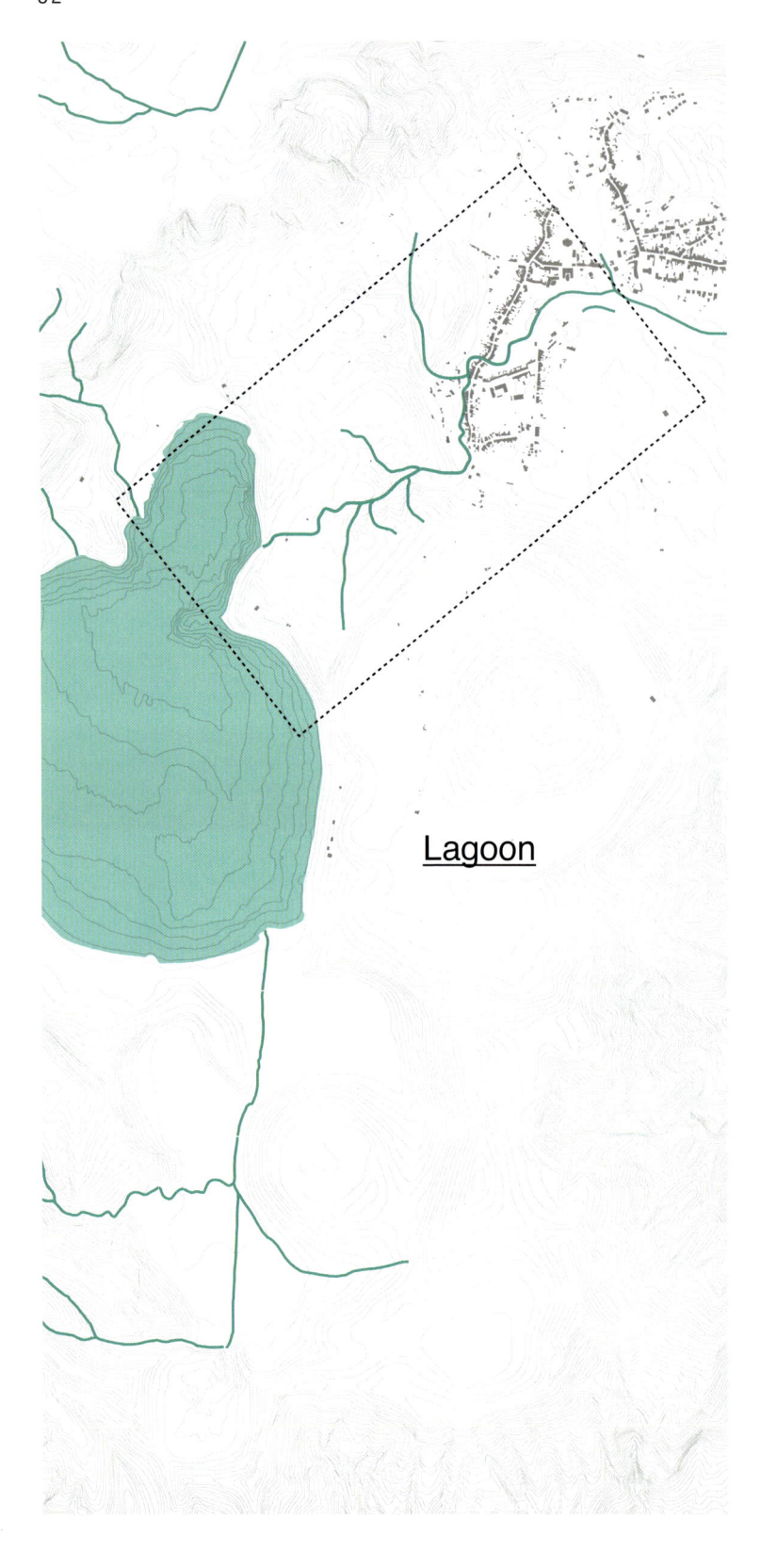

Alexander Cassini
MLA I, 2016

Lagoa das Furnas: A Dynamic Approach to a Landscape Project

Instructors
João Nunes,
João Gomes da Silva

Using cartography and qualitative and quantitative data gathered in cooperation with the University of the Azores, this studio explored elements of the Furnas Lagoon to learn how the landscape may function to produce architectonic space.

Mengchen Xia
MAUD, 2016

Moscow's Future: Tied Up in Traffic

Instructor
Martha Schwartz

Moscow's population is now close to seven million inhabitants but could grow to 17 million over the next 50 years. The existing transport structure is based on a medieval spoke-and-wheel organization, and the mega-structure of the roads (eight-lane highways) has created a range of problems that will eventually impede Moscow's ability to respond to population growth and engender a livable city. This studio examined ways of bringing positive change to these urban systems; the drawings here propose one possible solution.

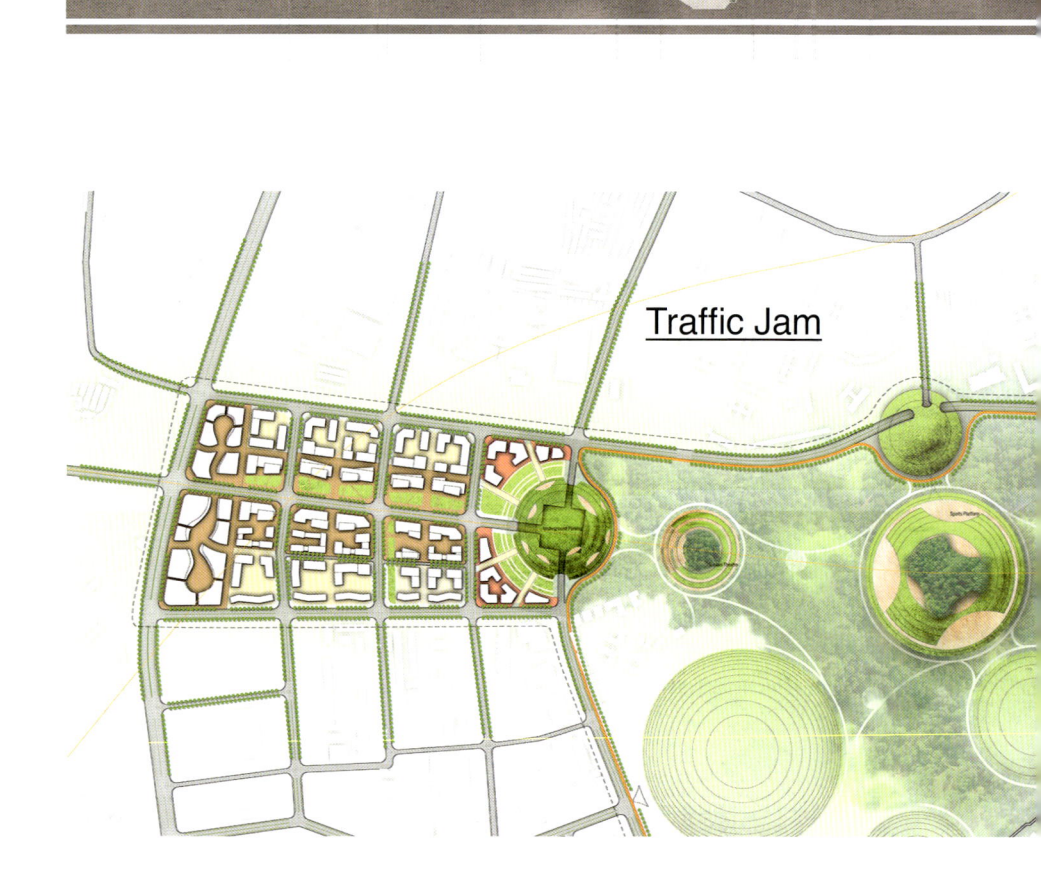

Traffic Jam

SALON Option Studio 55

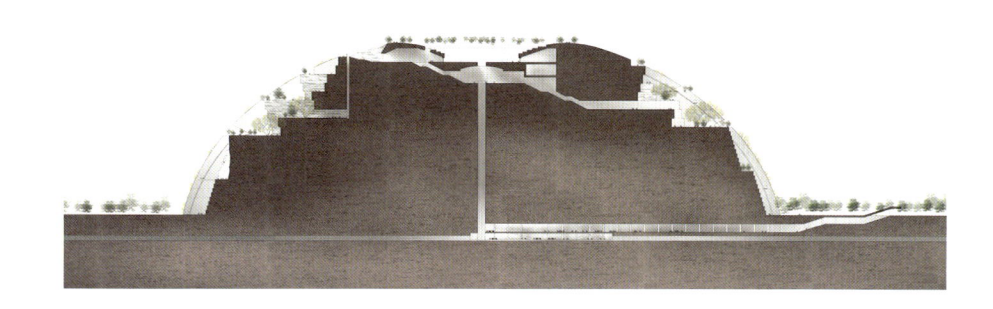

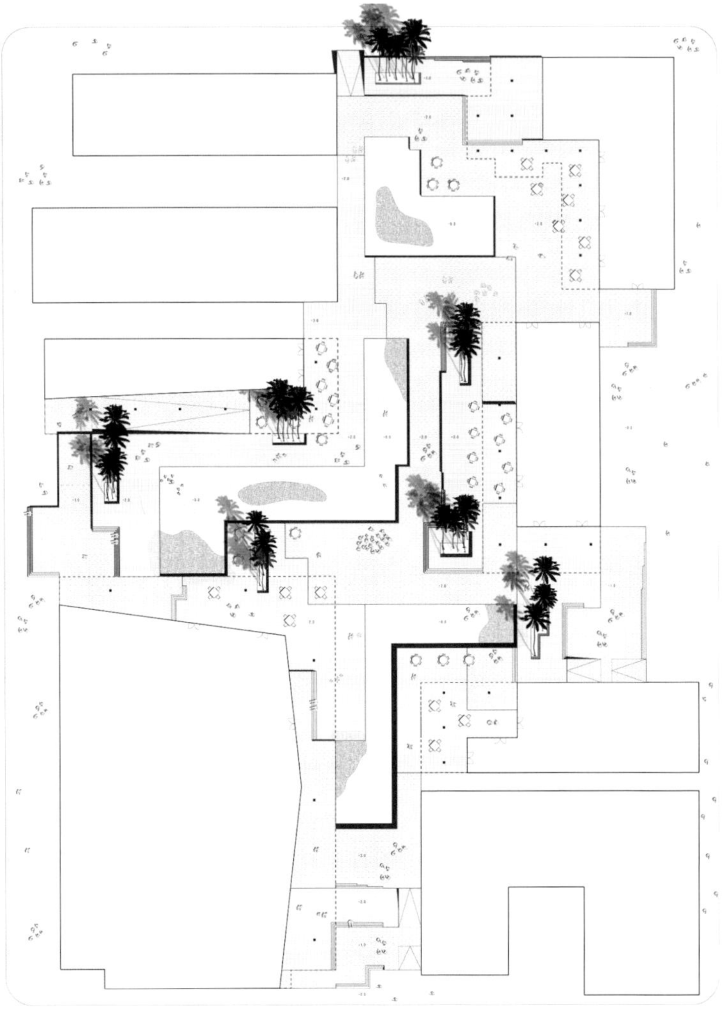

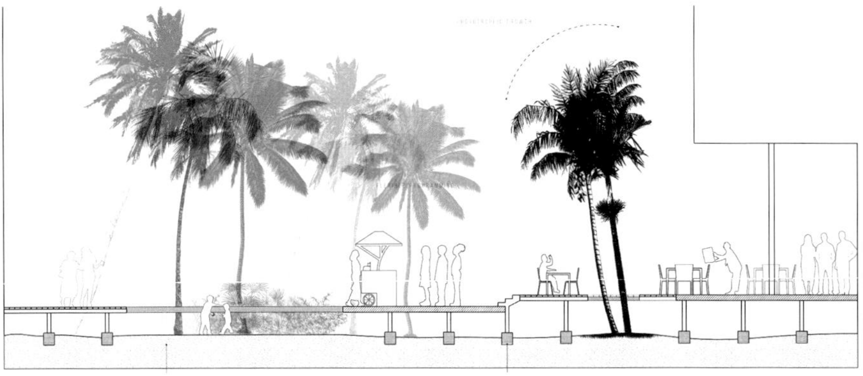

SALON Option Studio 57

Daniel Widis
MLA I, 2016

Miami Rise and Sink: Design for Urban Adaptation

Instructor
Rosetta Elkin

Miami's barrier islands are one of the most recognizable and singularly valuable cultural landscapes in the world. The conditions in Miami Beach reveal the potential for ecological and infrastructural strategies to act as alternatives to large, single-purpose engineering solutions. This project addresses contemporary conditions for "urban adaptation" in an era of sea-level rise.

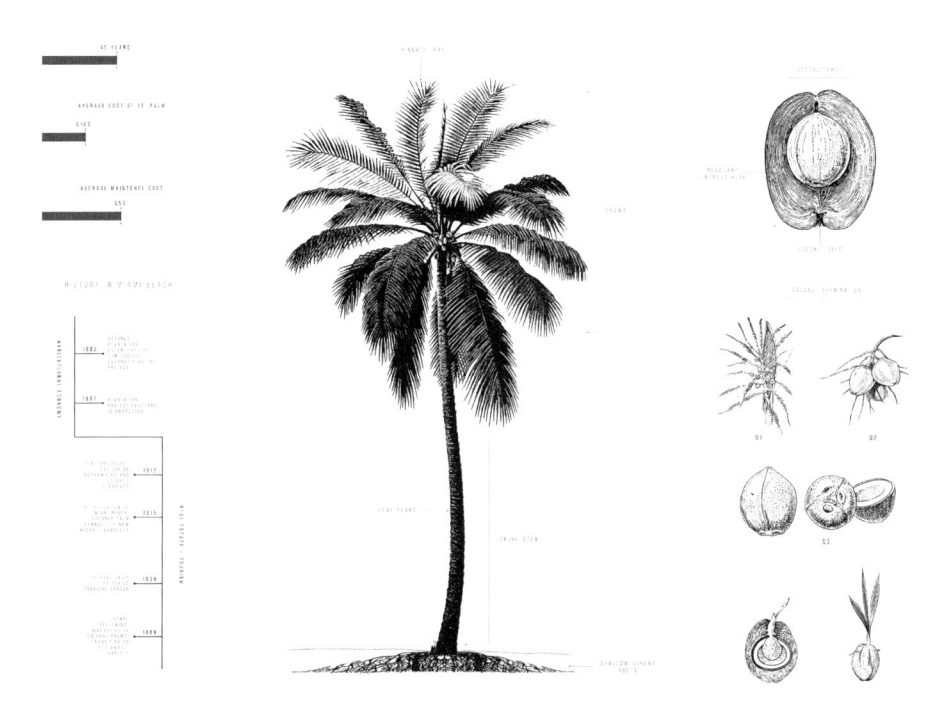

<u>Cocos nucifera</u>

What is that model? What is it made of? What software was used? These questions often circulate the production of new work in an effort to discern a technique or materiality. Some of the models arranged here capitalize on typical modelling strategies—3D printing, mat board, Plexiglas—but not all. A Master of Design Studies thesis project, titled Projectors: Experiments in Image Tectonics, appears to have used an industrial sand-printing machine. But the designer didn't stop there—the objects are enhanced (or maybe further obscured?) with layers of white semi-gloss, and then coated with clear iridescent paint. Another project gets "glammed up" in gold, elevating the site context to a new level.

It is worth noting that this collection of work uses formal methods to create cavities and holes with concavity and convexity in order to, say, top-off a roof, punctuate the bottom of a massing, and control an interior. A first-semester Architecture Core project renders the cavity of a "hidden room" in deep shadows. Another project does not differentiate between structural bay and room. Finally, a third denies extrusion in a mid-rise tower by torqueing the plan. The editors discover a contradiction, which is that ordinary materials do indeed yield challenging formal gaps and holes.

Glam Craft

60

GLAM CRAFT

62

1 Scalloped

Danielle Kasner
MArch I, 2018
Architecture Core III: Integrate
Instructor: Renata Sentkiewicz

2 Single Surface

Morgan Starkey
MArch I, 2019
Architecture Core II: Situate
Instructor: Tomás dePaor

3 Wedge

Evan Farley
MArch I, 2017
Readymade Architecture
Instructor: Preston Scott Cohen

[4 Disruptions p. 64](#)

Zeina Koreitem
MDes AP, 2016
Thesis: Projectors:
  Experiments in
  Image Tectonics
Advisor: Andrew Witt

5 Torque

Naureen Mazumdar
MArch I, 2018
Architecture Core III: Integrate
Instructor: Elizabeth Whittaker

[6 Hidden p. 66](#)

Radu-Remus Macovei
MArch I, 2019
Architecture Core I: Project
Instructor: Mariana Ibañez

[7 Mineral p. 68](#)

Marrikka Trotter
PhD Candidate
Still Life: Ruskin's
  Inorganic Ethics
Advisor: Antoine Picon

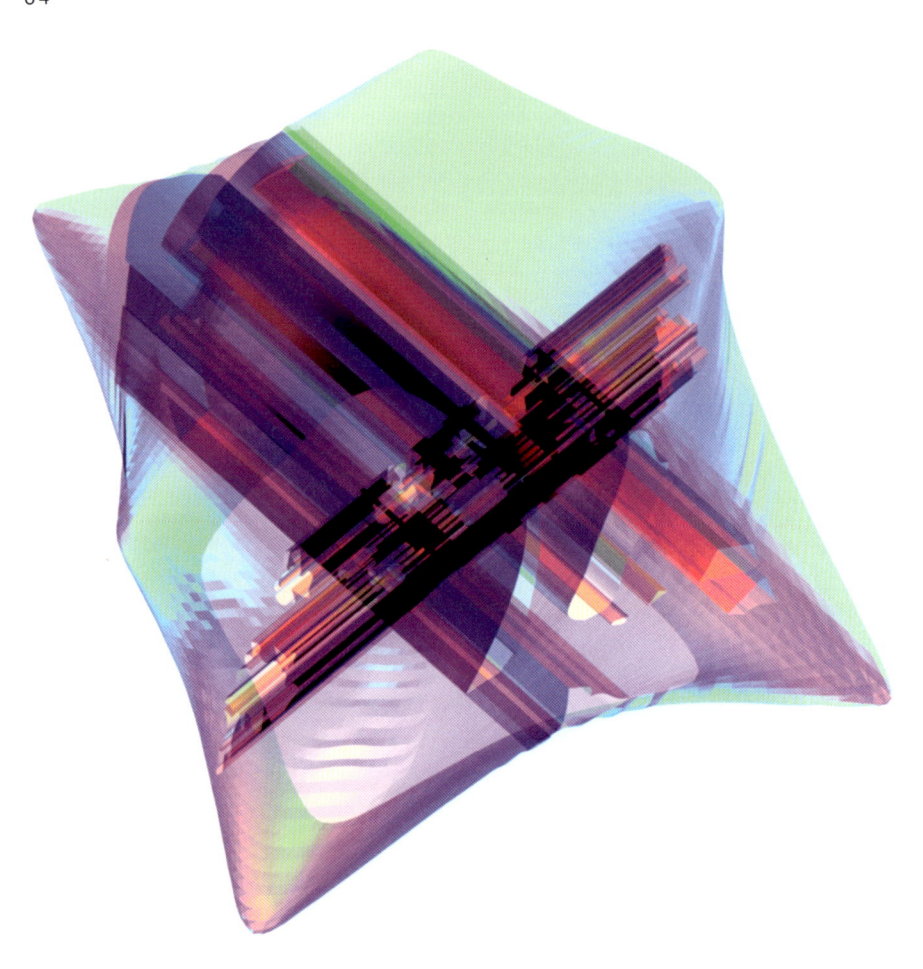

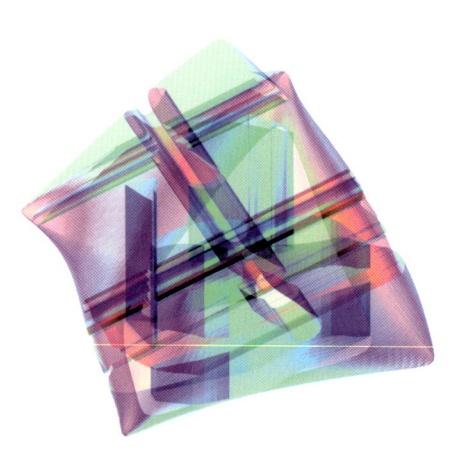

This project takes up the question of "image tectonics." To pursue this approach, image-based strategies of disruption must be viewed as essential elements of the architectural process, rather than imprecisions to be eliminated. This thesis tests strategies of image projection, such as ray tracing, parsing, sorting, scanning, and other forms of algorithmic pixel manipulation. It received the Daniel L. Schodek Award for Technology and Sustainability.

Zeina Koreitem
MDes AP, 2016

Thesis
Projectors: Experiments in Image Tectonics

Advisor
Andrew Witt

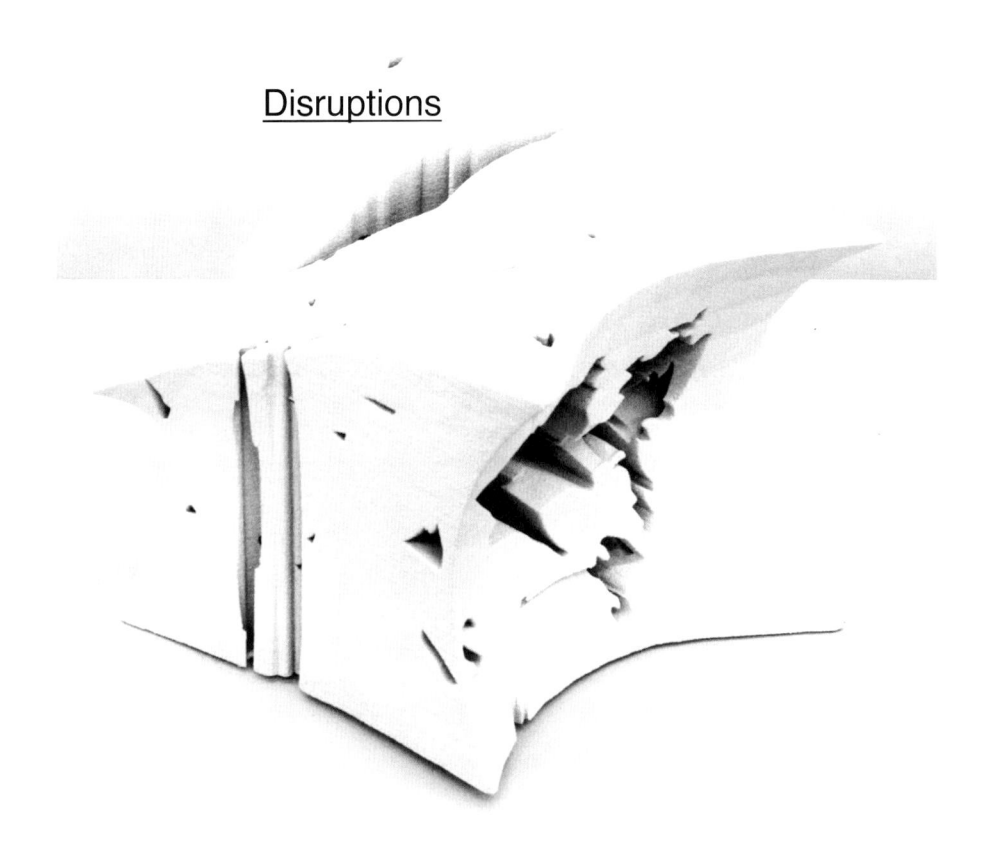

Disruptions

Radu-Remus
Macovei
MArch I, 2019

Architecture Core I:
Project

Instructor
Mariana Ibañez

The first-semester Architecture Core studio, Project, consists of a series of focused design exercises requiring students to investigate fundamental issues of practice and representation. Pictured here is a response to the assignment to create a "hidden room," a room no one can see. It utilizes nested shells, similar to the domes of St. Paul's Cathedral and St. Peter's Basilica, in order to carve concentric spaces for the room to appear in the overall volume.

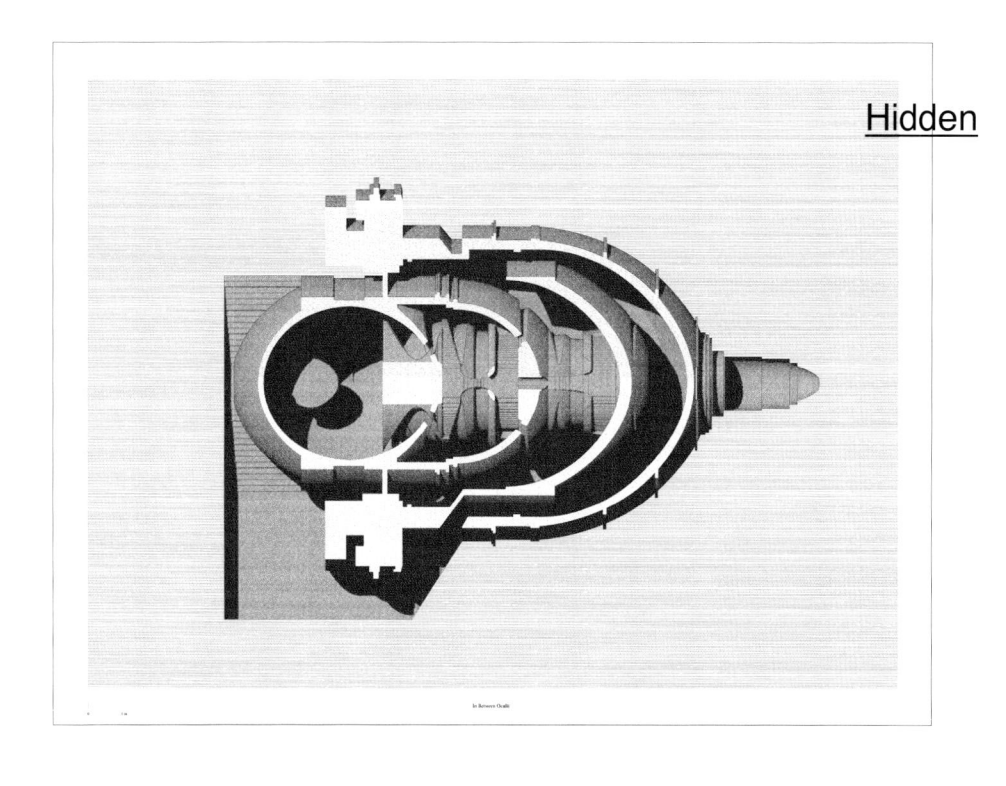

Hidden

GLAM CRAFT Core Studio 67

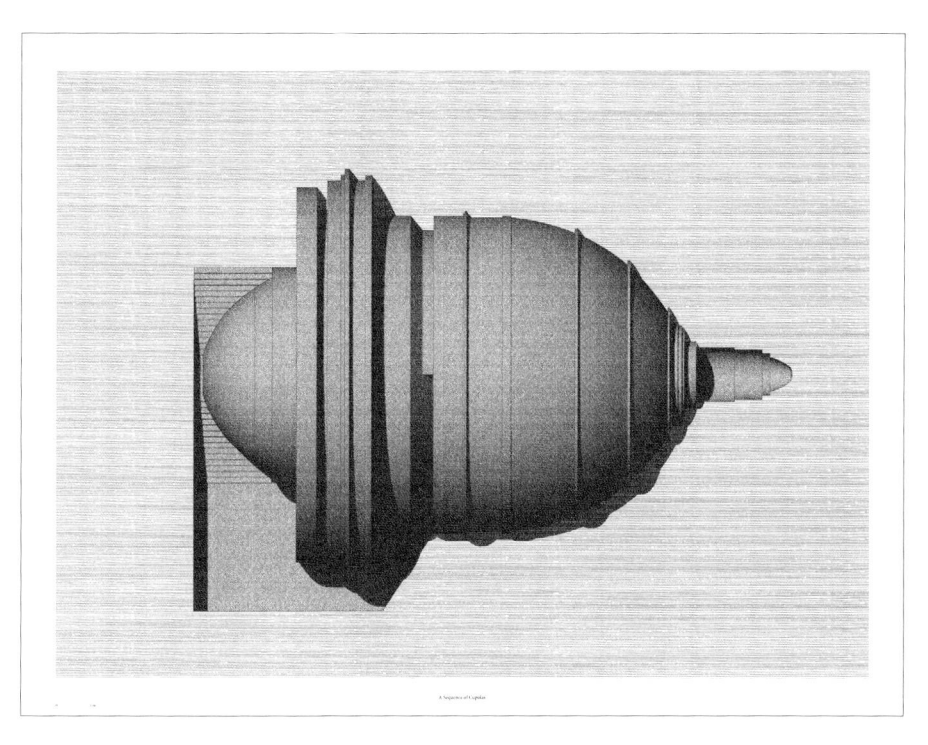

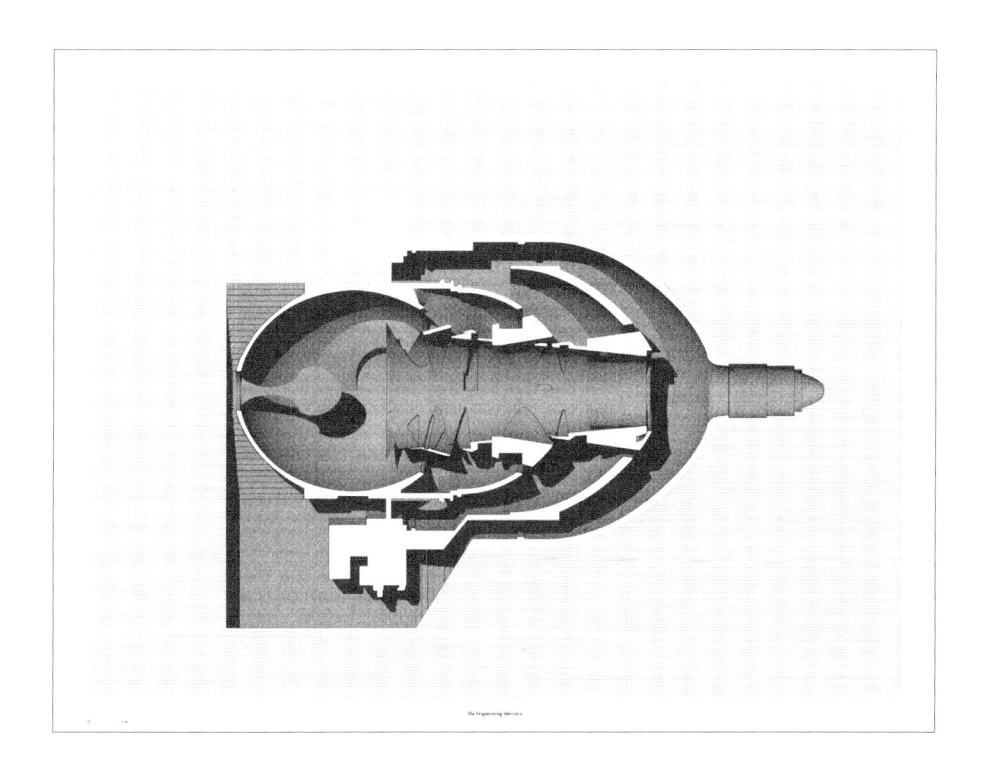

Marrikka Trotter
PhD Candidate

Still Life: Ruskin's
Inorganic Ethics[1]

Advisor
Antoine Picon

When John Ruskin, the influential Victorian critic who also happened to be a skilled amateur geologist, collected his geological and mineralogical papers for publication, he titled his book *Deucalion: Collected Studies of the Lapse of Waves, and Life of Stones* (1879).[2] Typically for Ruskin, what might seem a merely poetic turn of phrase is intended quite literally: he was discussing waves that actually lapse—notwithstanding the fact that they are sometimes formed of solid rock—and stones that actually live.

Ruskin characterized life as a self-organizing system. For him, the difference between the mineral world and the animal kingdom was one of degree rather than kind, and he believed that fundamental similitudes existed at all scales and within all systems of nature. Moreover, Ruskin followed the Protestant exegetical tradition of typology, in which nature's forms and the processes by which they came into being were seen as "types": embodiments of eternal truths and models of correct human behavior.[3] It is because of this typological link between literal attributes and moral lessons that Ruskin's various objects of concern are disparate only on the surface; they connect in ever-tighter and more factual ways the deeper down one goes. Apparent leaps in magnitude and duration, as, for example, when Ruskin discussed similarities between geological weathering patterns and the curve of a bird's wing, are often more productively viewed as shifts in the observer's distance from or angle on a single unified system. Indeed, Ruskin found such moves necessary to correctly observe the analogies between silicates and spires; between the crystalline logic of mountains and the native moral sense of humans; between the shaping of landscape by nature and the shaping of landscape by art. For Ruskin, the mineral world was particularly suited for this kind of revelatory seeing. The same formational principles applied to both a stone and a mountain, and geological change occurred so slowly that its examples were enduring.

Within this privileged field, Ruskin identified a fundamental principle that he felt constituted his major contribution to inorganic science. He detected it first in banded silicates, a group of rocks that includes agate and jasper. Close observation of the striations that characterize such stones revealed that bands of unique color and chemical composition had pulled apart from each other via an internally motivated process Ruskin called "tranquil division."[4] This ran counter to standard mineralogy, which interpreted these stones as a sequence of individual deposits welded together by external forces. For Ruskin, "tranquil division" was a process that operated across all scales. In his view, for example, even the large-scale strata visible on cliff faces and in railway cuts were not always to be interpreted as successive layers of sediment laid down in physical superimposition. Rather, he speculated that they were just as often the result of a process in which the constituent minerals of an originally undifferentiated and gelatinous chunk of rock slowly repelled and attracted, crystallized and formed, until they self-sorted and hardened into clean stripes.[5] Thus, for Ruskin, one of the great self-organizing principles of the mineral world was differentiation, whereby things arranged themselves into evermore refined and sharply delineated categories.

Ruskin scaled this principle of self-differentiation up to an essential ethic for human society. His ideal sociopolitical structure was one of strict hierarchies and absolute obedience—a naturalized take, in other words, on the traditional British class system that by the mid-19th century was threatened by wide-scale urbanization and industrialization. Yet Ruskin was a relentless critic of the existing state of things, which he believed to have been fatally corrupted by exploitative short-term profit taking on the part of wealthy landowners, coupled with a counterproductive pursuit of freedom on the part of the masses. On the second count, Ruskin insisted that nature offered no examples with which to justify such striving. He began his section on "The Lamp of Obedience," in *The Seven Lamps of Architecture* (1849), by denying "that treacherous phantom which men call Liberty":

> There is no such thing in the universe. There can never be. The stars have it not; the earth has it not; the sea has it not; and we men have the mockery and semblance of it only for our heaviest punishment.[6]

This is where the pedagogical counterexample of minerals was particularly valuable. In *The Ethics of the Dust*, or *Ten Lessons to Little Housewives on the Elements of Crystallization* (1866), Ruskin instructed his 11 female pupils, ages nine through 20, to persist in their own "unconquerable purity of vital power, and strength of crystal spirit" and develop according to plan, as it were.[7] Aside from what strikes us today as Ruskin's chauvinism—for his time, his view of female education was considered quite liberal[8]—perhaps the most repellent aspect of Ruskinian ethics to modern minds is that it demanded total submission to an unchanging and unquestionable pattern.

Here a wrinkle or pleat, both in typological thought in general and in Ruskin's thought in particular, comes into view. Nature was not only an example but also an instantiation; minerals and morals resembled each other because they both were obedient to the same natural law. In fact, Ruskin wrote, the chemical and the conscious differed from each other only by degree.[9] For Ruskin, the mineral landscape was the fundament from which all organic life, including human thought and activity, sprung: a biologically "lifeless seed of life."[10] He therefore attempted to identify and implement ways of living that would both maximize a population's geological settings and be congenial with this substrate's unchangeable chemical attributes. There were thus composite natural-artificial landscape "orders" akin to those of classical architecture:

> ... corresponding not only to the several species of rock, but to the particular circumstances of the rock's deposition or after-treatment, and to the incalculable varieties of climate, aspect, and human interference.[11]

Ideally such "human interference" would take the form of large-scale environmental cultivation tailored to the most useful and beautiful qualities of a particular inorganic landscape. For Ruskin, the proper work of the nation included shaping the critical physical junction between mineral and social life: averting floods, draining fens, checking sea erosion, constructing breakwaters—"dig the moor and dry the marsh," Ruskin urged, "to bid the morass give forth instead of engulfing, and to wring the honey and oil out of the rock."[12]

In the context of an ethical society, a correct alignment between human creativity and geological particulars could produce spectacular urban results. This is precisely the way Ruskin approached Venice. The underlying geomorphology of the Venetian archipelago, including its shallow seas; the narrow bandwidth of the tides and their regularity (which enabled sewage to be naturally scoured from the city's canals); and the gradual but immense deposition of fine sediment by the Po and other rivers—all of these inorganic vectors combined to provide what Ruskin emphasized as *"the only preparation possible"* for such a unique cultural achievement.[13]

At a smaller scale, minerals allowed to fully inhabit their chemical blueprints were literally better for humans than they would be in any artificially arrested or induced state. For example, when Ruskin lectured on "The Work of Iron" in 1858, he described unrefined iron's tendency to oxidize as a desire to breathe, and thus to live. As rust, iron exemplified the virtue of an imbrication between the physical and the spiritual akin to that between individual atoms of metal and oxygen, but it was also materially more valuable than its purified form. Iron oxide supplied nutrients to the soil, color to both the landscape and the proper building materials of brick, stone, and wood, and was generally so interfused with human life that it tinted the blood: rust, Ruskin argued, allows us to blush. On the other hand, refined iron, including iron wrought or cast into architectural components, was suspended in an unnatural and ultimately treacherous state that Ruskin called "anarchy."[14] He wrote in 1880 that "no builder has true command over the changes in the crystalline structure of iron, or over its modes of decay," and went on to reference "the definition of iron by the Delphic oracle: 'calamity upon calamity.'"[15] "Nay," he concluded in 1858, "in a certain sense, and almost a literal one, we may say that iron rusted is Living; but when pure or polished, Dead."[16]

Embedded in Ruskin's critique of the Industrial Revolution's basic materiality was a highly anomalous model of life and death. The breath that sent oxygen foliating through iron tamed that metal's energy within a stable compound, while the so-called deadness of its refined form was marked by an unquiet tendency to spring into unexpected chemical action. The static, replicable, and eternal qualities Ruskin ascribed to optimal mineral life raise perplexing issues when applied to the moral activities of human beings. Biological struggle is absent in Ruskin's "life of stones." To predicate human ethics on the self-organizational properties of minerals thus attempts to strip a critical animal faculty from the human subject: the ability to develop and change via precisely the kind of disruptive fluctuation Ruskin rejects in refined iron.

Historically, Ruskin's project coincides with that of Charles Darwin. If Darwin's publication of *On The Origin of Species* in 1859 demonstrated that there is no organic life without conflict and adaptation, Ruskin's embrace of inorganic stability reveals itself to be a conservative impulse that attempts to negate precisely the ways in which humans are *other* than their natural contexts. This includes architecture in the largest sense: the intellectual, cultural, and physical edifices we erect to temporarily exclude or contravene the biophysical laws to which our bodies are ultimately subject. The paradox at the heart of Ruskin's project boils down to this: there is no such thing as still life.

1. What follows is a short and necessarily partial summary of one chapter from my forthcoming dissertation. I am indebted to my colleagues in the PhD program, Ateya Khorakiwala and Peter Sealy, for their productive and insightful comments on this text.
2. "Deucalion" is a figure from Greek mythology who roughly corresponds to that of Noah in the Mosaic tradition. In the classical myth, Deucalion is instructed by the oracle to repopulate the earth by scattering "the bones of their mother"—the stones of the earth. For Ruskin, this resonated with two biblical passages: "God is able of these stones to raise up children . . . " (Matthew 3:19); and "If these [followers of Christ] should hold their peace, the very stones would immediately cry out" (Luke 19:40). See E. T. Cook and Alexander Wedderburn's detailed and authoritative introduction to Ruskin's *Collected Works* (London: George Allen, 1906), 26: xlvi–xlvii. All subsequent references to Ruskin's writing and Cook and Wedderburn's commentary are from this edition.
3. The most helpful discussion of Ruskin's typological thought remains Patricia M. Ball, *The Science of Aspects: The Changing Role of Fact in the Work of Coleridge, Ruskin and Hopkins* (London: The Athlone Press, 1971). See also Robert Hewison, *John Ruskin: The Argument of the Eye* (London: Thames and Hudson, 1976), 26–27.
4. Postscript to "On the Distinctions of Form in Silica" (1884), *Works* XXVI: 386.
5. "On Banded and Brecciated Concretions" (1861–1870), *Works* XXVI: 44.
6. *The Seven Lamps of Architecture* (1849), *Works* VIII: 287.
7. *The Ethics of the Dust: Ten Lectures to Little Housewives on the Elements of Crystallization* (1866), *Works* XVIII: 263.
8. Jeffrey L. Spear, *Dreams of an English Eden: Ruskin and his Tradition in Social Criticism* (New York: Columbia University Press, 1984), 167–177.
9. "Notes on the Construction of Sheepfolds" (1851), *Works* XXII: 526.
10. John Ruskin, "English versus Alpine Geology" (letter to the editor), *The Reader*, December 3, 1864, *Works* XXVI: 555. This is a position he shared with Alexander von Humboldt, the enormously influential Prussian explorer and scientist. See Humboldt's *Cosmos: a Sketch of a Physical Description of the Universe*, trans. E. C. Otté (New York: Harper & Brothers, 1856), I: 340–341. Ruskin first read Humboldt's narrative of his famous journey across the Americas in 1836. In response to readers who noticed similarities between his and Humboldt's work, Ruskin claimed to have never read *Cosmos*, and referred to its totalizing attempt to describe universal order in slighting terms. See Cook and Wedderburn's biographical note to Ruskin's *Essay on Literature* (1836), *Works* I: 369 n; *Modern Painters* III, Appendix III: "Plagarism," *Works* V: 428; and *Proserpina*, *Works* XXV: 369.
11. *Modern Painters I: Of General Principles and of Truth*, (1843), *Works* III: 39.
12. "*A Joy Forever:*" *being the Substance (with additions) of Two Lectures on the Political Economy of Art* (1857, 1880), *Works* XVI: 23.
13. Emphasis in the original. *The Stones of Venice II: The Sea Stories* (1853), *Works* X: 15. I am following David Wayne Thomas's analysis in *Cultivating Victorians: Liberal Culture and the Aesthetic* (Philadelphia: University of Pennsylvania Press, 2004), 52–53.
14. "The Work of Iron, in Nature, Art, and Policy" (1858), *Works* XVI: 375–411.
15. *Seven Lamps*, *Works* VIII: 68–70, n. As Cook and Wedderburn note, Ruskin is referring to Heroditus i: 68, which literally translates from the Greek as "trouble laid upon trouble by the thought that iron had been discovered for the evil of mankind." Ruskin goes on to reference sudden structural failures in iron infrastructure and damage inflicted to ships as evidence of refined iron's unruly nature.
16. "Work of Iron," *Works* XVI: 376–7.

The (Still) Life of Objects

The image is offered to me as a still life. I am preconditioned to a reading produced by a context that has been determined. Or not.

In a still life, the objects are specifically arranged to create a tableau. Some would say the result is meant to give extraordinary presence to ordinary things. The position of each element is as important as the resulting composition. The composition doesn't change the nature of the objects in it. They remain still. Inanimate. Or not.

It is inevitable to attempt an interpretation of the arrangement. To find meaning in the composition. The examination of individual objects is still possible. But we don't need to choose. The choice not to choose would center on the deictic function described exactly in Roland Barthes's *Empire of Signs* as signifiers and consciousness. Both exist. Both are relevant. Big to small. Curvy to square. Singles to multiples. Seriality. Structure. Center, edges, and grids. Maybe a still life, yet I cannot "unsee" the new world that it proposes. And the infinite number of new worlds it might generate. Still Alive. I swear I saw a bird soaring somewhere in there.

Mariana Ibañez
Associate Professor of Architecture

This still life is sure to "raise a ruckus." The option studio Extreme Urbanism, which focused on the neighborhood of Dongri in Mumbai, works on form via a perimeter housing block. Abutting this form are four red study models from an architecture studio that deal with figural flatness for an urban proposal for Boston. Working with singular material logics, four projects have different formal results: spirals, torqued bricks, truncated octahedrons, and structural aggregates. Shiny beans, ziggurats, and landscape samples might be categorized as primitive forms or versions of things we know. In an option studio tackling the readymade in art practice, a shotgun and a dinosaur find their way toward architectural form. Piles of inexpensive building systems are mined for a thesis project confronting cheap forms. Exercises in mapping and parametric modelling explore logical form-making, if there is such a thing. All figures and forms collected from the GSD's disorderly studio spaces (affectionately referred to as "the trays") are organized using "knolling," a process that highlights formal relationships and brings a new perspective to seemingly unrelated objects by juxtaposing them.

Form Ruckus

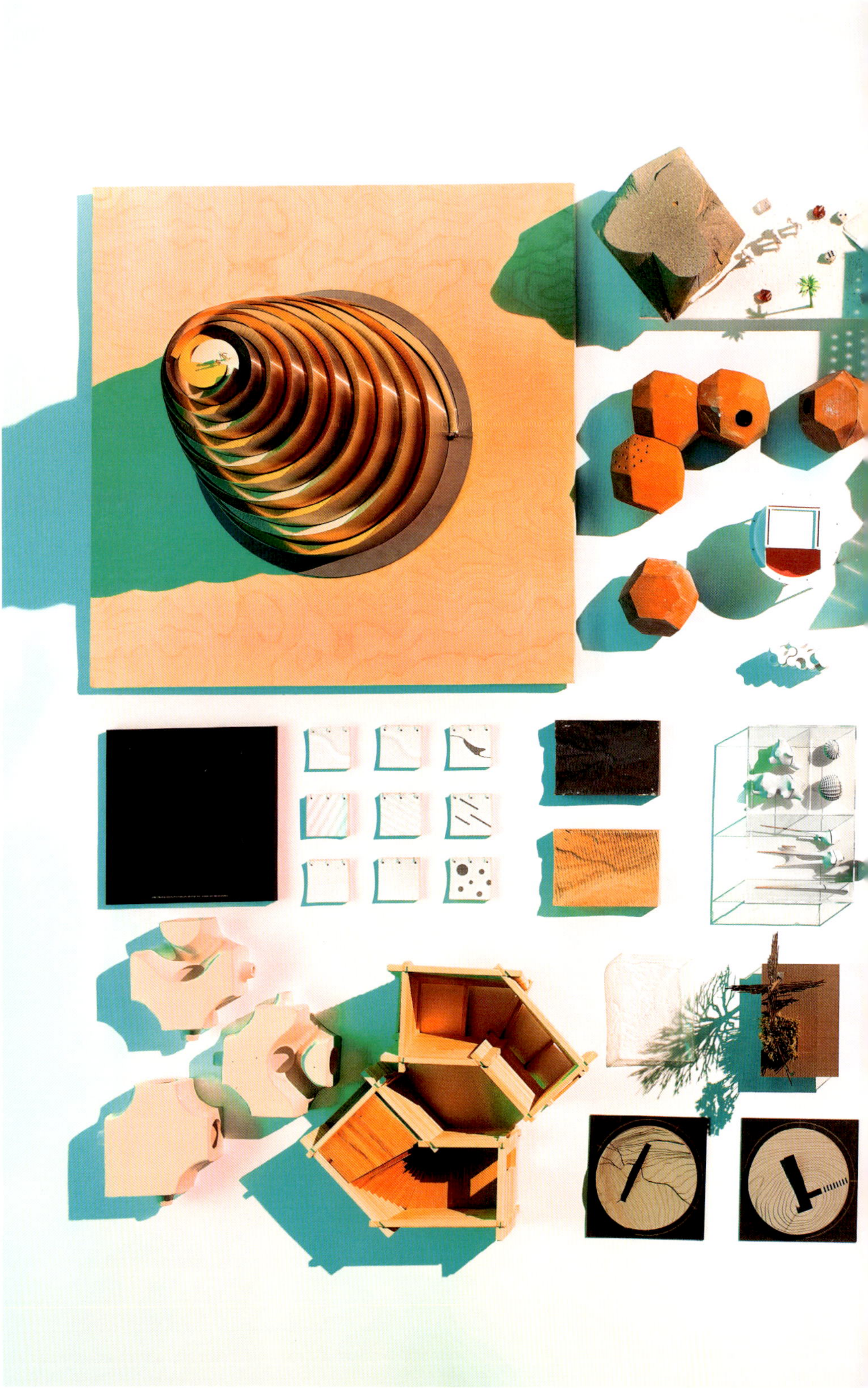

FORM RUCKUS

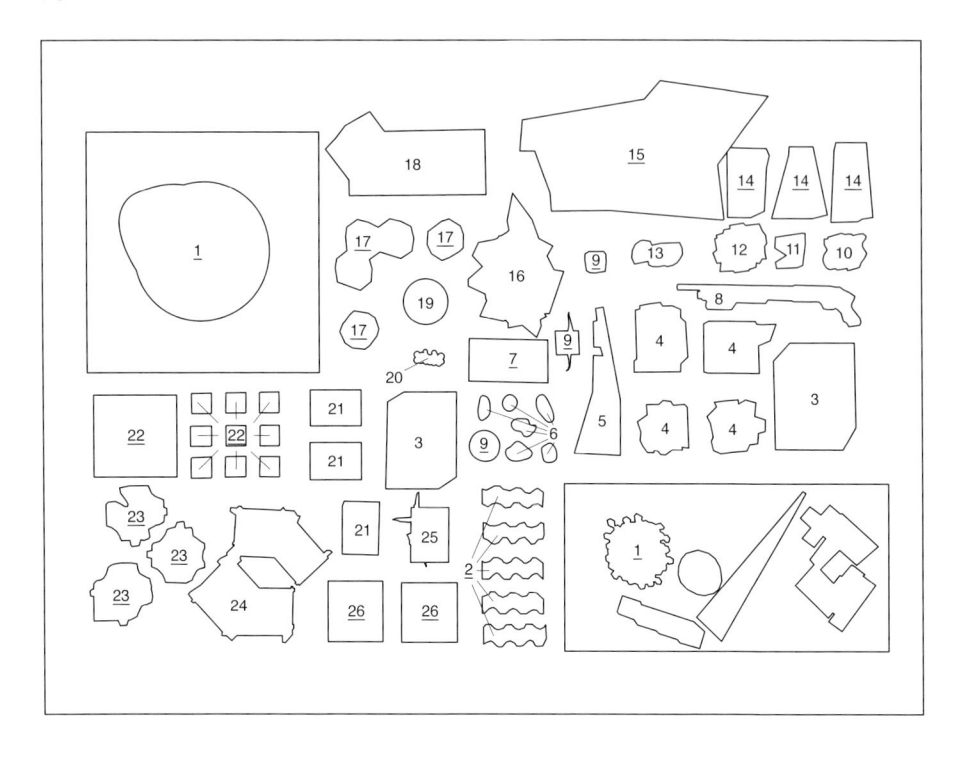

1 Cheap
p. 80
Ivan Ruhle
MArch I, 2016
Thesis: What is Good is
   Easy to Get, or Cheap
   Architecture
Advisor: Kiel Moe

2 Spirals
p. 82
Sizhi Qin
MArch II, 2017
Andrew Kim, Zhiwei Liao,
   Tanuja Mishra
MDes, 2017
Material Practice as Research:
   Digital Design and
   Fabrication
Instructor: Leire Asensio Villoria

3 Specimens
Zahra Safaverdi
MArch II, 2017
Third Natures: London's
   Typological Imagination
Instructors: Cristina
   Díaz Moreno, Efrén
   García Grinda

4 Pure Perversions
Madeline Lenaburg, Alexander
   Porter, Ho Cheung Tsui
MArch I, 2018
Architecture Core IV: Relate
Instructor: Andrew Holder

5 45,150 m²
Taylor Brandes
MArch I, 2017
Extreme Urbanism IV:
   Looking at Hyper Density—
   Dongri, Mumbai
Instructor: Rahul Mehrotra

6 Beans
Matthew Conway
MArch I, 2016
Thesis: The Visual Device
   Will Laugh
Advisor: Jeffry Burchard

7 Intensive
p. 84
Khorshid Naderi-Azad
MArch I, 2019
Architecture Core I: Project
Instructor: Mariana Ibañez

8 Shotgun
Evan Farley
MArch I, 2017
Readymade Architecture
Instructor: Preston Scott Cohen

9 Dinosaur
p. 86

Jonathan Rieke
MArch I, 2017
Readymade Architecture
Instructor: Preston Scott Cohen

10 Automation

Zeina Koreitem
MDes AP, 2016
Zachary Matthews
MArch II, 2017
Digital Media II
Instructor: Andrew Witt

11 Opposition

David Solomon
MArch I, 2019
Architecture Core II: Situate
Instructor: Grace La

12 Generative

Shaina Kim, Hyojin Kwon
MArch I, 2018
Digital Media II
Instructor: Andrew Witt

13 Inversion Illusions

Iman Fayyad
MArch I, 2016
Thesis: The Phantom Projective
Advisors: Preston Scott Cohen, Cameron Wu

14 Pug Mill
p. 82

Oliver Bucklin
MArch I, 2016
John Going, Kathryn Sonnabend
MArch I, 2017
Material Practice as Research: Digital Design and Fabrication
Instructor: Leire Asensio Villoria

15 A Vegas Motel
p. 88

Alexander Porter
MArch I, 2018
Architecture Core III: Integrate
Instructor: Jeffry Burchard

16 Inscribed Surfaces

Shani Cho, Felipe Oropeza, Scott Smith
MArch I, 2017
Mapping: Geographic Representation and Speculation
Instructor: Robert Pietrusko

17 Terracotta
p. 82

Alejandro Fernandez-Linares Garcia
MArch II, 2017
Palak Gadodia
MDes, 2016
Aaron Mendonca, Gabriel Munoz Moreno, Santiago Serna
MDes, 2017
Material Practice as Research: Digital Design and Fabrication
Instructor: Leire Asensio Villoria

18 Dice

Benzion Rodman
MArch I, 2017
etceteras
Instructor: Mack Scogin

19 Hot Pink

Bijan Thornycroft
MArch I, 2019
Architecture Core II: Situate
Instructor: Tomás dePaor

20 Undulating

Paris Nelson
MArch I, 2019
Architecture Core II: Situate
Instructor: Grace La

21 Molded

Nada AlQallaf
MArch II / MLA I AP, 2018
Landscape Core IV
Instructor: Sergio Lopez-Pineiro

22 Flip Books
p. 90

Siobhan Feehan Miller
MLA I, 2017
Xun Liu, Alexandra Mei
MLA I AP, 2017
Landscape Core IV
Instructor: Robert Pietrusko

23 Modular Filtration
p. 82

Giancarlo Montano
MArch I, 2016
Michael Clapp, Leonardo Rodriguez, Joseph Varholick
MArch II, 2017
Material Practice as Research: Digital Design and Fabrication
Instructor: Leire Asensio Villoria

24 Wood

Michael Piscitello
MArch II, 2016
Wood, Urbanism: From the Molecular to the Territorial
Instructors: Jane Hutton, Kiel Moe

25 Seaport

Marisa Villarreal
MLA I, 2018
Landscape Core I
Instructor: Jane Hutton

26 Ravine
p. 92

Jessica Booth
MLA I, 2016
Lagoa das Furnas: A Dynamic Approach to a Landscape Project
Instructors: João Nunes, João Gomes da Silva

Cheap

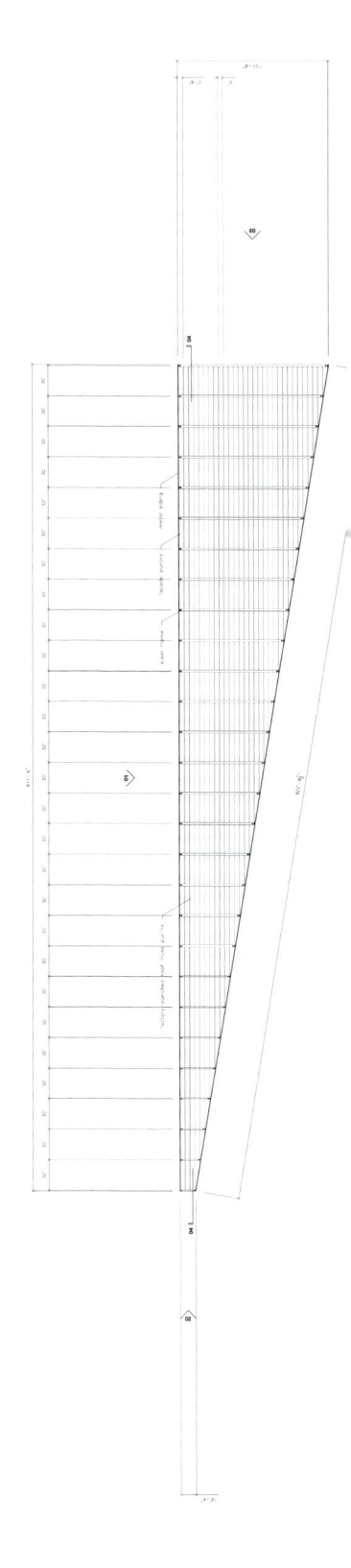

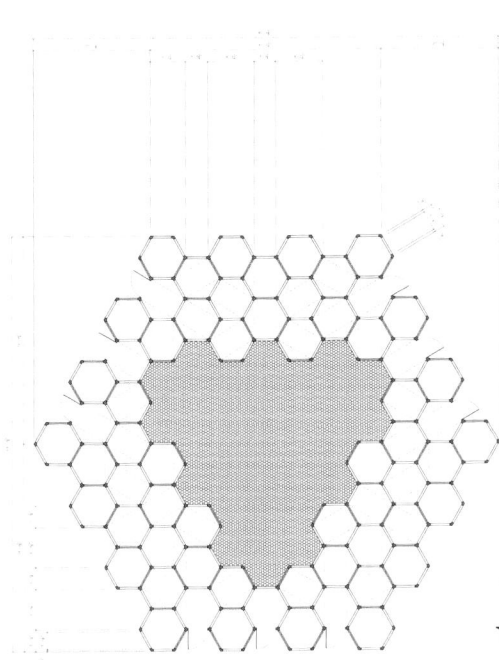

Ivan Ruhle
MArch I, 2016

Thesis
What is Good is Easy to Get, or Cheap Architecture

Advisor
Kiel Moe

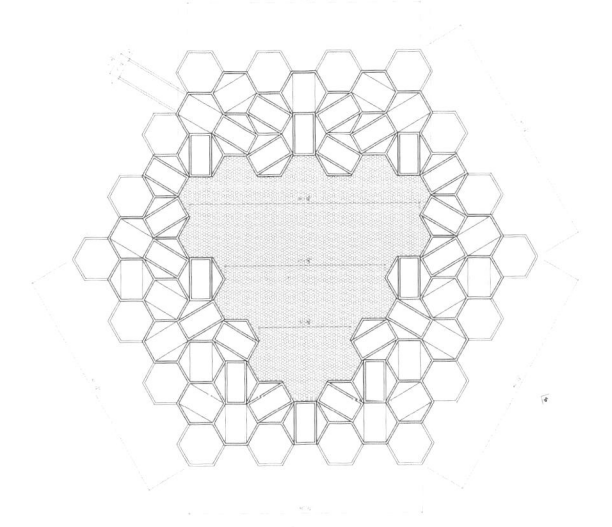

This thesis questions the meaning and application of what is considered "cheap" in architecture. The dual meaning of the word "cheap" serves as both description and inducement, with "cheap" accurately describing the contemporary state of material culture—the ground on which all architecture is built—while also serving as a challenge to reconsider the role of economy in construction.

Material Practice as Research: Digital Design and Fabrication

Instructor
Leire Asensio Villoria

In this course, ceramics served as the framework for research, discussion, and experimentation in digital design and fabrication technologies. While ceramics has one of the longest histories as a material in architecture, it holds the potential to generate a range of novel applications by engaging with emerging digital fabrication processes and by rethinking craft-based and high-volume industrial production traditionally associated with clay-based ceramics.

Terracotta

Modular Filtration

FORM RUCKUS — Seminar — 83

Pug Mill

Ceramic Material Formation

Harvard Graduate School of Design

Spirals

84

Khorshid Naderi-Azad
MArch I, 2019

Architecture Core I: Project

Instructor
Mariana Ibañez

ntensive

The "intensive/extensive" project in the first-semester Architecture Core I studio asks students to find solutions to questions of energy flows and duration. This project submerges the building, using an internal stepped and angular structure, to facilitate air circulation.

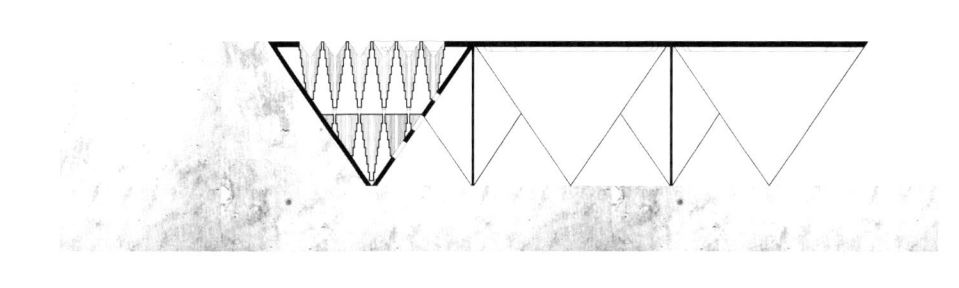

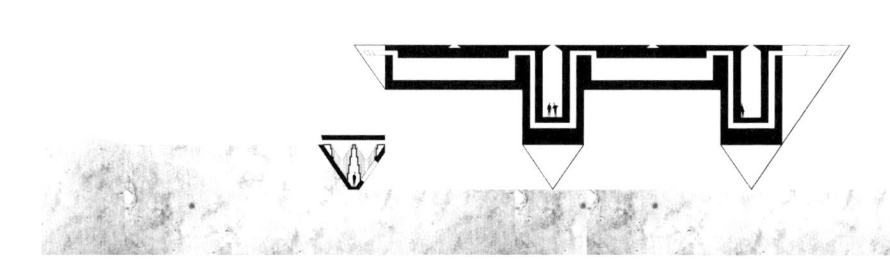

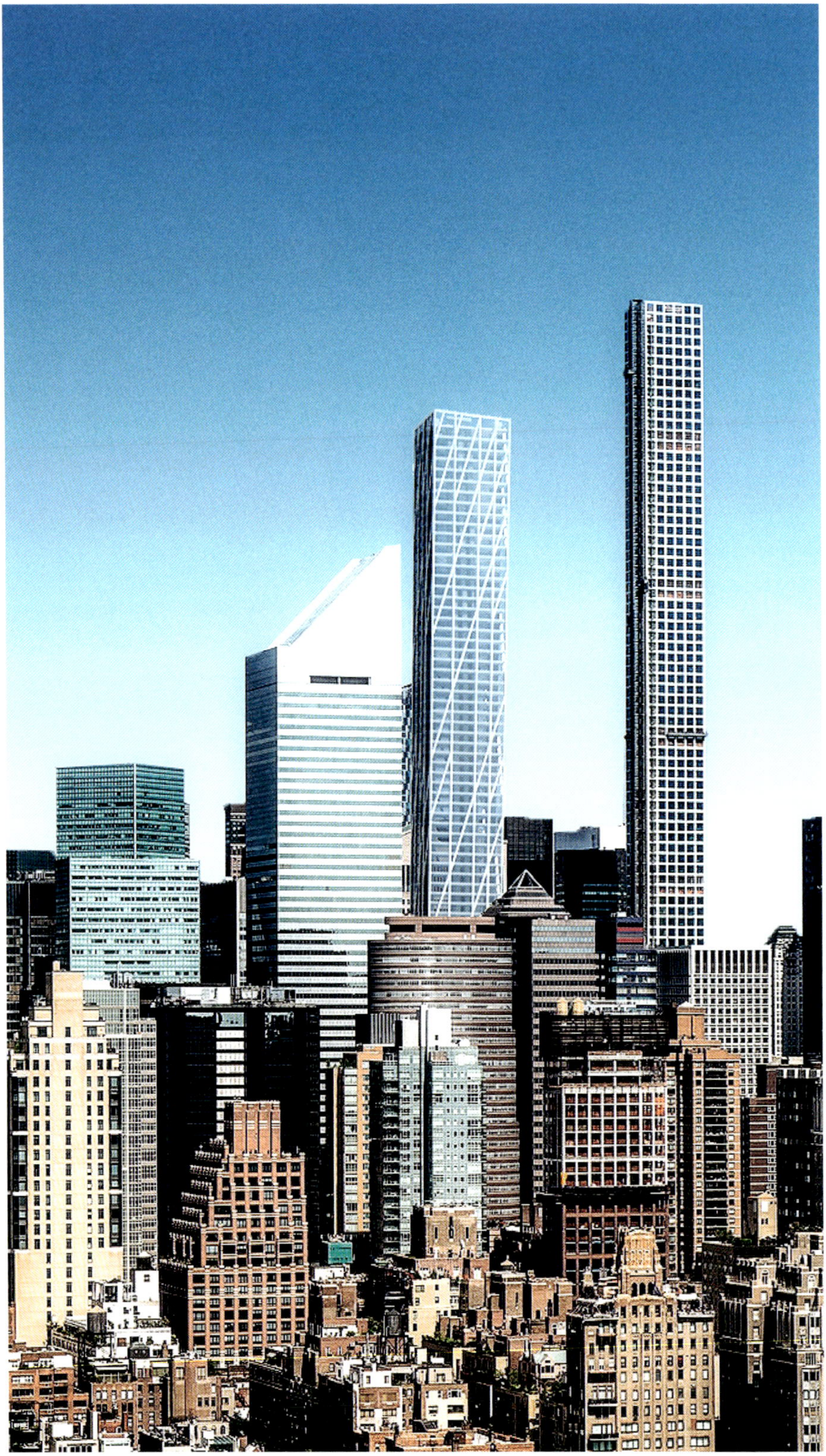

FORM RUCKUS | Option Studio | 87

Dinosaur

Readymade is a concept at once seemingly compatible with and inapplicable to architecture. On the one hand, architecture can be interpreted to embody the requisite ordinariness associated with found objects. On the other, architecture's context, whether the city or the countryside, does not act explicitly as a venue of legitimation. Here, both are considered as the project bends away from its orthogonal origin.

Jonathan Rieke
MArch I, 2017

Readymade Architecture

Instructor
Preston Scott Cohen

Architecture is fundamentally a part-to-whole problem, involving the complex integration of building components, systems, and processes into a synthetic whole. Situated in Las Vegas (off of the Strip), a mid-rise motel expands its interior space via the design of a folding envelope.

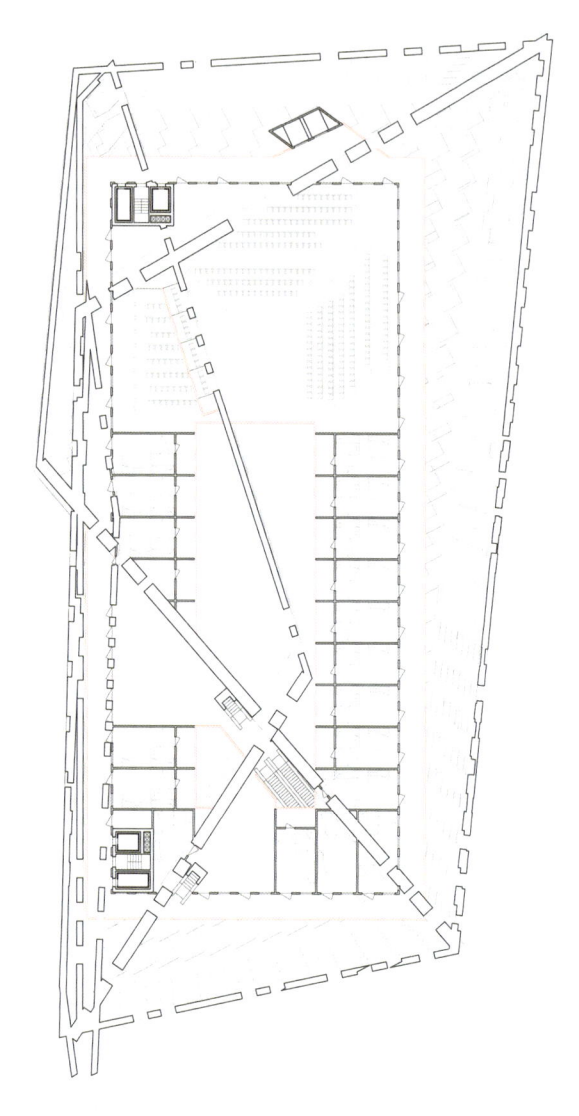

Alexander Porter
MArch I, 2018

Architecture Core III: Integrate

Instructor
Jeffry Burchard

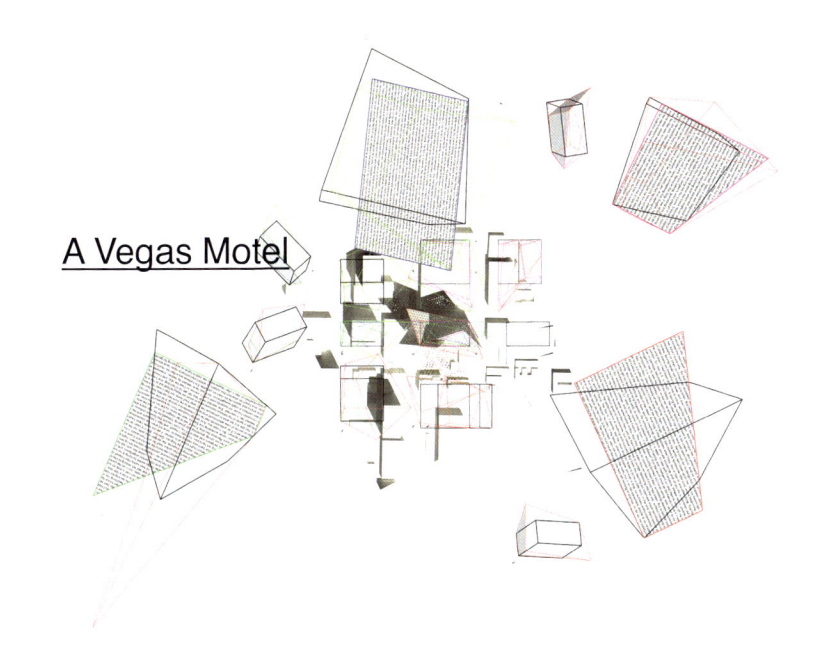

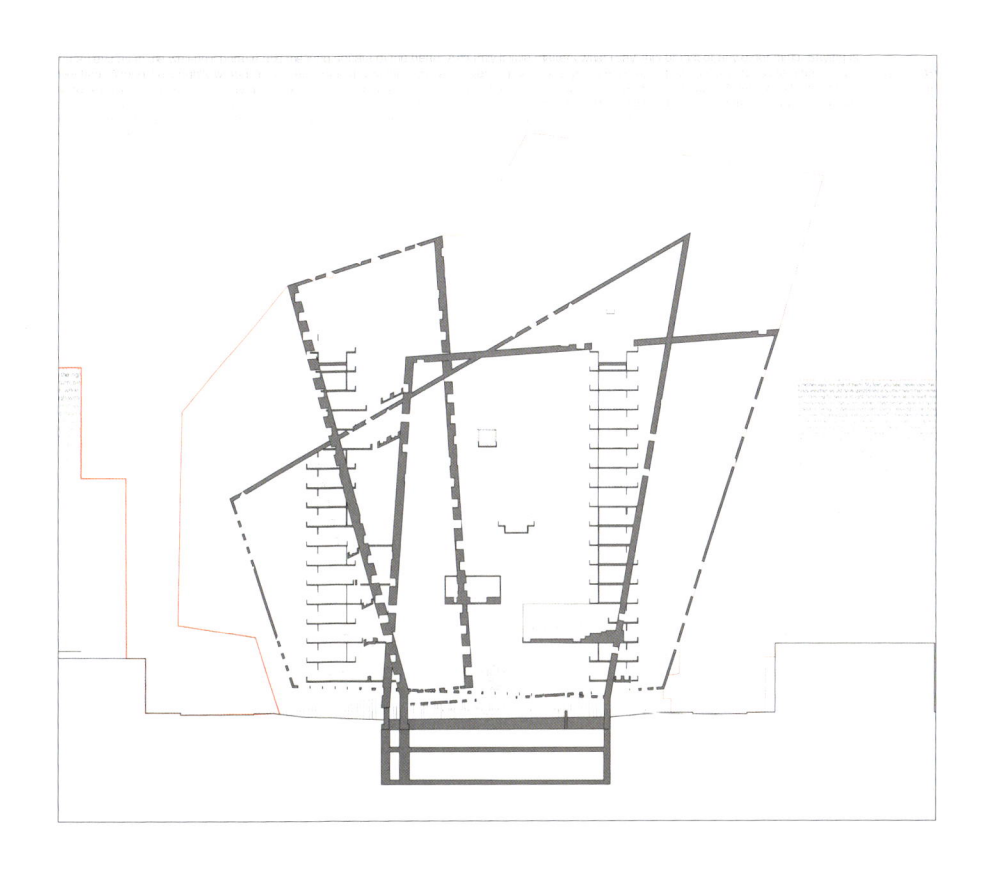

FORM RUCKUS   Core Studio   89

A Vegas Motel

Xun Liu, Alexandra Mei
MLA I AP, 2017

Siobhan Feehan Miller
MLA I, 2017

Landscape Core IV

Instructor
Robert Pietrusko

Flip Books

Addressing the inertia of urban planning and the overexertion of civil engineering in the 20th century, this fourth-semester Landscape Core studio focuses on the design of large, complex, contaminated brownfield sites via a regional, ecological, and infrastructural outlook. It employs regional ecology and landscape infrastructure as the dominant drivers of design to develop biodynamic and biophysical systems that provide flexible yet directive patterns for future urbanization.

FORM RUCKUS	Core Studio	91

Laurel Path
2 m

Dome Lookout
18 m

Dome Stairway
1 m

Creek Side
2 m

Lava Field
3 m

Pasture Lookout
10 m

The Furnas Lagoon is located on São Miguel Island in the Azores of Portugal. This studio studied how this unique and dynamic landscape was formed, paying attention to different rates of metabolism and the anthropic and cultural impact on the eutrophication of the Lagoon. This project studies the transformation of a path through sectional and detailed studies as it traverses a diverse array of environmental and intervened conditions.

Ravine

Jessica Booth
MLA I, 2016

Lagoa das Furnas: A Dynamic Approach to a Landscape Project

Instructors
João Nunes, João Gomes da Silva

Unlike the old part-to-whole relationship, utilized in past classical works or current aggregate projects, sampling is not a compositional tool; instead, it offers a representational device for various disciplines, including architecture, landscape architecture, and urban design. Sampling in design requires the author to select a fragment (a sample) of something in order to understand the whole. In a landscape architecture studio, studies of an airport plan using a circular clipping boundary yield three physical samples. Applying sampling to a much larger system, an architecture thesis project titled Transient Transition demonstrates how healthcare, urban development, and infrastructure merge into one public ground in a linear bar typology alongside a major roadway in Nanjing, China. A landscape architecture thesis project samples the fluvial landscape of the Los Angeles River with a robotic arm; the results are represented here in a series of petri dishes. Finally, New Neighbors, an architecture thesis project, samples endless circulation systems in order to reconfigure the architectural core for a housing proposal.

Sample Samples

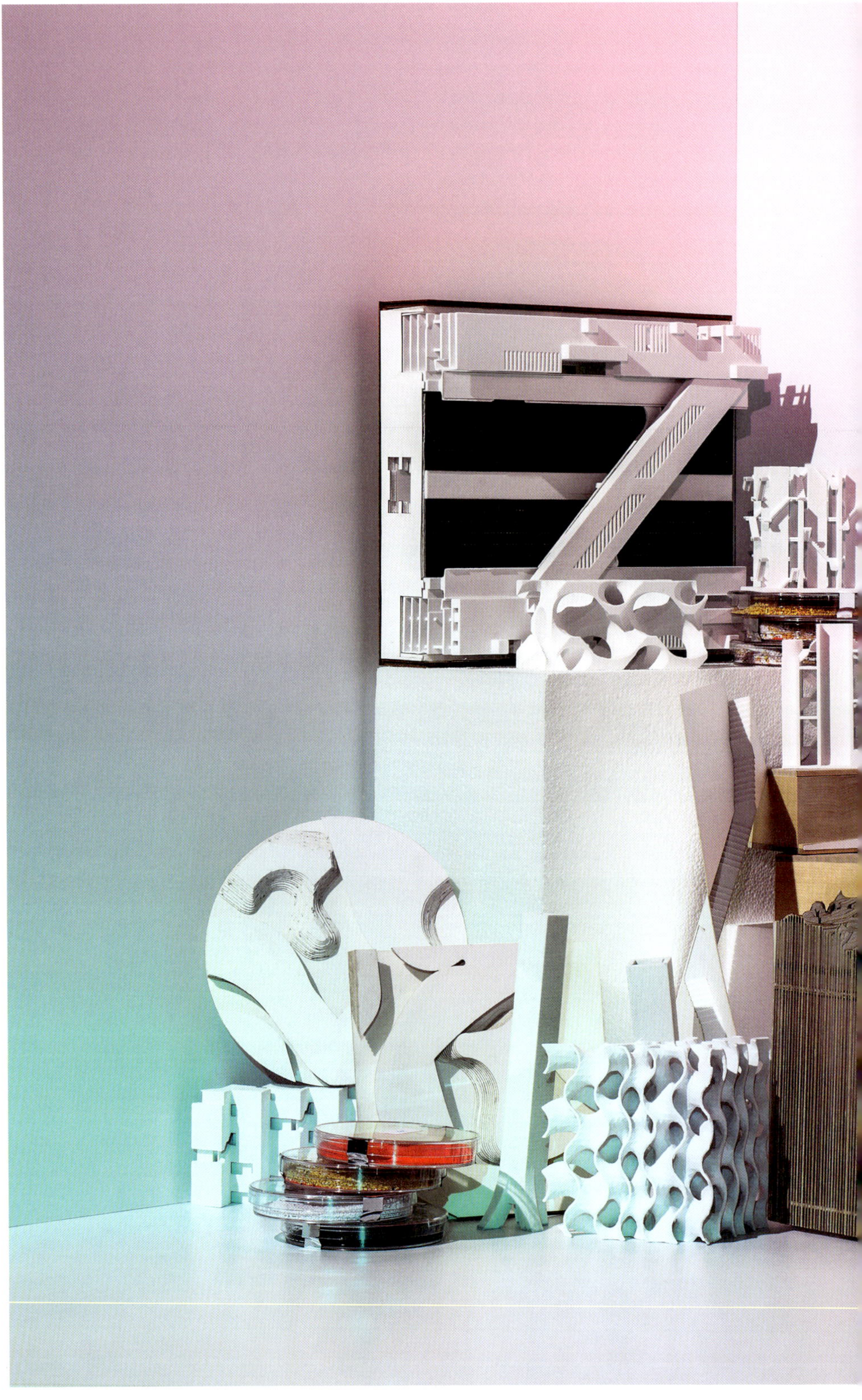

SAMPLE SAMPLES

98

SAMPLE SAMPLES

1   Nanjing

Xuanyi Nie
MArch I, 2016
Thesis: Transient Transition
Advisor: Alex Krieger

2   Re-Core
p. 100

Nancy Nichols
MArch I, 2016
Thesis: New Neighbors
Advisor: Mariana Ibañez

3   Petri Dish
p. 102

Leif Estrada
MDes / MLA I AP, 2016
Thesis: Towards Sentience:
    Attuning the Los Angeles
    River's Fluvial Morphology
Advisor: Bradley Cantrell

4   Ascent
p. 104

Allison Cottle
MArch I, 2017
Portals & Passages
Instructors: Billie Tsien,
    Tod Williams

5   Airport Plan
p. 106

Gideon Finck
MLA I, 2018
Landscape Core I
Instructor: Zaneta Hong

6   Steepness

Alica Meza
MLA I, 2016
Lagoa das Furnas:
    A Dynamic Approach to
    a Landscape Project
Instructors: João Nunes,
    João Gomes da Silva

7   Leaning
Tower

Jonathan Rieke
MArch I, 2017
Readymade Architecture
Instructor: Preston
    Scott Cohen

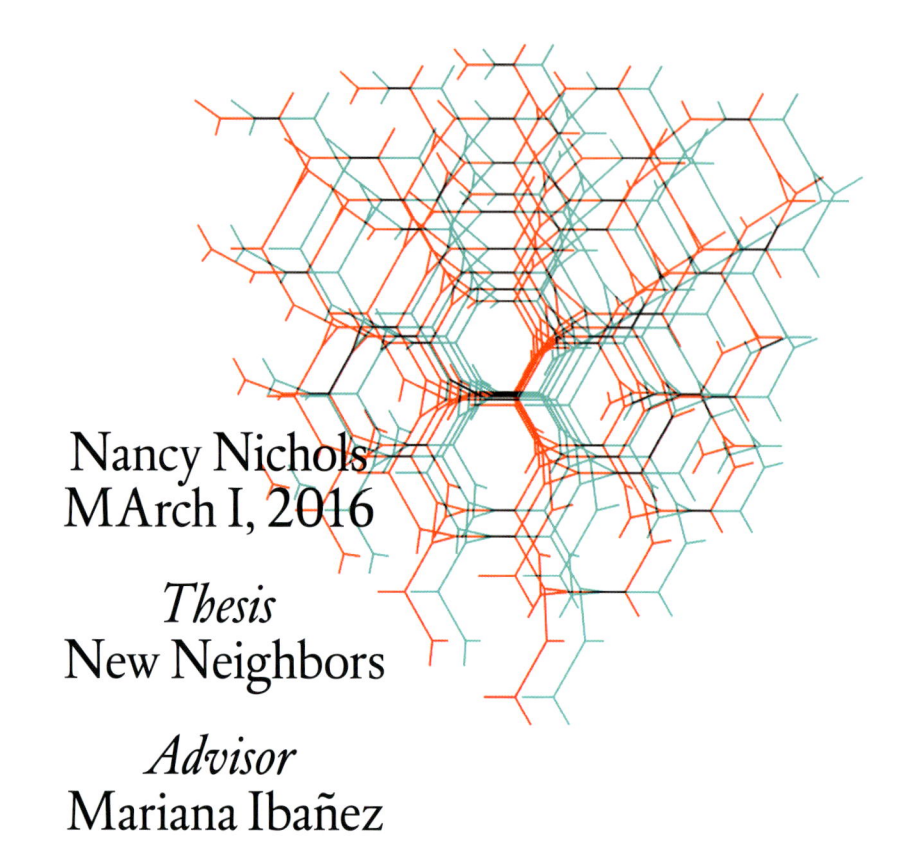

Nancy Nichols
MArch I, 2016

Thesis
New Neighbors

Advisor
Mariana Ibañez

Re-Core

Circulation structures society. It assigns users an identity in the form of an address and tells them who else is in their community. New Neighbors borrows its protagonists from Jonathan Swift's *Gulliver's Travels*, in which Gulliver describes uneasy relations between the ever-pragmatic citizens of the realm of Balnibarbi and their transcendentally inclined overlords, inhabitants of the floating island of Laputa. Reimagined in a contemporary postcolonial context, the two societies must dwell together, recognizing and reconciling their differences in a space of symbiotic exchange.

Leif Estrada
MDes / MLA I AP, 2016

Thesis
Towards Sentience: Attuning the Los Angeles River's Fluvial Morphology

Advisor
Bradley Cantrell

Awarded the Landscape Architecture Thesis Prize, this project explores the temporal morphology of the Los Angeles River through real-time sensing and responsive manipulations tested by a built machine and robot. Through advanced technology, the riverine landscape is constantly altered and modified to privilege ecological development.

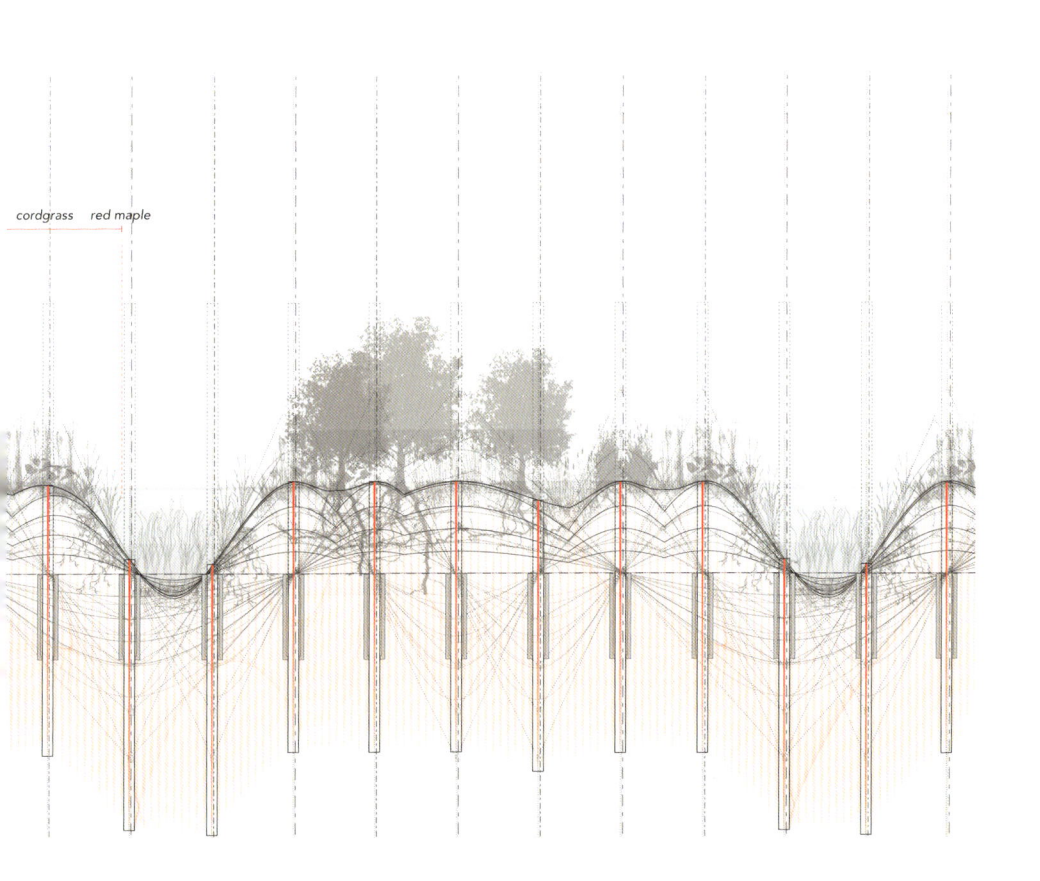

SAMPLE SAMPLES — Thesis Project — 103

cordgrass   red maple

clay loam

104

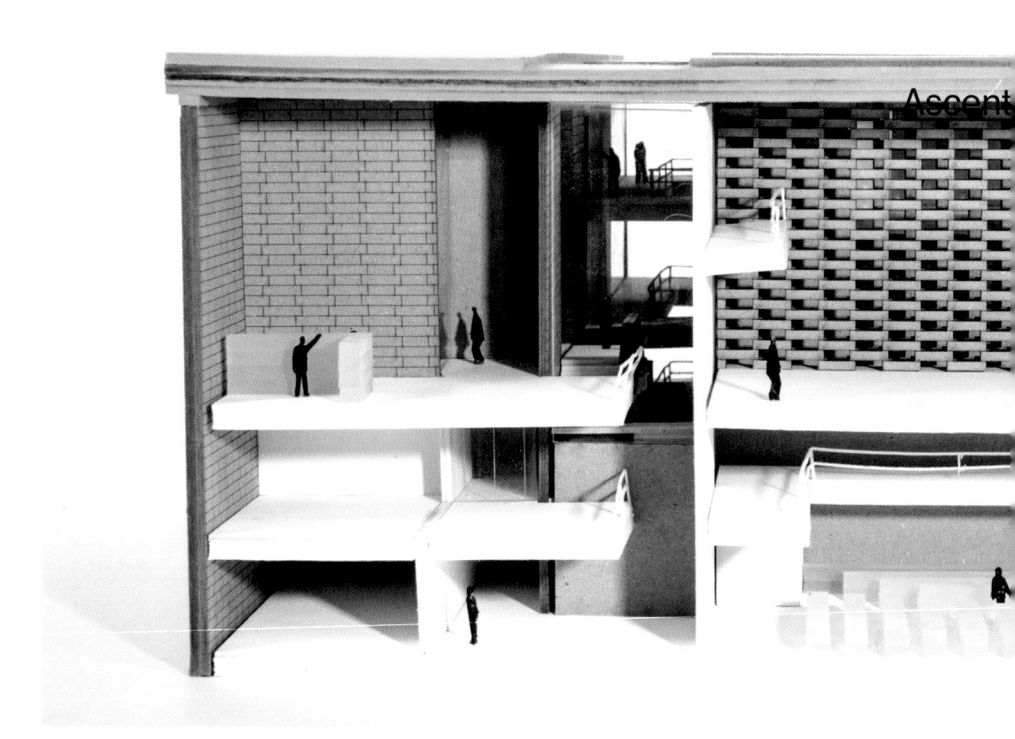

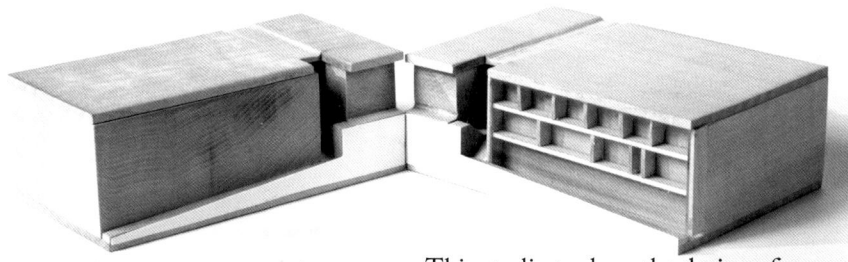

Allison Cottle
MArch I, 2017

Portals & Passages

Instructors
Billie Tsien,
Tod Williams

This studio took on the design of a performing arts center on the historic Cranbrook campus in Bloomfield Hills, Michigan. This resulting project strengthens the connection between the performing arts center and the city of Detroit, where a new renaissance of artistic activity is taking place.

106

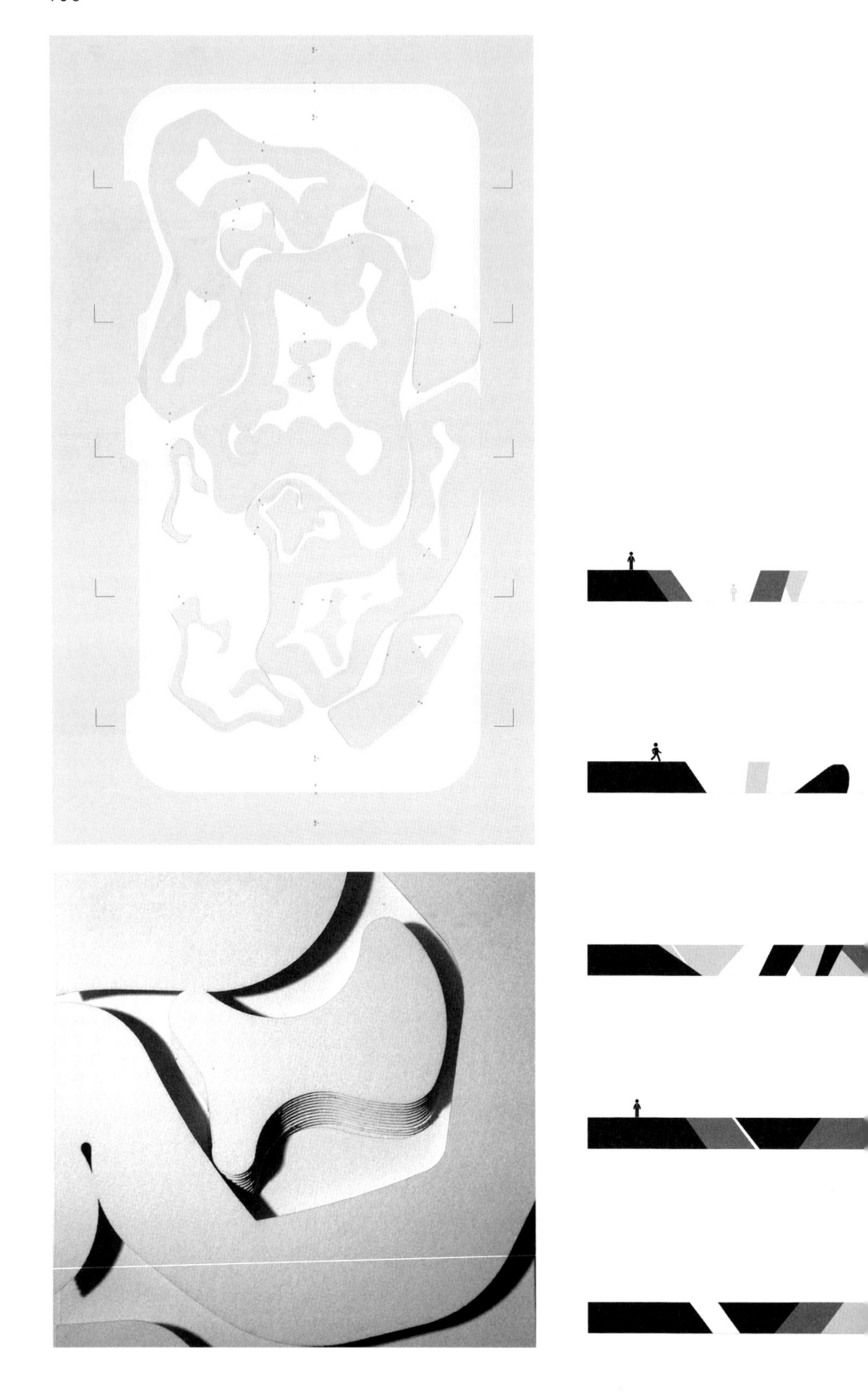

This Landscape Core studio used precedent projects, in this case the Praça Senador Salgado Filho by Roberto Burle Marx, to generate new spatial conditions through extruding and obscuring the original plan. The goal was to explore ways of connecting or disconnecting spaces both physically and visually.

Gideon Finck
MLA I, 2018

Landscape Core I

Instructor
Zaneta Hong

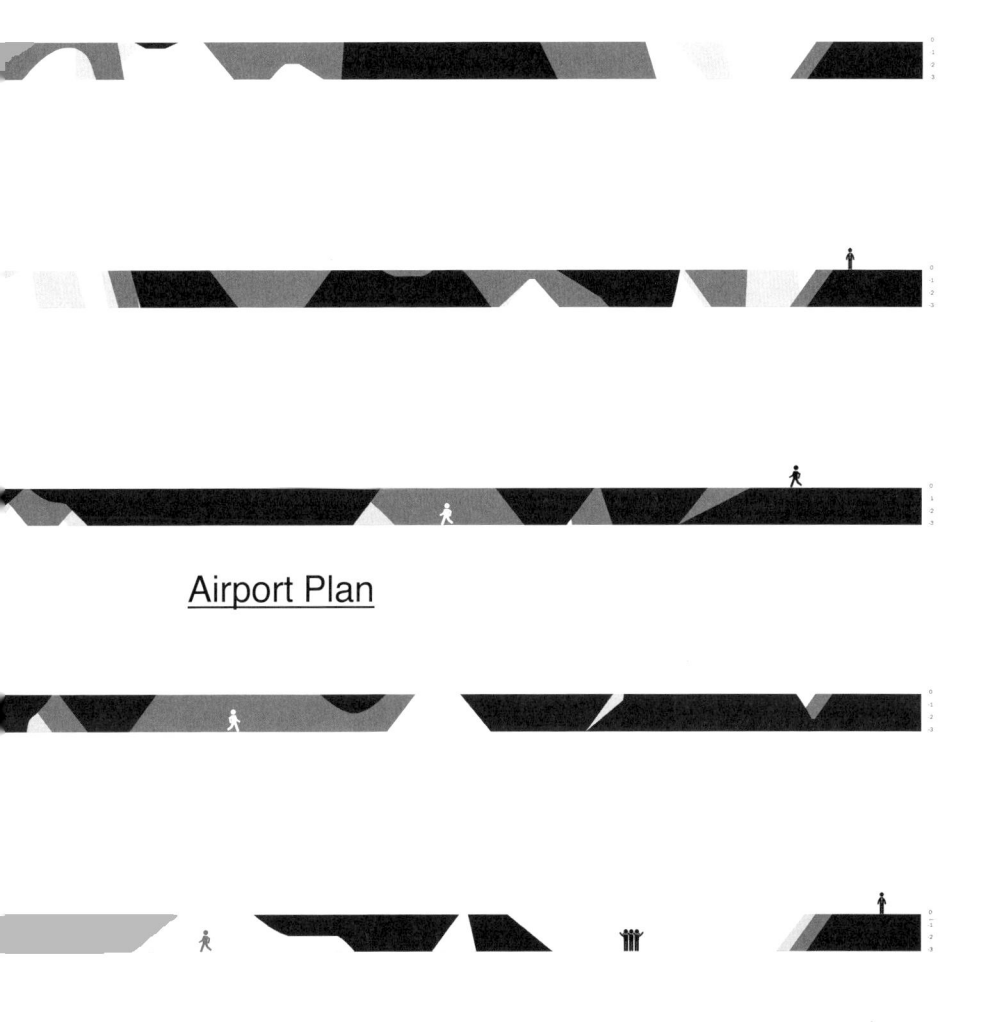

Airport Plan

Activating the Still Life

A desirable city is anything but a still life. What most gives a city its appeal is dynamism, constant movement, and open-ended change. The question thus becomes how to design for change, or even how to provoke urban dynamism through design. These collages begin to evoke a city's potential in these regards, through the sheer heterogeneity and juxtaposition of whimsical forms. But such a configuration also raises important questions about connectivity, the spatial ordering of parts and whole, the multiple scales of urbanism, and the role of the designer. A fragmented canvas of eclectic typologies and forms may capture the visual imagination, but that does not mean that, if materialized, it would necessarily be a desirable place to inhabit. What conditions must be met for a single building or parcel to be recognized as creatively contributing to the broader urban landscape? What makes it possible for discretely elegant projects to shape experiences beyond their immediate location so as to help activate urbanism at the scale of the city? To what extent can the aggregate production of individual projects produce a desirable city; or must some collective authorship be at play? Ongoing dialogue among architects, urban designers, and planners will lead the way in answering these questions, which are key to our profession and to the future of cities worldwide.

Diane E. Davis
Chair of the Department of Urban Planning and Design; Charles Dyer Norton Professor of Regional Planning and Urbanism

Vast territories, urban infills, leftover infrastructural spaces, abandoned centers, and waterfronts are the types of sites on view here. These charged site conditions promote exploration beyond the immediate site, as well as, and especially, beyond individual disciplines. In this still life, disciplinary silos crumble: architects study urbanism; urbanists work on landscapes; and landscape architects design urban form and architecture. An architectural thesis project titled Black | Mold: The City of Pride and Purpose starts by looking at chronic illnesses associated with subsidized housing (an approach that transcends disciplinary boundaries) and concludes with dueling, racked towers (pertinent to the discipline). The designer insists that "this is a project about mold"—full stop. Projects on water drainage, water scarcity, and recreational water represent a range of topics central to landscape architecture, yet all move past this discipline by proposing urban form. Not simply breaking the rules, but productively misbehaving, these projects go beyond disciplinary limits to write their own rules.

Out of Bounds

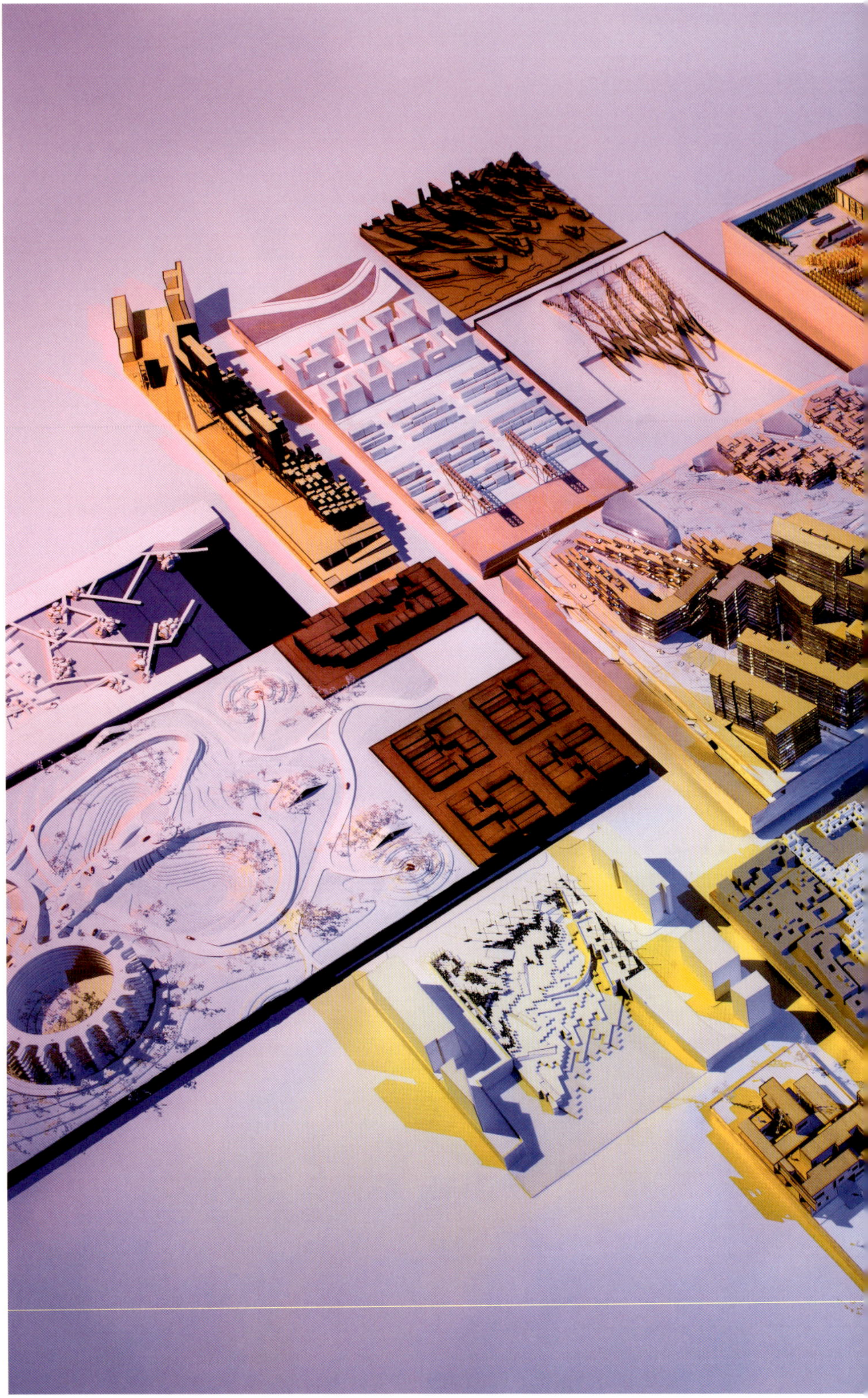

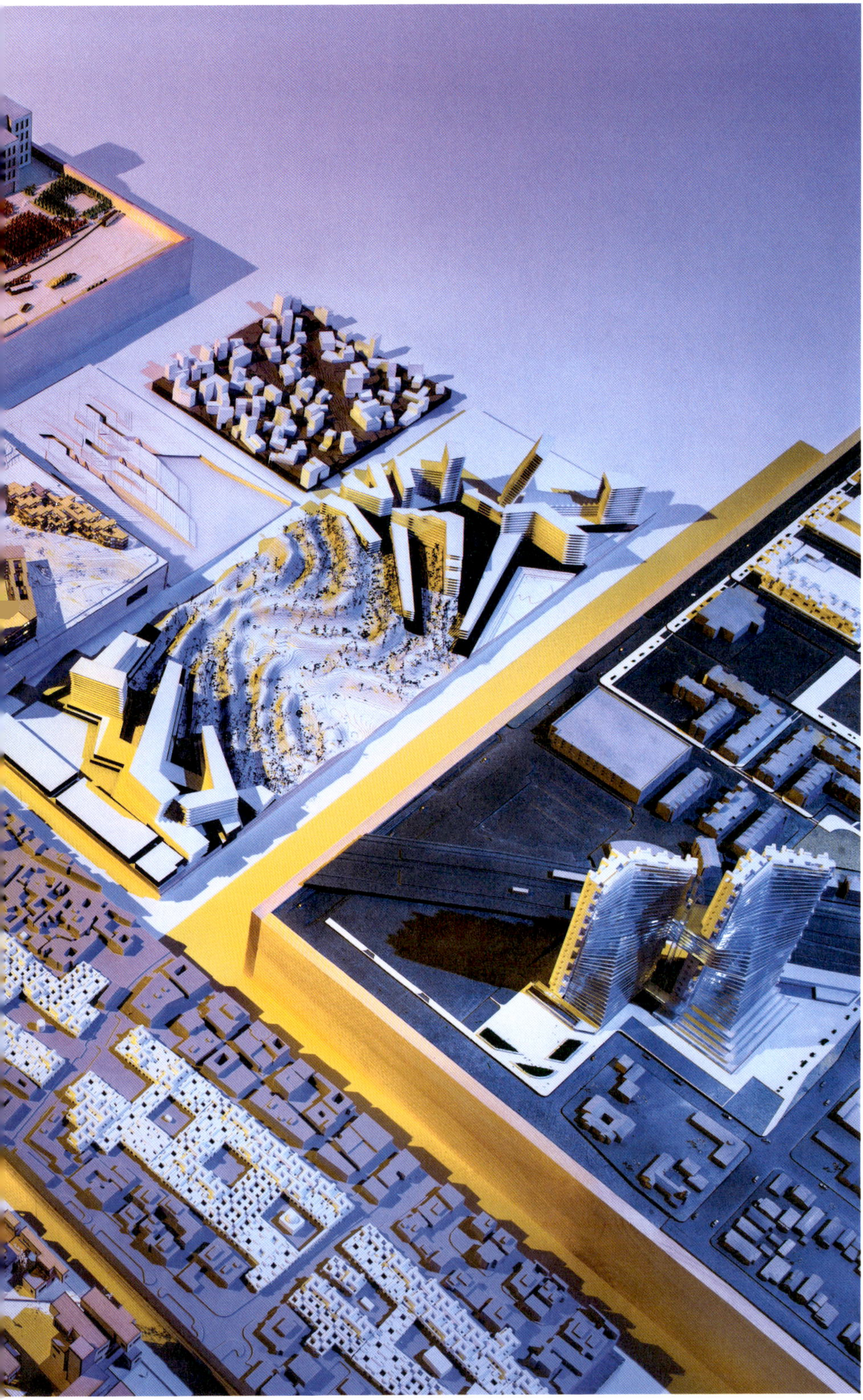

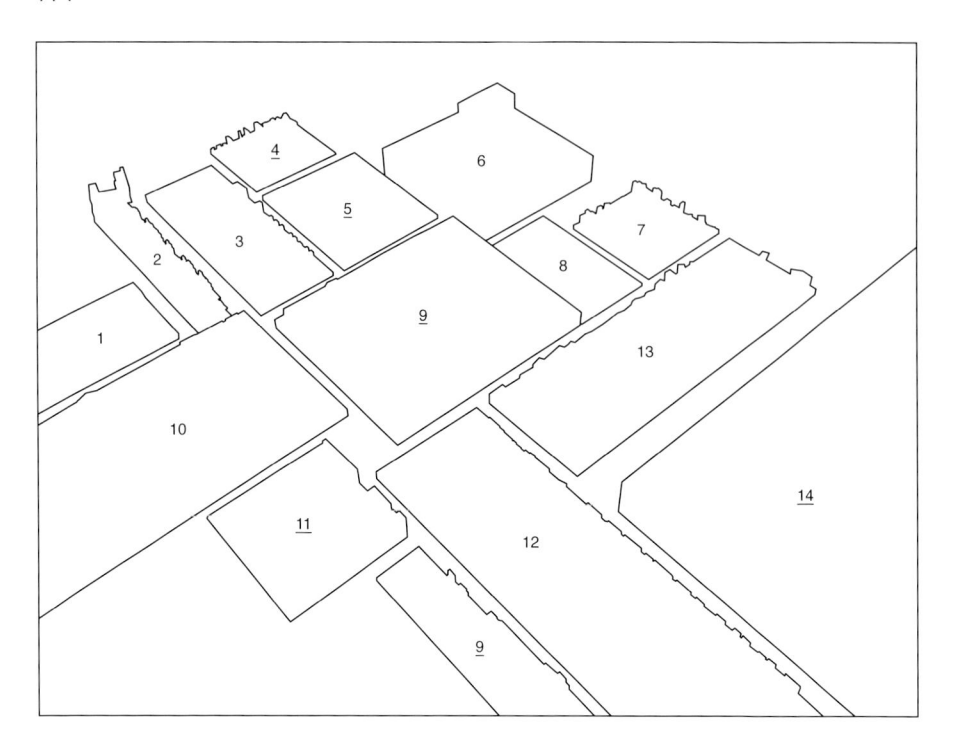

OUT OF BOUNDS

1 Waterfront
Alison Malouf
MLA I, 2018
Landscape Core I
Instructor: Zaneta Hong

2 Mat and Tower
Adam Himes, Jessy Yang
MAUD, 2017
Elements of Urban Design
Instructor: Felipe Correa

3 East 1st Street
Rekha Auguste-Nelson, Matthew Okazaki
MArch I, 2018
Aleksis Bertoni
MArch I AP, 2018
Architecture Core IV: Relate
Instructor: Carles Muro

4 [Runoff](p. 116)
Jianwu Han
MLA I AP, 2017
Xun Liu
MLA I, 2017
Landscape Core III
Instructor: Chris Reed

5 [Boardwalk](p. 118)
Mengfan Sha
MLA I, 2018
Landscape Core I
Instructor: Zaneta Hong

6 Legacy
Lou Langer
MLA I AP, 2016
The MLK Way: Building on Black America's Main Street
Instructor: Daniel D'Oca

7 Scatterplan
Andrew Taylor
MLA I AP, 2017
Lu Wang
MLA I, 2017
Landscape Core III
Instructor: Sergio Lopez-Pineiro

8 Rising Tide
Naoko Asano
MLA I, 2018
Landscape Core I
Instructor: Zaneta Hong

9 [Collective](p. 120)
Ethan Levine, Yen Shan Phoaw, Isabelle Verwaay, Hanguang Wu
MArch I, 2018
Architecture Core IV: Relate
Instructor: Carles Muro

10 Vehicular
Leif Estrada
MDes / MLA I AP, 2016
Moscow's Future: Tied Up in Traffic
Instructor: Martha Schwartz

11 [Tidal Pool](p. 122)
Michelle Benoit
MLA I, 2018
Landscape Core I
Instructor: Luis Callejas

12 Housing Units
Ali Karimi
MArch I, 2016
Thesis: Good Arab, ~~Bad City~~
Advisor: Christopher C.M. Lee

13 Brownfield
Jing Pan, Boxia Wang
MLA II, 2017
Landscape Core III
Instructor: David Mah

14 [Richmond](p. 124)
Whitney Hansley
MArch I, 2016
Thesis: Black | Mold The City of Pride and Purpose
Advisors: Iñaki Ábalos, K. Michael Hays, Peter Rowe

15 [Tijuana](p. 126)
Francisco Lara-Garcia
MUP, 2016
Thesis: ¿Te Vas o Te Quedas? Variations in Explanations for Housing Abandonment in Tijuana, Mexico
Advisor: Diane E. Davis

Runoff

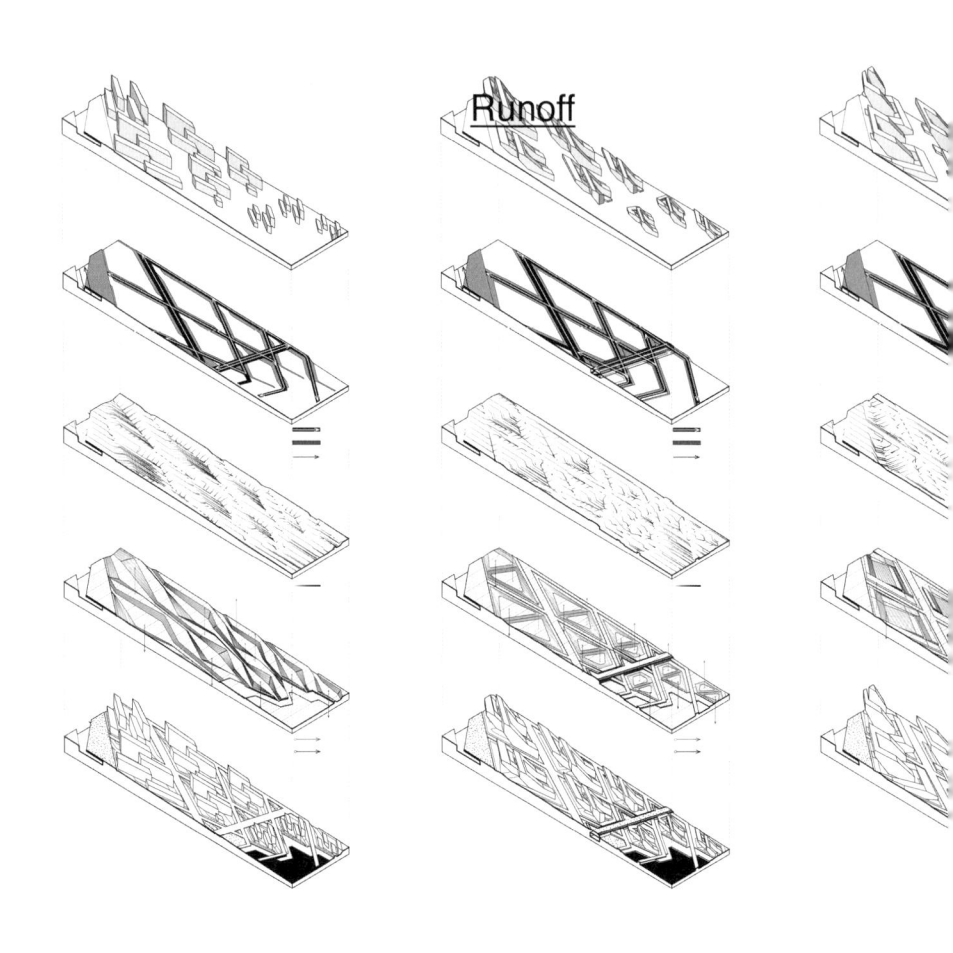

OUT OF BOUNDS   Core Studio   117

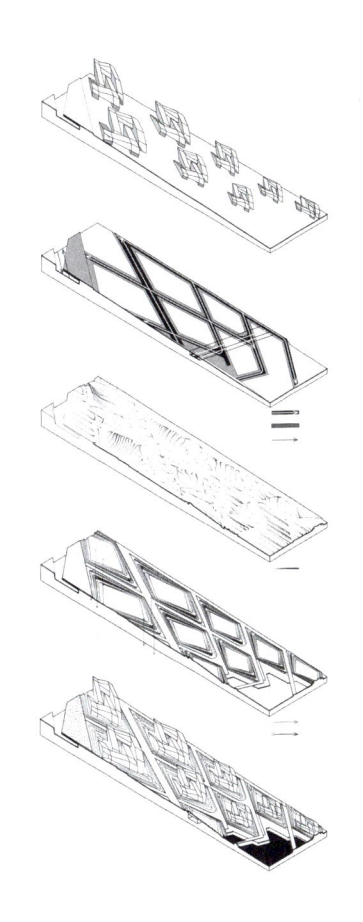

Jianwu Han
MLA AP, 2017

Xun Liu
MLA I, 2017

Landscape Core III

Instructor
Chris Reed

The third-semester Landscape Core studio introduces students to methods and representational techniques for describing urban form and the underlying ecologies that might be invoked to shape the urban fabric. This project aims to link the pedestrian circulation with a new hydrological network.

Boardwalk

The first of a four-term sequence of design studios, Landscape Core I helps students develop spatial literacy and proficiency in diverse modes of inquiry in landscape architecture. This project attempts to negotiate the growing residential and cultural hub of Boston's Seaport District with the tidal conditions of the harbor to create a new landscape for ecological pleasure.

Mengfan Sha
MLA I, 2018

Landscape Core I

Instructor
Zaneta Hong

Collective

OUT OF BOUNDS | Core Studio | 121

This studio, the last in the Architecture Core sequence, introduces students to the complexity of the urban condition and the different forms of negotiation between architecture and the city across multiple scales. Situated in South Boston, this project highlights the negotiation of vernacular urban grids to create new zones of housing and collective space.

Ethan Levine, Yen Shan Phoaw, Isabelle Verwaay, Hanguang Wu
MArch I, 2018

Architecture Core IV: Relate

Instructor
Carles Muro

Michelle Benoit
MLA I, 2018

Landscape Core I

Instructor
Luis Callejas

Tidal Pool

OUT OF BOUNDS — Core Studio — 123

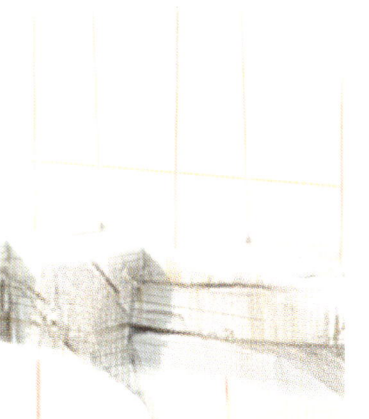

This first-semester Landscape Core studio examines issues of orientation and experience, scale and pattern, topographic form, climatic and vegetative influences, and varied ecological processes that help define urban public space. Due to inevitable rising tides, this project accepts water as its main programmatic driver, activating its movement through a designed waterfront quarry.

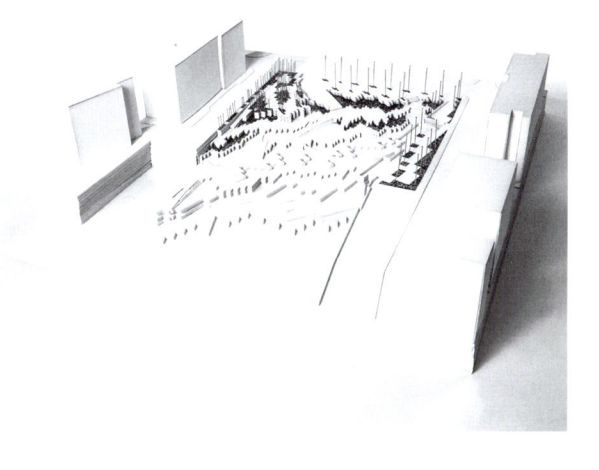

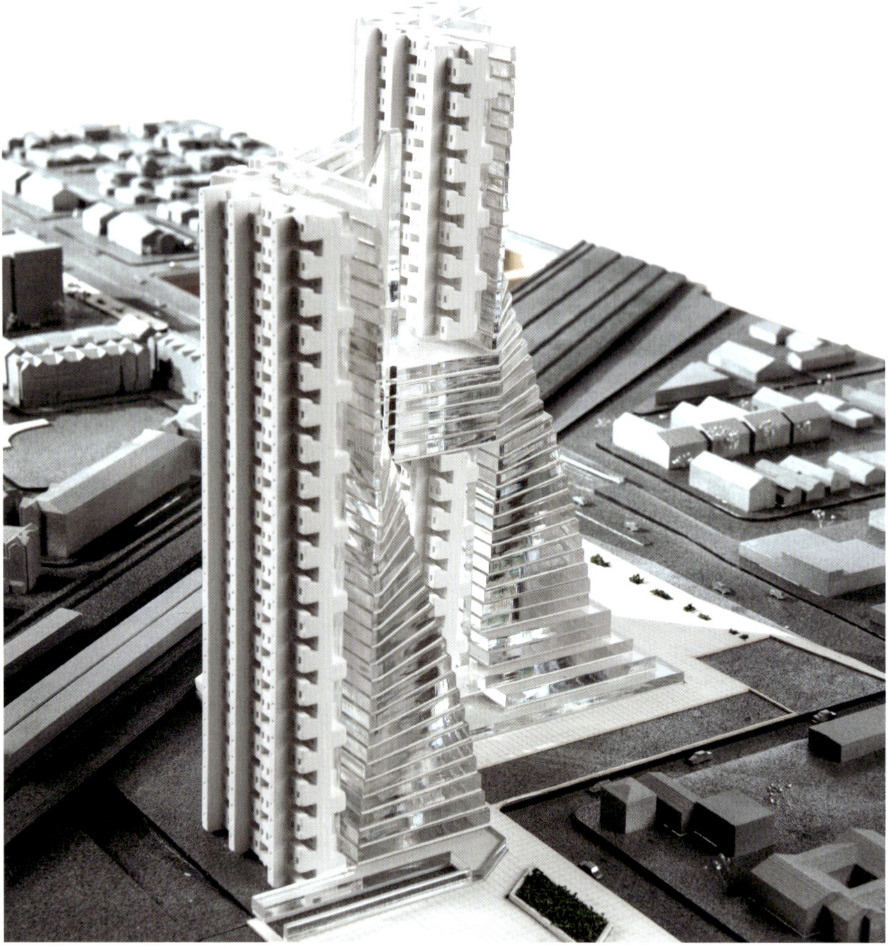

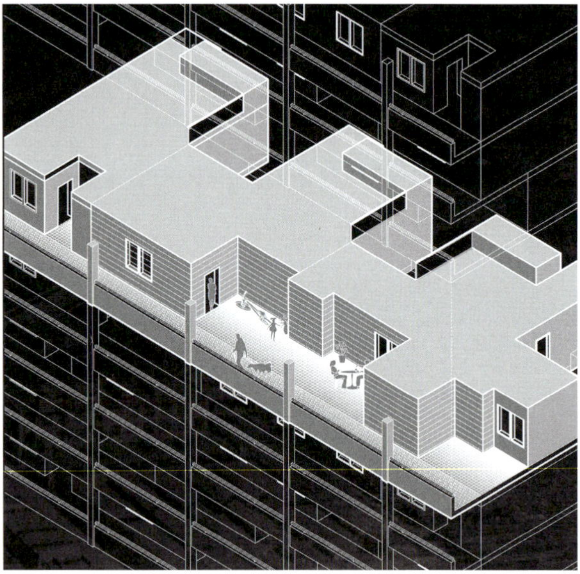

This thesis aims to revoke the American misinterpretation of modernist values that has led to the present equation of the minimum as the optimum. It abandons all self-satisfying notions of "adequate" or "satisfactory" or "tolerable" and assumes that the only truly fair solution is the one that produces the maximum utility for those who are most in need. It focuses on Richmond, California as a way to test the thesis through site-specific work indebted to the history and current life of the place.

Whitney Hansley
MArch I, 2016

Thesis
Black | Mold
The City of Pride and Purpose

Advisors
Iñaki Ábalos,
K. Michael Hays,
Peter Rowe

Francisco Lara-García
MUP, 2016

Thesis
¿Te Vas o Te Quedas? Variations in Explanations for Housing Abandonment in Tijuana, Mexico

Advisor
Diane E. Davis

There is a housing abandonment crisis in Tijuana, Mexico—evidenced by the monumental landscapes of residential vacancies conspicuous across the city. Recent reports released by the Mexican government estimate that there are more than five million vacant homes across the country, giving the nation a vacancy rate of 14 percent—the highest in Latin America. Tijuana is one of the metropolitan areas with the highest rates of abandonment, with roughly a fifth of its housing stock sitting empty. Policy makers and experts offer various explanations: the economic downturn; the overproduction of housing; low housing quality; high rates of violence; and presence of migration. Yet these explanations fail to address the uneven distribution of vacancy in Tijuana. Using Tijuana as a case study, my thesis accounts for variations in the explanations of housing abandonment.

Using a mixed-methods approach that included in-depth interviews and statistical modeling, I tested differing explanations. My research showed that "distance"—an analytical frame consisting of the scale of action (territorial scale in which an actor works) and locus of analysis (the degree of personal interaction with residents)—has a noticeable effect on the complexity of explanations that

Abandoned housing in Tijuana. Photograph by Francisco Lara-García.

stakeholders were likely to offer. Actors who had the shortest distance gave rich descriptions of the process of abandonment, offering sociophysical explanations that overlapped, interrelated, and covaried across time and space. Conversely, actors who were the most removed, having the farthest "distance," provided much simpler explanations that focused on discrete social and physical levers that were driving housing abandonment.

These results hint at three general conclusions. First, they reaffirm the value of conducting mixed-methods study, not only for the strength that triangulation brought toward the adequate representation of a phenomenon, but also for each methodology's ability to speak to a different spatial scale of analysis. Second, evaluation and program design should carefully consider the locus of analysis and scale of action because "distance" affects the type of explanations that agents are likely to give for housing abandonment. Finally, Mexican housing agencies should engage in the localized definition of problems and solutions because it promotes policy functionality and incorporates a multiplicity of perspectives.

The first conclusion cautions us to more seriously consider how the locus of analysis and the scale of action that actors have at their disposal affect how policy makers, practitioners, and researchers understand problems and devise solutions. As it stands, the predisposition to hypothesize the causes of abandonment at a predominantly quantitative and macro-level perspective that emanates from centralized agencies has allowed neither government officials nor the academy to provide a complete assessment of the housing abandonment phenomenon, or to avoid the worst excesses of state simplification described by James Scott, namely the state's penchant for destructively simplifying dynamic social and natural phenomena.[1] Thus, one of the conclusions of this work is to encourage varied methodologies in government evaluations of housing programs, as well as different scales of evaluation and problem-definition within abandonment assessments.

Second, this thesis has findings that complement Diane E. Davis's recent call to begin to treat the house as more than a simple "object" and instead begin conceiving it as a "subject."[2] In addition to this crucial cognitive shift, an epistemological reconfiguration that demands a move away from the territorial confines of the housing unit, my analysis further argues that the subject of housing should be treated at varying loci of analysis, which will allow the varied housing "subjects"—definitions that differ significantly depending on the institutional and scalar positionality of actors—to participate in policy initiatives and interventions. By shifting the scale of problem-definition, I argue that stakeholders will be able to create policies that treat housing as part and parcel of a healthy urban fabric, and also lead to housing that is appropriate for its context.

Finally, Mexican housing agencies should engage in localized problem-definition because it promotes better functionality and incorporates a multiplicity of perspectives.[3] To a degree, state simplifications are inevitable. However, the recognition that big housing agencies are not going to be able to represent everyone's interests should be built into the institutional DNA of any new policy approach, being devised in a way that maximizes diversity of perspective (disciplinary, scalar, sectoral, etc.) and prevents the interests of a single group from monopolizing policy directives. A way to do this is by allowing Infonavit (*Instituto del Fondo Nacional de la Vivienda para los Trabajadores*), Mexico's largest housing provident, to relinquish its leading role in problem-definition, and begin embracing an expanded role as facilitator of localized problem-definition and creator of urban value.

My work closes on an optimistic note. A study of Mexican social housing policy shows that it is in a constant state of flux, that housing policy undergoes "translations" depending on the exigencies of particular moments.[4] The present "translation," with its commitment to economic rationality above all, is the furthest from the housing ideals espoused during the Mexican Revolution. This can be seen as failure, or an opportunity. I believe we are due for the next translation of housing policy in Mexico, but it requires a shift away from traditional understandings of housing. This thesis is one part of that agenda; a crucial task if we are to be more successful at building housing that is responsive to the needs of Mexicans. Ultimately, if we are to stem the abandonment of houses, not just in Tijuana but throughout Mexico, changing our perspective is our primary task.

1   James C. Scott, *Seeing Like a State: How Certain Schemes to Improve the Human Condition Have Failed* (New Haven: Yale University Press, 1998).
2   Diane E. Davis, "The Urbanization-Development Nexus: Rethinking the Role of Housing in Sustainable Urbanism," (unpublished manuscript, 2015).
3   Matt Andrews, Lant Pritchett, and Michael Woolcock, "Escaping Capability Traps through Problem Driven Iterative Adaptation (PDIA)," *World Development* 51 (2013): 234–44.
4   In my thesis, I argue that Mexican housing policy has gone through discrete phases that reflect the political and social environment of the country over the last century. I refer to these different stages as housing "translations" because although these initiatives have nominally preserved a commitment to dignified housing for Mexican workers, their application was restyled significantly to serve the political purposes of Mexico's ruling class.

Tijuana

Mass housing in Valle de las Palmas, a development in Tijuana's periphery.
Photograph by Francisco Lara-García.

Basins, brownfields; coastal deserts that try to resist the gravitational pull of informal urban development; corridors that form a wildlands network for migratory animals; deltas; derricks that are remnants of an industrial landscape; factories that inspire alternate forms of urbanization; forests, hills, islands, lagoons, marshes, mountains, oceans, riverbanks, tropics, valleys.

Locations, locations, locations: All the models here engage forms and sites that inspire specific interventions. The design and siting of a mosque-church-temple take the visitor on a pilgrimage to Sart, Turkey. In a rural village of Tokyo, a proposal for a cultural building sources local wood while also designing a construction process for labor. An architecture thesis suggests four projects at four different global sites. These projects incite discourse by representing a range of locations that embrace a diversity of people, places, and cultures.

Locations

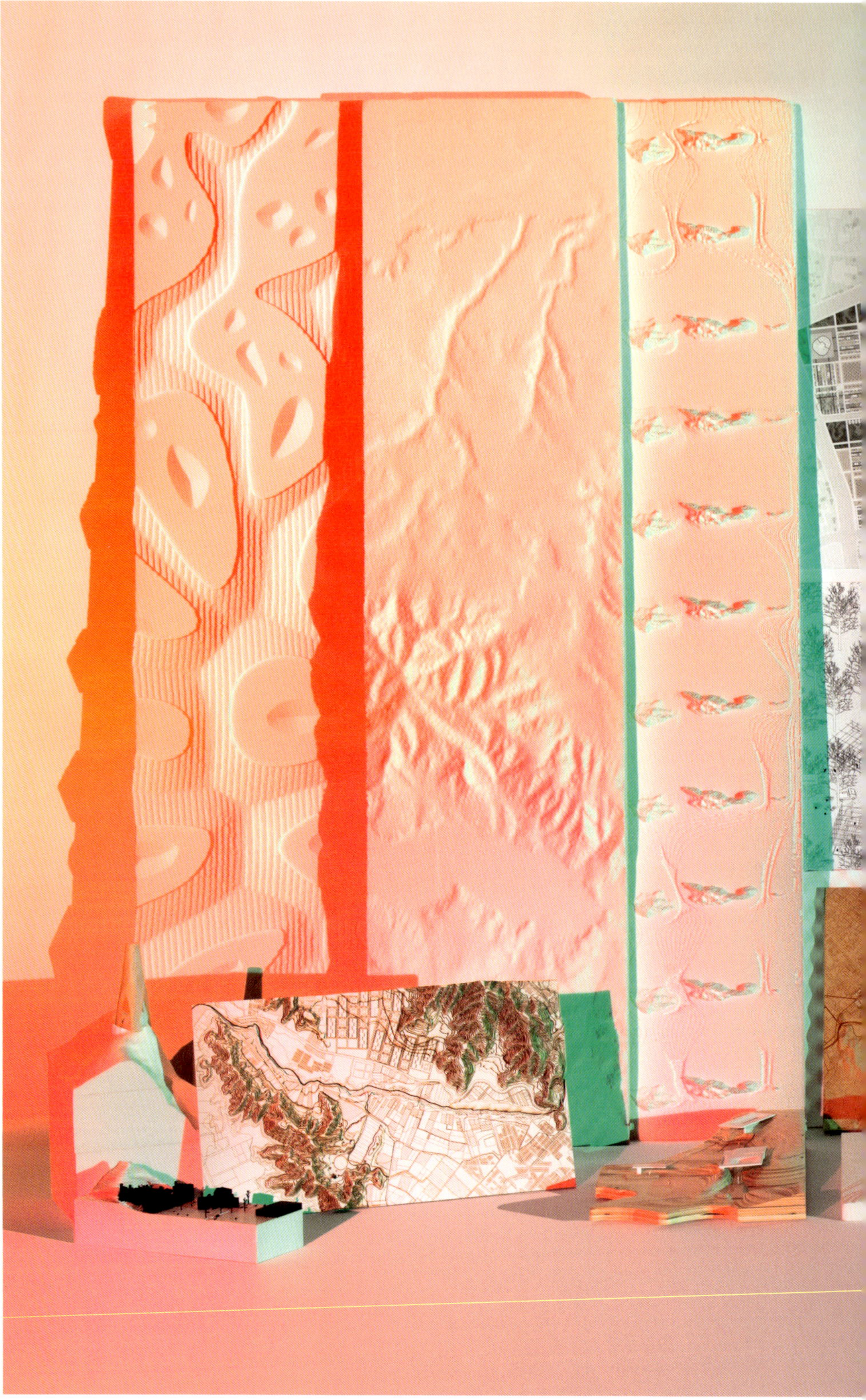

LOCATIONS 133

134

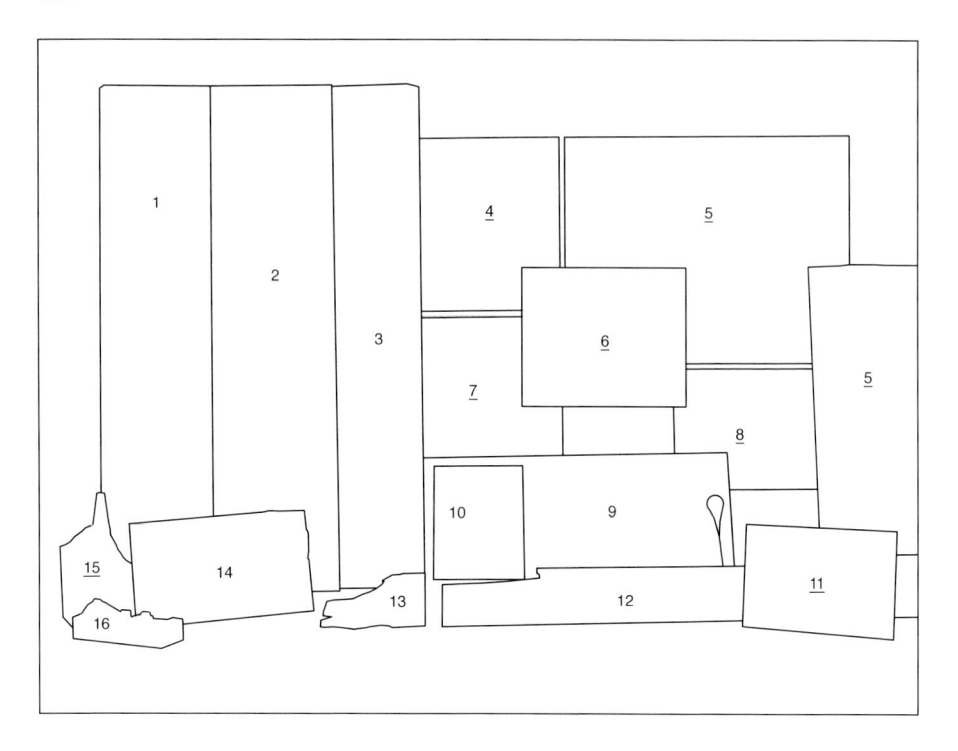

LOCATIONS

1 Ridge

Keith Scott
MLA I, 2017
Dandi Zhang
MLA I AP, 2017
Landscape Core IV
Instructor: Nicholas Pevzner

2 Spine

Gandong Cai, Xun Liu,
    Alexandra Mei
MLA I AP, 2017
Johanna Cairns, Leandro
    Couto de Almeida, Siobhan
    Feehan Miller, Sophia
    Geller, Maria Robalino,
    Diana Tao, Lu Wang,
    Malcom Wyler, Xin Zhao
MLA I, 2017
Gary Hon
MLA II, 2017
Landscape Core IV
Instructor: Robert Pietrusko

3 Serial

Gary Hon
MLA II, 2017
Maria Robalino
MLA I, 2017
Xin Zhao
MDes / MLA I, 2017
Landscape Core IV
Instructor: Robert Pietrusko

4 New Neighborhoods
p. 136

Elaine Kwong
MAUD, 2017
Poap Panusittikorn
MArch II, 2017
The Factory and the
    City: Rethinking the
    Industrial Spaces of the
    Developmental City
Instructor:
    Christopher C.M. Lee

5 Wild
p. 138

Mary Miller
MDes / MLA I AP, 2017
Thesis: Field and Valley:
    Disturbing Interfaces in the
    Colorado Western Slope
Advisor: Rosetta Elkin

6 Peru
p. 140

Mengdan Liu
MArch II, 2016
Long Zuo
MAUD, 2016
Urban Blackholes:
    Development and Heritage
    in the Lima Metropolis
Instructor: Jean
    Pierre Crousse

7 Construction
p. 142

Yutian Wang
MAUD, 2016
Redesigning the Actor
    Network in Rural Areas
    around Tokyo
Instructors: Momoyo Kaijima,
    Yoshiharu Tsukamoto

8 Circle
p. 144

Azzurra Cox
MLA I, 2016
Lagoa das Furnas: A
    Dynamic Approach to a
    Landscape Project
Instructors: João Nunes, João
    Gomes da Silva

9 Undulating

Gandong Cai
MLA I AP, 2017
Johanna Cairns, Diana Tao,
    Malcolm Wyer
MLA I, 2017
Landscape Core IV
Instructor: Robert Pietrusko

10 Heritage

Carol Jin Jin Chiu
MArch I, 2017
Devin Dobrowolski
MLA I, 2016
Urban Blackholes:
    Development and Heritage
    in the Lima Metropolis
Instructor: Jean
    Pierre Crousse

11 Los Angeles
p. 146

Michelle Shofet
MLA I, 2016
Thesis: Divine Seepage
Advisor: Sergio Lopez-Pineiro

12 Palace

Sofia Blanco Santos,
    Caio Barboza
MArch II, 2016
Dualisms: A House, a Palace
Instructor: Iñaki Ábalos

13 Hillside

Collin Cobia
MLA I AP, 2017
Imprecise Tropics
Instructor: Camilo
    Restrepo Ochoa

14 Valley

Thomas Nideroest
MLA II, 2016
Ruben Segovia
MArch II, 2017
Urban Blackholes:
    Development and Heritage
    in the Lima Metropolis
Instructor: Jean
    Pierre Crousse

15 Church
p. 148

Emma Silverblatt
MArch I, 2017
etceteras
Instructor: Mack Scogin

16 Hole-Whole

Mingyu Kim, Madelyn Willey,
    Tianze Tong
MArch I, 2018
Shaowen Zhang
MArch I AP, 2018
Architecture Core IV: Relate
Instructor: Andrew Holder

Elaine Kwong
MAUD, 2017

Poap Panusittikorn
MArch II, 2017

The Factory and the City: Rethinking the Industrial Spaces of the Developmental City

Instructor
Christopher C. M. Lee

The rise of the "Maker Movement" has brought the revitalization and revalidation of a forgotten building type: the factory. The history and evolution of the factory reflect the transformation of the nature of industries and the factory's relation to the city and its economy: once a polluting, large, Spartan shed exiled to the periphery, the factory has since become a sterile assembly plant, a lush business park for research and management, and, most recently, a "hip" space for collaboration. This studio aimed to imagine a "Maker's Factory" that could act as a new urban core in Singapore: a self-sufficient place that could support a dynamic economy in a revitalized industrial zone and provide cultural and intellectual stimulation—in other words, a factory that could serve as a city in itself.

LOCATIONS • Option Studio • 137

ew Neighborhoods

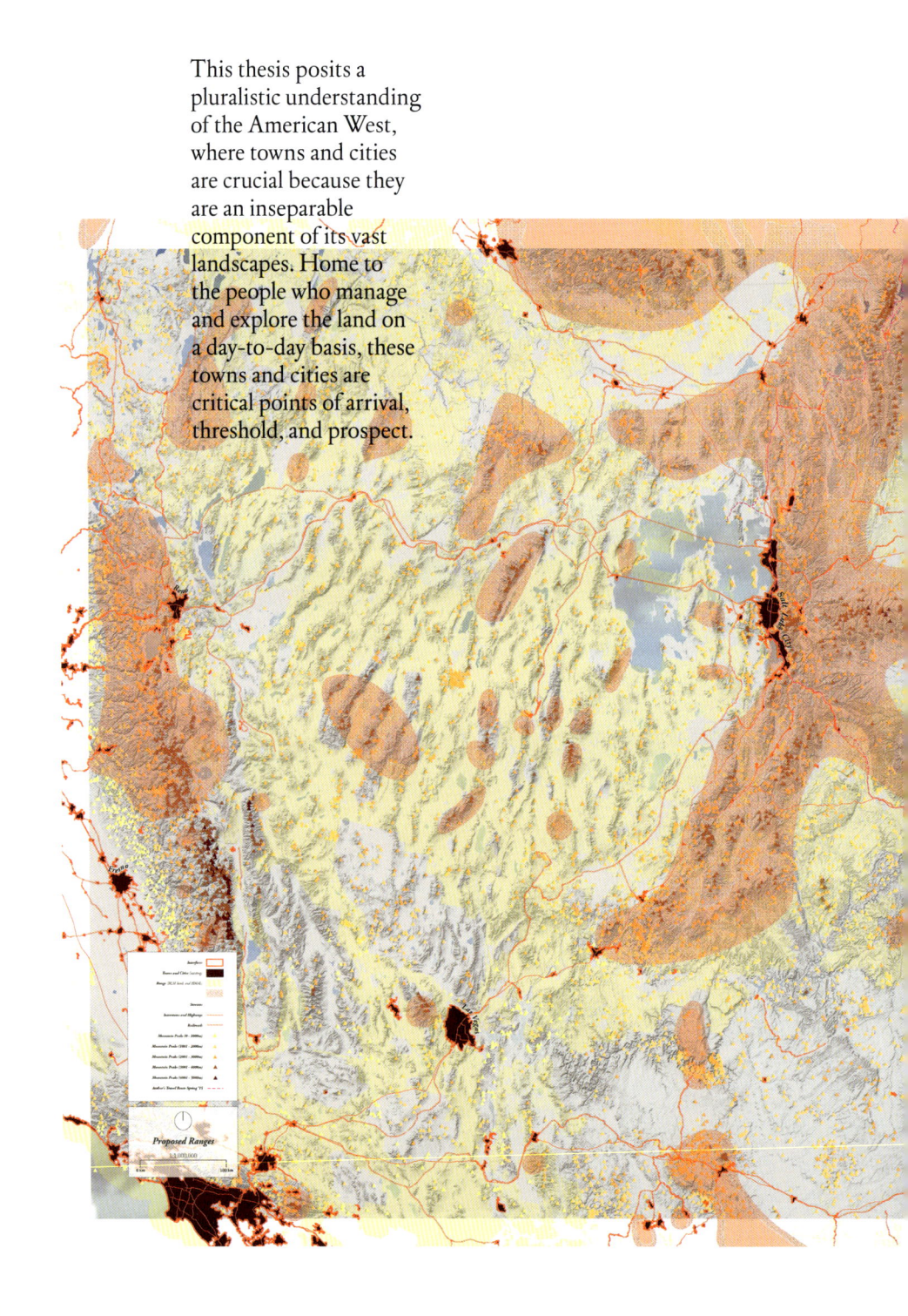

This thesis posits a pluralistic understanding of the American West, where towns and cities are crucial because they are an inseparable component of its vast landscapes. Home to the people who manage and explore the land on a day-to-day basis, these towns and cities are critical points of arrival, threshold, and prospect.

| LOCATIONS | Thesis Project | 139 |

Wild

Mary Miller
MDes / MLA I AP, 2017

Thesis
Field and Valley: Disturbing Interfaces in the Colorado Western Slope

Advisor
Rosetta Elkin

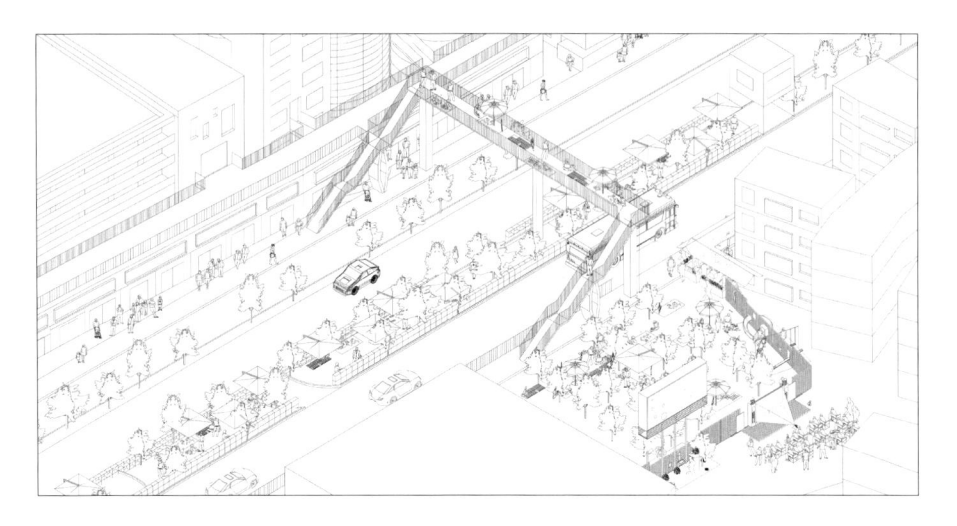

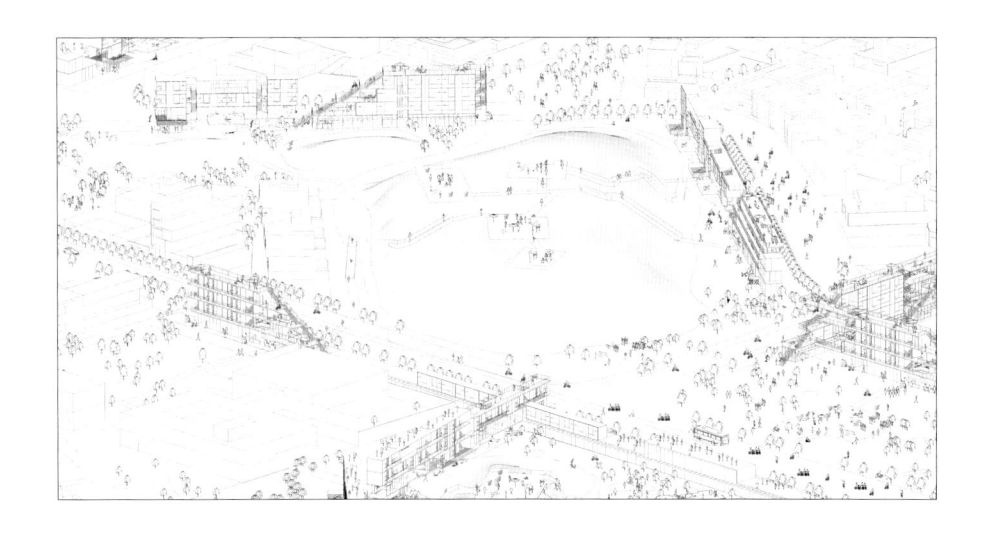

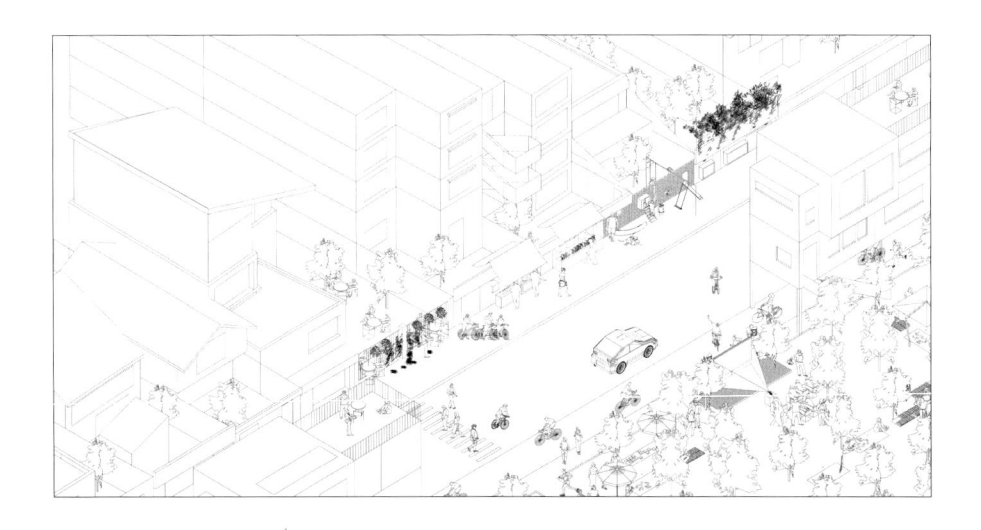

Mengdan Liu
MArch II, 2016

Long Zuo
MAUD, 2016

Urban Blackholes: Development and Heritage in the Lima Metropolis

Instructor
Jean Pierre Crousse

Cities with rapid growth, heritage, and development have often created frictional zones where economic logic collides with preservation policy. The absence of urban planning in Lima, Peru, over the past 30 years has transformed these zones into genuine blackholes within the urban grid—hopelessly attracting formal and informal growth. This studio explored multiple scales of intervention that could effectively integrate these "urban blackholes" with urban life in a lasting way.

Peru

This studio proposed instrumental space in the rural areas around Tokyo based on Bruno Latour's alternative actor-network theory. Here, the designer draws a "construction process scene" and specifies the use of wood to make a cultural building.

Yutian Wang
MAUD, 2016

Redesigning the Actor Network in Rural Areas around Tokyo

Instructors
Momoyo Kaijima, Yoshiharu Tsukamoto

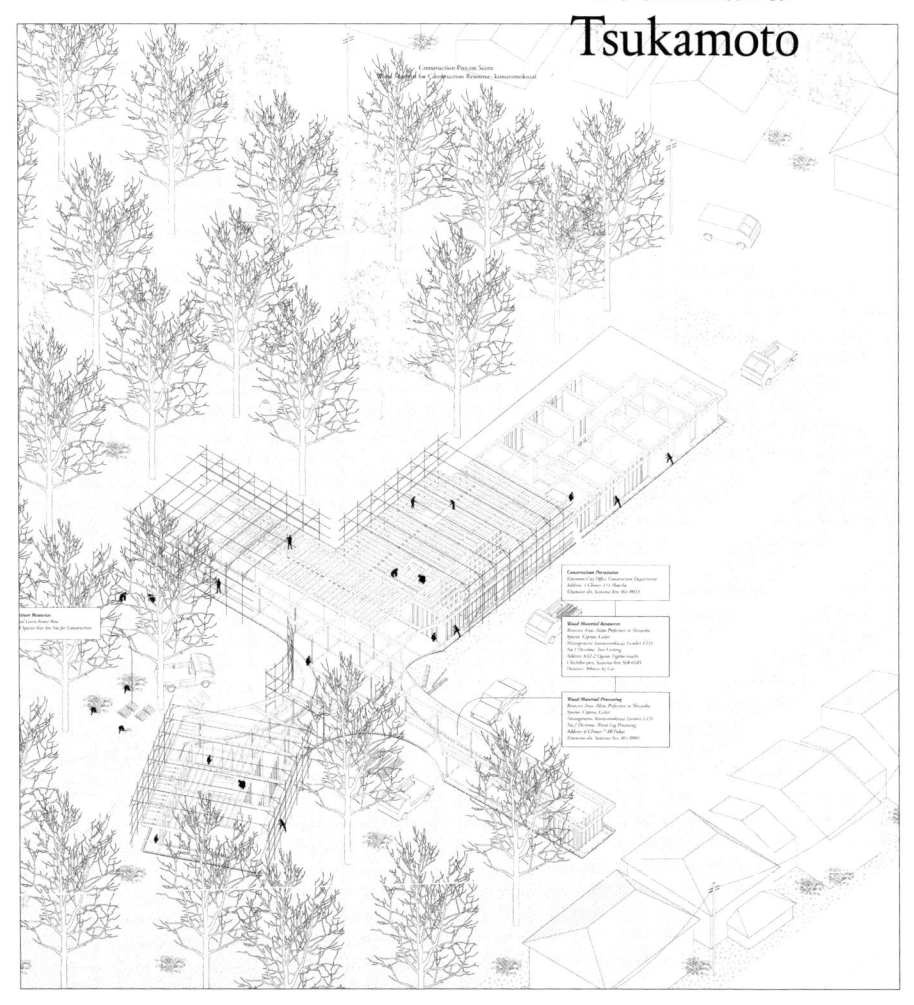

LOCATIONS   Option Studio   143

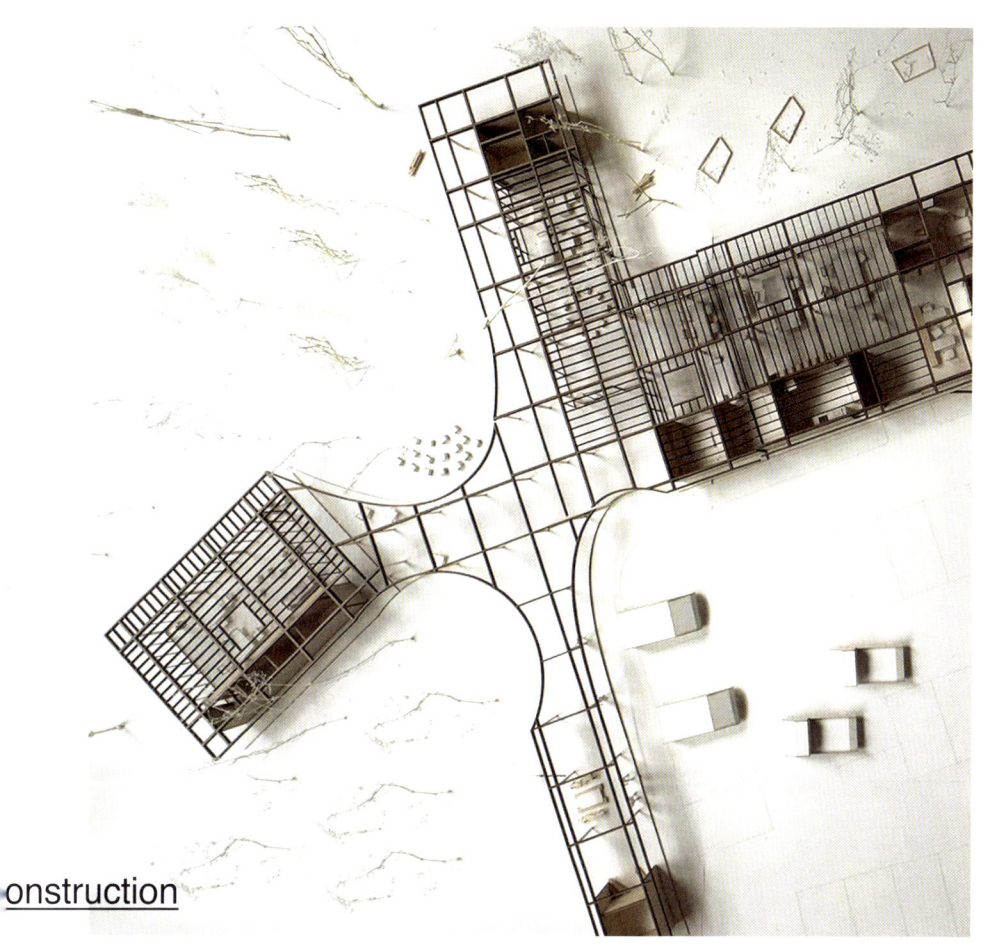

onstruction

Azzurra Cox
MLA I, 2016

Lagoa das Furnas: A Dynamic Approach to a Landscape Project

Instructors
João Nunes,
João Gomes da Silva

This studio intended to examine the questions raised by the dynamic generation of the Furnas landscape in the Azores and its classification as unique and iconic. Particular emphasis was given to the cultural and anthropic dimensions of the landscape, as well as the different cycles characteristic of these islands. Through serial sectioning and simple interventions, this project aims to highlight these distinctions.

LOCATIONS
Option Studio
145

Circle

Michelle Shofet
MLA I, 2016

Thesis
Divine Seepage

Advisor
Sergio Lopez-Pineiro

An irrevocable and unbiased seepage has long permeated Los Angeles. Its omnipresence manifests in derricks shrouded in lace curtains of greenery; in pools of primordial ooze on museum grounds; in puddles of seepage curing on the sidewalk; on the soles of one's feet at the beach. Despite the lengths gone to in order to mitigate its presence, the reality is that Los Angeles is mired in this substance. This thesis calls for a transformation of our cultural relationship to both nature and the hypertechnologized landscape.

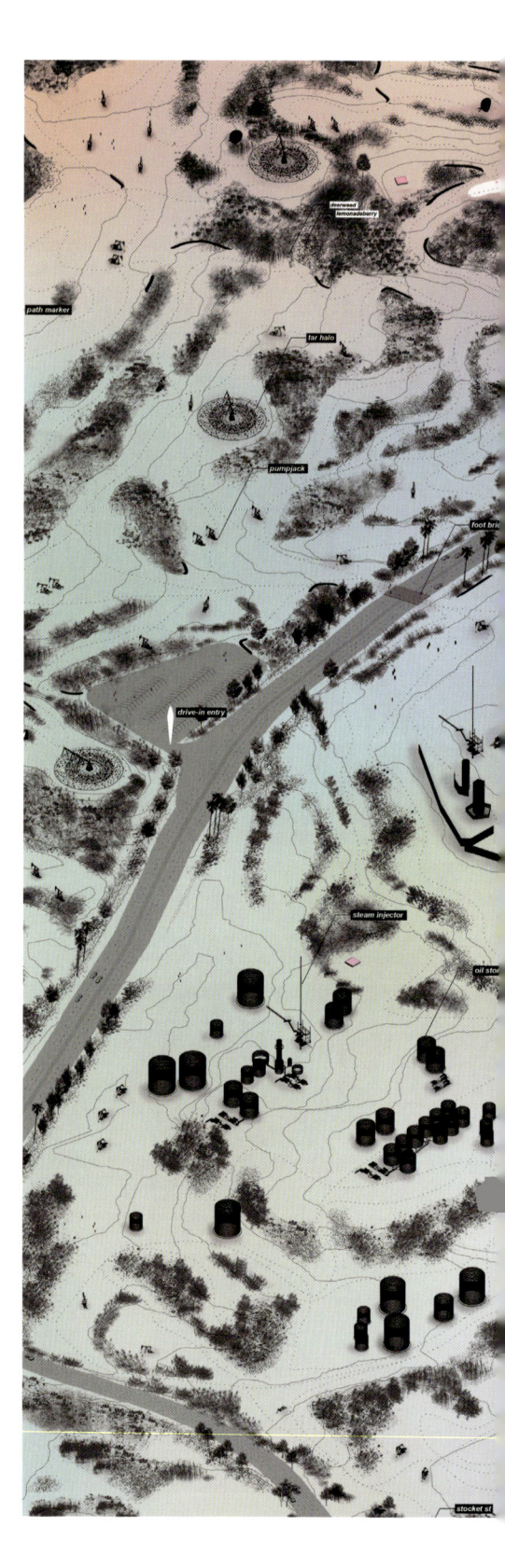

LOCATIONS · Thesis Project · 147

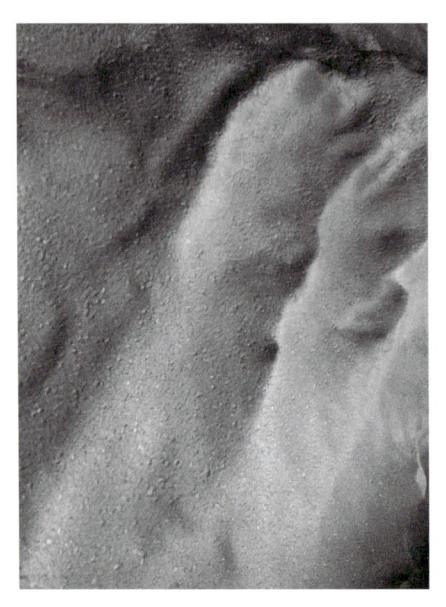

Emma Silverblatt
MArch I, 2017

etceteras

Instructor
Mack Scogin

Church

LOCATIONS Option Studio 149

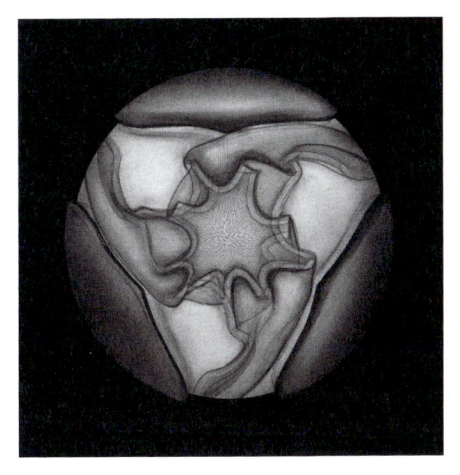

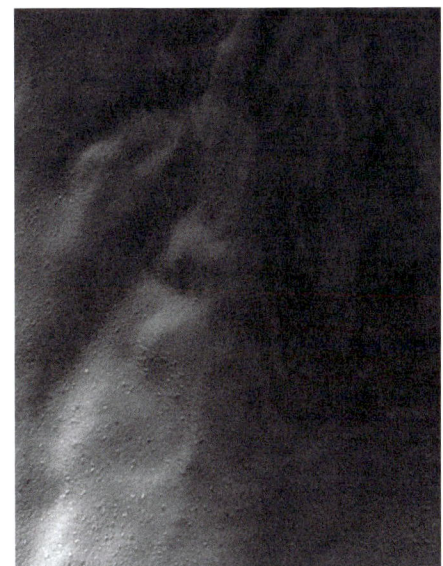

"When I was two, my family went to Maine. We hiked up a steep, spiraling mountain path. The mountain was surrounded by lapping waves. I could smell salty air. I ran far ahead of my parents, around and around the mountain, racing to get to the top. I didn't notice the very last turn of the path. I fell off a cliff into thin air. I died in the waiting waves. I was caught from below. I never fell."
—Emma Silverblatt

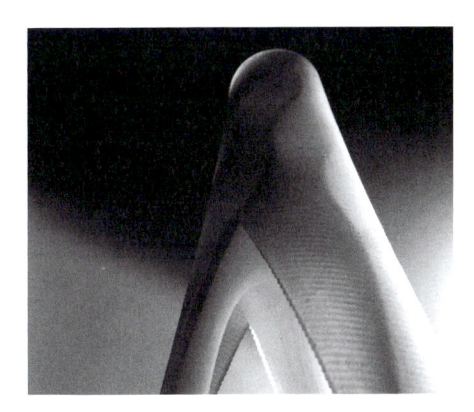

No More Self-Portraits Please

To understand how much architectural pedagogy has changed over the past two decades, it is helpful to use a pictorial analogy. The period of the Iconic Turn was nothing but the blooming of self-portraiture as the only architectural reaction to our own pettiness. That pathetic, autistic narcissism contributed to transforming architects into simply exterior decorators.

The still life genre means accepting that answers should be more complex than burying our heads or gazing at ourselves in the mirror. Still life is a cosmogony built from the double tension of objects and space in between, organic and inorganic, dead and alive. In architecture it can demonstrate that creative conversations and architecture/design, city/landscape cross-curricular dialogues are essential to finding the right path to a broadened, enriched experience of daily life.

Iñaki Ábalos
Chair of the Department of Architecture;
Professor in Residence of Architecture

The sectional model is alive and well at the GSD. Here, 27 models reveal their inner workings in what appears to be a sectional fête. Three projects for the studio The Architectural Double in the Museum City demonstrate spatial circulatory systems through the section. Some sectional models cut through ground, as in a housing proposal designed to accompany a waste-to-energy facility located in Johannesburg. Architecture students work on the "hidden room" project by submerging the mass in ground and section. A landscape architecture studio uses soil and vegetation to explore thermal mass, microclimates, and renewed ideas of pleasure within a historic park.

    Some models appear to be conceived of in section, while others were merely constructed for the final review in section. Either way, the sectional model encourages another view of design, one with depth and precision.

Sectional

154

SECTIONAL

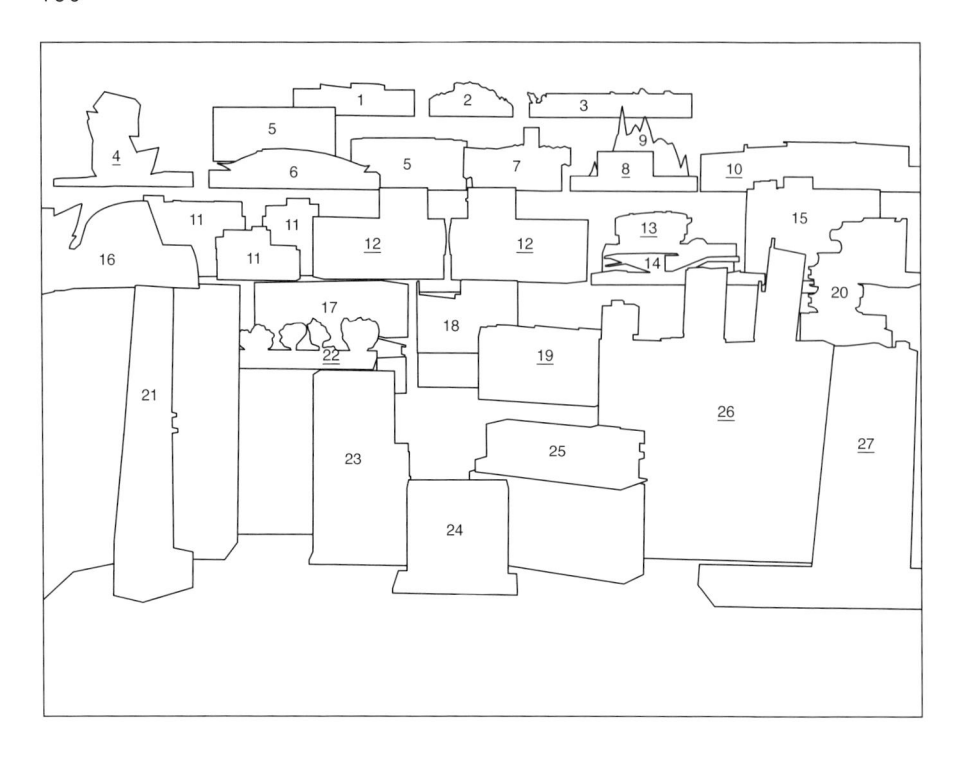

1   -56 Ft.

Jihoon Hyun
MArch I, 2019
Architecture Core I: Project
Instructor: Megan Panzano

2   Carbon

InHye Jang
MLA I, 2016
Wood, Urbanism: From the
    Molecular to the Territorial
Instructors: Jane Hutton,
    Kiel Moe

3   Academy

Chase Jordan
MArch I, 2017
The Function of Education:
    The 21st Century School
Instructors: Farshid Moussavi,
    James Khamsi

4   Skewered
p. 158

Emily Ashby
MArch I, 2019
Architecture Core II: Situate
Instructor: Jeffry Burchard

5   Curved Extrusion

Stephanie Conlan
MArch I, 2017
The Architectural Double in the
    Museum City
Instructors: Sharon
    Johnston, Mark Lee

6   Concentric Domes

Kai-hong Chu
MArch I, 2019
Architecture Core I: Project
Instructor: Andrew Holder

7   Hillside Mosque

David Hamm,
    Yu Kun Snoweria Zhang
MArch I, 2017
(Re) planned Obsolescence . . .
    Rethinking the
    Architecture of Waste
Instructors: Hanif Kara, Leire
    Asensio Villoria

8   Duration
p. 160

Khoa Vu
MArch I, 2019
Architecture Core I: Project
Instructor: Mariana Ibañez

9   Blue Data

Anita Helfrich, Chase Jordan,
    Niki Murata
MArch I, 2017
Mapping: Geographic
    Representation and
    Speculation
Instructor: Robert Pietrusko

SECTIONAL 157

10 Workplace
p. 162

Justin Jiang, LeeAnn Suen
MArch I, 2017
Junyoung Lee
MArch II, 2017
Work Environments 2:
    Glass Works
Instructor: Florian Idenburg

11 Embedded

Andrejs Rauchut
MArch II, 2017
Center for the Performing
    Arts at the Cranbrook
    Educational Community
Instructors: Billie Tsien,
    Tod Williams

12 Affected Ramp
p. 164

Benjamin Halpern
MArch I, 2017
The Architectural Double in the
    Museum City
Instructors: Sharon
    Johnston, Mark Lee

13 Santiago
p. 166

Caio Barboza, Sofia
    Blanco Santos
MArch II, 2016
Thesis: On Adapting: A
    House, a Palace
Advisor: Iñaki Ábalos

14 Cones

Chris Grenga
MArch I, 2019
Architecture Core II: Situate
Instructor: Jeffry Burchard

15 Respite

Xiaodi Yan
MLA II, 2016
Seoul Remade: Design of the
    "Kool" and the Everyday
Instructor: Niall Kirkland

16 Theatre

Iman Fayyad
MArch I, 2016
Thesis: The Phantom
    Projective
Advisors: Preston Scott
    Cohen, Cameron Wu

17 Intersected Stair

John Going
MArch I, 2017
The Architectural Double in the
    Museum City
Instructors: Sharon
    Johnston, Mark Lee

18 Waste Facility

Michael Haggerty
MArch I, 2017
Dana McKinney
MArch I / MUP, 2017
(Re) planned Obsolescence . . .
    Rethinking the
    Architecture of Waste
Instructors: Hanif Kara,
    Leire Asensio Villoria

19 Sawtooth
p. 168

Evan Farley
MArch I, 2017
"The English and the
    Americans Expect
    Everyone to be
    Well-dressed" or A Building
    for a Fashion House
Instructors: Emanuel Christ,
    Christoph Gantenbein

20 Sloterdijk

Nancy Nichols
MArch I, 2016
Thesis: New Neighbors
Advisor: Mariana Ibañez

21 Hanging

William Adams
MArch I AP, 2018
Architecture Core III: Integrate
Instructor: Jonathan Lott

22 Inside Out
p. 170

Jiawen Chen
MLA I, 2018
Landscape Core I
Instructor: Silvia Benedito

23 Stepped

Jeffrey Burges
MArch I, 2017
Architecture Core III: Integrate
Instructor: Elizabeth Whittaker

24 Slabs

Jihoon Hyun
MArch I, 2019
Architecture Core II: Situate
Instructor: Jennifer Bonner

25 Michigan

Yurina Kodama
MArch I, 2017
Center for the Performing
    Arts at the Cranbrook
    Educational Community
Instructors: Billie Tsien,
    Tod Williams

26 South Africa
p. 172

Joshua Feldman
MArch I, 2016
Thesis: Heterotic Architecture:
    Stacks, Chimneys, & Shoots
Advisors: Leire Asensio Villoria,
    Hanif Kara, Grace La

27 Balconies
p. 174

Bryant Nguyen
MArch I, 2018
Architecture Core III: Integrate
Instructor: Jennifer Bonner

Skewered

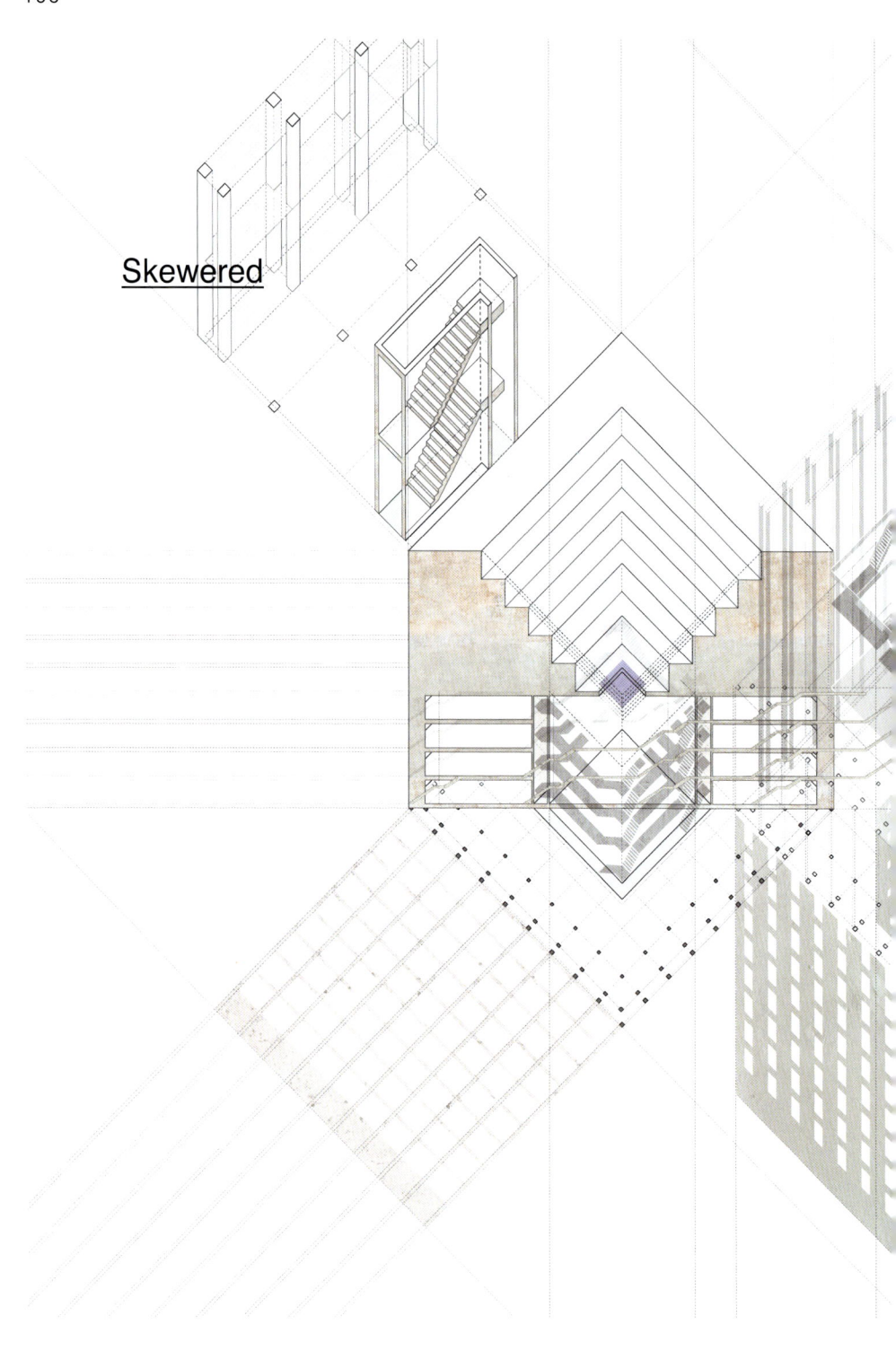

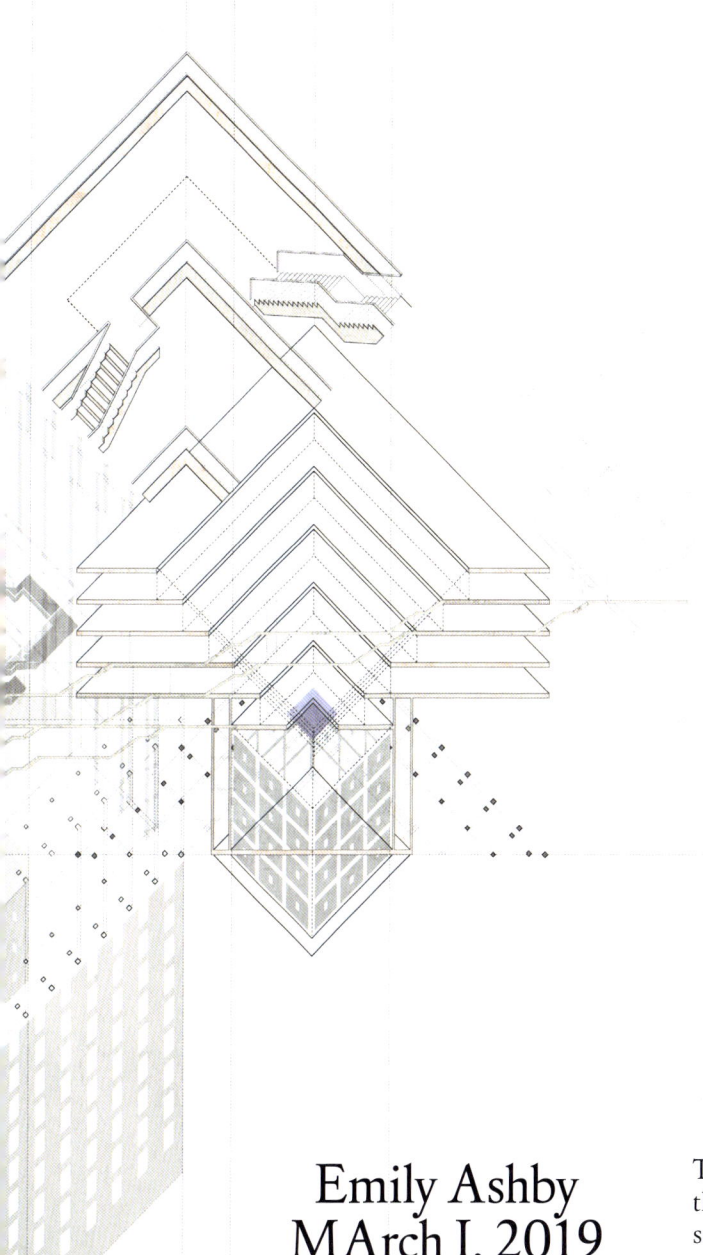

SECTIONAL   Core Studio   159

Emily Ashby
MArch I, 2019

Architecture Core II: Situate

Instructor
Jeffry Burchard

The second course of the Architecture Core sequence extends the subject matter to include the fundamental parameters of site and program, which are considered foundational to the discipline. This project explores these complex notions by situating a library in Boston's Back Bay Fens.

Khoa Vu
MArch I, 2019

Architecture Core I: Project

Instructor
Mariana Ibañez

The Architecture Core sequence begins by challenging students through progressive projects that test the rigor of architectural themes and principles and evolve into contextual, site-specific programs in the "intensive/extensive" and "perimeter plan" projects. Here, the first project appropriates form into a reading of thermal duration, while the project on the following page highlights a stair transformation's effects on the movement of the facade.

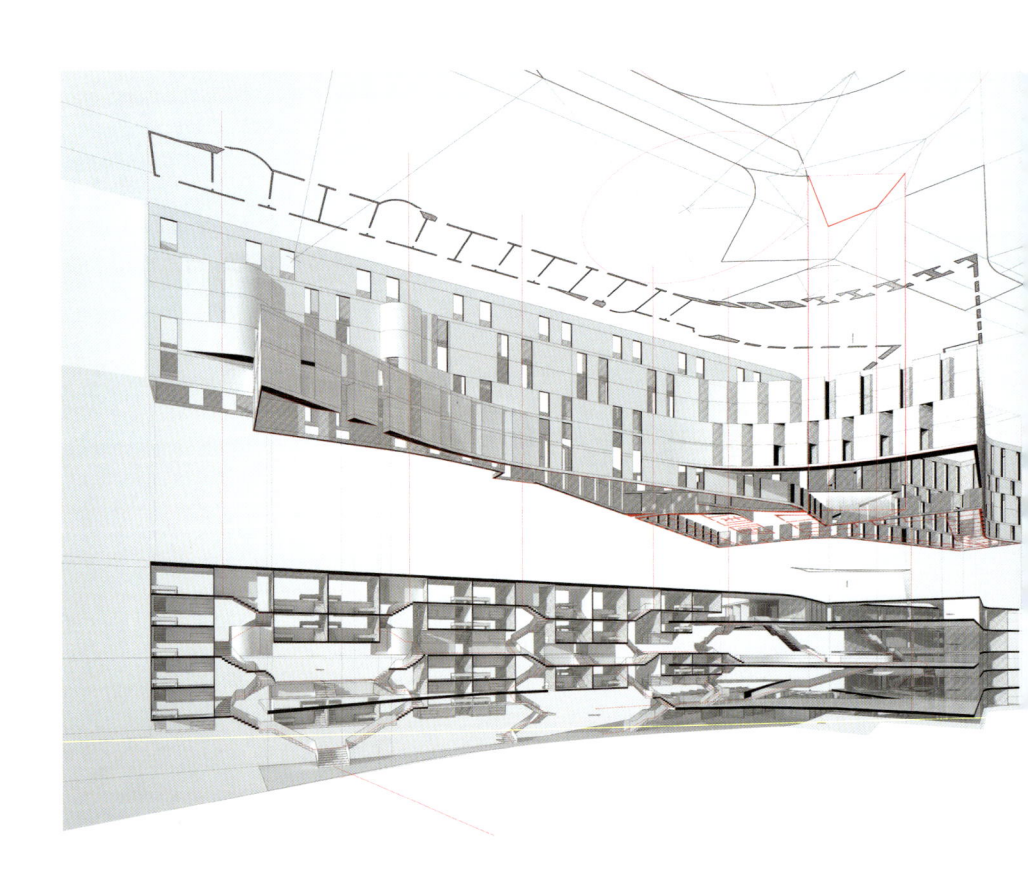

SECTIONAL Core Studio 161

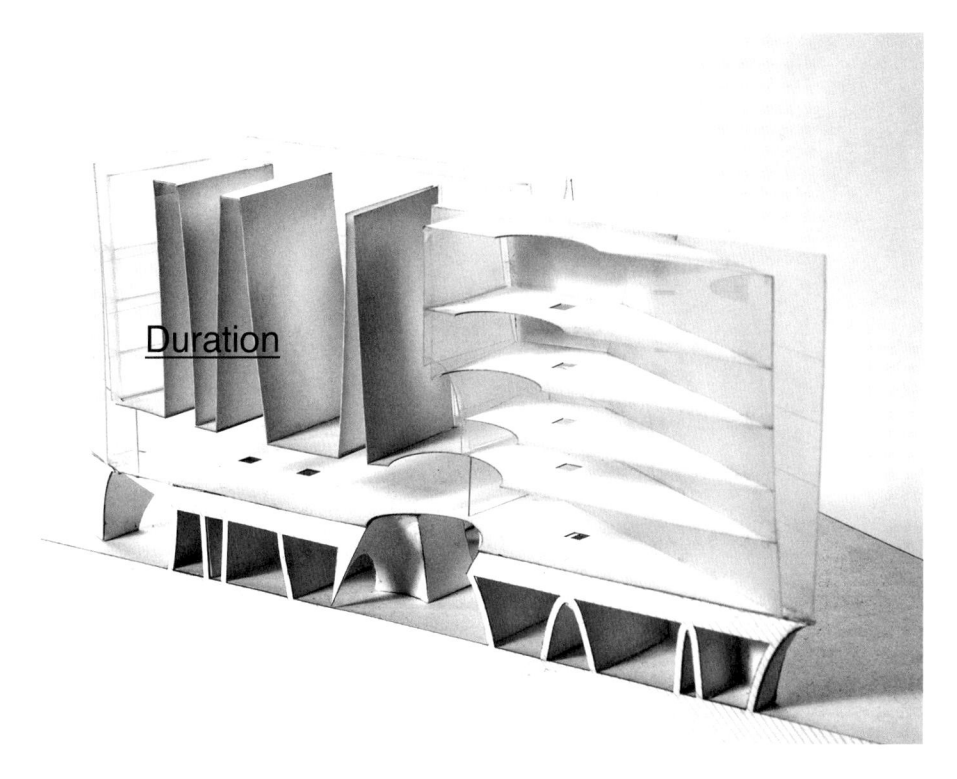

Duration

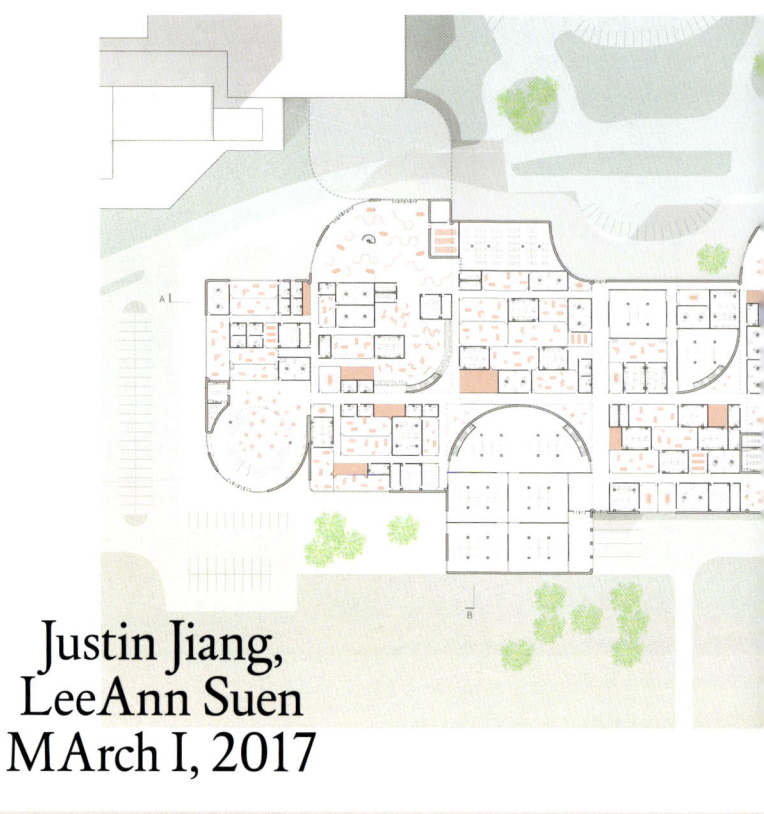

Justin Jiang,
LeeAnn Suen
MArch I, 2017

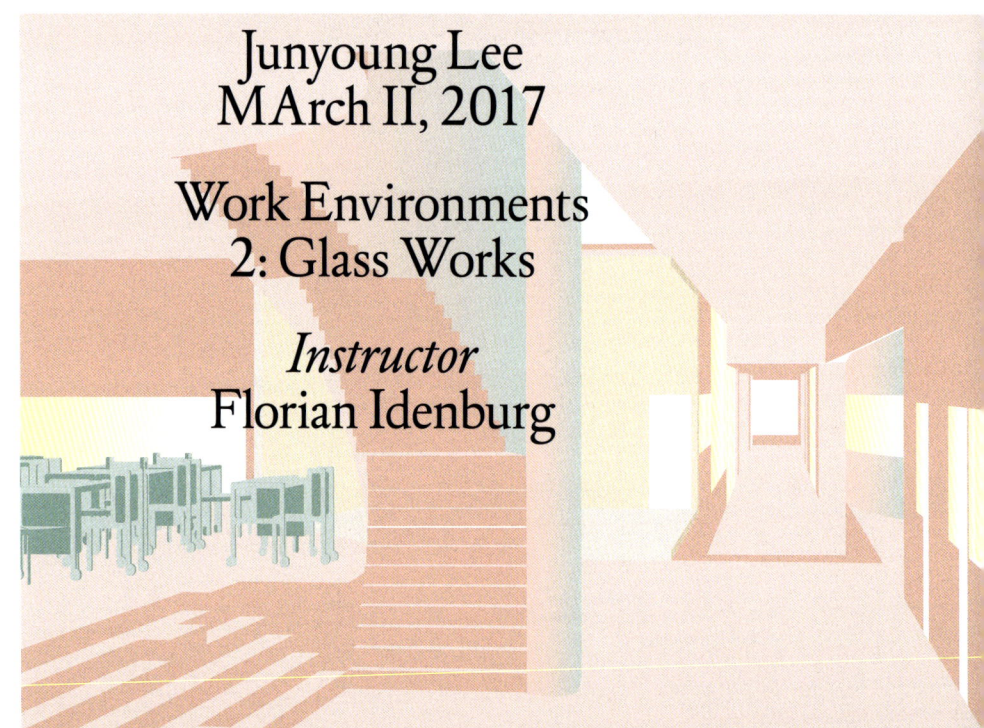

Junyoung Lee
MArch II, 2017

Work Environments
2: Glass Works

Instructor
Florian Idenburg

Workplace

In the second of three studios sponsored by Knoll, an international company creating workplace and residential furnishings, this studio examined, through research and design, the disruptive transformations that occur in work environments around the world. This project focuses on how furniture connects and grows at the corner, effecting the scale of the office to that of the building.

This studio examined the design of a new, freestanding building for the Museum of Contemporary Art in Chicago. The museum has the potential to affect and respond to the development and growth of its surroundings. The project presented here represents the dichotomy of wrapper and central atrium.

Benjamin Halpern
MArch I, 2017

The Architectural Double in the Museum City

Instructors
Sharon Johnston, Mark Lee

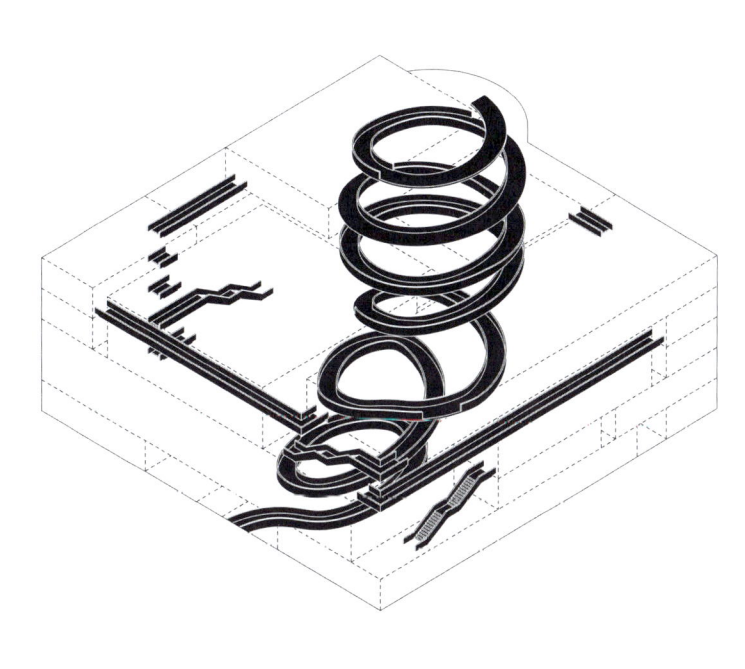

SECTIONAL   Option Studio   165

Caio Barboza, Sofia Blanco Santos
MArch II, 2016

Thesis
On Adapting:
A House, a Palace

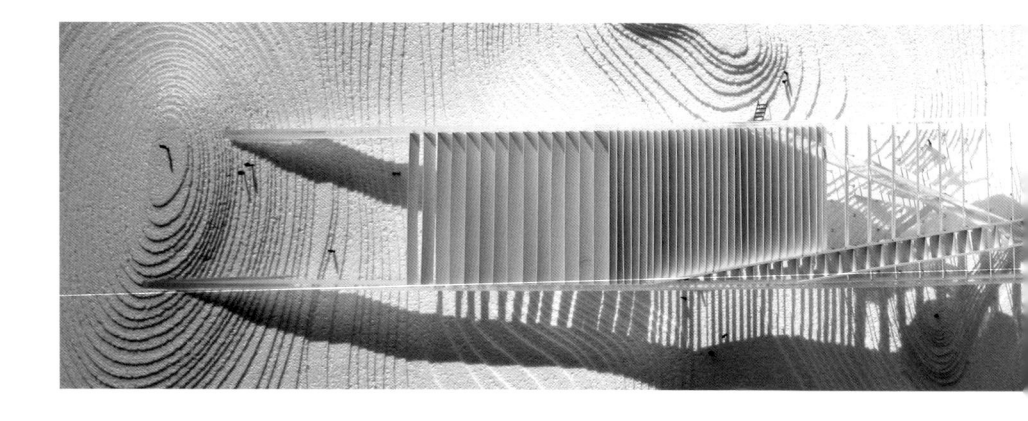

Advisor
Iñaki Ábalos

This project explores life and work, culture and thermodynamics, and architecture and philosophy, and identifies site-specific explorations in the cities of Santiago, Chile; Rio de Janeiro and São Paulo, Brazil; and Finistère, France. This thesis project was awarded the James Templeton Kelley Prize in Architecture for the Master in Architecture II program.

Santiago

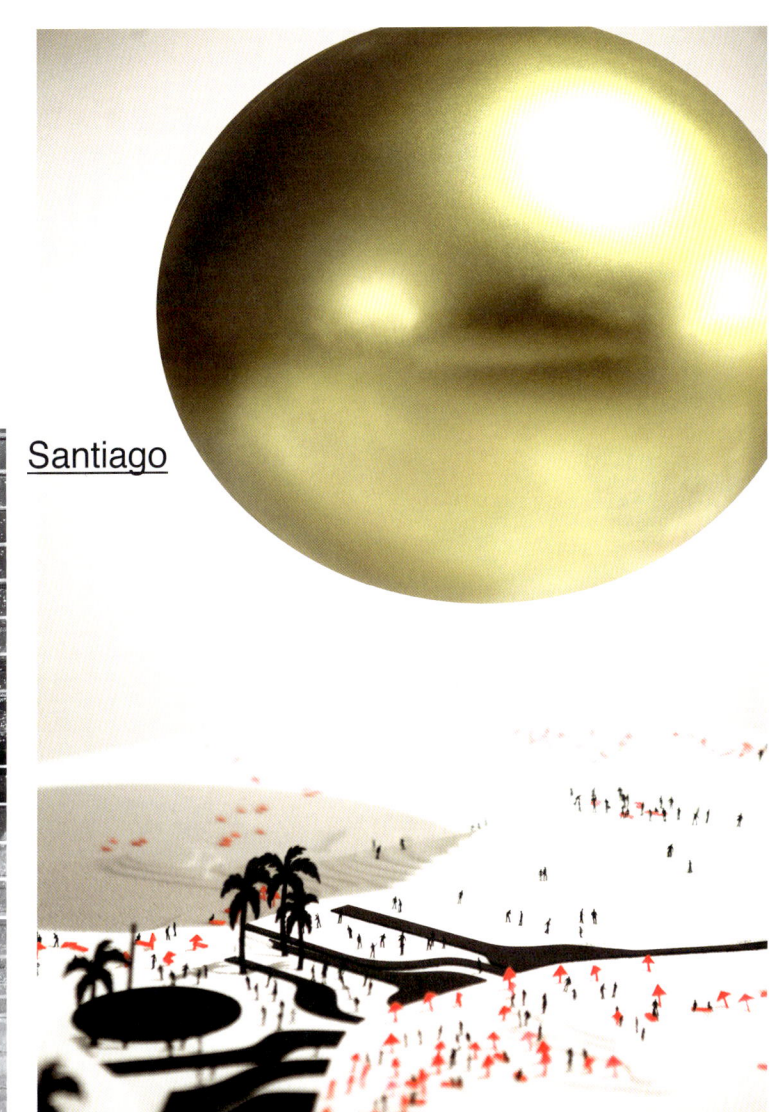

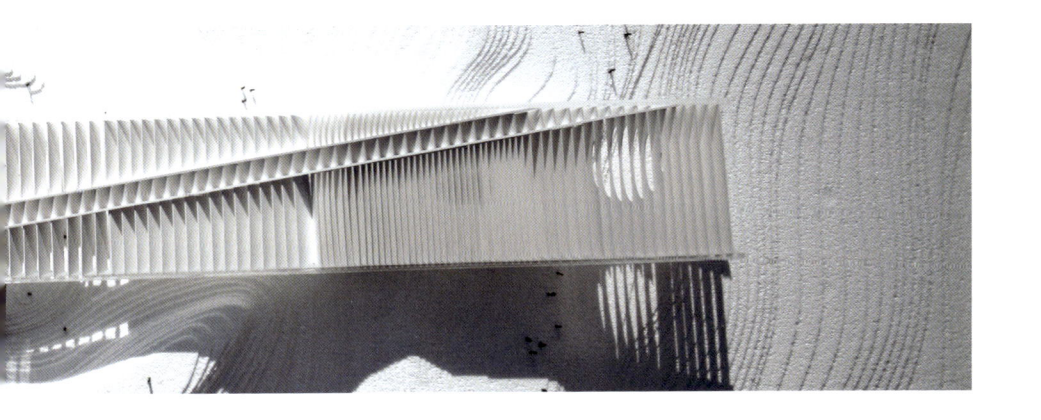

In Adolf Loos's words, "the English and the Americans expect everyone to be well-dressed." This studio drew connections between contemporary architecture and fashion. Here, a sawtooth roof form allows for a free plan while catwalks negotiate the spaces between a factory and the surrounding context.

Evan Farley
MArch I, 2017

"The English and the Americans Expect Everyone to be Well-dressed" or A Building for a Fashion House

Instructors
Emanuel Christ, Christoph Gantenbein

SECTIONAL Option Studio 169

Sawtooth

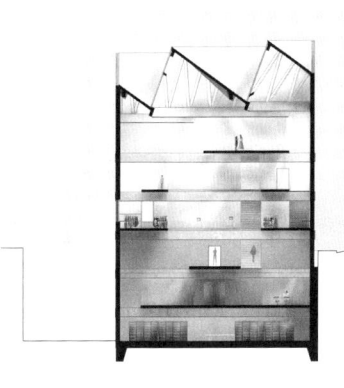

This studio, the first in the Landscape Core sequence, explores the challenges associated with interventions in complex urban conditions: layered interventions; issues of connectivity, accessibility, and identity; and a need for contemporary programs. This project does so specifically through the use of experiential sunken gardens along a pedestrian route.

Inside Out

SECTIONAL Core Studio 171

Jiawen Chen
MLA I, 2018

Landscape Core I

Instructor
Silvia Benedito

Joshua Feldman
MArch I, 2016

Thesis
Heterotic Architecture: Stacks, Chimneys, & Shoots

Advisors
Leire Asensio Villoria, Hanif Kara, Grace La

SECTIONAL　　　　　　　　　　　Thesis Project　　　　　　　　　　　173

Heterotic Architecture seeks to foster synergistic relationships through its urbanistic, functional, and formal exchanges. A merging of housing and waste-to-energy programs through thermal exchange results in new social and economic urban conditions. This thesis project was awarded the James Templeton Kelley Prize in Architecture for the Master in Architecture I program.

South Africa

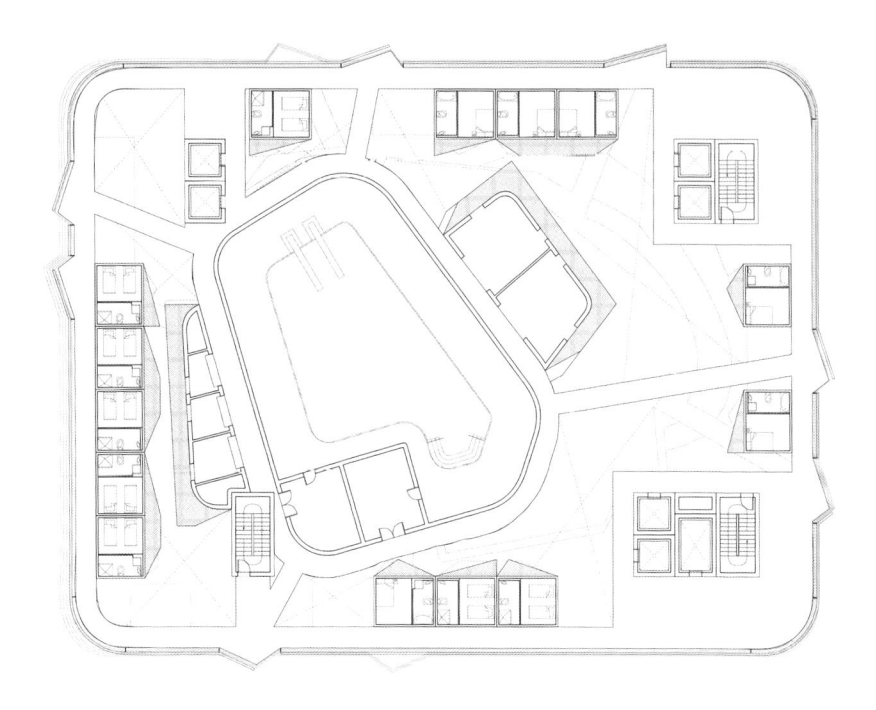

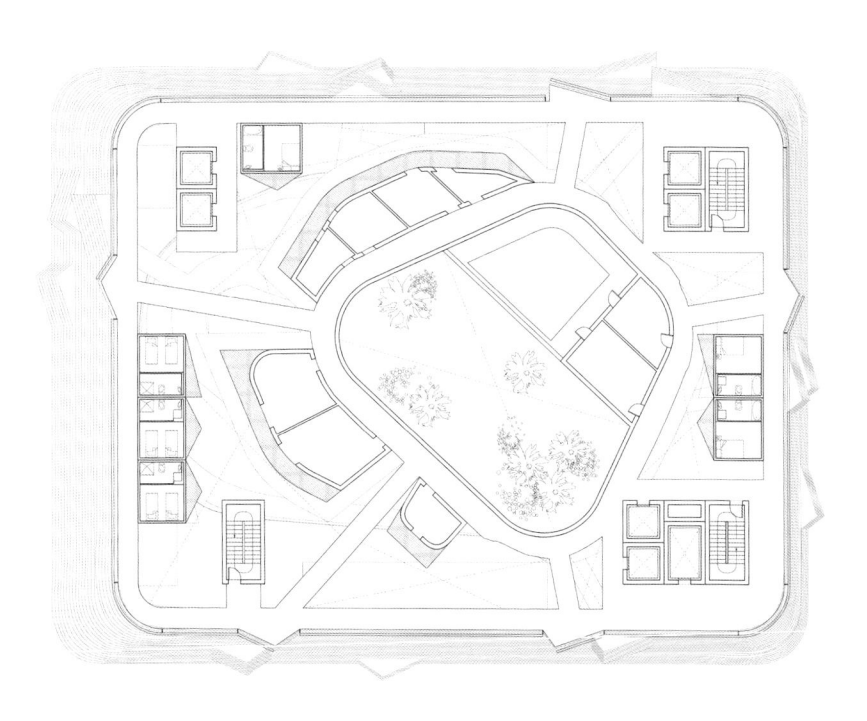

SECTIONAL Core Studio 175

Bryant Nguyen
MArch I, 2018

Architecture Core III: Integrate

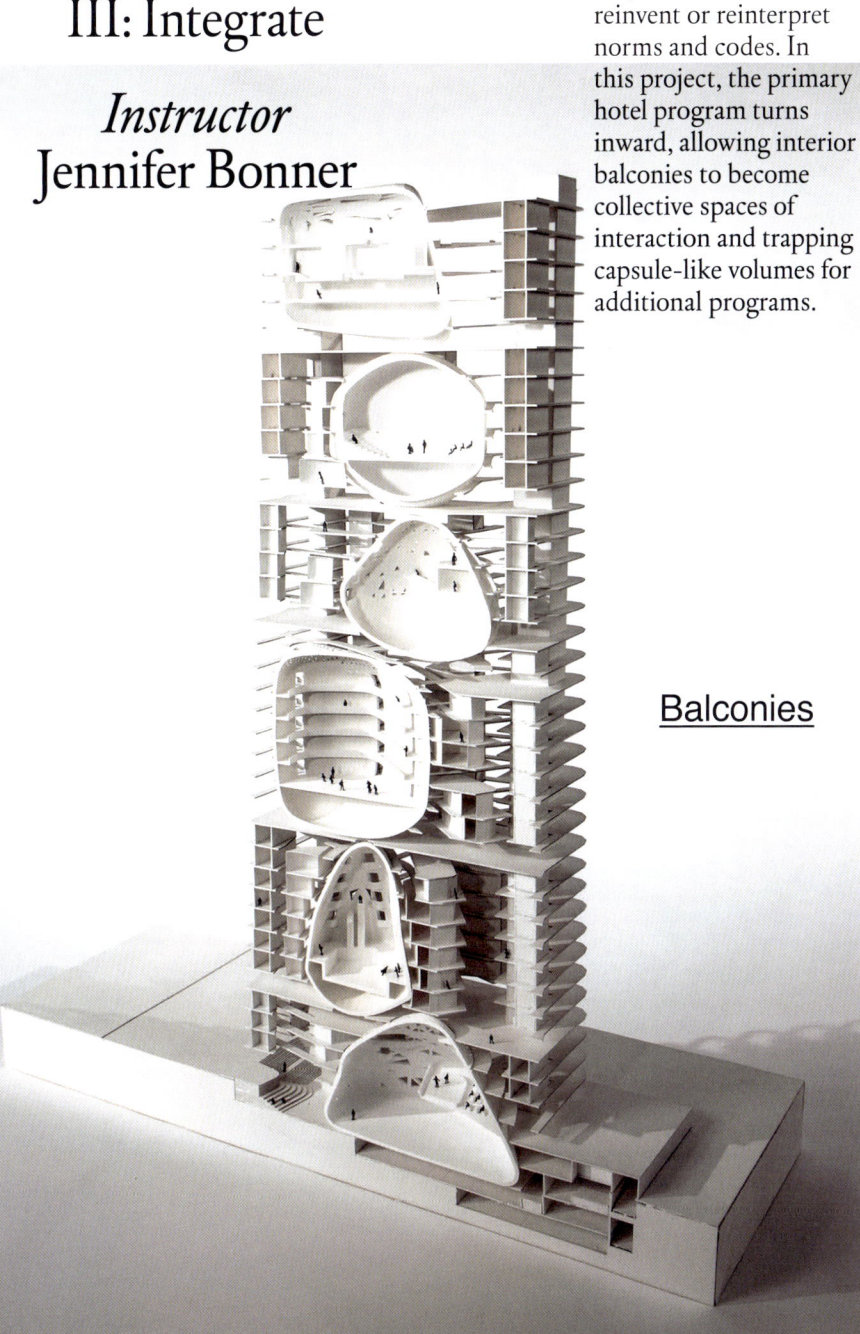

Instructor
Jennifer Bonner

This studio's comprehensive outline required students to consider notions of structure, energy, systems, program, site, and more. Projects were tasked to reinvent or reinterpret norms and codes. In this project, the primary hotel program turns inward, allowing interior balconies to become collective spaces of interaction and trapping capsule-like volumes for additional programs.

<u>Balconies</u>

Samples

Out of
Bounds

Locations

Sectional

Lightness

AN OVERVIEW OF
LIFE AND WORK
AT THE GSD

180
Lectures

196
In Memoriam:
Zaha Hadid

200
Publications

204
Exhibitions

206
Labs & Centers

209
Courses

216
GSD Leadership

217
Faculty

222
Loeb Fellowship;
Fellowships & Prizes

226
Staff

229
Students

↑ Christopher Riley, May 3, 2016

GSD etc.

↑ Farshid Moussavi

FARSHID MOUSSAVI
"The Function of Style"
September 3, 2015

"... Style relates to the way we arrange buildings. But when discussing the function of style, we are asking, What is the agency of style as objects in everyday life? The agency of human subjects in everyday experience has been discussed in the field of phenomenology, in terms of how humans gain access to the being of objects. This being is assumed as either already existing, such as matter, or being governed by natural laws, or as having a metaphysical reality. Although more recent investigations in everyday experience—for example, by speculative realism—question the privileging of the human being over other entities and propose the flattening of human subjects and objects, they still investigate objects as given, whether natural or artificial.

In architecture, the object-subject relationship is unavoidable, as buildings are part of everyday experience. But buildings don't exist as ready-made objects. They are arranged with our architectural process. And because style relates to the way we arrange buildings, it is central to the discussion of agency of buildings in everyday experience.

Traditionally, 'style' has been the word employed to describe a narrative around which architects unite buildings. However, since the 1990s, three pivotal changes in the way buildings are designed and used force us to define style differently. First, unity seems not to apply to contemporary architecture, which is characterized by immense diversity. If this diversity is not the product of mere eclecticism or the market, style must account for the coherence that underlies it."

CHARLES WALDHEIM
"A General Theory"
Olmsted Lecture
September 8, 2015

ERIC BUNGE, HILDE HEYNEN, NIKLAS MAAK, IRÉNÉE SCALBERT
"Housing—What Next?"
September 10, 2015

KERSTEN GEERS, JONATHAN OLIVARES, DAVID VAN SEVEREN
"2×2"
Rouse Visiting Artist Program
September 15, 2015

SCOTT PASK
"Scripts in Space"
Rouse Visiting Artist Program
September 17, 2015

FRÉDÉRIC BONNET
"The Countryside I—Ruralism"
September 21, 2015

CLAUDIA CASTILLO, MIGUEL COYULA, MICHAEL HOOPER, ORLANDO INCLAN, PATRICIA RODRIGUEZ
"The Challenge of Change: The Future of Havana"
September 24, 2015

ANGELA GLOVER BLACKWELL
John T. Dunlop Lecture
September 29, 2015

Harvard Design: Chicago | Adaptive Architectures and Smart Materials Conference
Chicago, IL
October 1–3, 2015

GEORGE BAIRD
"Writings on Architecture and the City"
GSD Talks Series
October 6, 2015

Black in Design Conference
October 9–10, 2015

"... Not only because the events in Ferguson and Baltimore made national news last year, but because these events are unfortunately not uncommon, we felt that it was imperative to make a new contribution to this dialogue, and to use our training as designers to convene a conversation about how to intervene in these cycles of injustice."
—CARA MICHELL, conference organizer (MUP '16)

"... The radicalized place that black Americans live in has compelled them to develop different optics. George Lipsitz, from UC Santa Barbara, stresses that black people have had to, out of necessity, turn segregation into congregation."
—K. MICHAEL HAYS, Associate Dean for Academic Affairs, GSD

"... I want to talk about the potential of Black in Design in a black city from the perspective of a black designer who is now entrusted with shaping and forming urban life for 700,000 residents, 80 percent of whom are black—so no small task ... Detroit is demolishing 70,000 structures at the rate of 250 a week. What happens when a city is destroying its urban fabric, and that gives us another problem to solve, which is fallow land? We have a few ideas. One is that it is an extraordinary opportunity to reforest the city, and to do it in the instance of land stewardship ... The city has decided that for every house that comes down, a grove of trees will be planted."
—MAURICE COX, Planning Director for the City of Detroit (Loeb Fellow '05)

↑ From left: Deanna Van Buren, Jeanine Hays, Mitch McEwen, and Dana McKinney.

"... I decided to go back to school when I came across a rural development program that allowed me to study the on-the-ground conditions of the rural South while earning an advanced degree. My first project was a solar irrigation project for socially disadvantaged farmers in the Alabama Black Belt; farmers excluded from access to cutting-edge information and technologies. And Sustainable Rural Regenerative Enterprises for Families (SURREF) was the first minority-and-women-led organization to introduce solar-powered water and drip irrigation systems to the state of Alabama. With our solarized irrigation and pumping systems we have improved diets and boosted income in agricultural communities in the rural Black Belt South."
—EUNEIKA ROGERS-SIPP, artist (Loeb Fellow '16)

"... Empathy is very different than sympathy. When we talk about practicing in some of these communities, we're like, 'those poor people who are living in those very severely depressed environments.' That is sympathy, and that's not going to help anyone. Empathy is about emotional intelligence and using that to create something that can build capacity and improve lives. It's really about this idea of looking at people as individuals and hearing their stories and using that as a platform for development."
—LIZ OGBU, architect (MArch '04)

"... There were some projects that I just wouldn't work on, which led me to other projects that were much more fulfilling and made a positive impact on the communities where they were built. So there were no prisons, no strip shopping centers, no casinos in my portfolio. It was a very, very simple standard to measure against. If we couldn't complete the project feeling good about what we had contributed as architects, we weren't interested in doing the work. And so 25 years later, we are still doing the kind of work that I think is meaningful and that we are certainly proud of."
—PHILIP FREELON, architect (Loeb Fellow '90)

RICHARD TUTTLE
"An Open Door"
Rouse Visiting Artist Program
October 13, 2015

Why do I, an artist, like art and design, too?
When I pick up "T" Magazine, why do I abandon
Restraint and when put down, feel impoverished?
Lacking interest? Exhausted from its poor quality?
Who speaks? Athena or Zeus? both is singular?
Athena, goddess of opposites, no way, singular..,
Or multiple? Why is "design" in nature? Why is art
Against nature? How much is "nature", a human
Concept? Is the "concept" in the design? Is there
Any 'issue' free of "design"? If, that things grow up,
Defines design that art knocks down, why is art
Design? Is, the-variety-of-any-given-thing-real-
Defines-design-without-making-the-thing-real,
The reason the designed thing (which comes close
To stating the thing), why, the "thing" is so welcome?-
In "itself"? Is "design" like letters, art, like numbers?
Is the singular, plural in design? Is the design
Singular, in plural? Is there no telling design from
Plural, plural from singular in "design"? How does
A singular… lost while arriving at train terminus.

↑ Richard Tuttle

JOÃO NUNES
Daniel Urban Kiley Lecture
October 14, 2015

PIERRE BÉLANGER,
  CHUCK HOBERMAN,
  MARIANA IBAÑEZ,
  SANFORD KWINTER,
  CIRO NAJLE, LLUIS
  ORTEGA, ANDREW WITT
"Organization or Design?"
Symposium on Architecture
October 15, 2015

VIJAY IYER, WADADA LEO
  SMITH
"Work in Progress"
Rouse Visiting Artist Program
October 20, 2015

ERIC HÖWELER
GSD Talks | Technologies of
  Design
October 21, 2015

CALEDONIA CURRY
  (SWOON)
"An Uncompromising Vision"
Loeb Fellowship 45th
  Anniversary Lecture
October 22, 2015

"... About a year after the earthquake in Haiti, we were there opening a community center. I remember this moment, about six months after the quake, when we were in full go-mode. We were in total building mode. And people were coming by, saying 'Oh, my God, how are you guys doing this? All of the organizations that we know of have their materials stuck in customs. They're stuck in gridlock. How are you guys already in full construction?'

For me it was a really beautiful moment. I get that we don't look qualified to be doing this. I get that we're just a group of scraggly artists. I get that we're not a massive NGO. We're not first responders.

But I have this hunch that as people who intensely believe in possibility and are willing to work at this very small scale, we have something that can be uniquely powerful at this moment. In Haiti, that has turned out to be true. We connected with this community. We built a community center."

JUN SATO
GSD Talks | Technologies of
  Design
October 26, 2015

CHUCK HOBERMAN, ROB
  MACCURDY, CONOR
  WALSH, ROBERT WOOD
"Informal Robotics"
Rouse Visiting Artist Program
October 27, 2015

↑ Caledonia Curry (Swoon)

REM KOOLHAAS
"The Countryside"
October 28, 2015

"... The countryside is considered as a kind of enormous canvas. Almost any form of organized activity which would be difficult to make compatible with urban life, and with the city, is now spreading over the countryside. Looking into the complexity of the nuclear waste stations for example, you realize that their system is not limited to a two-dimensional organization on the ground but is actually a deeply three-dimensional configuration, extending two thousand feet below the surface. It is incredible how elaborate and artificial all of this is becoming.

The unnatural things that are forced into the countryside are phenomenal. The scale of server farms is almost unimaginable. This is a colossal factory covered in solar panels and surrounded by wind farms. It is an incredibly intense piece of architecture, without almost any need for inhabitation, an architecture that nobody is prepared for. None of us have thought that a building could be this radical, perhaps, this extremely abstract, this codified, this unaffected by human need, this distant from us, and, nevertheless, produced by us, and needed by us."

EMANUEL CHRIST,
 CHRISTOPH
 GANTENBEIN
Lecture
October 29, 2015

↑ Rem Koolhaas

Lectures

CALVIN KLEIN
Rouse Visiting Artist Program
November 2, 2015

ANDREW HOLDER
"Bricks Like You"
GSD Talks | Innovate Series
November 3, 2015

"... I have this dichotomy. I love very sensual, soft fabrics that move on a woman's body or man's body. But I also love fabrics that have structure and shape and that you can do all sorts of interesting things with."

↑ Calvin Klein

PAOLA ANTONELLI,
 ELIJAH ANDERSON,
 ERIC DE BROCHE DES
 COMBES, ALEXA CLAY,
 JANE FULTON SURI
"Hybrid: The Space in
 Between"
Rouse Visiting Artist Program
November 3, 2015

"... Hybrid space, coming from the idea of merging different worlds—especially the digital and physical—is one of the most important fields of practice for architects. Hybridity has helped us get through so many different and difficult spots."

HCGBC Conference |
 Sustainability in
 Scandinavia
LORD NORMAN FOSTER,
 Keynote
November 5, 2015

JONATHAN LOTT
"Holes 'N' Clokwork"
GSD Talks | Innovate Series
November 10, 2015

RICHARD HASSELL,
 WONG MUN SUMM
"Garden City, Mega City"
November 10, 2015

BERNARD KHOURY
Open House Lecture
November 13, 2015

SERGIO LOPEZ-PINEIRO
"Things as Holes"
GSD Talks | Kiley Fellow Talk
November 17, 2015

RAHUL MEHROTRA
UD 50 Lectureship in
 Urban Design
November 17, 2015

CARLOS BENAÏM,
 FRÉDÉRIC MALLE
Rouse Visiting Artist Program
November 19, 2015

↑ Paola Antonelli

↑ Dean Mohsen Mostafavi and Jacques Herzog

JACQUES HERZOG
"... Hardly Finished Work..."
January 27, 2016

"... A project always has potential, always. And good architecture is made when you exploit that potential... I like the comparison to football. There you have 11 players and you have two different trainers. Each trainer coaches the team for one season; one is more successful than the other. Why? Because the good one is better at exploiting the potential of the team.

Is the given talent on the offensive side... or the defensive? Should you, therefore, train and instruct them to play for ball-possession... or rather focus on fast counterattacks? That seems ridiculous as a comparison. But it's pretty much what you do as an architect. You can do a building that has the potential to open up part of a city, to make it public and lively. Or you miss that opportunity and the consequence is a hermetic architecture with no appeal to stimulate communication among people. It would be a waste of money.

Appreciating architecture is not about whether you like it or not. That's personal. But determining if it is good is not personal. Beauty is a major driving force... but beauty has nothing to do with decoration. Beauty is much more complex. It is not about taste. It is about politics. It is about making you more political, more radical. It is about making you keen to explore more, to go further, to stimulate you to go beyond your imagination."

HANIF KARA, GEORGE LEGENDRE
GSD Talks | Organization or Design?
January 29, 2016

GIOVANNA BORASI
GSD Talks | Organization or Design?
February 2, 2016

MADRID RIO: BURGOS & GARRIDO, PORRAS LA CASTA, RUBIO & ÁLVAREZ-SALA, and WEST 8
Award Ceremony | Veronica Rudge Green Prize In Urban Design
February 2, 2016

Conference | On Atmospheres
Rouse Visiting Artist Program
Organized by SILVIA BENEDITO
February 4–5, 2016

BILLIE TSIEN, TOD WILLIAMS
"Inside Out"
February 16, 2016

↑ Toyo Ito and Julia Lee (translator)

DEV RAJ PAUDYAL
"The Scope of Spatial Data and Technology for Building Resilience of Vulnerable Groups: A Case of 2015 Nepal Earthquake and Informal Settlements in Kathmandu"
MDes Risk and Resilience
February 18, 2016

JENNIFER BONNER
"Close Reading of the Good Ol' Ordinary"
GSD Talks | Innovate Series
February 23, 2016

JEAN-LOUIS COHEN
"The Art of Zigzag: Le Corbusier's Politics"
February 25, 2016

GEETA PRADHAN
"The Privileged City: Cambridge and the Pursuit of Equity"
Department of Urban Planning and Design Lecture
March 1, 2016

TOYO ITO
"Tomorrow's Architecture"
Kenzo Tange Lecture
March 7, 2016

"... This evening I want to speak about how I create places. I never like to divide spaces. For me, space is just a void, expanding unlimitedly.
  This sketch shows a really fundamental principle behind my architecture. During the sakura season, people congregate under the sakura blossom trees. In the past, they used a fabric screen to create a place.

The most important thing is that people choose where they want to be. How do people choose? In this situation, they find the tree they want to be under, or, more importantly, they decide based on the views at that place, whether the ground is dry or wet, whether the wind blows enough or not. They choose their place with almost animal instincts.

This is an image of ripples dissipating in water. The way the waves dissipate is very similar to how Japanese language is structured. The way that the language is positioned in space is similar to how a ripple dissipates in a void.

So, unlike English, the Japanese language is basically structured so that there are these key elements floating in space.

There's no strict structure for composing a sentence. In Japanese, the speaker can choose their own words and how they structure a sentence.

The same principle is behind my architecture."

DIANA AL-HADID,
　JULIA KING,
　DR. ATYIA MARTIN,
　SUSAN SURFACE
"Radical Practice"
Organized by Harvard GSD
　Women in Design
March 8, 2016

Doctoral Program Conference
　| #Decoding: Operating
　Between Fixed Protocols
　and Dynamic Ecologies
March 11, 2016

FLORIAN IDENBURG,
　BENJAMIN PARDO
GSD Talks | Knoll Studio
"The Future of Work"
March 22, 2016

ANDREA COCHRAN,
　JAMES LORD, KEN
　SMITH
"Material Provocations"
March 22, 2016

ROSS LOVEGROVE
Margaret McCurry Lecture
Rouse Visiting Artist Program
March 24, 2016

DAVID HARVEY
Senior Loeb Scholar Lecture
March 28, 2016

". . . Now, what do you want to do as an urban planner or architect? Do you want to spend all your time trying to figure out how to create investment opportunities for middle- and upper-class people so that they can invest in a place but not necessarily live in it? Or do you want to actually build an alternative

↑ David Harvey

that embodies what people need and want? It's no surprise that over the last 15 years some of the major outbreaks of discontent in the world have been about urban issues. Gezi Park wasn't a working-class uprising; it was a cultural uprising against the qualities of urban life, and the authoritarianism and the lack of democracy. And while there are all sorts of crazy things being done and said in the United States that are totally misguided, a lot of that, it seems to me, is connected to the foreclosure crisis. People lost their security. They lost their houses. They're angry. They need somebody to blame."

Conference | Voices & Visions of St. Louis: Past, Present, Future
Organized by DIANE E. DAVIS
March 30–April 1, 2016

PIER VITTORIO AURELI
"Territory and Archetypes"
April 5, 2016

"... For us, the villa was very interesting as an archetype ... Because in a way, the villa is the quintessential domestic space ... The urban villa, unlike the traditional villa, is a multi-family house ... a typology that could fit a community of 50 or so people who want to live together as one domestic unit. The fundamental gesture here is to reclaim the land. The villa was built not just to offer habitation, but also to allow the owner to define his own ownership of the land. In this case, the villa does the opposite. In a way, it relieves the land from any appropriation from property. It signals the possibility to use the city and not to own the city.

This is how, even within the finite scale of an architectural object, and also from within the interior of domestic space, it is possible to address a territorial project."

↑ Pier Vittorio Aureli

ABDOUMALIQ SIMONE
"On the Concept of
   Global South"
Aga Khan Program Lecture
April 6, 2016

"... Almost all representations of urban processes raise the question about divides... For no matter how non-linear actual relationships may be, political entities that speak and act in the name of some collective always need to figure boundaries. Boundaries between what counts and what doesn't count, what is relevant or not, what is necessary to pay attention to or what is not, because nobody can pay attention to everything. One has to decide. One has to decide what it is to pay attention. And even as all these decisions are really difficult... and even as more decisions are made for us through algorithmic interoperability, the pragmatic necessity of boundary-making remains."

LEWIS JONES, GILES
   SMITH (ASSEMBLE)
Open House Lecture
Rouse Visiting Artist Program
April 7, 2016

↑ AbdouMaliq Simone

DIDIER FAUSTINO
"Building Intimacy"
Rouse Visiting Artist Program
April 11, 2016

MEGAN PANZANO
"The Edge"
GSD Talks | Innovate Series
April 12, 2016

JAN GEHL
"Livable Cities for the 21st
　Century"
Rachel Dorothy Tanur Lecture
April 12, 2016

"Bound and Unbound:
　The Sites of Utopia"
Doctoral Program Conference
　| Cambridge Talks X
April 14–15, 2016

ANITA BERRIZBEITIA,
　MICHEL DESVIGNE
"On the Limits of Progress:
　The Case for Precision in
　Landscape"
April 14, 2016

↑ Liu Yichun

LIU YICHUN
"Structure Matters"
April 19, 2016

"... The site of the Long Museum used to be a wharf for transporting coals near the Huangpu River. When we started this project, the basement was already built. However, this coal-uploading bridge was preserved. It is around 100 meters long and eight meters wide. We were very inspired by this bridge. When engineers design a bridge, aesthetics might not be a priority. However, after many years, after its original function has been lost, it becomes a purely visual and spatial artifact—a beautiful object. As that structure falls into ruin, it also becomes neutralized. Today people like to play under the coal-hopper bridge. They like to take photos here."

XIANGNING LI
"Tradition and Interiority in Chinese Architecture"
GSD Talks | Innovate Series
April 21, 2016

ALBERT POPE
"Modernism and Urban Ecology"
April 21, 2016

Symposium on Architecture | Interior Matters
Organized by KIEL MOE
April 22, 2016

"IN MEMORIAM: ZAHA HADID"
Essay by Emma Silverblatt
Originally composed as an assignment for The Poetics
 of Place: Critical Writing for Designers, instructed by
 Alastair Gordon

Over the wrought-iron gate in front of the former school that is Zaha Hadid Architects' London office is a Victorian-age inscription: "Girls & Infants." The words evoke a not-so-distant past when women were second-class citizens. Zaha's career was the metaphoric equivalent of a 12-ton wrecking ball against that gate.

But Zaha's work exists independent of the past. With her buildings, there is only ever the future: a future beyond orthogonality, beyond the perceived capabilities of construction, beyond industry biases. Her work is a departure from historical burdens of the field, subtly echoing the Malevich-laced revolution promised in her earliest drawings. I used to think it was a shame that she abandoned this aesthetic. I now understand it as a necessary step towards establishing her own tabula rasa.

Her oeuvre is the most effective outline of the new world order she developed. It demonstrates a utopian design equality, where a ski jump in Austria and a factory in Germany have the same grinning, cantilevered facade; a museum in Italy and a parking lot in France are both precariously perched on angled tiptoe; and the sumptuous curves of an Olympic stadium find new purpose as a homeware collection. Scaleless, programless, and fearless, her designs envisioned a total environment without regard for convention.

Regardless of one's opinion of her work, the moment her passing was announced, everyone felt the lurch in our field. On hearing of her death the morning of March 31, 2016, I was immobilized by a rapid succession of thoughts: It was impossible. She was among the youngest of the living architecture heroes. The only woman to ever attain such success in this field, her career was cut short right at its peak. It was excruciating to those of us who cheered her meteoric rise with our own dreams in mind. Perhaps hardest to grasp was the loss of her singular imagination. It was to this vision that she devoted her life, and for this vision that the field of architecture would canonize her—but then what? Now that she is gone, has anything actually changed? Will we ever live in her unfinished reality, or will all the walls she tore down be rebuilt?

Maybe to ask such questions is to miss the point. Zaha never needed anyone to follow her lead. She never required the blessing of the establishment or allowed it to limit her sense of possibility. For her, life was like the Victorian school housing her practice. She simply took her place in the building, with its delimiting inscription over the gate, and she remade it as her own.

198

↑ Nada AlQuallaf, April 28, 2016

GSD etc. 199

RECENT GSD PUBLICATIONS

HARVARD DESIGN MAGAZINE

Harvard Design Magazine 40: Well, Well, Well. Edited by JENNIFER SIGLER and LEAH WHITMAN-SALKIN. Cambridge, MA: Harvard University Graduate School of Design. Spring/Summer 2015.

Harvard Design Magazine 41: Family Planning. Edited by JENNIFER SIGLER and LEAH WHITMAN-SALKIN. Cambridge, MA: Harvard University Graduate School of Design. Fall/Winter 2015.

Harvard Design Magazine 42: Run for Cover! Edited by JENNIFER SIGLER and LEAH WHITMAN-SALKIN. Cambridge, MA: Harvard University Graduate School of Design. Spring/Summer 2016.

NEW GEOGRAPHIES

New Geographies 7: Geographies of Information. Edited by ALI FARD and TARANEH MESHKANI. Cambridge, MA: Harvard University Graduate School of Design, 2015.

THE INCIDENTS

HERMÉ, PIERRE. *The Incidents: The Architecture of Taste.* Cambridge, MA: Harvard University Graduate School of Design; Berlin: Sternberg Press, 2015.

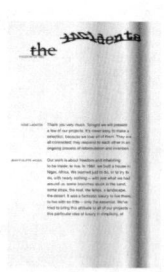

LACATON, ANNE and JEAN-PHILIPPE VASSAL, *The Incidents: Freedom of Use.* Cambridge, MA: Harvard University Graduate School of Design; Berlin: Sternberg Press, 2015.

STUDIO REPORTS

BARKOW, FRANK and ARNO BRANDLHUBER. *Poor but Sexy: Berlin, the New Communal.* Cambridge, MA: Harvard University Graduate School of Design, 2016.

DESVIGNE, MICHEL and INESSA HANSCH. *The Barracks of Pion.* Cambridge, MA: Harvard University Graduate School of Design, 2016.

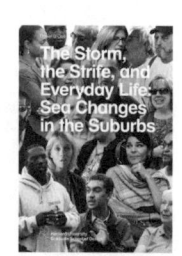

D'OCA, DANIEL. *The Storm, the Strife, and Everyday Life: Sea Changes in the Suburbs.* Cambridge, MA: Harvard University Graduate School of Design, 2016.

Publications

IDENBURG, FLORIAN. *Work Environments: Campus and Event.* Cambridge, MA: Harvard University Graduate School of Design, 2015.

ISHIGAMI, JUNYA. *Another Nature.* Cambridge, MA: Harvard University Graduate School of Design, 2015.

JOHNSTON, SHARON and MARK LEE. *The Architectural Double in the Museum City.* Cambridge, MA: Harvard University Graduate School of Design, 2016.

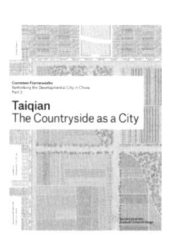

LEE, CHRISTOPHER C. M. *Taiqian: The Countryside as a City.* Cambridge, MA: Harvard University Graduate School of Design, 2015.

MENGES, ACHIM. *Material Performance: Fibrous Tectonics & Architectural Morphology.* Cambridge, MA: Harvard University Graduate School of Design, 2016.

OMAN, ROK and SPELA VIDECNIK. *Habitation in Extreme Environments.* Cambridge, MA: Harvard University Graduate School of Design, 2015.

WANG, BING and A. EUGENE KOHN. *Global Leadership in Real Estate and Design.* Cambridge, MA: Harvard University Graduate School of Design, 2015.

HARVARD DESIGN STUDIES

AIDOO, FALLON SAMUELS and DELIA DUONG BA WENDEL, eds. *Spatializing Politics: Essays on Power and Place.* Cambridge, MA: Harvard University Graduate School of Design, 2015.

DÜMPELMANN, SONJA and CHARLES WALDHEIM, eds. *Airport Landscape: Urban Ecologies in the Aerial Age.* Cambridge, MA: Harvard University Graduate School of Design, 2016.

LEE, CHRISTOPHER C. M., ed. *Common Frameworks: Rethinking the Developmental City in China.* Cambridge, MA: Harvard University Graduate School of Design, 2016.

COPUBLICATIONS

HONG, ZANETA, ed. *Platform 8*. New York: Actar; Cambridge, MA: Harvard University Graduate School of Design, 2015.

MOSTAFAVI, MOHSEN and GARETH DOHERTY. *Ecological Urbanism*. Revised edition. Cambridge, MA: Harvard University Graduate School of Design; Zurich: Lars Müller Publishers, 2016.

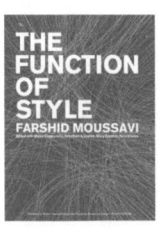

MOUSSAVI, FARSHID. *The Function of Style*. New York: Actar; Cambridge, MA: Harvard University Graduate School of Design; London: FUNCTIONLAB, 2015.

MUMFORD, ERIC, ed. *The Writings of Josep Lluís Sert*. Cambridge, MA: Harvard University Graduate School of Design; New Haven: Yale University Press, 2015.

OSHIMA, KEN TADASHI, ed. *Kiyonori Kikutake: Between Land and Sea*. Cambridge, MA: Harvard University Graduate School of Design; Zurich: Lars Müller Publishers, 2016.

FACULTY BOOKS

BECHTHOLD, MARTIN. *Ceramic Material Systems in Architecture and Interior Design*. Basel: Birkhauser, 2015.

BÉLANGER, PIERRE and Project OPSYS. *Pamphlet Architecture 35. Going Live: From States to Systems*. New York: Princeton Architectural Press, 2015.

BERRIZBEITIA, ANITA, ed. *Urban Landscape*. London: Routledge, 2015.

CANTRELL, BRADLEY and Wes Michaels. *Digital Drawing for Landscape Architecture: Contemporary Techniques and Tools for Digital Representation in Site Design*, Second edition. Hoboken, NJ: Wiley, 2015.

CANTRELL, BRADLEY and Justine Holzman. *Responsive Landscapes: Strategies for Responsive Technologies in Landscape Architecture*. New York: Routledge, 2016.

CASTILLO, JOSE and DIANE E. DAVIS. *The Flexible Leviathan: Reconsidering Scale and Fixity in Iztapalapa, Mexico City = El Leviatán Flexible: Reconsiderar Escala y Fijeza en Iztapalapa, Ciudad de México*. Cambridge, MA: Harvard University Graduate School of Design, 2016.

DAVIS, DIANE E., JOSE CASTILLO, and Yuxiang Luo. *Housing and Habitus: Craft, Politics, and the Production of Housing in Oaxaca, Mexico*. Cambridge, MA: Harvard University Graduate School of Design, 2016.

DOHERTY, GARETH and CHARLES WALDHEIM. *Is Landscape... ? Essays on the Identity of Landscape*. New York: Routledge, 2016.

DÜMPELMANN, SONJA and John Beardsley. *Women, Modernism, and Landscape Architecture.* New York: Routledge, Taylor and Francis Group, 2015.

ELKIN, ROSETTA S. *Live Matter.* Cambridge, MA: Radcliffe Institute for Advanced Study. Harvard University, 2015.

HARGREAVES, GEORGE, Mary Margaret Jones, Gavin McMillan. *Landscapes & Gardens.* Oro Editions, 2015.

Harvard Symposia on Architecture Editorial Committee: IÑAKI ÁBALOS, Aurora Fernandez Per, Javier Mozas, Collin Gardner. *Design Techniques.* Vitoria-Gasteiz, Spain: a+t architecture publishers, 2015.

KIRKWOOD, NIALL and Kate Kennen. *Phyto: Principles and Resources for Site Remediation and Landscape Design.* New York: Routledge, 2015.

LAIRD, MARK. *A Natural History of English Gardening, 1650–1800.* New Haven: Published for the Paul Mellon Centre for Studies in British Art by Yale University Press, 2015.

MEHROTRA, RAHUL and Felipe Vera, eds. *Disolviendo Umbrales = Dissolving Thresholds*, first edition. Santiago: ARQ ediciones, 2015.

MEHROTRA, RAHUL and Felipe Vera with José Mayoral. *Ephemeral Urbanism: Cities in Constant Flux.* Santiago: ARQ ediciones, 2016.

MEHROTRA, RAHUL and Felipe Vera, eds. *Kumbh Mela: Mapping the Ephemeral Megacity.* Ostfildern: Hatje Cantz; Cambridge, MA: Harvard University; South Asia Institute, 2015.

MOE, KIEL. *Our Model of Models / My Model of Model.* CreateSpace Independent Publishing Platform, 2016.

MOE, KIEL. *Rain Gravity Heat Cold.* Toronto, Ontario: superkul, 2015.

MOSTAFAVI, MOHSEN and Helene Binet. *Nicholas Hawksmoor: London Churches.* Zurich: Lars Müller Publishers, 2015.

PICON, ANTOINE. *Smart Cities: A Spatialised Intelligence.* Chichester, West Sussex: Wiley, 2015.

KUO, JEANNETTE, ed. *Space of Production: Projects and Essays on Rationality, Atmosphere, and Expression in the Industrial Building.* Zurich: Park Books, 2015.

Srinivasan, Ravi and KIEL MOE. *The Hierarchy of Energy in Architecture: Emergy Analysis.* New York: Routledge, 2015.

STILGOE, JOHN R. *What is Landscape?* Cambridge, MA: MIT Press, 2015.

WALDHEIM, CHARLES. *Landscape as Urbanism: A General Theory.* Princeton, NJ: Princeton University Press, 2016.

STUDENT PUBLICATIONS

Masks: Quarterly Journal of Dissimulation in Art | Architecture | Design. Issue 0, 2016. Edited by Clemens Finkelstein and Anthony Morey.

Open Letters. Edited by Sarah Bolivar, Sarah Canepa, Azzurra Cox, Ellen Epley, Justin Kollar.
"Davis Owen writes to Stephan Petermann." Issue 37. March 25, 2016.
"Olga Semenovych writes to AASU & Women in Design." Issue 35. December 14, 2015.
"Francesca Romana Forlini writes to Franceso di Salvo." Issue 34. November 13, 2015.
"Scott March Smith writes to Preston Scott Cohen." Issue 33. October 30, 2015.
"Black in Design writes to the GSD." Issue 32. October 16, 2015.
"The Shrimper and the Coastal Protection Officer write to 'Resilience.'" Issue 31. September 25, 2015.
"Taylor Dover writes to Olafur Eliasson." Issue 30. September 11, 2015.

Process: Journal of the GSD Design Research Forum. Vol. 1, Issue 1, March 4, 2016. Edited by Kate Cahill, Justin Henceroth, Carly James, and Jane Zhang.

Process: Journal of the GSD Design Research Forum. Vol. 1, Issue 2, April 14, 2016. Edited by Kate Cahill, Justin Henceroth, Carly James, and Jane Zhang.

Very Vary Veri, No. 2, 2016. Edited by Simon Battisti, Ali Karimi, Erin Ota, Lukas Pauer, and Etien Santiago.

2015–2016 EXHIBITIONS

MAIN EXHIBITIONS

Living Anatomy: An Exhibition About Housing
August 24–October 18, 2015
Curators: MEGAN PANZANO, *Design Critic in Architecture;* Daniel V. Rauchwerger; Matthew Gin; *Curatorial Research:* Patrick Herron.

This exhibition captures the fullness of the conversation about housing that is happening at the GSD and at Harvard more broadly, focusing primarily on research and projects from the last 50 years.

Green Prize in Urban Design: Madrid Río—Burgos & Garrido, Porras La Casta, Rubio & Álvarez-Sala, and West 8
January 19–March 6, 2016
Faculty Curator: RAHUL MEHROTRA, *Professor of Urban Design and Planning;* Curatorial Researcher: Nupoor Monani; Curatorial Researcher and Exhibition Design: Daniel V. Rauchwerger.

Madrid Río illustrates the transformative potentials of architecture, landscape, urban design, and planning for the city of Madrid.

Platform 8: An Index of Design & Research
March 21–May 13, 2016
Faculty Curator: ZANETA HONG, *Lecturer in Landscape Architecture.*

Platform 8 catalogs a curated selection of work generated in the past year at the Harvard University Graduate School of Design.

EXPERIMENTS WALL

BANG! BANG! BANG! Housing Policy and the Geography of Fatal Police Encounters
August 31–October 18, 2015
GSD African American Student Union (GSD AASU), Map the Gap Committee; Marcus Mello, *Project Coordinator;* Lindsay Woodson, *Project Coordinator;* Dana McKinney, *AASU President;* Héctor Tarrido-Picart, *Summer Fellow.*

The GSD African American Student Union's exhibition critically examines how the evolution of the Fair Housing Act of 1968 and subsequent housing policies have adversely impacted disadvantaged populations, namely black communities, on a national scale.

+360 Weathers
October 26, 2015–February 28, 2016
Curators: SILVIA BENEDITO, *Assistant Professor of Landscape Architecture,* and Alexander Häusler. *Collaborators:* Velania Cervino, Joe Liao, Ziyi Zhang, and Ken Chongsuwat.

+360 Weathers celebrates the 16th-century circle of landscape painters known as the "Danube School," as well as highlights the 21st-century landscapes of the Danube River Valley as affected by environmental stress, overbuilt infrastructure, energetic demands, and pressing civic aspirations for the river edges.

12 Instigations for a Becoming Middle East
March 6–May 13, 2016
Ramzi Naja, *Thesis Advisor:* MACK SCOGIN; Faisal Al Mogren, *Thesis Advisor:* PETER ROWE; Ali Karimi, *Thesis Advisor:* CHRISTOPHER C. M. LEE; Weaam Al Abdallah, *Thesis Advisors:* SILVIA BENEDITO *and* ANITA BERRIZBEITIA; Wen Wen, *Thesis Advisor:* JORGE SILVETTI; Noor Boushehri, *Thesis Advisor:* SUSAN SNYDER; Rawan AlSaffar, *Project Advisor:* RANIA GHOSN; Nada Tarkhan, *Project Advisor:* HOLLY SAMUELSON; Myrna Ayoub, *Project Advisor:* PAUL NAKAZAWA; Dana Sheikh Soleiman, *Project Advisor:* ROBERT PIETRUSKO; Aziz Barbar, *Project Advisor:* ANDREW WITT; Sama ElSaket, *Project Advisor:* NABEEL HAMDI.

This exhibition collects the work of 12 students addressing the Middle East in its present condition. The work approaches the Middle East by looking at different scales, from different perspectives, and in different materialities, in order to generate an understanding of the region that is critical and collective, but not uniform.

FRANCES LOEB LIBRARY

A Poetry of the Ordinary: Life in Alison & Peter Smithson's Robin Hood Gardens, 1972
August 31–November 2, 2015
Curator: Daniel V. Rauchwerger.

Set within the wider framework of *Living Anatomy: An Exhibition About Housing*, this exhibition focuses on Robin Hood Gardens—Alison and Peter Smithson's housing project in East London, completed in 1972.

Exhibitions

A Sustainable Future for Exuma
November 9–December 20, 2015
Mariano Gomez Luque, Rob Daurio, Suryani Dewa Ayu.
Faculty Advisor: GARETH DOHERTY, *Assistant Professor of Landscape Architecture.*

This multi-year ecological planning project, aiming for a more sustainable future for the Exuma archipelago, and the Bahamas more generally, is a collaboration among the Government of The Bahamas, the Bahamas National Trust, and Harvard University Graduate School of Design.

The Nine Square Grid
January 25–March 20, 2016
Caio Barboza, Sofia Blanco Santos, Daniel Hemmendinger.
Faculty Advisor: K. MICHAEL HAYS, *Eliot Noyes Professor of Architectural Theory and Associate Dean for Academic Affairs.*

This exhibition pays tribute to architect, professor, and GSD alumnus John Hejduk (MArch '53) by exploring the development of the Nine Square Grid Exercise, first proposed in the University of Texas at Austin in the early 1950s. The pedagogical context surrounding "9SG" seeks to explore and emphasize Hejduk's contribution as a professor, as the Nine Square Grid has influenced architects since its inception.

Interior Matters
March 28–May 13, 2016
Faculty Curator: KIEL MOE, *Associate Professor of Architecture and Energy, Codirector of the Master in Design Studies program.*

Architecture's interior matters in new ways today. The question of the interior challenges architecture's assumed boundaries, such as the conventional dichotomies of "inside" and "outside." The project also raises many topics that the discipline has yet to fully address, and explores a radically evolved epistemology through which to think about interior and matter simultaneously, and to exercise their propensities in novel ways.

DEAN'S WALL

A Non-Urban Apparatus
September 7–October 18, 2015
Winner of the Clifford Wong Housing Prize: Jyri Eskola (MArch I AP '16), Shaoliang Hua (MArch II '15), Radhya Adityavarman (MLA II '15).

As an endeavor to regain the agency, productivity, and economic independence of the Chinese rural, this thesis proposes an alternative to the current trend in new development where farmers' land-ownership rights are overlooked and the connection to the "land" is lost.

Zhabei New Gateway: Designing a New Global Centrality for Shanghai
January 25–March 23, 2016
Kyriaki Kasabalis, Michael Keller, Kitty Tinhung Tsui, and in collaboration with Dingliang Yang. Faculty Advisor: JOAN BUSQUETS, *Martin Bucksbaum Professor in Practice of Urban Planning and Design.*

The team's winning proposal is titled "Zhabei New Gateway: Designing a New Global Centrality for Shanghai," and features an elevated railway platform with asymmetrical cross-section. The plan also prioritizes the establishment of large-scale parks and plazas and a system of semi-private open spaces and pedestrian walkways that connect the north and south ends of the area. Meanwhile, towers on the east and west ends of the area offer a gateway to the reimagined district.

Alpine Shelter, Skuta, Slovenia
April 1–May 13, 2016
Spela Videcnik and Rok Oman (Ofis Arhitekti) with Frederick Kim, Katie MacDonald, and Erin Pellegrino.

Designed for Skuta Mountain in Slovenia, the Peak House is a mountain shelter nestled in the scenic Alps that offers an intimate refuge for eight visitors. Deployed by helicopter as three modules, the building was joined on site.

FORTY KIRKLAND GALLERY

Curators: Jiyoo Jye; Vero Smith; Scott Valentine

Invaluable
September 25–October 7, 2015
WorkingGSD

Baugruppe GSD
October 9–21, 2015
Julian Funk, Giancarlo Montano, Elizabeth Pipal, Chris Soohoo, Dana Wu

Chasing Gold
November 6–18, 2015
Alica Meza and Althea Northcross

Cloudtime Fantasy
November 20–December 2, 2015
Anthony Morey

Ephemeral Formwork
February 12–24, 2016
Daniel Carlson, Alexander Timmer

Traces of Urbanization / Stereoscope
February 26–March 9, 2016
Sonja Vangjeli, Dana Kash, Eunice Wong

Spaces from Syria
March 17–30, 2016
Myrna Ayoub, Ramzi Naja

I See What I See Clearly
April 1–13, 2016
Whitney Hansley, Allison Green, Brian Palmiter, Courtney Sharpe

Light Hive
April 15–May 9, 2016
Aziz Barbar, Akshay Goyal

GSD DESIGN LABS

ANTOINE PICON,
G. Ware Travelstead Professor of the History of Architecture and Technology and Director of Research; Anne Mathew, Director, Research Administration; Nony Rai, Research Coordinator.

The Design Labs synthesize theoretical and applied knowledge to produce innovative and speculative research that enables design to be an agent of change in society.

City Form Lab
Principal Investigator: ANDRES SEVTSUK, Assistant Professor of Urban Planning. Affiliate: Michael Mekonnen.

The City Form Lab focuses on urban design, planning, and real-estate research. It develops new software tools for researching city form; uses cutting-edge spatial analysis and statistics to investigate how the physical pattern of urban development affects the social, environmental, and economic quality of urban environments; and develops creative design and policy solutions for contemporary urban challenges.

Energy, Environments & Design
Lab Principals: KIEL MOE, Associate Professor of Architecture and Energy; JANE HUTTON, Assistant Professor of Landscape Architecture.

The Energy, Environments & Design Lab investigates novel agendas for energy at a range of design scales. From overlooked thermal parameters at the molecular level to global-scale emergy analysis, the design disciplines urgently need alternate intellectual frameworks, research methodologies, and practices for energy in the 21st century. Materials, buildings, landscapes, cities, and urbanization are all overtly connected energy hierarchies that must be lucidly understood as the basis of any design agenda for energy today.

Geometry Lab
Research Principal: PRESTON SCOTT COHEN, Gerald M. McCue Professor in Architecture. Faculty: ANDREW WITT, Professor in Practice of Architecture; CAMERON WU, Associate Professor of Architecture; HANIF KARA, Professor in Practice of Architectural Technology; GEORGE LEGENDRE, Associate Professor in Practice of Architecture; PANAGIOTIS MICHALATOS, Assistant Professor of Architectural Technology; MARIANA IBAÑEZ, Associate Professor of Architecture; CHUCK HOBERMAN, Lecturer in Architecture.

The Geometry Lab is a new research unit that engages core questions of architectural geometry and computational design. Focused on the use of advanced geometry in the discipline of architecture, the research scope of the lab includes issues of digital fabrication, constructability, structural geometry, performance, infrastructural optimization, formal research, and the historical role of geometry in design. The objective of the lab is to produce and disseminate new knowledge, to generate broad scalable solutions to big problems, and to explore the associated cultural and human implications.

The Just City Lab
Research Principal: TONI L. GRIFFIN, Professor in Practice of Urban Planning.

The Just City Lab investigates the definition of urban justice and the just city and examines how design and planning contribute to the conditions of justice and injustice in cities, neighborhoods, and the public realm.

Material Processes and Systems Group
Research Principal: MARTIN BECHTHOLD, Kumagai Professor of Architectural Technology. Faculty: PANAGIOTIS MICHALATOS, Assistant Professor of Architecture; LEIRE ASENSIO VILLORIA, Lecturer in Architecture.

The Material Processes and Systems (MaP+S) Group, founded and led by Professor Martin Bechthold, is a research unit that analyzes, develops, and deploys innovative material technologies for buildings. The group evolved from the previously established Design Robotics Group. MaP+S looks at materiality as starting points for design research, with a special interest in robotic and computer-numerically controlled (CNC) fabrication processes as well as small-scale work on nano-materials. Current work includes the development of novel ceramic material systems, robotic 3D printing or clay-based and cementitious material, as well as a range of studies under the umbrella of "design robotics."

Responsive Environments and Artifacts Lab
Research Principal: ALLEN SAYEGH, Associate Professor of Practice in Architectural Technology. Research Faculty: BRADLEY CANTRELL, Associate Professor of Landscape Architecture Technology. Research Associates: Edith Ackermann, Senior Research Associate; Stefano Andreani, Research Associate; Jock Herron, Senior Research Associate.

The Responsive Environments and Artifacts Lab (REAL) is a research lab that pursues the design of digital, virtual, and physical worlds as an indivisible whole. It recognizes the all-pervasive nature of digital information and interaction at scales ranging from our bodies to the larger urban contexts we occupy and the infrastructures that support them.

Social Agency Lab
Research Principal: MICHAEL HOOPER, *Associate Professor of Urban Planning. Research Fellows:* Brian Goldberg, Andy Gerhart, Andrew Perlstein, Lily Canan Reynolds.

The Social Agency Lab studies the ways in which individuals, institutions, and organizations shape social outcomes in cities. The lab leads a number of funded research projects related to this theme. These projects currently include research efforts focused on the social dimensions of urban change in sub-Saharan Africa, Haiti, Mongolia, and aboriginal communities in Canada.

Urban Theory Lab
Lab Director: NEIL BRENNER, *Professor of Urban Theory. Faculty Researcher:* ROBERT PIETRUSKO, *Assistant Professor of Landscape Architecture and Urban Planning; Postdoctoral Fellow:* Martín Arboleda, *Urban Studies Foundation Postdoctoral Fellow; Lab Research Manager:* Daniel Ibañez.

Over four decades ago, Henri Lefebvre put forward the radical hypothesis of the complete urbanization of society. This required, in his view, a radical shift from the analysis of urban form to the investigation of urbanization processes. The Urban Theory Lab builds upon Lefebvre's approach to investigate emergent sociospatial formations under early 21st-century capitalism. Our research starts from the proposition that inherited frameworks of urban knowledge must be radically reinvented to illuminate emergent forms of 21st-century urbanization.

GSD CENTERS AND RESEARCH INITIATIVES

Center for Green Buildings and Cities
Founding Director: ALI MALKAWI, *Professor of Architectural Technology; Codirector:* RICHARD FREEMAN, *Faculty Codirector of the Labor and Worklife Program at Harvard Law School and Senior Research Fellow in Labour Markets at London School of Economics' Centre for Economic Performance.*

The Harvard Center for Green Buildings and Cities aims to transform the building industry through a commitment to design-centric strategy that directly links research outcomes to the development of new processes, systems, and products.

By strongly emphasizing innovation and multidisciplinary collaboration, the Center works to promote holistic change within the built environment, namely the creation and continued improvement of sustainable, high-performance buildings and cities.

Joint Center for Housing Studies
Managing Director: CHRISTOPHER HERBERT; *Senior Associate Director:* Pamela Baldwin; *Senior Research Fellow and Project Director of the Remodeling Futures Program:* Kermit Baker.

The Joint Center advances understanding of housing issues and informs policy. Through its research, education, and public outreach programs, the center helps leaders in government, business, and the civic sectors make decisions that effectively address the needs of cities and communities. Through graduate and executive courses, as well as fellowships and internship opportunities, the Joint Center also trains and inspires the next generation of housing leaders.

Aga Khan Program for Islamic Architecture
SIBEL BOZDOGAN, *Lecturer in Urban Planning and Design;* HANIF KARA, *Professor in Practice of Architectural Technology;* RAHUL MEHROTRA, *Professor of Urban Design and Planning.*

The Aga Khan Program for Islamic Architecture at GSD and MIT is dedicated to the study of Islamic art and architecture, urbanism, landscape design, and conservation. The GSD program is invested in the application of that knowledge to contemporary design issues.

Health and Places Initiative
LEIRE ASENSIO VILLORIA, *Lecturer in Architecture;* ANN FORSYTH, *Director of the Master in Urban Planning Degree Program and Professor of Urban Planning;* DAVID MAH, *Lecturer in Landscape Architecture;* PETER ROWE, *Raymond Garbe Professor of Architecture and Urban Design and Harvard University Distinguished Service Professor.*

This project investigates how to create healthier cities in the future, with a specific emphasis on China. Bringing together experts from the Harvard Graduate School of Design and the Harvard T. H. Chan School of Public Health (HSPH), it creates a forum for understanding the multiple issues that face cities in light of rapid urbanization and an aging population worldwide.

Transforming Urban Transport
DIANE E. DAVIS, *Chair, Department of Urban Planning and Design and Charles Dyer Norton Professor of Regional Planning and Urbanism; Lily Song, Research Associate; Antya Waegemann, Project Assistant.*

A research project led by Diane E. Davis, this project seeks to advance our knowledge of how, when, and where political leadership has been critical to the successful implementation of path-breaking transportation policies. TUT-POL is conducting case study research in eight cities—Los Angeles, Mexico City, New York City, Paris, San Francisco, Seoul, Stockholm, and Vienna—where political leadership has been central to the adoption and implementation of significant, transformative, and innovative transportation policies in their locales.

Zofnass Program for Sustainable Infrastructure
ANDREAS GEORGOULIAS, *Lecturer in Architecture and Senior Research Associate;* SPIRO N. POLLALIS, *Professor of Design Technology and Management.*

The mission of the Zofnass Program for Sustainable Infrastructure is to develop and promote methods, processes, and tools that quantify sustainability for infrastructure. Its goal is to facilitate the adoption of sustainable solutions for infrastructure projects and systems, and expand the body of knowledge for sustainable infrastructure.

GSD COURSES FALL 2015

VISUAL STUDIES AND COMMUNICATION

Meteorological Reveries: On Atmosphere, Sensation, and the Design of Public Space
SILVIA BENEDITO

Landscape Representation III: Landform and Ecological Process
BRADLEY CANTRELL, DAVID MAH

Relational Urban Modeling
EDUARDO RICO CARRANZA, ENRIQUETA LLABRES VALLS

Paper or Plastic: Reinventing Shelf-life in the Supermarket Landscape
TEMAN EVANS, TERAN EVANS

Drawing for Designers: Technics of Expression, Articulation, and Representation
EWA HARABASZ

Visual Studies
EWA HARABASZ

Landscape Representation I
ZANETA HONG, SERGIO LOPEZ-PINEIRO

Communication for Designers
EMILY WAUGH

Digital Media II
ANDREW WITT

Public Projection: Projection as a Tool for Expression and Communication in Public Space
KRZYSZTOF WODICZKO

Projective Representation in Architecture
CAMERON WU

DESIGN THEORY

States of Design: The Present and Future of the Field in Thirteen Parts
PAOLA ANTONELLI

Theories of Landscape as Urbanism, Landscape as Infrastructure: Paradigms, Practices, Prospects
PIERRE BÉLANGER

Interdisciplinary Art Practices
SILVIA BENEDITO

Teaching Techniques
PRESTON SCOTT COHEN

The Idea of Environment
DILIP DA CUNHA

The Aperture Analyzed: The Form and Space of Openings
GRACE LA

Learning from The Function of Style
FARSHID MOUSSAVI, JAMES KHAMSI

Conservation of Older Buildings: Techniques and Technics
ROBERT SILMAN

Culture, Conservation, and Design
SUSAN SNYDER, GEORGE THOMAS

Art, Design, and the Public Domain Proseminar
KRZYSZTOF WODICZKO

HISTORY AND THEORY

Reconceptualizing the Urban: Berlin as Laboratory
EVE BLAU

Histories of Landscape Architecture I: Textuality and the Practice of Landscape Architecture
EDWARD EIGEN

Buildings, Texts, and Contexts III: The Tower and the Sphere: Architecture and Modernity
K. MICHAEL HAYS, HILDE HEYNEN, BRYAN NORWOOD

Buildings, Texts, and Contexts I
K. MICHAEL HAYS, ERIKA NAGINSKI

Walking: The Art of Walking and its Culture
JOHN HUNT

The History of Plants and Animals in Landscape Design: Antiquity to Present
MARK LAIRD

Urbanization in the East Asian Region
PETER ROWE

Authority and Invention: Medieval Art and Architecture
CHRISTINE SMITH

Structuring Urban Experience: From the Athenian Acropolis to the Boston Common
CHRISTINE SMITH

Studies of the Built North American Environment: 1580 to the Present
JOHN STILGOE

North American Seacoasts and Landscapes: Discovery Period to the Present
JOHN STILGOE

SOCIO-ECONOMIC STUDIES

The Spatial Politics of Land: A Comparative Perspective
SAI BALAKRISHNAN

Cities by Design I
EVE BLAU, NEIL BRENNER, JOAN BUSQUETS, FELIPE CORREA, ALEX KRIEGER, RAHUL MEHROTRA, PETER ROWE

Staging the City: Urban Form and Public Life in Istanbul
SIBEL BOZDOGAN

Policy Making in Urban Settings (at HKS)
JAMES CARRAS

Analytic Methods: Qualitative
ANN FORSYTH

Healthy Places
ANN FORSYTH

Transportation Policy and Planning (at HKS)
JOSE GOMEZ-IBANEZ

Design, Development, and Democracy in the Future City
STEPHEN GRAY

Deciding Interventions in Urban Development: A Practical Guide to Strategic Design
NABEEL HAMDI

Community Action Planning: Principles and Practices
NABEEL HAMDI

Analytic Methods of Urban Planning: Quantitative
MICHAEL HOOPER

Land Use and Environmental Law
DAVID KARNOVSKY

Real Estate Finance and Development Fundamentals for Public and Private Participants (at HKS)
EDWARD MARCHANT

Structural Design 1
PATRICK MCCAFFERTY

Housing and Urbanization in the United States
JENNIFER MOLINSKY, JAMES STOCKARD

Cases in Contemporary Construction
MARK MULLIGAN

Architecture and its Texts (1650–1800)
ERIKA NAGINSKI

Markets and Market Failures with Cases (at HKS)
ALBERT NICHOLS

Tokyo Study Abroad Seminar: The Japan Syndrome
KAYOKO OTA

Real Estate Finance and Development
RICHARD PEISER

Modern Housing and Urban Districts: Concepts, Cases, and Comparisons
PETER ROWE

Field Studies in Real Estate, Planning, and Urban Design: Innovation District and New Community Development on Goose Island, Chicago and Waterfront, TOD, and Entertainment Redevelopment in Revere, MA
RICHARD PEISER

Spatial Analytics of the Built Environment
ANDRES SEVTSUK

Urban Governance and the Politics of Planning in the Developing World
ENRIQUE SILVA

Market Analysis and Urban Economics
RAYMOND TORTO

SCIENCE AND TECHNOLOGY

The Innovative Practice: Finding, Building, and Leading Good Ideas with Others (at SEAS)
BETH ALTRINGER

Changing Natural and Built Coastal Environments
STEVEN APFELBAUM, KATHARINE PARSONS

Nano Micro Macro: Adaptive Material Laboratory
MARTIN BECHTHOLD, JAMES WEAVER

Innovation in Science and Engineering: Conference Course (at SEAS)
PAUL BOTTINO

Construction Lab
SALMAAN CRAIG

The Nature and Culture of Plants
PETER DEL TREDICI

Ecologies, Techniques, Technologies III: Introduction to Ecology
PETER DEL TREDICI, ERLE ELLIS, CHRISTOPHER MATTHEWS

Ecologies, Techniques, Technologies I
ROSETTA ELKIN, MATTHEW URBANSKI

Informal Robotics / New Paradigms for Design & Construction
CHUCK HOBERMAN

Tokyo Study Abroad Seminar on Structure and Material in Japan
MITS KANADA

Brownfields Practicum: Regeneration and Reuse of Brownfield Lands: Research, Remediation, and Design Practices
NIALL KIRKWOOD

Building Simulation
ALI MALKAWI

Architectural Acoustics (module)
BEN MARKHAM

Poetics of Landscape Construction
ALISTAIR MCINTOSH

Introduction to Computational Design
PANAGIOTIS MICHALATOS

Energy in Architecture
KIEL MOE

Water Engineering (at SEAS)
CHAD VECITIS

Material Practice as Research: Digital Design and Fabrication
LEIRE ASENSIO VILLORIA

Architecture in the Daylight (module)
DANIEL WEISSMAN

Mechatronic Optics
ANDREW WITT

Computer Vision (at SEAS)
TODD ZICKLER

PROFESSIONAL PRACTICE

Urban Design Trajectories: Perspectives on Practice
STEPHEN GRAY

Practices of Landscape Architecture
JANE HUTTON

Innovation in Project Delivery
MARK R. JOHNSON

Frameworks of Contemporary Practice
PAUL NAKAZAWA

PROPAEDEUTIC AND ADVANCED RESEARCH

Ecology, Infrastructure, Power
PIERRE BÉLANGER

Urban Design Proseminar
EVE BLAU, CARLES MURO

Proseminar in Landscape, Ecology, and Urbanism
GARETH DOHERTY

Preparation of Design Thesis Proposal for Master in Landscape Architecture
GARETH DOHERTY, ROSETTA ELKIN

Courses

Independent Thesis in Satisfaction of Degree MArch
EDWARD EIGEN

South Florida Rise and Sink: the Case of Miami Beach
ROSETTA ELKIN

The Architecture of Waste
ANDREAS GEORGOULIAS, LEIRE ASENSIO VILLORIA

Preparation for Independent Thesis Proposal for MUP, MAUD, or MLAUD
MICHAEL HOOPER

Doctoral Program Proseminar
PETER ROWE

MArch II Proseminar
JORGE SILVETTI

Independent Thesis in Satisfaction of the Degree MLA

Architecture Thesis in Satisfaction of the Degree Doctor of Design

STUDIOS

First Semester Architecture Core: Project
ANDREW HOLDER, MARIANA IBAÑEZ, MEGAN PANZANO (Coordinator), CRISTINA PARRENO ALONSO, CAMERON WU

Third Semester Architecture Core: Integrate
JENNIFER BONNER, JEFFRY BURCHARD, JONATHAN LOTT (Coordinator), JOHN MAY, RENATA SENTKIEWICZ, ELIZABETH WHITTAKER

Landscape Architecture I: First Semester Core Studio
LUIS CALLEJAS, GARY HILDERBRAND (Coordinator), ZANETA HONG, JANE HUTTON (Coordinator), with ALISTAIR MCINTOSH

Landscape Architecture III: Third Semester Core Studio
JAVIER ARPA, FIONN BYRNE, BRADLEY CANTRELL, SERGIO LOPEZ-PINEIRO, DAVID MAH, CHRIS REED (Coordinator)

First Semester Core Urban Planning Studio
SAI BALAKRISHNAN, ANA GELABERT-SANCHEZ, ANDRES SEVTSUK, with ROBERT PIETRUSKO and KAIROS SHEN

Elements of Urban Design
ANITA BERRIZBEITIA, FELIPE CORREA (Coordinator), CARLOS GARCIAVELEZ, CARLES MURO, with MICHAEL MANFREDI and ROBERT PIETRUSKO

Dualisms: A House, A Palace
IÑAKI ÁBALOS

"The English and the Americans expect everyone to be well-dressed" or A Building for a Fashion Label
EMANUEL CHRIST, CHRISTOPH GANTENBEIN

Urban Blackholes: Development and Heritage in the Lima Metropolis
JEAN PIERRE CROUSSE

The MLK Way: Building on Black America's Main Street
DANIEL D'OCA

Lisbon Story: Architecture between Atmosphere and Tectonics
RICARDO BAK GORDON

Metroport on the Rhine: Strasbourg-Kehl
HENRI BAVA

Architecture without Content 15
KERSTEN GEERS, DAVID VAN SEVEREN

The Naked Eye: Medusae & other stories
EELCO HOOFTMAN, BRIDGET BAINES

Making Omishima the Best Island to Live on in Japan: Tokyo Studio Abroad
TOYO ITO

The Architectural Double in the Museum City
SHARON JOHNSTON, MARK LEE

When the Future Looked Bright We Didn't Wear Shades
BERNARD KHOURY

Material Performance: Fibrous Tectonics & Architectural Morphology
ACHIM MENGES

The Function of Education: The 21st Century School
FARSHID MOUSSAVI, JAMES KHAMSI

Lagoa das Furnas: A Dynamic Approach to a Landscape Project
JOÃO NUNES, JOÃO GOMES DA SILVA

Meteorological Architecture
PHILIPPE RAHM

Imprecise Tropics
CAMILO RESTREPO OCHOA

Moscow's Future: Tied Up in Traffic
MARTHA SCHWARTZ and instructors from Strelka Institute for Media, Architecture and Design

Iceberg Alley
LOLA SHEPPARD, MASON WHITE

Alimentary Design: The Final Course
SHOHEI SHIGEMATSU, CHRISTINE CHENG

East New York Open Space System
KEN SMITH

↑ Matthew Wong and Ernest Haines, May 6, 2016

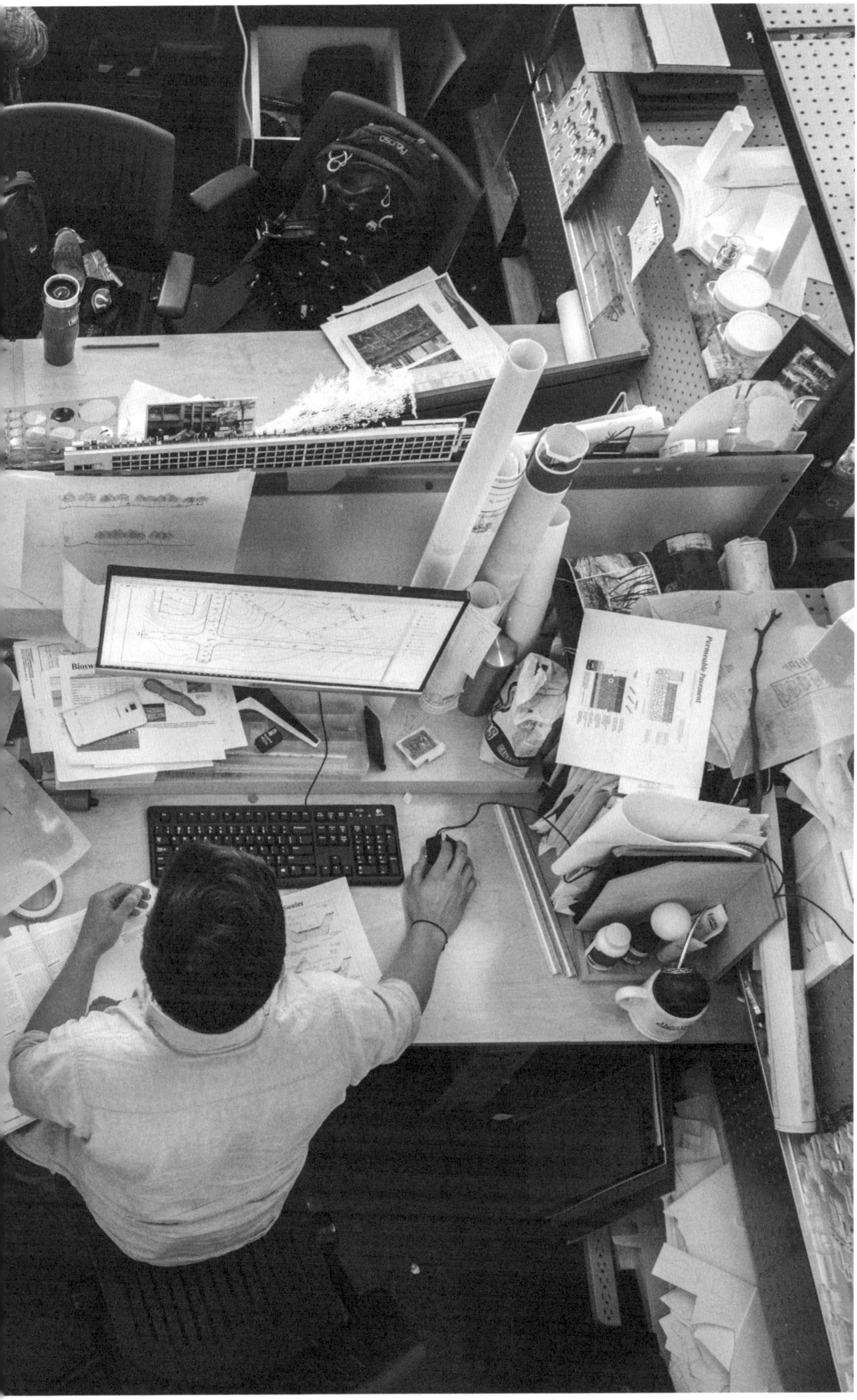
Permeable Pavement
Swales

SPRING 2016

VISUAL STUDIES AND COMMUNICATION

Immersive Landscape: Representation through Gaming Technology
ERIC DE BROCHE DES COMBES

Landscape Representation II
FIONN BYRNE, DAVID MAH

Painting for Designers: Techniques, Methods, and Concepts
EWA HARABASZ

The Poetics of Place: Critical Writing for Designers
ALASTAIR GORDON

Digital Design and Making: Landscape and Ecological Approaches
DAVID MAH

Responsive Environments: Bergamo eMotion
ALLEN SAYEGH

Conic and Developable Surfaces
CAMERON WU

DESIGN THEORY

Theories of Landscape Architecture
ANITA BERRIZBEITIA

Urban Grids: Open Form for City Design
JOAN BUSQUETS

Landscape as Urbanism in Latin America
LUIS CALLEJAS

Designing the American City: Civic Aspirations and Urban Form
ALEX KRIEGER

Type and the Idea of the City
CHRISTOPHER C. M. LEE

Political Landscapes (Rotterdam Study Abroad Seminar)
NIKLAS MAAK

Today's Architecture as Seen through Enduring Concerns
RAFAEL MONEO

Fieldwork in Conservation Design
MARK MULLIGAN

Potential Architecture
CARLES MURO

The Architecture of Health: Power, Technology, and the Hospital
MICHAEL MURPHY, ALAN RICKS

Philosophy of Technology
ROBERT SILMAN

Socio-Environmental Responsive Design
JOSE LUIS VALLEJO, BELINDA TATO

HISTORY AND THEORY

Advanced Real Estate Finance
FRANK APESECHE

Building and Leading Real Estate Enterprises and Entrepreneurship
FRANK APESECHE

Film Theory, Visual Thinking
GIULIANA BRUNO

Screens: Media Archaeology and the Visual Arts Seminar
GIULIANA BRUNO

Discourses and Methods: Conservation, Destruction, and Curating Impermanence
NATALIA ESCOBAR CASTRILLON, K. MICHAEL HAYS

Shifting Terrains 1930–1970: Cambridge Modern Architecture and Landscape
CAROLINE CONSTANT

Histories of Landscape Architecture II: Design, Representation, and Use
SONJA DÜMPELMANN

Super Landscapes, Super Sports
SONJA DÜMPELMANN

Buildings, Texts, and Contexts II
ED EIGEN, ERIKA NAGINSKI

Le Corbusier: Themes/Discourse/Figures
K. MICHAEL HAYS, ANTOINE PICON

Property in Common: The Nexus between Architecture and Real Estate
CATHERINE INGRAHAM

Selected Topics on Contemporary Chinese Architecture and Urban Planning
XIANGNING LI

Countryside versus Cityside: A Seminar in Environmental History (Rotterdam Study Abroad Seminar)
SEBASTIEN MAROT

Interiors, Environments, Atmosphere
KIEL MOE, ANTOINE PICON

The Ruin Aesthetic: Episodes in the History of an Architectural Idea
ERIKA NAGINSKI

Modern Architecture and Urbanism in China
PETER ROWE

Making Sacred Space
CHRISTINE SMITH

Power & Place: Culture and Conflict in the Built Environment
SUSAN SNYDER, GEORGE THOMAS

Modernization in the Visual United States Environment, 1890–2035
JOHN STILGOE

SOCIO-ECONOMIC STUDIES

Urbanization and International Development
SAI BALAKRISHNAN

Environmental Planning & Sustainable Development
ANN FORSYTH

Urban Design for Planners
DAVID GAMBLE

Cities by Design II: Projects, Processes, and Outcomes
STEPHEN GRAY

Courses

Design for the
Just City
TONI GRIFFIN

Creating Real Estate
Ventures: a Legal
Perspective
MICHAEL HAROZ

Markets and Market
Failures
CHRISTOPHER
HERBERT

Urban Inequality after
Civil Rights (at FAS)
ELIZABETH
HINTON

Affordable and
Mixed-Income Housing
Development, Finance,
and Management
EDWARD
MARCHANT

The Space of Conflict
MARIANNE
POTVIN

Transportation
Planning and
Development
PAUL SCHIMEK

Public and Private
Development
LAURA
WOLF-POWERS

Economic Development
in Urban Planning
DONALD ZIZZI

SCIENCE AND TECHNOLOGY

Design Survivor:
Experiential Lessons
in Designing for
Desirability (at SEAS)
BETH
ALTRINGER

Structural Design 2
MARTIN
BECHTHOLD

Cyborg Coasts:
Responsive
Hydrologies
BRADLEY
CANTRELL

The Thermal
Allometry of Massive
Buildings, Breathing
Buildings, and
Breathing Walls
SALMAAN CRAIG

Poetics of Plant Design
DANIELLE
CHOI, KIMBERLY
MERCURIO

Construction Systems
BILLIE
FAIRCLOTH

Interdisciplinary
Design Practice
ANDREAS
GEORGOULIAS,
HANIF KARA

Urban and Town
Ecology
RICHARD T.T.
FORMAN

Survey of Energy
Technology (at SEAS)
DAVID KEITH

Ecologies, Techniques,
Technologies IV
NIALL
KIRKWOOD,
ALISTAIR
MCINTOSH

Structures in
Landscape
Architecture
ALISTAIR
MCINTOSH

Digital Structures and
Material Distribution
PANAGIOTIS
MICHALATOS

Innovative
Construction in Japan
MARK
MULLIGAN

Mapping: Geographic
Representation and
Speculation
ROBERT
PIETRUSKO

Ecologies, Techniques,
Technologies II
THOMAS RYAN,
LAURA SOLANO

Environmental Systems
in Architecture
HOLLY
SAMUELSON

Structural Surfaces
ANDREW WITT

PROFESSIONAL PRACTICE

The Practice as Project
FLORIAN
IDENBURG

Issues in Architectural
Practice and Ethics
CARL SAPERS,
MARYANN
THOMPSON

PROPAEDEUTIC AND ADVANCED RESEARCH

Independent Thesis
in Satisfaction of
the Degree MAUD,
MLAUD, or MUP
SAI
BALAKRISHNAN

Life-Cycle Design
MARTIN
BECHTHOLD

Discourse and
Methods II
NEIL BRENNER

Urban Theory Lab
Research Practicum:
"Operational
Landscapes" of
Planetary Urbanization
NEIL BRENNER

Surplus Housing:
Models of Collective
Living in South America
FELIPE CORREA

Independent Thesis
in Satisfaction of the
Degree MLA
GARETH
DOHERTY

Independent Thesis
in Satisfaction of The
Degree MArch
EDWARD EIGEN

Art, Design, and
the Public Domain
Pre-Final Project
Workshop
FRIDA
ESCOBEDO

Vegetal City:
Projecting Urban
Canopy
GARY
HILDERBRAND

Living in the Kinetic
City: Mapping Housing
in a Landscape of Flux,
Mumbai
RAHUL
MEHROTRA

What Is a Thesis?
Conversations on
Means and Methods of
the Thesis Project
MOHSEN
MOSTAFAVI,
JONATHAN LOTT,
JOHN MAY

Visualization (at SEAS)
HANSPETER
PFISTER

REAL: Genome of the
Built Environment:
Measuring the Unseen
ALLEN SAYEGH

Research Methods
in Landscape
Architecture
ASHLEY
SCHAFER

Master of Design
Studies Final Project

STUDIOS

Second Semester
Architecture Core:
Situate
JENNIFER
BONNER,
JEFFRY
BURCHARD
(Coordinator),
TOMÁS DEPAOR,
MAX KUO, GRACE
LA (Coordinator),
PATRICK
MCCAFFERTY

Fourth Semester
Architecture Core:
Relate
LUIS CALLEJAS,
ANDREW
HOLDER,
MARIANA IBAÑEZ,
JEANNETTE
KUO (Coordinator),
CARLES MURO
(Coordinator),
BELINDA TATO

Landscape
Architecture II
NADIR
ABDESSEMED,
SILVIA
BENEDITO
(Coordinator),
ANITA
BERRIZBEITIA
(Coordinator), ERIC
DE BROCHE
DES COMBES,
DANIELLE
CHOI, PETER
DEL TREDICI,
JILL DESIMINI,
MARTHA
SCHWARTZ

Landscape
Architecture IV
PIERRE
BÉLANGER
(Coordinator),
FIONN BYRNE,
PETER DEL
TREDICI,
SERGIO
LOPEZ-PINEIRO,
NICHOLAS
PEVZNER,
ROBERT
PIETRUSKO

Second Semester Core
Urban Planning Studio
DANIEL D'OCA
(Coordinator),
STEPHEN
GRAY, KATHY
SPIEGELMAN

"Regular City" in
Chongqing: Searching
for Domesticated
Superstructures
JOAN BUSQUETS

Readymade
Architecture
PRESTON SCOTT
COHEN

Jakarta: Models of
Collective Space for the
Extended Metropolis
FELIPE CORREA

Housing in Mérida
Yucatán: The Urban
and the Territorial
DIANE E. DAVIS,
JOSE CASTILLO

Southampton Quay
MICHEL
DESVIGNE,
INESSA HANSCH

Third Natures:
London's Typological
Imagination
CRISTINA DÍAZ
MORENO, EFRÉN
GARCÍA GRINDA

Miami Rise and Sink:
Design for Urban
Adaptation
ROSETTA ELKIN

Frontier City
ADRIAAN GEUZE,
DANIEL VASINI

Wood, Urbanism: From
the Molecular to the
Territorial
JANE HUTTON,
KIEL MOE

Work Environments 2:
Glass Works
FLORIAN
IDENBURG

(Re)planned
Obsolescence . . .
Rethinking the
Architecture of Waste
HANIF KARA,
LEIRE ASENSIO
VILLORIA

Redesigning the Actor
Network in Rural
Areas around Tokyo
MOMOYO
KAIJIMA,
YOSHIHARU
TSUKAMOTO

Seoul Remade: Design
of the "Kool" and the
Everyday
NIALL
KIRKWOOD

Rotterdam Study
Abroad Option Studio:
Smart Countrysides
REM KOOLHAAS

Oh, Jerusalem: Eternal
Center / Generic
Periphery
ALEX KRIEGER

The Factory and the
City: Rethinking the
Industrial Spaces of the
Developmental City
CHRISTOPHER
C. M. LEE

Exrtreme Urbanism
IV: Looking at Hyper
Density—Dongri,
Mumbai
RAHUL
MEHROTRA

etceteras
MACK SCOGIN

Territorio Guaraní III
JORGE SILVETTI

Center for the
Performing Arts at the
Cranbrook Educational
Community
BILLIE TSIEN,
TOD WILLIAMS

GSD LEADER- SHIP

MOHSEN
MOSTAFAVI
Dean; Alexander
& Victoria Wiley
Professor of Design

PATRICIA J.
ROBERTS
Executive Dean

K. MICHAEL
HAYS
Associate Dean for
Academic Affairs; Eliot
Noyes Professor of
Architectural Theory

LAUREN BACCUS
Director of Human
Resources

W. KEVIN CAHILL
Facilities Manager,
Building Services

STEPHEN
MCTEE ERVIN
Assistant Dean for
Information Technology

RENA FONSECA
Director of Executive
Education &
International Programs

MARK GOBLE
Chief Financial Officer

BETH KRAMER
Associate Dean for
Development & Alumni
Relations

THERESA
A. LUND
Managing Director,
Office of the Dean

JACQUELINE
PIRACINI
Assistant Dean for
Academic Services

BENJAMIN
PROSKY
Assistant Dean for
Communications

Leadership

LAURA SNOWDON
Dean of Students & Assistant Dean for Enrollment Services

MELINDA STARMER
Director of Faculty Planning

ANN BAIRD WHITESIDE
Assistant Dean for Information Services & Librarian, Frances Loeb Library

ARCHITECTURE

IÑAKI ÁBALOS
Chair of the Department of Architecture; Professor in Residence of Architecture

GRACE LA
Director of the Master of Architecture Program; Professor of Architecture

LANDSCAPE ARCHITECTURE

ANITA BERRIZBEITIA
Chair of the Department of Landscape Architecture; Professor of Landscape Architecture

BRADLEY CANTRELL
Director of the Master in Landscape Architecture Program; Associate Professor of Landscape Architectural Technology

URBAN PLANNING AND DESIGN

DIANE E. DAVIS
Chair of the Department of Urban Planning and Design; Charles Dyer Norton Professor of Regional Planning and Urbanism

FELIPE CORREA
Director of the Master in Urban Design Program; Associate Professor of Urban Design

ANN FORSYTH
Director of the Master in Urban Planning Program; Professor of Urban Planning

MASTER OF DESIGN STUDIES

PIERRE BÉLANGER
Codirector of the Master in Design Studies Program; Associate Professor of Landscape Architecture

KIEL MOE
Codirector of the Master in Design Studies Program; Associate Professor of Architecture and Energy

MASTER IN DESIGN ENGINEERING

MARTIN BECHTHOLD
Codirector of Master in Design Engineering; Kumagai Professor of Architectural Technology

WOODWARD YANG
Codirector of Master in Design Engineering; Gordon McKay Professor of Electrical Engineering and Computer Science at SEAS

DOCTOR OF DESIGN AND PHILOSOPHY

MARTIN BECHTHOLD
Director of the Doctor of Design Studies Program; Kumagai Professor of Architectural Technology

ERIKA NAGINSKI
Director of the Doctoral Program; Professor of Architectural History

ANTOINE PICON
Director of Research; G. Ware Travelstead Professor of the History of Architecture and Technology

FACULTY

NADIR ABEDESSMED
Lecturer in Landscape Architecture

CARLOS GARCIAVELEZ ALFARO
Design Critic in Urban Planning and Design

BETH ALTRINGER
Lecturer on Innovation and Design, SEAS

ALAN ALTSHULER
Professor of Urban Planning and Design

FRANK APESECHE
Acting Director of the Harvard Real Estate Center; Lecturer in Architecture & Urban Planning and Design

STEVEN APFELBAUM
Lecturer in Landscape Architecture

JAVIER ARPA
Design Critic in Landscape Architecture

MICHAEL AZIZ
Gene and Tracy Sykes Professor of Materials and Energy Technologies, SEAS

BRIDGET BAINES
Design Critic in Landscape Architecture

RICARDO BAK GORDON
Design Critic in Architecture

SAI BALAKRISHNAN
Assistant Professor of Urban Planning

HENRI BAVA
Design Critic in Landscape Architecture

FRANCESCA BENEDETTO
Design Critic in Landscape Architecture

SILVIA BENEDITO
Assistant Professor of Landscape Architecture

IMOLA BERCZI
Instructor in Architecture

EVE BLAU
Adjunct Professor of the History and Theory of Urban Form and Design

JENNIFER BONNER
Assistant Professor of Architecture

SIBEL BOZDOGAN
Lecturer in Urban Planning, and Design

NEIL BRENNER
Professor of Urban Theory, Urban Planning and Design

GIULIANA BRUNO
Emmet Blakeney Gleason Professor of Visual and Environmental Studies, Architecture

JEFFRY BURCHARD
Design Critic in Architecture

JOAN BUSQUETS
Martin Bucksbaum Professor in Practice of Urban Planning and Design

FIONN BYRNE
Daniel Urban Kiley Fellow and Lecturer in Landscape Architecture

LUIS CALLEJAS
Lecturer in Architecture and Landscape Architecture

JAMES CARRAS
Adjunct Lecturer in Public Policy, HKS

JOSE CASTILLO
Design Critic in Urban Planning and Design

NATALIA ESCOBAR CASTRILLON
Instructor in Architecture and Urban Planning and Design

MARTHA CHEN
Affiliated Lecturer to the Department of Urban Planning and Design

CHRISTY CHENG
Design Critic in Architecture

DANIELLE CHOI
Design Critic in Landscape Architecture

EMANUEL CHRIST
Design Critic in Architecture

PRESTON SCOTT COHEN
Gerald M. McCue Professor of Architecture

CAROLINE CONSTANT
Visiting Professor Emerita in Landscape Architecture

SALMAAN CRAIG
Lecturer in Environmental Technology

JEAN PIERRE CROUSSE
Visiting Associate Professor in Urban Planning and Design

DILIP DA CUNHA
Lecturer in Urban Planning and Design

ERIC DE BROCHE DES COMBES
Lecturer in Landscape Architecture

TIM DEKKER
Lecturer in Landscape Architecture

PETER DEL TREDICI
Associate Professor in Practice of Landscape Architecture

TOMÁS DEPAOR
Design Critic in Architecture

JILL DESIMINI
Assistant Professor of Landscape Architecture

MICHEL DESVIGNE
Design Critic in Landscape Architecture

DANIEL D'OCA
Design Critic in Urban Planning and Design

WILLIAM DOEBELE
Frank Backus Williams Professor of Urban Planning and Design, Emeritus

GARETH DOHERTY
Assistant Professor of Landscape Architecture and Senior Research Associate

SONJA DÜMPELMANN
Associate Professor of Landscape Architecture

EDWARD EIGEN
Associate Professor of Architecture and Landscape Architecture

ROSETTA ELKIN
Assistant Professor of Landscape Architecture

ERLE ELLIS
Visiting Professor in Landscape Architecture

FRIDA ESCOBEDO
Lecturer in Architecture

TEMAN EVANS
Lecturer in Architecture

TERAN EVANS
Lecturer in Architecture

SUSAN FAINSTEIN
Senior Research Fellow

BILLIE FAIRCLOTH
Lecturer in Architecture

RICHARD T.T. FORMAN
Research Professor of Advanced Environmental Studies in the Field of Landscape Ecology

PETER GALISON
Affiliated Professor to the Department of Landscape Architecture

DAVID GAMBLE
Lecturer in Urban Planning and Design

CHRISTOPH GANTENBEIN
Design Critic in Architecture

EFRÉN GARCÍA GRINDA
Design Critic in Architecture

KERSTEN GEERS
Design Critic in Architecture

ANA GELABERT-SANCHEZ
Design Critic in Urban Planning and Design

Faculty

ANDREAS GEORGOULIAS
Lecturer in Architecture and Senior Research Associate

ADRIAAN GEUZE
Design Critic in Landscape Architecture

JOSE GOMEZ-IBANEZ
Derek Bok Professor of Urban Planning and Public Policy

ALASTAIR GORDON
Lecturer in Landscape Architecture

STEPHEN GRAY
Assistant Professor of Urban Design

TONI GRIFFIN
Professor in Practice of Urban Planning

NABEEL HAMDI
Visiting John T. Dunlop Professor in Urban Planning and Design

STEVEN HANDEL
Visiting Professor in Landscape Architecture

INESSA HANSCH
Design Critic in Landscape Architecture

EWA HARABASZ
Lecturer in Architecture, Landscape Architecture, and Urban Planning and Design

MICHAEL HAROZ
Lecturer in Urban Planning and Design

CHARLES HARRIS
Professor of Landscape Architecture, Emeritus

K. MICHAEL HAYS
Eliot Noyes Professor of Architectural Theory

CHRISTOPHER HERBERT
Lecturer in Urban Planning and Design Managing Director of the Joint Center for Housing Studies

HILDE HEYNEN
Lecturer in Architecture

GARY HILDERBRAND
Professor in Practice of Landscape Architecture

ELIZABETH KAI HINTON
Assistant Professor of History and of African and African American Studies at FAS

CHUCK HOBERMAN
Lecturer in Architecture

ANDREW HOLDER
Assistant Professor of Architecture

ZANETA HONG
Lecturer in Landscape Architecture

EELCO HOOFTMAN
Design Critic in Landscape Architecture

MICHAEL HOOPER
Associate Professor of Urban Planning

ERIC HÖWELER
Assistant Professor of Architecture

CHRISTOPHER HOXIE
Lecturer in Architecture

JOHN DIXON HUNT
Visiting Professor in Landscape Architecture

JANE HUTTON
Assistant Professor of Landscape Architecture

MARIANA IBAÑEZ
Associate Professor of Architecture

FLORIAN IDENBURG
Associate Professor in Practice of Architecture

CATHERINE INGRAHAM
Visiting Professor in Architecture

TOYO ITO
Kenzo Tange Design Critic in Architecture

MARK R. JOHNSON
Lecturer in Architecture

SHARON JOHNSTON
Design Critic in Architecture

JORRIT DE JONG
Lecturer in Public Policy at HKS

MOMOYO KAIJIMA
John T. Dunlop Visiting Professor in Architecture

MITS KANADA
Lecture in Architecture

HANIF KARA
Professor in Practice of Architectural Technology

DAVID KARNOVSKY
Lecturer in Urban Planning and Design

JEROLD KAYDEN
Frank Backus Williams Professor of Urban Planning and Design

STEPHANIE KAYDEN
Assistant Professor, Harvard Medical School and Harvard T. H. Chan School of Public Health

JAMES KHAMSI
Instructor in Architecture

BERNARD KHOURY
Design Critic in Urban Planning and Design

NIALL KIRKWOOD
Professor of Landscape Architecture

REM KOOLHAAS
Professor in Practice, Architecture and Urban Design

ALEX KRIEGER
Professor in Practice, Urban Design

JEANNETTE KUO
Assistant Professor in Practice, Architecture

MAX KUO
Design Critic in Architecture

MARK LAIRD
Lecturer in Landscape Architecture

CHRISTOPHER C. M. LEE
Associate Professor in Practice, Urban Design

MARK LEE
Design Critic in Architecture

XIANGNING LI
Visiting Professor in Architecture

GEORGE LEGENDRE
Associate Professor in Practice, Architecture

ENRIQUETA LLABRES VALLS
Lecturer in Landscape Architecture

SERGIO LOPEZ-PINEIRO
Lecturer in Landscape Architecture

JONATHAN LOTT
Design Critic in Architecture

NIKLAS MAAK
John T. Dunlop Lecturer of Housing and Urbanization

DAVID MAH
Lecturer in Landscape Architecture

ALI MALKAWI
Professor of Architectural Technology; Founding Director of the Harvard Center for Green Buildings and Cities

MICHAEL MANFREDI
Design Critic in Urban Planning and Design and Expert-in-Residence

EDWARD MARCHANT
Lecturer in Urban Planning and Design

BEN MARKHAM
Lecturer in Architecture

SEBASTIEN MAROT
Lecturer in Architecture

CHRISTOPHER MATTHEWS
Lecturer in Landscape Architecture

JOHN MAY
Design Critic in Architecture

PATRICK MCCAFFERTY
Lecturer in Architecture

GERALD MCCUE
John T. Dunlop Professor of Housing Studies, Emeritus

ALISTAIR MCINTOSH
Lecturer in Landscape Architecture

RAHUL MEHROTRA
Professor of Urban Design and Planning

ALEJANDRA MENCHACA
Lecturer in Architecture

ACHIM MENGES
Visiting Professor in Architecture

KIMBERLY MERCURIO
Lecturer in Landscape Architecture

PANAGIOTIS MICHALATOS
Lecturer in Architecture

JENNIFER MOLINSKY
Lecturer in Urban Planning and Design

RAFAEL MONEO
Josep Lluis Sert Professor in Architecture

CRISTINA DÍAZ MORENO
Design Critic in Architecture

TOSHIKO MORI
Robert P. Hubbard Professor in Practice of Architecture

FARSHID MOUSSAVI
Professor in Practice of Architecture

MOHSEN MOSTAFAVI
Dean, Alexander and Victoria Wiley Professor of Design

MARK MULLIGAN
Associate Professor in Practice of Architecture

CARLES MURO
Design Critic in Architecture and Urban Design

MICHAEL MURPHY
Lecturer in Architecture

PAUL NAKAZAWA
Associate Professor in Practice of Architecture

NICHOLAS NELSON
Lecturer in Landscape Architecture

ALBERT NICHOLS
Lecturer in Urban Planning and Design

BRYAN NORWOOD
Instructor in Architecture

JOÃO NUNES
Visiting Professor in Landscape Architecture

KAYOKO OTA
Lecturer in Architecture

MEGAN PANZANO
Design Critic in Architecture

CRISTINA PARRENO ALONSO
Design Critic in Architecture

KATHARINE PARSONS
Lecturer in Landscape Architecture

RICHARD PEISER
Michael D. Spear Professor of Real Estate Development

NICHOLAS PEVZNER
Design Critic in Landscape Architecture

HANSPETER PFISTER
An Wang Professor of Computer Science at SEAS

PABLO PEREZ-RAMOS
Lecturer in Landscape Architecture

ROBERT PIETRUSKO
Assistant Professor of Landscape Architecture and Urban Planning

SPIRO N. POLLALIS
Professor of Design Technology and Management

MARIANNE POTVIN
Instructor in Urban Planning and Design

GEETA PRADHAM
Lecturer in Urban Planning and Design

PHILIPPE RAHM
Design Critic in Architecture

CHRIS REED
Associate Professor in Practice of Landscape Architecture

DOUG REED
Lecturer in Landscape Architecture

CAMILLO RESTREPO OCHOA
Design Critic in Architecture

ALAN RICKS
Lecturer in Architecture

EDUARDO RICO CARRANZA
Lecturer in Landscape Architecture

Faculty

PETER ROWE
Raymond Garbe Professor of Architecture and Urban Design and Harvard University Distinguished Service Professor

THOMAS RYAN
Lecturer in Landscape Architecture

HOLLY SAMUELSON
Assistant Professor of Architecture

CARL SAPERS
Adjust Professor Emeritus in Architecture

ALLEN SAYEGH
Associate Professor in Practice of Architectural Technology

ASHLEY SCHAFER
Visiting Associate Professor in Landscape Architecture

PAUL SCHIMEK
Lecturer in Urban Planning and Design

JEFFREY SCHNAPP
Affiliated Professor to the Department of Architecture and Professor of Romance Languages & Literature at FAS

MARTHA SCHWARTZ
Professor in Practice of Landscape Architecture

MACK SCOGIN
Kajima Professor in Practice of Architecture

EDUARD SEKLER
Osgood Hooker Professor of Visual Art, Emeritus; Professor of Architecture, Emeritus

ANDRES SEVTSUK
Assistant Professor of Urban Planning

SHOHEI SHIGEMATSU
Design Critic in Architecture

KAIROS SHEN
Consultant in Urban Planning and Design

LOLA SHEPPARD
Visiting Associate Professor in Architecture

ROBERT SILMAN
Lecturer in Architecture

ENRIQUE SILVA
Lecturer in Urban Planning and Design

JOÃO GOMES DA SILVA
Design Critic in Landscape Architecture

JORGE SILVETTI
Nelson Robinson Jr. Professor of Architecture

CHRISTINE SMITH
Robert C. and Marian K. Weinberg Professor of Architectural History

KEN SMITH
Design Critic in Landscape Architecture

SUSAN SNYDER
Lecturer in Architecture

LAURA SOLANO
Associate Professor in Practice of Landscape Architecture

KATHY SPIEGELMAN
Design Critic in Urban Planning and Design

CARL STEINITZ
Alexander and Victoria Wiley Professor of Landscape Architecture and Planning, Emeritus

JOHN STILGOE
Robert and Lois Orchard Professor in the History of Landscape Development

JAMES STOCKARD
Lecturer in Housing Studies

BELINDA TATO
Design Critic in Architecture

GEORGE THOMAS
Lecturer in Architecture

MARYANN THOMPSON
Professor in Practice of Architecture

RAYMOND TORTO
Lecturer in Urban Planning and Design

BILLIE TSIEN
John C. Portman Design Critic

YOSHIHARU TSUKAMOTO
John T. Dunlop Visiting Associate Professor in Architecture

MATTHEW URBANSKI
Associate Professor in Practice of Landscape Architecture

JOSE LUIS VALLEJO
Design Critic in Architecture

DAVID VAN SEVEREN
Design Critic in Architecture; Charles Eliot Professor in Practice of Landscape Architecture

DANIEL VASINI
Design Critic in Landscape Architecture

CHAD VECITIS
Associate Professor of Environmental Engineering, SEAS

LEIRE ASENSIO VILLORIA
Lecturer in Architecture

ALEXANDER VON HOFFMAN
Lecturer in Urban Planning and Design

JAMES VOORHIES
Lecturer in Architecture

CHARLES WALDHEIM
John E. Irving Professor of Landscape Architecture; Director of the Office for Urbanization

BING WANG
Associate Professor in Practice of Real Estate and the Built Environment

EMILY WAUGH
Lecturer in Landscape Architecture

JAMES WEAVER
Senior Research Scientist-Adaptive Materials, HMS, Wyss Institute

DANIEL WEISSMAN
Lecturer in Architecture

ELIZABETH WHITTAKER
Assistant Professor in Practice of Architecture

JAY WICKERSHAM
Associate Professor in Practice of Architecture

TOD WILLIAMS
John C. Portman
Design Critic

ANDREW WITT
Assistant Professor
in Practice of
Architecture

KRZYSZTOF
WODICZKO
Professor in Residence
of Art, Design, and the
Public Domain

ANNA LAURA
WOLF-POWERS
Lecturer in Urban
Planning and Design

CAMERON WU
Associate Professor of
Architecture

TODD ZICKLER
William and Ami Kuan
Danoff Professor of
Electrical Engineering
and Computer
Science, SEAS

DONALD ZIZZI
Lecturer in Urban
Planning and Design

LOEB FELLOWSHIP

JOHN PETERSON
Curator

SALLY YOUNG
Program Coordinator

2015–2016 FELLOWS

NEHA BHATT
Planner and
smart-growth advocate
(Washington, DC)

LILIANA CAZACU
Architect and historic
preservationist
(Sibui, Romania)

JANELLE CHAN
Executive Director,
Asian Community
Development
Corporation
(Boston, MA)

KIMBERLY DRIGGINS
Planner and
community developer
(Washington, DC)

ALEJANDRO ECHEVERRI
Architect, planner,
and urban designer
(Medellín, Colombia)

SHANE ENDICOTT
Founding Director,
Our United Villages
(Portland, OR)

ARIF KHAN
Urban planner,
community organizer,
disaster-and-relief
manager
(New York, NY)

BRETT MOORE
Architect and
humanitarian shelter,
infrastructure, and
reconstruction advisor
(Victoria, Australia)

EUNEIKA ROGERS-SIPP
Community developer,
social-impact designer,
and artist (Atlanta, GA)

FELLOWSHIPS & PRIZES

Wheelwright Prize
ANNA PUIGJANER

Veronica Rudge Green
Prize in Urban Design
MADRID RÍO

HARVARD GSD STUDENT FELLOWSHIPS, PRIZES & TRAVEL PROGRAMS

Druker Traveling
Fellowship
Kyriaki Thalia
Kasabalis (MAUD '16)

Award for Outstanding
Leadership in Urban
Planning
Paul Andrew
Lillehaugen (MUP '16)

Award for Outstanding
Leadership in Urban
Design
William J. Rosenthal
(MAUD '16)

Award for Academic
Excellence in Urban
Planning
Nathalie Maria Janson
(MUP '16)

Award for Academic
Excellence in Urban
Design
Michael Keller (MAUD
/ MLA I AP '16)

Award for Excellence
in Urban Design
Kyriaki Thalia
Kasabalis (MAUD '16)

Award for Excellence
in Project-Based
Urban Planning
Shani Adia Carter
(MUP '16); Kathryn
Hanna Casey (MUP
'16); Warren E. A.
Hagist (MUP '16)

Fellowships & Prizes

Department of Urban Planning and Design Thesis Prize in Urban Planning
Francisco Lara Garcia (MUP '16)

Department of Urban Planning and Design Thesis Prize in Urban Design
Yinan Wang (MAUD '16)

American Institute of Certified Planners Outstanding Student Award
Paige Elizabeth Peltzer (MUP '16)

Howard T. Fisher Prize in Geographic Information Science
Elena Chang (MUP '16); Elliot Kilham (MUP '16); Russell Philip Koff (MUP '16); Alexander John Mercuri (MUP '16); Sarah Madeleine Winston (MUP '16)

Ferdinand Colloredo-Mansfeld Prize for Superior Achievement in Real Estate Studies
Dongmin Chung (MDes '16)

UD Shanghai's 2015 International Student Urban Design Competition for Shanghai Railway Station Area
Kyriaki Thalia Kasabalis (MAUD '16), Michael Keller (MAUD / MLA I AP '16), and Kitty Tin Hung Tsui (MAUD '16)

Pollman Fellowship in Real Estate and Urban Development
Can Cui

Plimpton-Poorvu Design Prize
Anna Hermann (MArch I '17) and Felipe Oropeza, Jr. (MArch I '17)

Dimitris Pikionis Award
Eliyahu Keller (MDes '16)

The Daniel L. Schodek Award for Technology and Sustainability
Zeina Koreitem (MDes AP '16); David George Kennedy (MDes '16); Jacob Wayne Mans (MDes '16); Benjamin Lee Peek (MDes '16), for a group thesis.

Project Prize (MDes)
Josselyn Francesca Ivanov (MDes AP '16)

AIA Henry Adams Medal
Nancy Nichols (MArch I '16)

AIA Henry Adams Certificate
Iman Fayyad (MArch I '16)

Alpha Rho Chi Medal
Alexander Timmer (MArch I '16)

Araldo A. Cossutta Annual Prize for Design Excellence
Elizabeth McEniry (MArch I / MLA I AP '18)

Clifford Wong Prize
Liang Wang (MAUD '16) and Lu Zhang (MAUD '16)

ETH Zurich Exchange Program
Kathryn Sonnabend (MArch I '17) and Douglas Harsevoort (MArch I '18)

Department of Architecture Faculty Design Award
MArch I: Iman Fayyad (MArch I '16)
MArch II: Sofia Blanco Santos (MArch II '16)

Julia Amory Appleton Traveling Fellowship
John Kirsimagi (MArch I '16)

John E. Thayer Award
Alexander Timmer (MArch I '16)

James Templeton Kelley Prize
MArch I: Joshua Feldman (MArch I '16)
MArch II: Sofia Blanco Santos and Caio Barboza (MArch II '16)

Kevin V. Kieran Award
Caio Barboza (MArch II '16)

Peter Rice Internship Program at Renzo Piano Building Workshop
Royce Perez (MArch I AP '17)

Takenaka Summer Internship
Johanna Faust (MArch I '17)

Charles Eliot Traveling Fellowship in Landscape Architecture
Thomas Nideroest (MLA II '16)

Jacob Weidenman Prize
Michael Keller (MAUD / MLA I AP '16)

Peter Walker and Partners Fellowship for Landscape Architecture
Foad Vahidi (MLA I '16)

Landscape Architecture Thesis Prize
Leif Estrada (MDes / MLA I AP '16)

American Society of Landscape Architects Awards
Certificate of Merit: Christianna Bennett (MLA I AP '16); Devin Dobrowolski (MLA I '16); Ambrose Luk (MLA I '16)
Certificate of Honor: Bruce Cannon Ivers (MLA II '16); Ruichao Li (MLA I AP '16); Elaine Stokes (MLA I AP '16)

Norman T. Newton Prize
Natasha Polozenko (MLA II '16)

Penny White Student Projects Fund
Oliver Curtis (MDes '17); Alberto Embriz de Salvatierra (MLA I AP, MDes '17); Ellen Epley (MLA I '17); Kent Hipp (MLA II '17); Jia Joy Hu (MLA I AP '17); Justin Kollar (MArch I AP / MUP '17); Qi Xuan (Tony) Li (MLA I '17); Sophie Maguire (MLA I '17); Kira Sargent (MLA I '17); Julia Smachylo (DDes '19); Jonah Susskind (MLA I '17); Jane Zhang (MDes '17)

Olmsted Scholar
Azzurra Cox (MLA I '16)

Peter Rice Prize
Manuel Martínez Alonso (MDes '17)

↑ Sophia Geller, April 28, 2016

GSD etc.

STAFF

JOSEPH AMATO
Maintenance Technician

KATHLEEN ANDERSON
Staff Assistant, Executive Education

ELIZABETH ANTONELLIS
Coordinator, Research Administration

MERIDITH APFELBAUM
Career Services Counselor

ALLA ARMSTRONG
Financial Manager, Academic Programs

JOHN ASLANIAN
Director of Student Affairs and Recruitment

PAMELA BALDWIN
Assistant Dean of Faculty Affairs

KERMIT BAKER
Program Director for Remodeling Studies, Joint Center for Housing Studies

CLAIRE BARLIANT,
Managing Editor, Communications

KATE BAUER
Executive Assistant to the Dean

LAUREN BACCUS
Assistant Dean of Human Resources

LAUREN BEATH
Accounting Assistant

TODD BELTON
Web Developer

JENNA BJORKMAN
Administrative Coordinator, Center for Green Buildings & Cities

SHANTEL BLAKELY
Public Programs Manager

SUSAN BOLAND
Web Administrator

DAN BORELLI
Director of Exhibitions

EDWARD BREDENBERG
Administrative Manager, Academic Programs & Executive Dean

KEVIN CAHILL
Facilities Manager

HEIDI CARRELL
Communications and Outreach Manager, Joint Center for Housing Studies

MAGGIE CARTER
Development Coordinator

JAMES CHAKNIS
Communications and Outreach Coordinator, Joint Center for Housing Studies

JOSEPH CHART
Senior Major Gifts Officer, Development

TOM CHILDS
Operations Supervisor

JOANNE CHOI
Staff Assistant, Frances Loeb Library

ANNA CIMINI
Staff Assistant, Computer Resources

CARRA CLISBY
Assistant Director of Development Communications and Donor Relations

SEAN CONLON
Registrar

ANNE CREAMER
Coordinator, Career Services

TRAVIS DAGENAIS
Communications Specialist

CAITLIN DECOSTA-KUPSC
Academic Appointments & Payroll Assistant

SARAH DICKINSON
Research Support Services Librarian

STEPHEN ERVIN
Assistant Dean for Information Technology

JEFFREY FITTON
Outreach and Events Manager, Green Buildings & Cities

ANGELA FLYNN
Staff Assistant, Joint Center for Housing Studies

RENA FONSECA
Director of Executive Education & International Programs

NICOLE FREEMAN
Associate Director of Development

JENNIFER GALA
Associate Director, Executive Education and International Programs

HEATHER GALLAGHER
Financial Associate

ERICA GEORGE
Program Coordinator, Coordinator of Student Activities and Outreach

KEITH GNOZA
Director of Financial Assistance & Assistant Director of Student Services

MARK GOBLE
Chief Financial Officer

MERYL GOLDEN
Director of Career and Community Services

SANTIAGO GOMEZ
Staff Assistant, Student Services

DESIREE GOODWIN
Library Assistant

SARA GOTHARD
Program Coordinator, Landscape Architecture and Urban Planning & Design

HAL GOULD
Manager of User Services, Computer Resources

LINDSEY GRANT
Campaign Event Manager

NORTON GREENFELD
Development Information Systems Manager

ARIN GREGORIAN
Financial Associate, Academic Programs

HYEYON GRIMBALL
Accounting Assistant, Academic Programs

DEBORAH GROHE
Staff Assistant, Building Services

GAIL GUSTAFSON
Director of Admissions

MARK HAGEN
Windows System Administrator

TESSALINA HALPERN
Staff Assistant, Student Services

Staff

RYANNE HAMMERL
Student Services Staff Assistant

CHRISTOPHER HANSEN
Digital Fabrication Technical Specialist

BARRY HARPER
Staff Assistant, Building Services

CHRISTOPHER HERBERT
Managing Director, Joint Center for Housing Studies

THOMAS HEWITT
Research Assistant, Administration & Academic Programs

JOHANN HINDS
Help Desk Technician, Computer Resources

TIMOTHY HOFFMAN
Faculty Planning Coordinator

TAYLOR HORNER
Department Administrator, Architecture

SARAH HUTCHINSON
Executive Assistant, Academic Programs & Executive Dean

RYAN JACOB
Program Coordinator, Architecture

MAGGIE JANIK
Multimedia Producer, Communications

BETH KAPLAN
Assistant Director of Alumni Communications

JOHANNA KASUBOWSKI
Design Resources Librarian

KAREN KITTREDGE
Associate Director of Finance

JEFFREY KLUG
Director, Career Discovery

SARAH KNIGHT
Annual Fund and Alumni Relations Coordinator

HELEN KONGSGAARD
Research Associate, Office for Urbanization

ARDYS KOZBIAL
Collections and Outreach Librarian

BETH KRAMER
Associate Dean for Development & Alumni Relations

ELIZABETH LA JEUNESSE
Research Assistant, Joint Center for Housing Studies

MARY LANCASTER
Senior Financial Manager, Joint Center for Housing Studies

ASHLEY LANG
Department Administrator, Landscape Architecture and Urban Planning & Design

AMY LANGRIDGE
Finance Manager, Executive Education

KEVIN LAU
Head of Instructional Technology Group and Library

BURTON LEGEYT
Digital Fabrication Technical Specialist

IRENE LEW
Research Assistant, Joint Center for Housing Studies

ANNA LYMAN
Director of External Administration, Office of the Dean

SONALI MATHUR
Research Assistant III, Demographics

BOB MARINO
Finance and Grant Manager, Center for Green Buildings & Cities

EDWIN MARTINEZ
Help Desk Technician, Computer Resources

ELLEN MARYA
Research Assistant, Joint Center for Housing Studies

ANNE MATHEW
Director, Research Administration

DANIEL MCCUE
Research Manager, Joint Center for Housing Studies

BETH MILLSTEIN
Associate Director of Development

MARGARET MOORE DE CHICOJAY
Program Manager, Executive Education

ROCIO MOYANO-SANCHEZ
Research Assistant, Joint Center for Housing Studies

JANESSA MULEPATI
Coordinator, Landscape Architecture and Urban Planning & Design

JANINA MUELLER
Design Data Librarian

MICHELLE MULIRO
Human Resources and Payroll Coordinator

GERI NEDERHOFF
Director of Admissions and Diversity Recruitment Manager

CAROLINE NEWTON
Director of Internal Administration, Office of the Dean

KETEVAN NINUA
Staff Assistant, Development & Alumni Relations

CHRISTINE O'BRIEN
Accounting Assistant, Communications

TREVOR O'BRIEN
Assistant Manager, Building Services

BARBARA PERLO
Program Manager, Executive Education

JOHN PETERSON
Curator, Loeb Fellowship Program

JACQUELINE PIRACINI
Assistant Dean for Academic Services

LISA PLOSKER
Assistant Director of Human Resources

DAVID BRAD QUIGLEY
Director of Alumni Relations & Annual Giving

NONY RAI
Coordinator, Research Administration

PILAR RAYNOR JORDAN
Financial Associate, Academic Programs

ALIX REISKIND
Digital Initiatives Librarian

PATRICIA J. ROBERTS
Executive Dean

MEGHAN SANDBERG
Publications Coordinator

JOCELYN SANDERS
Senior Major Gifts Officer, Development

MADELIN SANTANA
Project Manager, Executive Education

RONEE SAROFF
Assistant Director, Digital Content & Strategy, Communications

JENNIFER SIGLER
Editor in Chief, Communications

GOSIA SKLODOWSKA
Associate Director of Administration, Center for Green Buildings & Cities

MATTHEW SMITH
Media Services Manager, Computer Resources

LAURA SNOWDON
Assistant Dean for Enrollment Services; Dean of Students

JOHN SPADER
Senior Research Associate, Joint Center for Housing Studies

SUSAN SPAULDING
Building Services Coordinator

WHITNEY STONE
Campaign Coordinator

AMBER STOUT
Development Assistant

DAVID STUART-ZIMMERMAN
Exhibitions Coordinator

JEN SWARTOUT
Program Administrator, Advanced Studies Program

AIMEE TABERNER
Director of Academic Programs Administration

ELLEN TANG
Assistant Director of Financial Aid

ELIZABETH THORSTENSON
Program Coordinator, Advanced Studies Program

KATHAN TRACY
Director of Development, Major and Principal Giving

JENNIFER VALLONE
Accounting Assistant

EDNA VAN SAUN
Program Coordinator, Faculty Planning

RACHEL VROMAN
Manager, Digital Fabrication Laboratory

ANTYA WAEGEMANN
Staff Assistant

LIZ WALAT
Director of Financial Planning and Analysis

ANN BAIRD WHITESIDE
Assistant Dean for Information Services and Librarian, Frances Loeb Library

SARA WILKINSON
Director of Human Resources

ABBE WILL
Research Analyst, Joint Center for Housing Studies

KELLY TEIXEIRA WISNASKAS
Manager of Special Programs for Student Services

SALLY YOUNG
Coordinator, Loeb Fellowship Program

INES ZALDUENDO
Special Collections Archivist & Reference Librarian

KATHRYN ZIRPOLO
Center Coordinator, Center for Green Buildings & Cities

GSD STUDENTS 2015–2016

MASTER OF ARCHITECTURE

Clare Adrien
Chantine Akiyama
Cari Alcombright
Miriam Alexandroff
Majda AlMarzouqi
Ahmad Altahhan
Nastaran Arfaei
Alice Armstrong
Emily Ashby
Cheuk Fan Au
Rekha Auguste-Nelson
Sofia Balters
Peiying Ban
Esther Bang
Patrick Baudin
Sasha Bears
Sandra Bonito
Taylor Brandes
Benjamin Bromberg Gaber
Jacob Bruce
Oliver Bucklin
Jeffrey Burgess
Nathan Buttel
Yaqing Cai
Daniel Carlson
Maria Carriero
Stanislas Chaillou
Ruth Chang
Abigail Chang
YuanTung Chao
Caroline Chao
Yu Chen
Shiyang Chen
Joanne Cheung
Sean Chia
Chieh Chih Chiang
Carol Chiu
Shani Cho
Sukhwan Choi
Kai-hong Chu
Yewon Chun
Stephanie Conlan
Matthew Conway
Allison Cottle
Carly Dickson
Claire Djang
Eliana Dotan
Anna Falvello Tomas
Valeria Fantozzi
Evan Farley
Johanna Faust
Iman Fayyad
Joshua Feldman
Martin Fernandez
Paul Fiegenschue
Julian Funk
Arianna Galan Montas
Bennett Gale
Justin Gallagher
Yuan Gao
Ya Gao
John Going
Marianna Gonzalez
Christian Gonzalez
Chris Grenga
Jia Gu
Yun Gui
Yuqiao Guo
Fabiola Guzman Rivera
Michael Haggerty
Taylor Halamka
Benjamin Halpern
David Hamm
Rebecca Han
Whitney Hansley
Douglas Harsevoort
Spencer Hayden
Benjamin Hayes
Chen He
Christina Hefferan
Anita Helfrich
Anna Hermann
Carlos Hernandez-Tellez
Patrick Herron
Kelley Hess
Olivia Heung
Kevin Hinz
Kira Horie
Yousef Hussein
Jihoon Hyun
Tomotsugu Ishida
Shi Yu Jiang
Suthata Jiranuntarat
Chase Jordan
Young Eun Ju
Hyeyun Jung
Mazyar Kahali
Sarah Kantrowitz
Ali Karimi
Danielle Kasner
Andrew Keating
Thomas Keese
Gerrod Kendall
Shaina Kim
Mingyu Kim
Jason Kim
Insu Kim
Haram Kim
Frederick Kim
John Kirsimagi
Arion Kocani
Yurina Kodama
Wyatt Komarin
Lindsey Krug
Claire Kuang
Hyojin Kwon
Daniel Kwon
Hoi Ying Lam
Jungwoo Lee
Jamie Lee
Elizabeth Lee
Madeline Lenaburg
Naomi Levine
Ethan Levine
Yixin Li
Keunyoung Lim
Shao Lun Lin
Yanchen Liu
Kirby Liu
Gregory Logan
Anna Kalliopi Louloudis
Fan Lu
Yan Ma
Sicong Ma
Radu-Remus Macovei
Emily Margulies
Caleb Marhoover
Casey Massaro
Naureen Mazumdar
Lauren McClellan
Elizabeth McEniry
Patrick McKinley
Dana McKinney
Thomas McMurtrie
Marcus Mello
Aaron Menninga
Michael Meo
Steven Meyer
Dasha Mikic
Farhad Mirza
Chit Yan Paul Mok
Giancarlo Montano
Yina Moore
Niki Murata
James Murray
Khorshid Naderi-Azad
Paris Nelson
Yina Ng
Jing Yi Ng
Phi Nguyen
Bryant Nguyen
Duan Ni
Nancy Nichols
Xuanyi Nie
Matthew Okazaki
Felipe Oropeza
Kimberly Orrego
Davis Owen
Meric Ozgen
Sophia Panova
Jee Hyung Park
Andy Park
Maia Peck
Haibei Peng
Yen Shan Phoaw
David Pilz
Luisa Pineros Sanchez
Elizabeth Pipal
Philip Poon
Alexander Porter
Hannah Pozdro
Irene Preciado Arango
Jiayu Qiu
See Hong Quek
Yi Ren
Jonathan Rieke
Julia Roberts
Cara Roberts
Benzion Rodman
Matthew Rosen
Lane Rubin
Stuart Ruedisueli
Ivan Ruhle
Anne Schneider
Jennifer Shen
Yiliu Shen-Burke
Emma Silverblatt
Scott Smith
Lance Smith
David Solomon
Humbi Song
Kathryn Sonnabend
Christopher SooHoo
Morgan Starkey
Karen Stolzenberg
Constance Storie Johnson
LeeAnn Suen
Mahfuz Sultan
Adelene Tan
Noelle Tay
Lilian Taylor
Bijan Thornycroft
Alexander Timmer
Tianze Tong
Chun Ting Tsai
Ho Cheung Tsui
Rex Tzen
Samantha Vasseur
Isabelle Verwaay
Khoa Vu
Ping Wang
Jacob Welter
Wen Wen
Emily Wettstein
Madelyn Willey
Georgia Williams
Enoch Wong
Hanguang Wu
Dana Wu
Andrey Yakovlev
Bryan Yang
Jung Chan Yee
Tzyy Haur Yeh
Carolyn Yi
Hyunsuk Yun
Yu Kun
Snoweria Zhang
Huopu Zhang
Guowei Zhang
Eric Zuckerman

MASTER OF ARCHITECTURE AP

William Adams
Aleksis Bertoni
Patrick Burke
Andres Camacho
Jaewoo Chon
Collin Cobia
Jyri Eskola
Lauren Friedrich
Carly Gertler
Yoonjin Kim
Justin Kollar
Daniela Leon
Yi Li
Raffy Mardirossian
Paruyr Matevosyan
Patrick Mayfield
Chong Ying Pai
Royce Perez
Chang Su
Xuezhu Tian
Long Chuan Zhang
Shaowen Zhang
Yufeng Zheng
Yubai Zhou

MASTER OF ARCHITECTURE II

Nada AlQallaf
Sara Arfaian
Myrna Ayoub
Tam Banh
Caio Barboza
James Barclay
Mohamad Berry
Sofia Blanco Santos
Xiang Chang
Michael Charters
Konstantinos Chatzaras
Ji Hyuk Choi
Michael Clapp
Jose Pablo Cordero
Erin Cuevas
Niccolo Dambrosio
Ximena de Villafranca
Cameron Delargy
Sama El Saket
Alejandro Fernandez-Linares Garcia
Wei-Che Fu
Mikhail Grinwald
Zhuang Guo
Elena Hasbun
Daniel Hemmendinger
Feijiao Huo
Tamotsu Ito
Taehyun Jeon
Xin Ji

Michael Johnson
Joshua Jow
Chrisoula Kapelonis
Ranjit Korah
Dayita Kurvey
Christian Lavista
Junyoung Lee
Man Lai Manus Leung
Hongjie Li
Yatian Li
Yi Li
Changyue Liu
Mengdan Liu
Timothy Logan
Ping Lu
Yuxiang Luo
Feifan Ma
Katherine MacDonald
Hana Makhamreh
Jana Masset
Zachary Matthews
Christopher Meyer
Yuyangguang Mou
Andrew Nahmias
Ramzi Naja
Erin Ota
Poap Panusittikorn
Fani-Christina Papadopoulou
Erin Pellegrino
Zhe Peng
Konstantina Perlepe
Michael Piscitello
Demir Purisic
Sizhi Qin
Daniel Quesada Lombo
Andrejs Rauchut
Christopher Riley
Marysol Rivas Brito
Leonardo Rodriguez
Zahra Safaverdi
Juan Sala
Ruben Segovia
Harsha Sharma
Joshua Smith
Stefan Stanojevic
Xin Su
Stephen Sun
Haotian Tang
Jeronimo Van Schendel Erice
Joseph Varholick
Cangkai Wang
Fan Wang
Tiantian Wei
Wei Xiao
Junko Yamamoto
Haoxiang Yang
Yujun Yin
Ni Zhan
Boya Zhang
Xi Zhang
Meng Zhu

MASTER OF LANDSCAPE ARCHITECTURE

Emily Allen
Jonathan Andrews
Madeleine Aronson
Maria Arroyo
Naoko Asano
Rachel Bedet
Larissa Belcic
Michelle Benoit
Emily Blair
Lanisha Blount
Lee Ann Bobrowski
Sarah Bolivar
Jessica Booth
Andrew Boyd
Laura Butera
Johanna Cairns
Sarah Canepa
Alexander Cassini
Jenna Chaplin
Jiawen Chen
Su-Yeon Choi
Timothy Clark
Kelly Clifford
Ashelee Collier
Emmanuel Coloma
Leandro Couto de Almeida
Azzurra Cox
Tiffany Dang
Devin Dobrowolski
Emily Drury
Ellen Epley
Enrico Evangelisti
Siobhan Feehan
Gideon Finck
Hannah Gaengler
Yufan Gao
Ana Garcia
Sophia Geller
Emma Goode
Ernest Haines
Jeremy Hartley
Mark Heller
Aaron Hill
Rayana Hossain
InHye Jang
Geunhwan Jeong
Diana Jih
Dana Kash
Yong Uk Kim
Bradley Kraushaar
Sirinya Laochinda
Yanick Lay
Xiaoshuo Lei
Charlotte Leib
Qi Xuan Li
Xinhui Li
Yuanjie Li
Annie Liang
Christopher Liao
Rebecca Liggins

Ho-Ting Liu
Ambrose Luk
Nicholas Lynch
Sophie Maguire
Alison Malouf
Alica Meza
Nathalie Mitchell
Althea Northcross
Ivy Pan
Nina Phinouwong
Maria Robalino
Lauren Robie
Gabriella Rodriguez
Louise Roland
Ann Salerno
Kira Sargent
Jennifer Saura
Elizabeth Savrann
Rachel Schneider
David Schoen
Keith Scott
Max Sell
Mengfan Sha
Yun Shi
Michelle Shofet
Vipavee Sirivatanaaksorn
Chella Strong
Jonah Susskind
Shanasia Sylman
Zixuan Tai
Diana Tao
Carly Troncale
Carlo Urmy
Foad Vahidi
Marisa Villarreal
Gege Wang
Hui Wang
Lu Wang
Na Wang
Yifan Wang
James Watters
Daniel Widis
Sarah Winston
Ahran Won
Eunice Wong
Matthew Wong
Malcolm Wyer
Zehao Xie
Han Xu
Yuan Xue
Xin Zhao

MASTER OF LANDSCAPE ARCHITECTURE AP

Alexander Agnew
Weaam Alabdullah
Nada AlQallaf
Rawan Alsaffar
Christianna Bennett
Sourav Biswas

Students

Elise Bluell
Gandong Cai
Shimin Cao
Mengqing Chen
Yijia Chen
Alberto
 Embriz-Salgado
Leif Estrada
Matthew
 Gindlesperger
Jianwu Han
Gary Hon
Jia Hu
Mark Jongman-Sereno
Thomas Keese
Michael Keller
Gyeong Kim
Lyu Kim
Lou Langer
Ruichao Li
Yifei Li
Xun Liu
Chen Lu
Alexandra Mei
Mailys Meyer
Mary Miller
Timothy Nawrocki
Yuqing Nie
Wenyi Pan
Linh Pham
Yuxi Qin
Christopher Reznich
Yue Shi
Soo Ran Shin
Andrea Soto Morfin
Elaine Stokes
Andrew Taylor
Sonja Vangjeli
Yujia Wang
Emily Wettstein
Sonny Meng Qi Xu
Tzyy Haur Yeh
Yujun Yin
Andrew Younker
Dandi Zhang
Xi Zhang
Ziwei Zhang

MASTER OF LANDSCAPE ARCHITECTURE II

Taylor Baer
Chenyuan Gu
Robert Hipp
Bruce Ivers
Qiyi Li
Andrew Madl
Christopher Merritt
Tyler Mohr
Thomas Nideroest
Jing Pan
Natasha Polozenko
Antonia Rudnay
Samantha Solano
Izgi Uygur
Boxia Wang
John Wray IV
Xiaodi Yan
David Zielnicki

MASTER OF ARCHITECTURE IN URBAN DESIGN

Clayton Adkisson
Lori Ambrusch
Jiachen Bai
Hovhannes Balyan
Jesica Bello
Yao Bo
Marios Botis
Nathalia Camacho
Difei Chen
Shiyu Chen
Mikela De Tchaves
Moises Garcia Alvarez
Rodrigo Guerra
Christopher Haverkamp
Adam Himes
Elizabeth Hollywood
Yang Huang
Seunghoon Hyun
Vasileios Ioannidis
Juan Diego
 Izquierdo Hevia
David Jimenez
Taro Kagami
Natalia Kagkou
Kyriaki Kasabalis
Michael Keller
Jeffrey Knapke
Elaine Kwong
Shiqing Liu
Shiyao Liu
Chenghao Lyu
Siwen Ma
Yasamin Mayyas
Paul Miller
Chi Yoon Min
Hyun-sik Mun
Qun Pan
Nishiel Patel
Chao Qi
Dai Ren
William Rosenthal
Gaby San
 Roman Bustinza
Juan Santa Maria
Dana Shaikh Solaiman
Jianwei Shi
Caroline Smith
Man Su
Claudia Tomateo
Daniel Toole
Tin Hung Tsui
Magdalena Valenzuela
Liang Wang
Yinan Wang
Yutian Wang
Ran Wei
Hayden White
Xiaohan Wu
Mengchen Xia
Teng Xing
Ruoyun Xu
Jessy Yang
Yiying Yang
Ting Yin
Ziming Yuan
Lu Zhang
Miao Zhang
Pu Zhang
Xiao Zhang
Yuting Zhang
Bin Zhu
Chang Zong
Long Zuo

MASTER OF LANDSCAPE ARCHITECTURE IN URBAN DESIGN

Zhuo Cheng
Gabriella Rodriguez
Janice Tung
Zehao Xie

MASTER OF URBAN PLANNING

Andrew Alesbury
Faisal Almogren
Cory Berg
Maira Blanco
Isabel Margarit Cantada
Omar Carrillo Tinajero
Shani Carter
Kathryn Casey
Cesar Castro
Elena Chang
Sohael Chowfla
Carissa Connelly
Katherine Curiel
Matthew Curtin
Omar De La Riva
Megan Echols
Omar Farroukh
Daniel Foster
Clara Fraden
Peimeizi Ge
Marco Gorini
Fernando
 Granados Franco
Carolyn Grossman
Arjun Gupta Sarma
Warren Hagist
Mark Heller
Tamara Jafar
Nathalie Janson
Jessica Jean-Francois
Howaida Kamel
Miriam Keller
Elliot Kilham
Mina Kim
Russell Koff
Justin Kollar
Francisco Lara-Garcia
Samuel LaTronica
Sarah Leitson
Alexander Lew
Paul Lillehaugen
Stephany Lin
John McCartin
Dana McKinney
Meghan McNulty
Marcus Mello
Andres
 Mendoza Gutfreund
Alexander Mercuri
Cara Michell
Katherine Miller
Yvonne Mwangi
Paige Peltzer
Lucy Perkins
Nina Phinouwong
Jack Popper
Angelica Quicksey
Andres Quinche
Rebecca Ramsey
Carlos Felipe Reyes
Aline Reynolds
Erica Rothman
Illika Sahu
Edgardo Sara Muelle
Jennifer Saura
Emma Schnur
David Schoen
Hanna Schutt
Laurel Schwab
Courtney Sharpe
Apoorva Shenvi
Jorge Silva
Brodrick Spencer
Alyson Stein
Andrew Stokols
Kevin Symcox
Antara Tandon
Carmen Jimena
 Veloz Rosas
Anna White
Sarah Winston
Lindsay Woodson

MASTER OF DESIGN STUDIES

Amira Abdel-Rahman
Annapurna Akkineni

Rawan Alsaffar
Spyridon Ampanavos
Tairan An
Jolin Ang
Rabih Anka
Pedro Aparicio
Aziz Barbar
George Bartulica
Megan Berry
Hernan
   Bianchi Benguria
Noor Boushehri
Adria Boynton
Jordan Bruder
Jihyeun Byeon
Mary Kate Cahill
Andrea Carrillo Iglesias
Marielsa Castro
Xin Chen
Tiffany Cheng
Xu Chi
HyoJeong Choi
Dongmin Chung
Oliver Curtis
Kritika Dhanda
Gerardo Diaz
Hao Ding
Peng Dong
Alexander Duffy
Farzaneh Eftekhari
Alberto Embriz-Salgado
Genevieve Ennis
Peter Erhartic
Leif Estrada
Yuan Fang
Carla Ferrer Llorca
Clemens Finkelstein
Francesca Forlini
Cristobal Fuentes
Palak Gadodia
Maria Letizia Garzoli
Cody Glen
Marcus Goodwin
Akshay Goyal
Mikhail Grinwald
Boya Guo
Liang Hai
Jacob Hamman
Dave Hampton
Huishan He
Justin Henceroth
Shanika Hettige
Yujie Hong
Gregory Hopkins
Elad Horn
Xinyun Huang
Lisa Joelle Jahn
Carlyn James
Tian Jiang
Xiong Jiang
Yiyi Jiang
Jiyoo Jye
Amir Karimpour
Apoorv Kaushik
Eliyahu Keller

David Kennedy
Andrew Kim
Haeyoung Kim
Seung Kyum Kim
Justin Kunz
Boram Lee
Jolene Wen Hui Lee
Jungwoo Lee
Namju Lee
Zongye Lee
Arthur Leung
Danlu Li
Hanwei Li
Lezhi Li
Yi Li
Yunjie Li
Zhiwei Liao
Karen Lin
Mariana Llano
Joyce Lo
Xuan Luo
Leeor Maciborski
Namik Mackic
Qurat-ul-ain Malick
Jacob Mans
Andrea Margit
Megan Marin
Manuel Martinez Alonso
Alkistis Mavroeidi
Ana Mayoral Moratilla
Daryl McCurdy
Evangeline McGlynn
Eric Melenbrink
Aaron Mendonca
Amanda Miller
Helen Miller
Guan Min
Tanuja Mishra
Thomas Montelli
Anthony Morey
Gabriel Munoz Moreno
Vivek Muralidhar
Oscar Natividad Puig
Rebecca Nolan
Stephen Nowak
Erin Ota
Javier Ors Ausin
Jacqueline Palavicino
Michail Papavarnavas
Dale Park
Roma Patel
Benjamin Peek
Benjamin Perdomo
Adam Pere
Jane Philbrick
Yu Ling Pong
Yu Qiao
Jake Rudin
Ambieca Saha
Olga Semenovych
Rodrigo Senties
Santiago Serna
Kevin Sievers
Razan Sijeeni
Keebaik Sim

Michael Sinai
Aman Singhvi
Vero Smith
Eli Sokol
Young Joo Song
Youngjin Song
Bryan Spatzner
Anthony Stahl
Joseph Steele
Elnaz Tafrihi
Nada Tarkhan
Ashley Thompson
Christine Tiffin
Shreejaya Tuladhar
Alejandro Valdivieso
Scott Valentine
Enol Vallina Fernandez
Phillip van Alstede
Cong Wang
Rufei Wang
Xueshi Wang
Karno Widjaja
Lindsay Woodson
Jung Hyun Woo
Longfeng Wu
Jia Yi Xia
Qi Xiong
Andrew Yam
HyeJi Yang
Dan Zhang
Jinjin Zhang
Xin Zhao

MASTER
OF DESIGN
STUDIES AP

Josselyn Ivanov
Yoonjee Koh
Zeina Koreitem

DOCTOR OF
DESIGN

Ozlem Altinkaya Genel
Nicole Beattie
Joelle Bitton
Ignacio Cardona
Somayeh Chitchian
Daniel Daou
Ali Fard
Wendy Fok
Yun Fu
Jose Garcia del
   Castillo Lopez
Mariano Gomez Luque
Jonathan Grinham
ChengHe Guan
Saira Hashmi
Vaughn Horn
Xiaokai Huang
Kristen Hunter
Daniel Ibanez

Aleksandra Jaeschke
Ghazal Jafari
Nikolaos Katsikis
Miguel Lopez Melendez
Yingying Lu
Taraneh Meshkani
Sarah Norman
Dimitris Papanikolaou
Daekwon Park
Pablo Perez Ramos
Carolina San Miguel
Julia Smachylo
Jihoon Song
Juan Ugarte
Bing Wang
Dingliang Yang
Arta Yazdanseta
Nari Yoon
Jeongmin Yu
Jingyi Zhang

DOCTOR OF
PHILOSOPHY

Fallon Michele
   Samuels Aidoo
Matthew Allen
Amin Alsaden
Maria Atuesta
Katarzyna Balug
Aleksandr Bierig
Christine Elizabeth
   Crawford
Brett Michael Culbert
John Dean Davis
Igor Ekstajn
Samaa Elimam
Tamer Elshayal
Natalia Escobar
Matthew Gin
Lisa Anne
   Haber-Thomson
Ateya Khorakiwala
Diana Louise Lempel
Manuel Lopez Segura
Bryan Norwood
Morgan Ng
Jason Nguyen
Sabrina Osmany
Sun Min Park
Marianne Potvin
Katherine Prater
Etien Santiago
Peter Sealy
Justin Stern
Adam Tanaka
Marrikka Trotter
Rodanthi Vardouli
Dimitra Vogiatzaki
Eldra D. Walker
Delia Duong Ba
   Wendel

On(e) Point

Heavy Matter

Variations on the Display

Hold the

A light-weight long-span roof for a cultural project in Medellín, Colombia, sits in front of experiments in carbon fiber, while spindly vertical members represent a structural strategy for a mid-rise tower, or map the distances between open space and hospitals in Cambridge, Massachusetts. All of the models presented here express lightness either through the physical weight of the materials or vis-a-vis the conceptual mood of the project. One architecture studio encourages the use of broken eggshells to construct a field, while a landscape architecture seminar constructs thin, fragile shells with an egg-crate definition in Rhino. The proportions of a tower are bulky, but the designer achieves lightness of materiality with slumped glass. Circulation models are almost always light and airy, momentarily ignoring the mass of the architecture. Spindly, fragile, airy, and light are ways of reading the works that follow.

Lightness

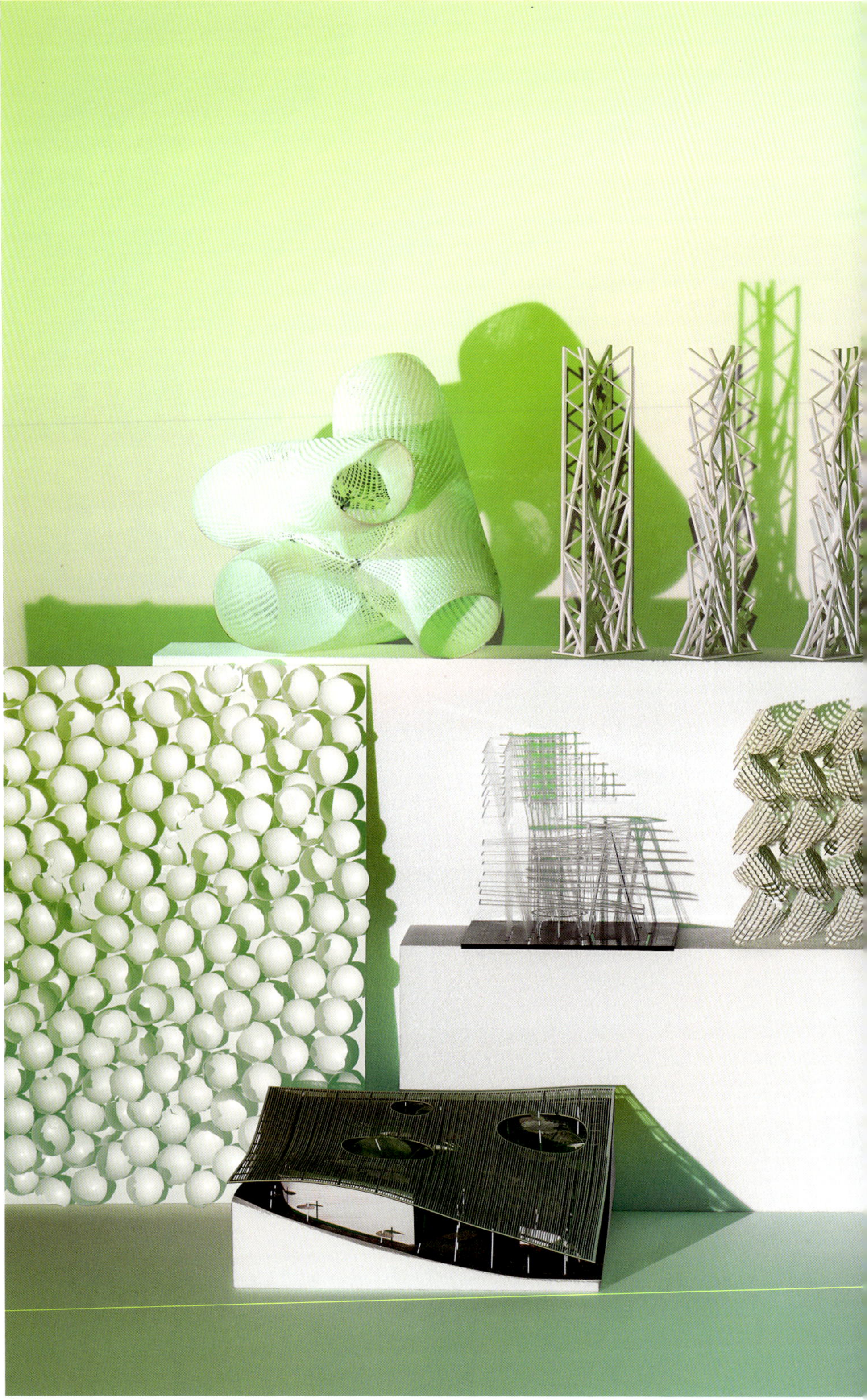

LIGHTNESS

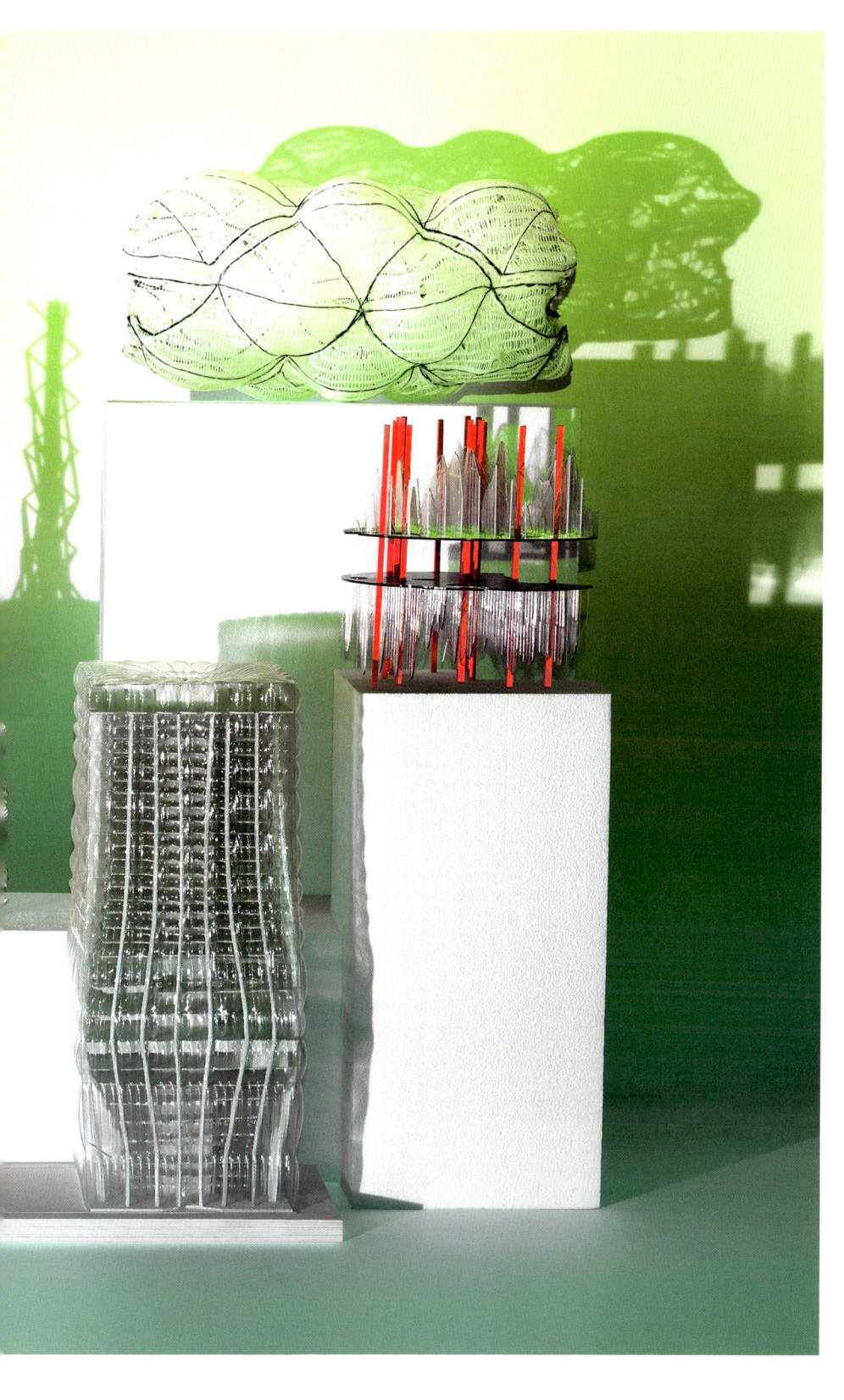

238

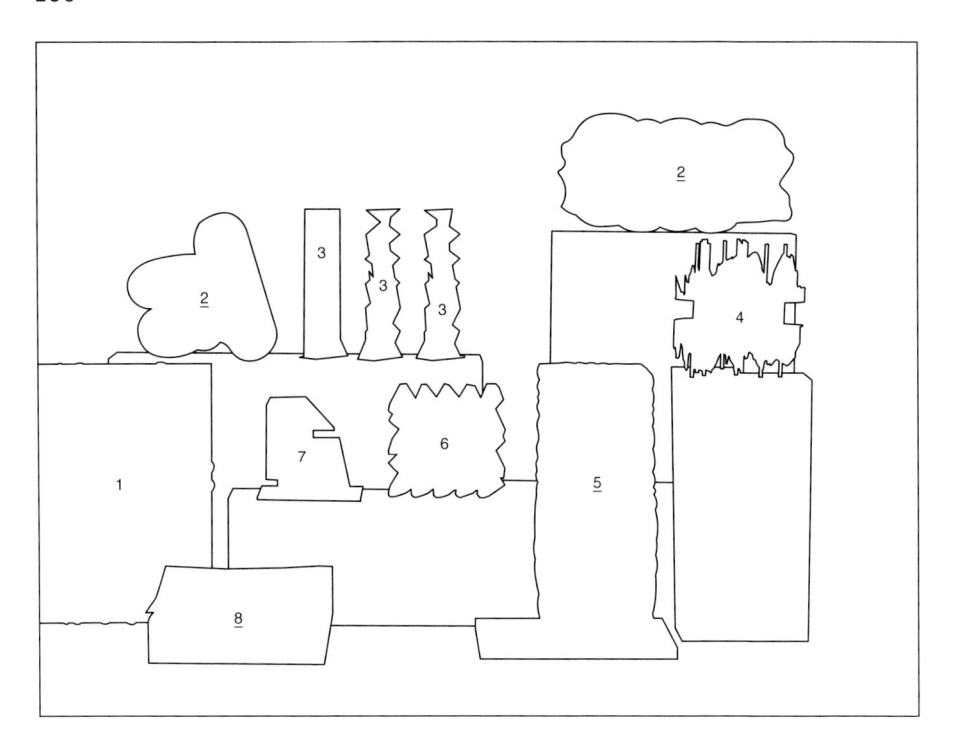

LIGHTNESS

1 Eggshells
Johanna Faust
MArch I, 2017
etceteras
Instructor: Mack Scogin

2 Fibrous
p. 240

Yuan Gao
MArch I, 2017
Demir Purisic, Zahra
    Safaverdi, Joseph Varholick
MArch II, 2017
Material Performance: Fibrous
    Tectonics & Architectural
    Morphology
Instructor: Achim Menges

3 Structural Members
Steven Meyer
MArch I, 2018
Architecture Core III: Integrate
Instructor: Jennifer Bonner

4 Datums
Caroline Chao, Taylor
    Halamka, Christina Hefferan
MArch I, 2019
Mapping: Geographic
    Representation and
    Speculation
Instructor: Robert Pietrusko

5 Vacuum Formed
p. 242

Elizabeth McEniry
MArch I / MLA I AP, 2019
Architecture Core III: Integrate
Instructor: Jonathan Lott

6 Waffle
Christopher Liao
MLA I, 2018
Landscape Representation I
Instructors: Zaneta Hong,
    Sergio Lopez-Pineiro

7 Circulation System
Shao Lun Lin
MArch I, 2018
Architecture Core III: Integrate
Instructor: Jeffry Burchard

8 No Stop
p. 244

James Murray
MArch I, 2017
Imprecise Tropics
Instructor: Camilo
    Restrepo Ochoa

Yuan Gao
MArch I, 2017

Demir Purisic, Zahra Safaverdi, Joseph Varholick
MArch II, 2017

Material Performance: Fibrous Tectonics & Architectural Morphology

Instructor
Achim Menges

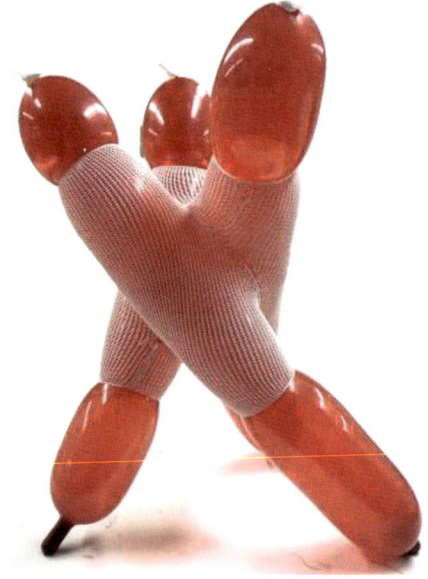

LIGHTNESS — Option Studio — 241

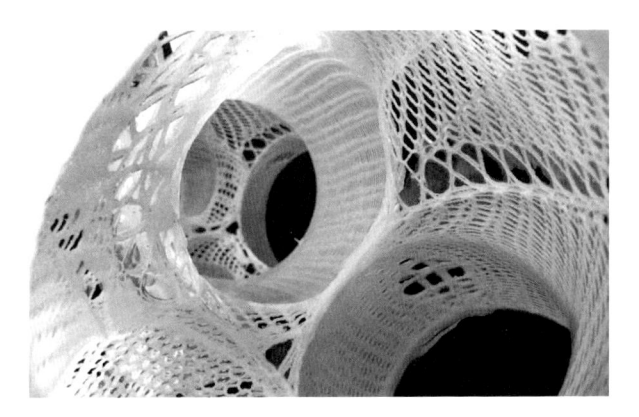

This studio explored the new role of materials, such as advanced fiber composites, as active generators of design that break away from predefined molds. The resulting designs reveal the morphic character of fibrous systems.

Elizabeth McEniry
MArch I / MLA I
AP, 2019

Architecture Core III: Integrate

Instructor
Jonathan Lott

This course, the third in the Architecture Core sequence, brought in facade engineer Marc Simmons to consult with students on their projects. Here, a double-cavity, slumped-glass envelope embraces circulatory exchanges between floor levels and various programs. The proposal challenges a deep floor plan with this thick, figural facade.

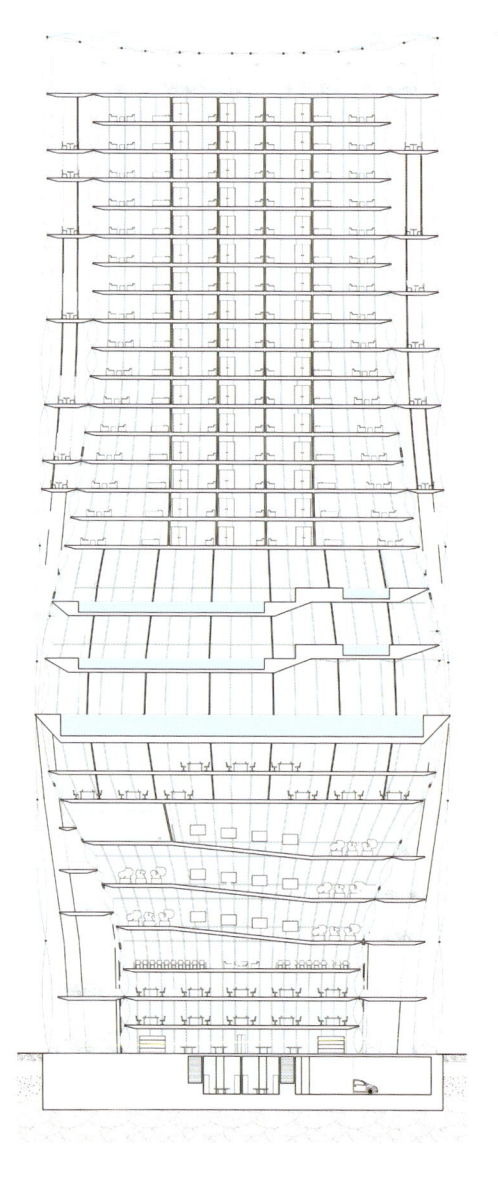

LIGHTNESS   Core Studio   243

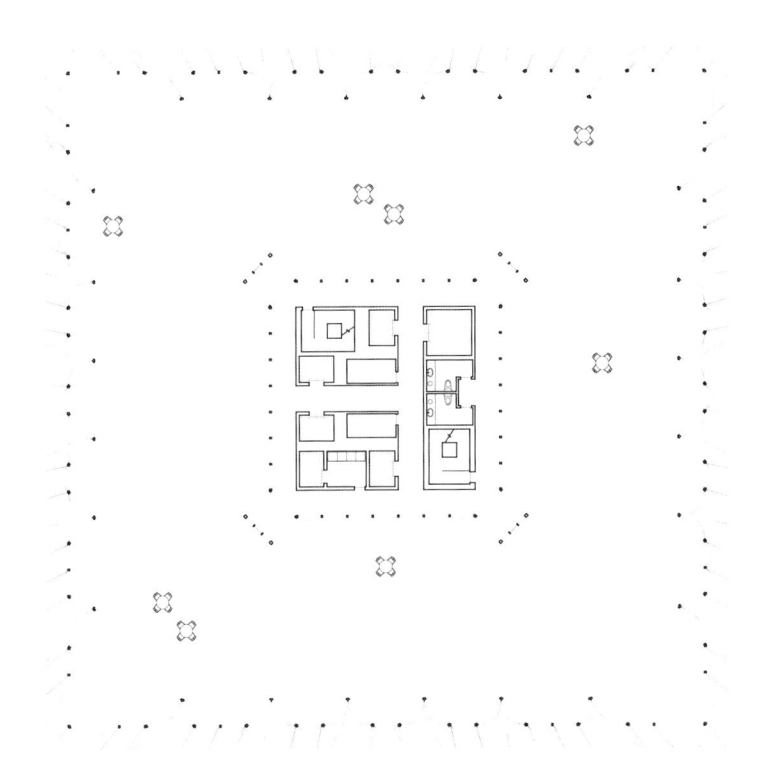

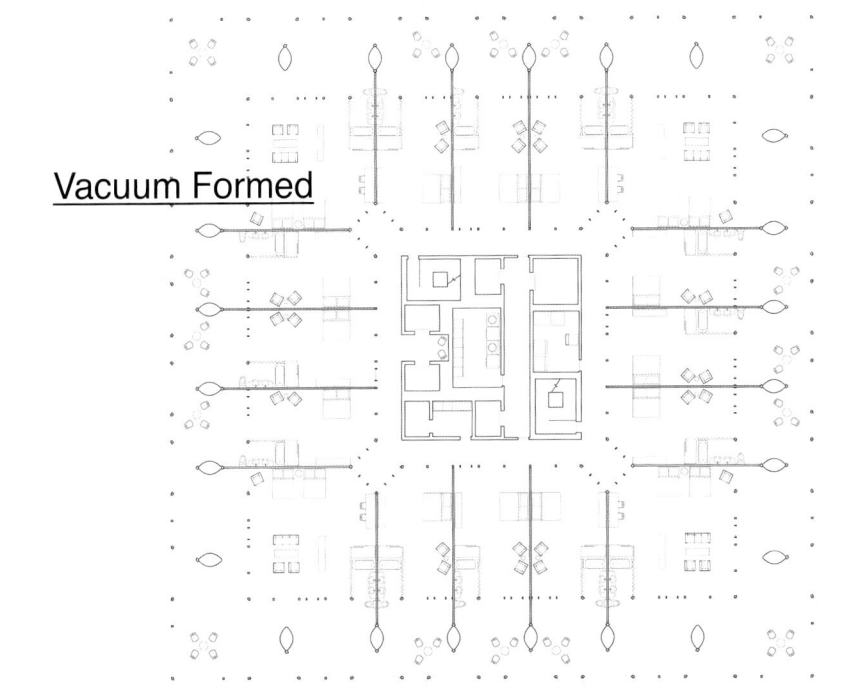

Vacuum Formed

No Stop

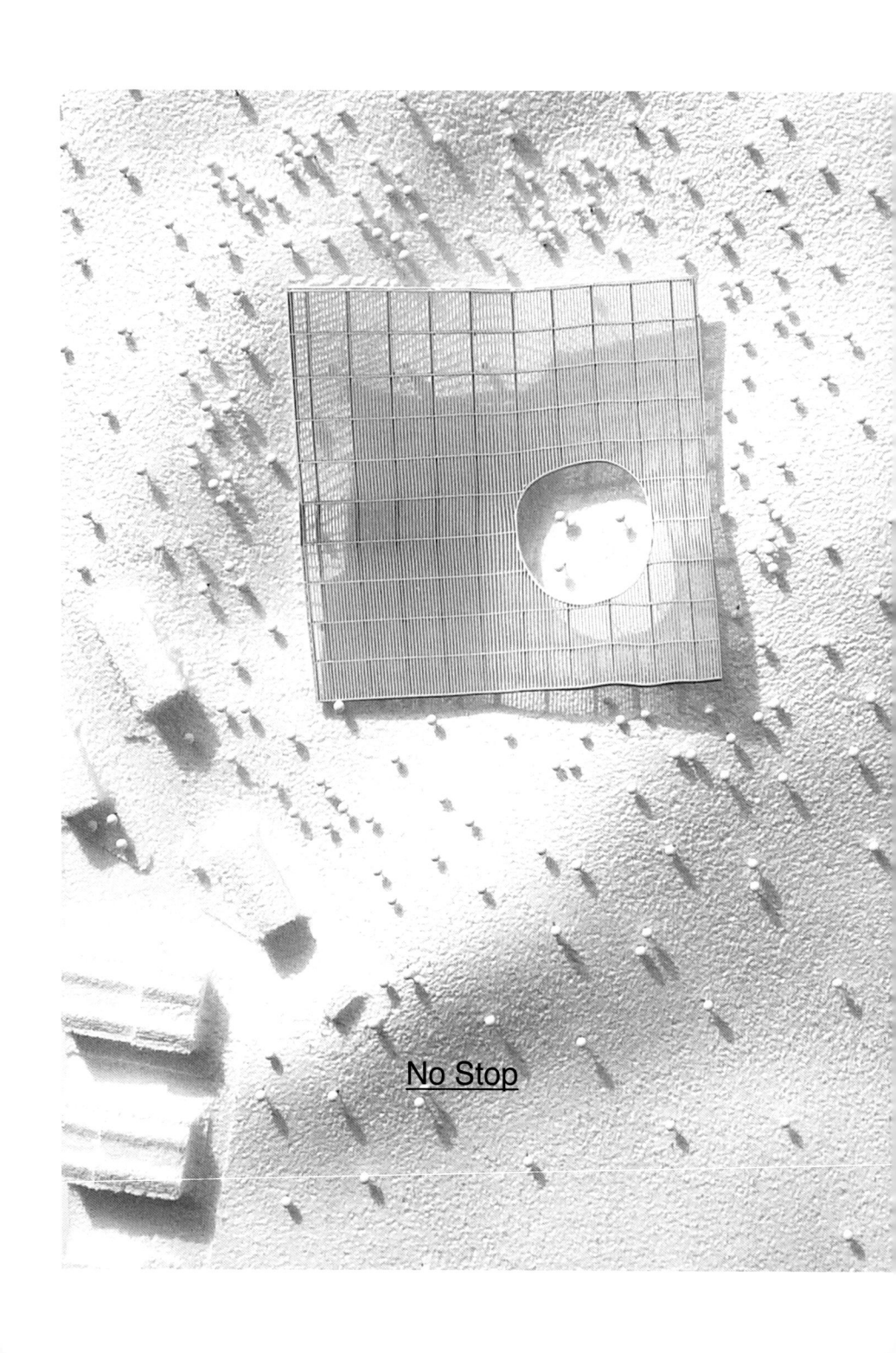

James Murray
MArch I, 2017

Imprecise Tropics

Instructor
Camilo Restrepo Ochoa

The tropic is precise in its definition only when it is referred to as latitude. It is imprecise in its architecture, in its spatial condition, and in the experience of its everyday life. This studio took inspiration from Medellín, Colombia, as a way to unravel the nontransparent tropical condition, and used its unique geography, climate, diversity, and material culture as resources to redefine the idea of tropical space.

Still Life with Pinks and Blues

The first still life was architecture. It was the pile of stones that the first traveler-*cum*-architect placed at the crossroads during his journey elsewhere—a setting-up of objects to claim a place, to confirm having been there, to insist on being other, to make a difference. Or the mark made on the stone at the moment just before Architecture separated from Text (arche-writing). As William Wordsworth recognized in *Essay upon Epitaphs*: "An Epitaph presupposes a Monument, upon which it is to be engraven." "Monument" here is not a valuation; it conveys rather an inert materiality to the monument as still life; not an availability so much as a thingness, obduracy, a lack of immanent meaning—like Hegel's pyramid awaiting the hieroglyphs. The pyramid as still-life fruit on the folded dessert.

Hermes was the first traveler-*cum*-architect who set up this monument, the gods themselves tossing the stones that encased him in his cairn: stilled life. (And in this sense, Le Corbusier's Ronchamp, for example, is an exquisitely hermetic still life, a pile of rubble from the old ruined chapel, encased in white, addressed to the "four horizons," resonant with the "acoustical landscape," and concerned, above all, not about us worshippers, but about its own being there.) Taken together as originary performances, what Wordsworth's monument and the hermetic cairn allow us to grasp is the necessary negativity of still life (the negativity which so many contemporary architects try to tame with more and more exuberance). For what the inscription "presupposes" of the monument is not a particular meaning, but a certain kind of potentiality, a non-semantic materiality, a non-referential construct. It presupposes the structure or system (or discipline?) in which the inscription could both take its place and find its material support. Indeed, it presupposes architecture as a certain kind of *being*.

The still life performs rather than represents the process of inscription.

K. Michael Hays
Associate Dean for Academic Affairs;
Eliot Noyes Professor in
Architectural Theory

Five one-point perspectives levitate here. They are arranged in a photograph that is also framed by the one-point, suggesting a one-point perspective on one-point perspectives. It is the representation of choice for several option studios that took place over fall 2015: Iceberg Alley; Alimentary Design: The Final Course; Architecture Without Content 15: Neon Palladian; and Imprecise Tropics. Renderings collage several materials without perspective, thus appearing (intentionally) flat, and, to push this aesthetic even further, shadow is used sparingly. It seems plausible that all of this concerted effort on the part of the designers is reactionary. More in the spirit of Mies's one-point perspectives, and contradictory to photo-realism of recent image-making trends, these one-points take another tack—this time, no lines are visible and collaged flat materials saturate the image.

Resting below these one-point perspectives, seven urban design and architecture proposals are carefully framed, representing the spaces where the editors imagine that these one-point perspectives reside. There, an architecture studio also confronts the one-point, not through flat drawings, but with large-scale interior models for a promising development on the one-point. Whether referencing old techniques or inventing new methods, both are on point.

On(e) Point

250

ON(E) POINT

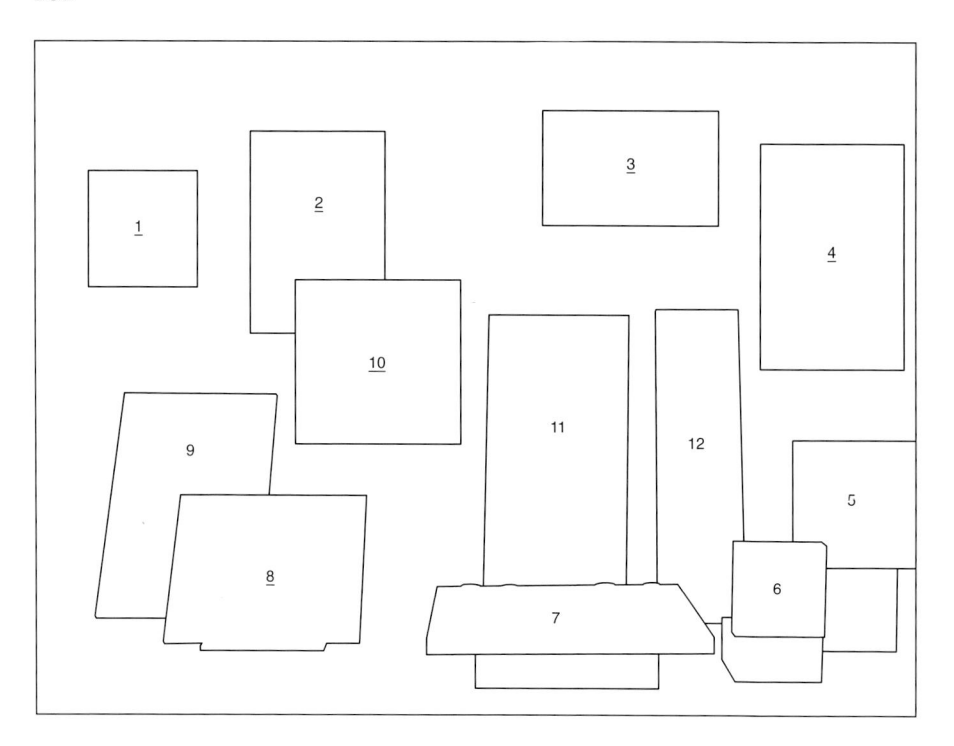

ON(E) POINT

1   Food
p. 254

Christopher Riley
MArch II, 2017
Alimentary Design: The Final Course
Instructors: Shohei Shigematsu, Christine Cheng

2   Dispensary
p. 256

Maia Peck
MArch I, 2017
Architecture Without Content 15: Neon Palladian
Instructors: Kersten Geers, David Van Severen

3   Domestic
p. 258

Konstantina Perlepe
MArch II, 2016
Imprecise Tropics
Instructor: Camilo Restrepo Ochoa

4   Canopy
p. 260

Sara Arfaian
MArch II, 2017
Architecture Without Content 15: Neon Palladian
Instructors: Kersten Geers, David Van Severen

5   Edge

Yaqing Cai
MArch I, 2017
Iceberg Alley
Instructors: Lola Sheppard, Mason White

6   Superimposition

Collin Cobia
MArch I AP, 2017
Territorio Guaraní III
Instructor: Jorge Silvetti

7   Fluid

Irene Preciado Arango
Valeria Fantozzi, Meriç Özgen
MArch I, 2018
Architecture Core IV: Relate
Instructor: Belinda Tato

8   Interior
p. 262

Ya Gao, Danielle Kasner, Naureen Mazumdar
MArch I, 2018
Architecture Core IV: Relate
Instructor: Jeannette Kuo

9   Archetypes

Sasha Bears, Yousef Hussein, Elizabeth McEniry
MArch I, 2018
Architecture Core IV: Relate
Instructor: Luis Callejas

10   Cloister
p. 264

Dai Ren
MAUD, 2016
Iceberg Alley
Instructors: Lola Sheppard, Mason White

11   Lincoln Road

Patrick Mayfield
MArch I AP, 2016
Thesis: From Water to Salt
Advisor: Kiel Moe

12   Hybrid

Gary Lin, Marcus Mello, James Zhang
MArch I, 2018
Architecture Core IV: Relate
Instructor: Belinda Tato

This studio was the third and final investigation in a series that explored the relationships among the alimentary (defined as of or relating to nourishment or nutrition), architecture, and urbanism. This project attempts to exploit these relationships by designing a factory and facility that highlight both the individual and the collective.

Food

ON(E) POINT   Option Studio   255

Christopher Riley
MArch II, 2017

Alimentary Design: The Final Course

Instructors
Shohei Shigematsu, Christine Cheng

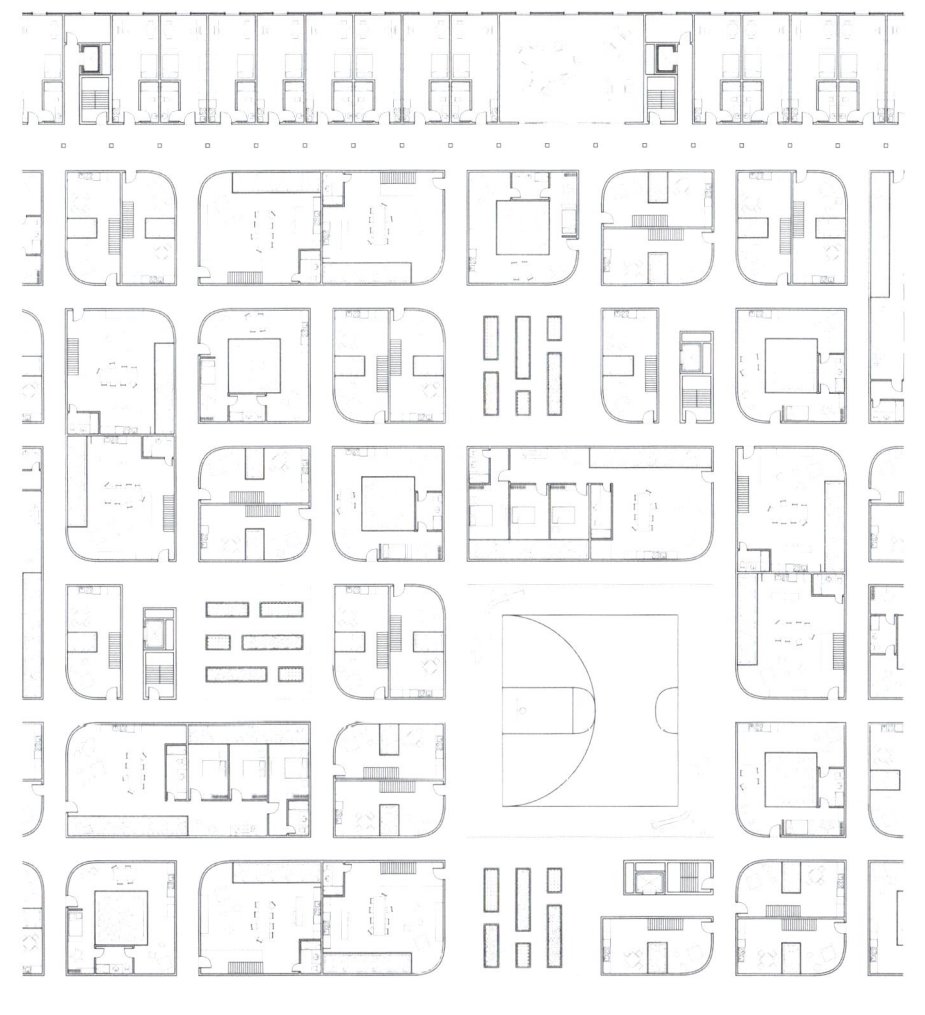

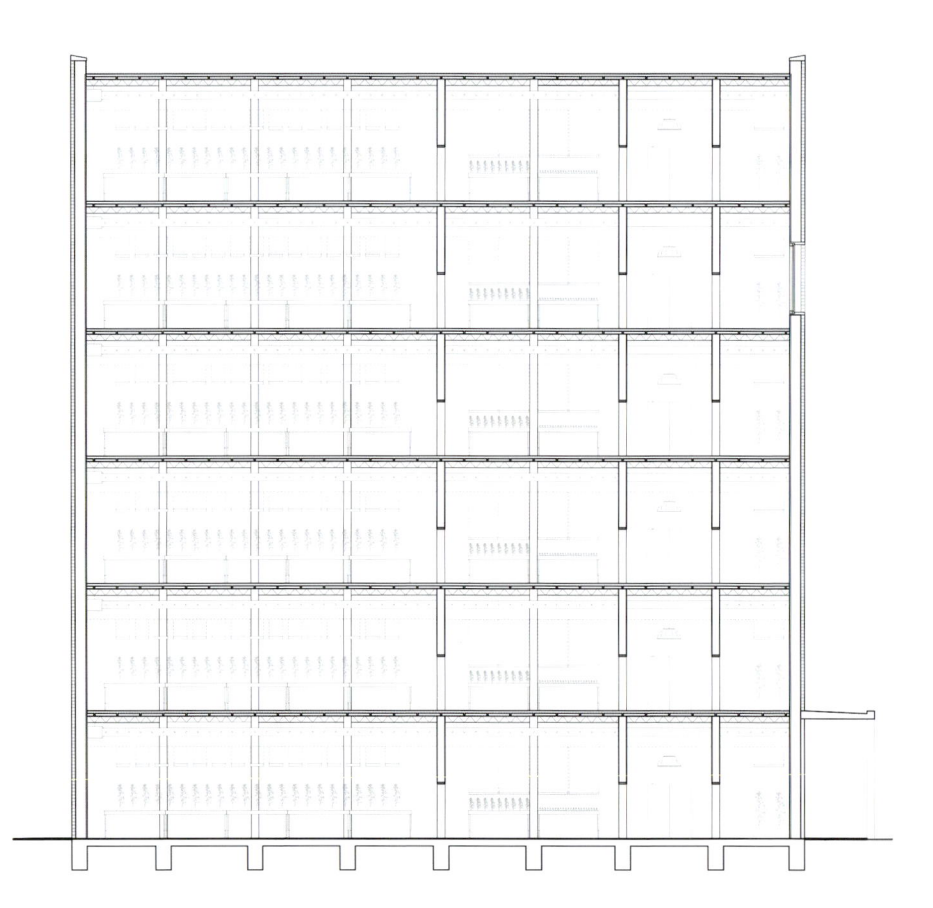

Dispensary

Maia Peck
MArch I, 2017

Architecture Without Content 15: Neon Palladian

Instructors
Kersten Geers, David Van Severen

This studio was part of an ongoing series looking at scale and precedents for American architecture. It investigated Neo-Palladianism, as Palladianism is a defining influence of early American architecture, and inflated it to the scale of the Las Vegas Strip: Neon Palladian. This project, situated on the outskirts of Rochester, New York, is a medical-marijuana dispensary.

This studio employed architecture as a device for experiencing the tropic in an ambiguous way, and to redefine tropical space and architecture in a manner that resists the usual clichés of leisure, white sands, and cocktails in coconut shells. The project featured here focuses on domestic space.

ON(F) POINT   Option Studio   259

Konstantina Perlepe
MArch II, 2016

Imprecise Tropics

Instructor
Camilo Restrepo Ochoa

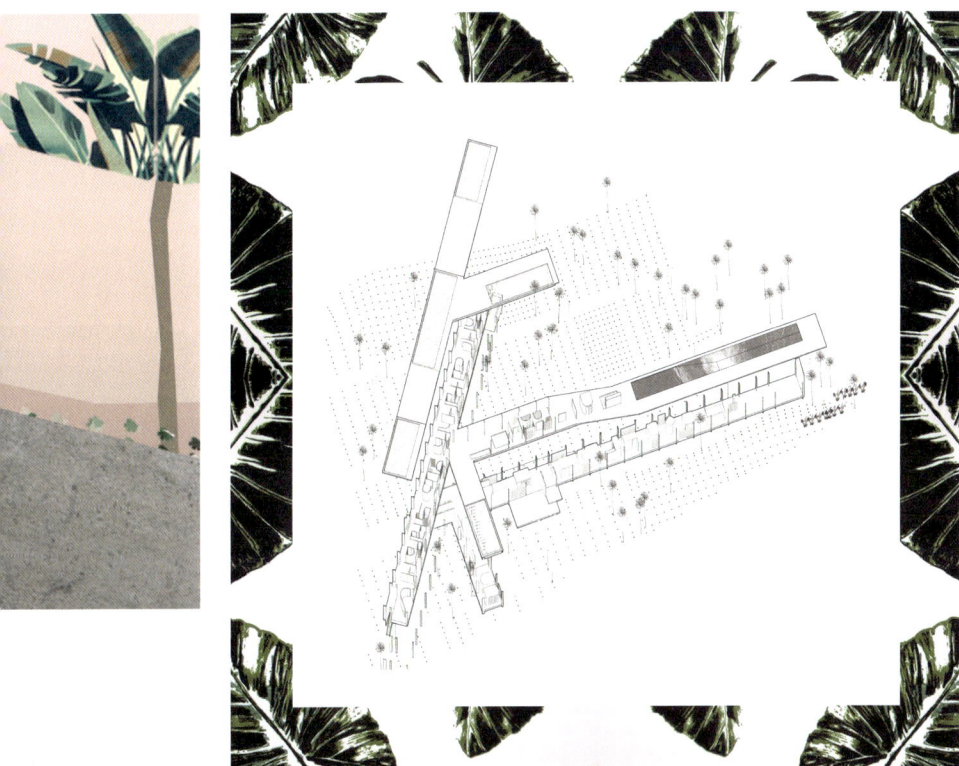

Sara Arfaian
MArch II, 2017

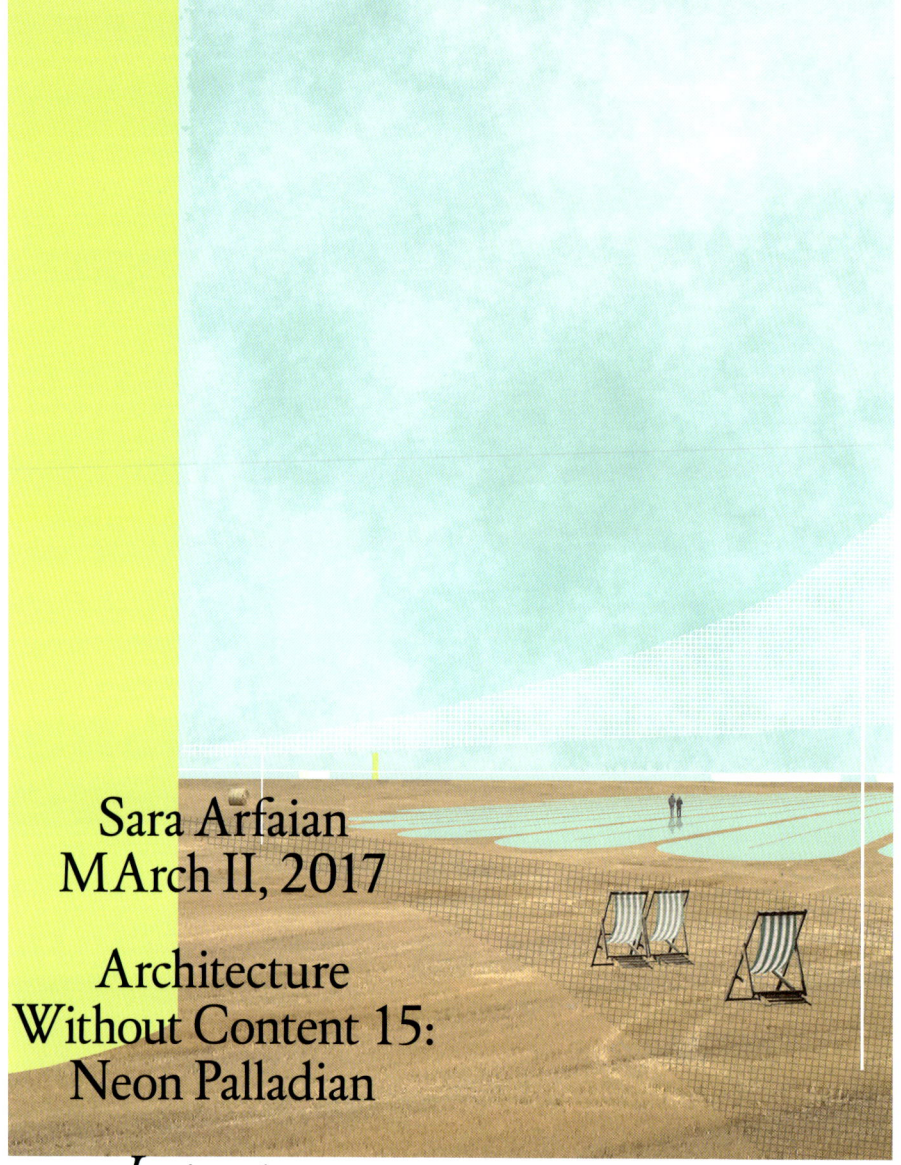

Architecture
Without Content 15:
Neon Palladian

Instructors
Kersten Geers,
David Van Severen

Among the many precedents for American architecture explored in the Neon Palladian studio was one that is omnipresent: Roman architecture. This project plays off of these antecedents by delineating space through the subtle intervention of a canopy that traps program and points of respite.

ON(E) POINT   Option Studio   261

Canopy

10 km

Troy Chen,
Chit Yan Paul Mok,
Jennifer Shen
MArch I, 2018

Architecture Core
IV: Relate

Instructor
Jeannette Kuo

Interior

The fourth course in the Architecture Core sequence, Relate, explores the role of housing as a central component of the physical fabric of the city and as the fundamental site of the negotiation between the individual and the collective in the search for new forms of inhabitation.

Ya Gao,
Danielle Kasner,
Naureen Mazumdar
MArch I, 2018

Architecture Core
IV: Relate

Instructor
Jeannette Kuo

Every year, about 40,000 icebergs calve from the edges of Greenland glaciers. After slipping into the ocean, the bergs float in frosty arctic bays, melting slowly as they pass through the Davis Strait and into the Labrador Current toward St. John's, Newfoundland. Only about 400 to 800 bergs make it so far south. This annual cycle has given this passage, which stretches across the eastern coast of Newfoundland, the nickname "iceberg alley." This studio developed projects that simultaneously serve and expand beyond the tourism and resource industry that exists in this area.

ON(E) POINT Option Studio 265

Dai Ren
MAUD, 2016

Iceberg Alley

Instructors
Lola Sheppard,
Mason White

From smoothly cast objects resembling pebbles, to rough, crumbling material retrieved from one of Robert Smithson's Non-sites, "heavy matter" is everywhere. The editors of *Platform* spotted dozens of rocks in the GSD's studio trays: rocks as sites, rocks as aggregate in concrete, and carved foam meant to look rock-like. A PhD scholar performs a close read of those "countless specks of white and grey fill" in an essay titled "The Rough Concrete Surfaces of Perret's Notre-Dame du Raincy." An architecture studio engages heavy matter through ruins in the South American region of Territorio Guaraní; it is paired with the history-theory seminar The Ruin Aesthetic: Episodes in the History of an Architectural Idea. In a search for non-modern design methodologies, with a proposition called Abductive Architecture, one architecture thesis project turns up the heat on heavy matter, using fire to unearth the overall mass.

Heavy Matter

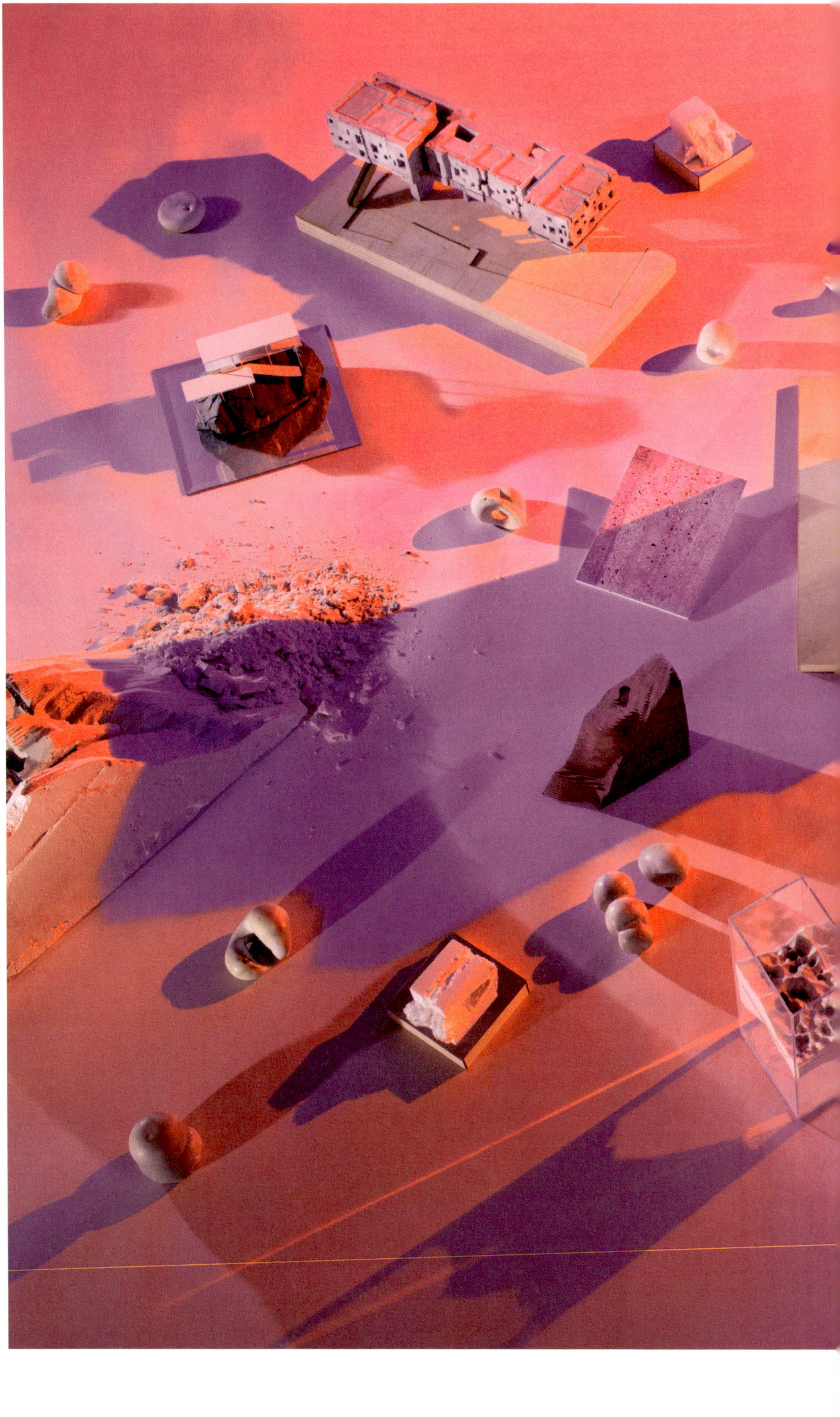

HEAVY MATTER

270

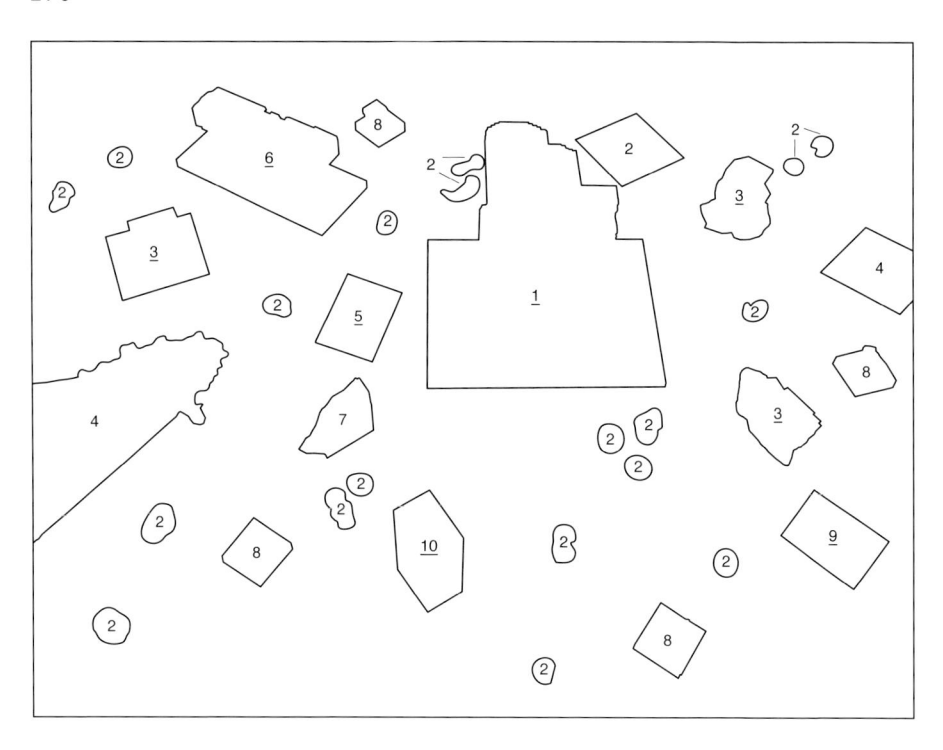

HEAVY MATTER

1 Cement
p. 272

Alexander Timmer
MArch I, 2016
Thesis: Abductive Architecture
Advisor: Kiel Moe

2 Carnival

Carol Jin Jin Chiu
MArch I, 2017
etceteras
Instructor: Mack Scogin

3 Bedrock
p. 274

Aaron Menninga
MArch I, 2016
Thesis: Figure Ground
Advisor: Kiel Moe

4 Crumble

Emily Wettstein
MArch I / MLA I AP, 2016
Thesis: Hinged Hinterlands
Advisor: Iñaki Ábalos

5 Reinforced Concrete
p. 276

Etien Santiago
PhD Candidate
The Rough Concrete Surfaces of Perret's Notre-Dame du Raincy
Advisor: Antoine Picon

6 Formwork
p. 282

Collin Cobia
MArch I AP, 2017
Territorio Guaraní III
Instructor: Jorge Silvetti

7 Asphalt

Tyler Mohr
MLA II, 2016
Moscow's Future: Tied Up in Traffic
Instructor: Martha Schwartz

8 Small Rocks

Martin Fernandez
MArch I, 2019
Architecture Core II: Situate
Instructor: Tomás dePaor

9 Paving Joints
p. 284

Nina Phinouwong
MLA I / MUP, 2016
Southampton Quay
Instructors: Michel Desvigne, Inessa Hansch

10 Crater
p. 286

Taylor Baer, Andrew Madl, Izgi Uygur
MLA II, 2017
Mapping: Geographic Representation and Speculation
Instructor: Robert Pietrusko

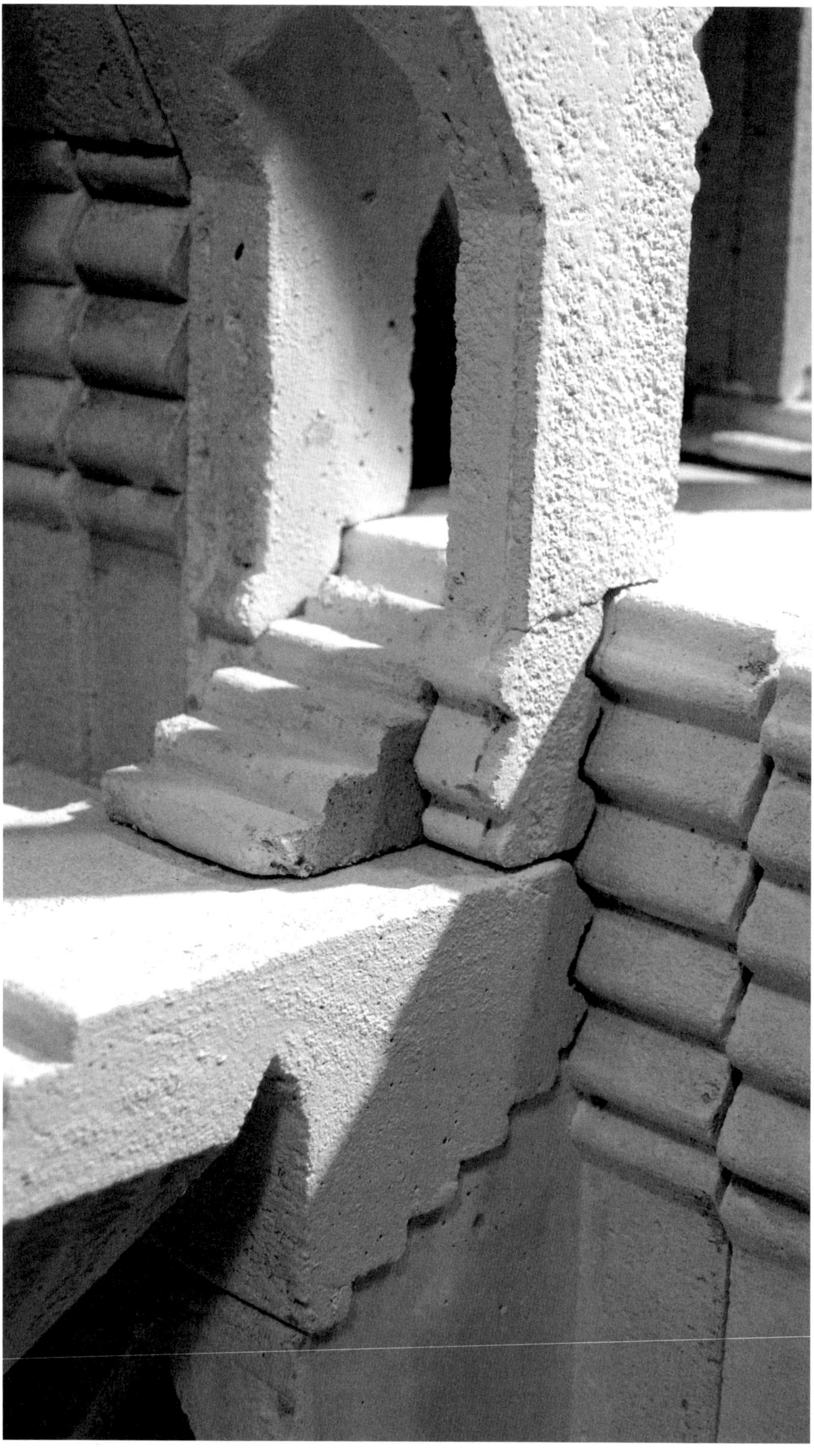

This thesis uses open thermodynamics, specifically fire, to demonstrate what an abductive convergence of mass around an energetic flow might look like. The goal is to compress the feedback loop that is design and construction to allow for more immediate innovation in design.

Alexander Timmer
MArch I, 2016

Thesis
Abductive Architecture

Advisor
Kiel Moe

274

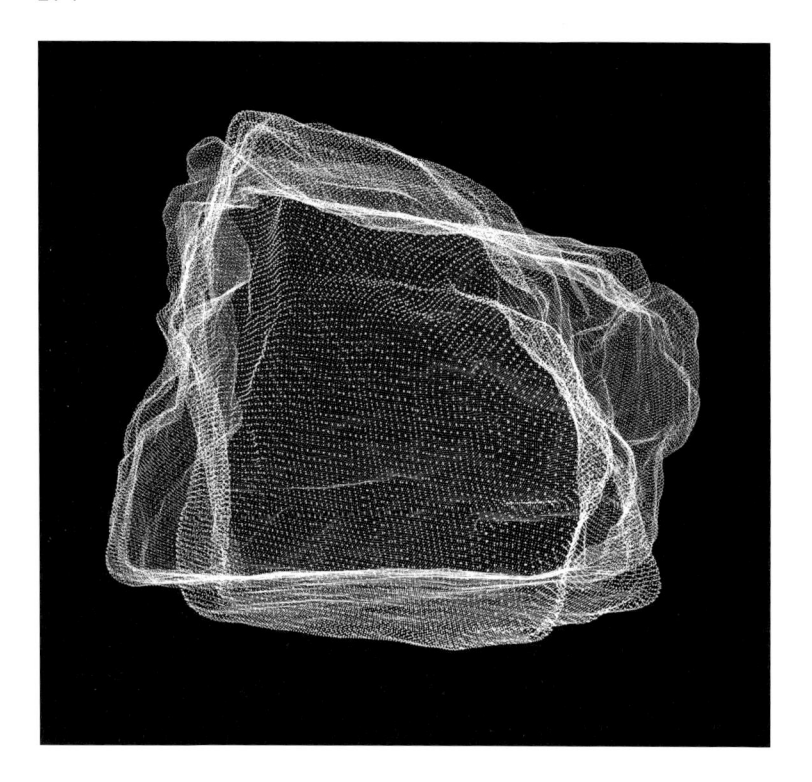

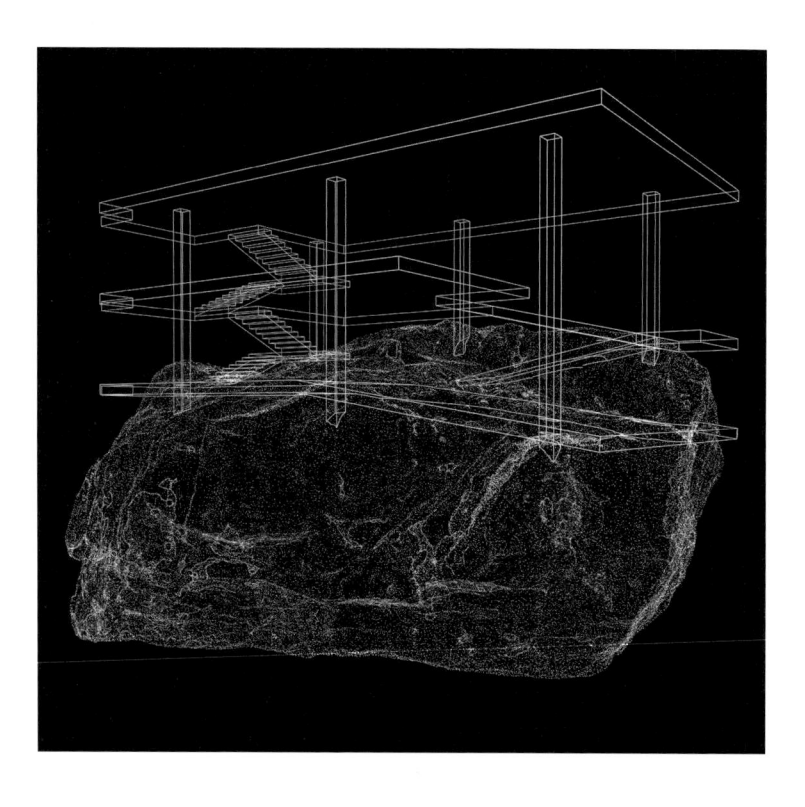

Aaron Menninga
MArch I, 2016

Thesis
Figure Ground

Advisor
Kiel Moe

Bedrock

The foundational drivers of an architectural proposal can be understood through surveying and interfacing with the ground. This thesis exposes the ways site data are collected and the effect that has on representation and building.

Etien Santiago
PhD Candidate

The Rough Concrete Surfaces of Perret's Notre-Dame du Raincy

Advisor
Antoine Picon

Alongside the main doors to the church of Notre-Dame du Raincy, just northeast of Paris, France, lies a patch of reinforced concrete wall much like any other. In it, uneven constellations of pebbles, small rocks, and broken bits of shells—in a gamut of colors including dusty reds, indigo blues, deep maroons, caramel oranges, and bone-hued beiges—float amid an ash grey field of granulated cement. At midrange, our eyes struggle to focus on a single part of the material; its finely dappled surface produces an effect akin to visual noise. Countless specks of white and grey fill our field of view, so numerous, dense, and varied that they appear to vibrate asynchronously like the static of a disconnected television screen. When viewed a bit closer, the cement almost appears soft, as if it were still a thick liquid oozing over and around the smooth, rounded aggregates. Small globular pockets of air have been caught within its flow, dotted with shallow indentations left by missing pieces of rock. Touching the concrete, however, results in an entirely different sensation: gritty and rough like sandpaper—but worse—its uneven bumps grate against our fingers. The cement is chalky at our touch, crumbling into a powder of fine particles. We can both see and feel ridgelines that indexically recall the location of the former joints in the wooden formwork. Certain splotches of the material have slightly different tones and textures than neighboring ones; they abut one another in sloppy bands that, if we use our imagination, vaguely recall the process of vertically pouring the concrete—like adjoining waterfalls of gravel whose motion has been frozen in the fixed frame of a film.

Upon first inspection, the material constituting Notre-Dame du Raincy appears utterly mundane: identical to many other gritty concrete surfaces that permeate the built environment. Yet this particular stretch of concrete stands apart due to its unique position in history and, most importantly, its seminal contribution to modernist architectural aesthetics. We know that it was poured sometime between April 30, 1922, when the first symbolic stone of the church was laid, and June 17, 1923, when the Bishop of Versailles consecrated the completed edifice.[1] We also know that the French architect Auguste Perret, born in Ixelles, Belgium in 1874, was responsible for the decision to use concrete in this building, its design, the management of its construction, and the choice to leave its industrial-grade concrete bare.[2] We possess some information about the technical processes used to produce its final forms. Yet, if we were to confine our discussion to only these factors, we would still not get to the heart of the matter regarding this object. What especially commands our attention is the fact that, here, unrefined concrete was willfully left exposed in a civic building with a monumental function—a revolutionary idea that simply had no precedent at the time.

Reinforced concrete is a mixture of cement (or lime), water, sand, and small stones that dries after being poured around metal reinforcing rods placed in a mold. It is a product of the 19th century, invented by several innovators working independently in different countries, after which developments in North America, England, France, and Germany fed off one another to create a mounting pile of experiments as well as publications devoted to it.[3] As the architectural historian Réjean Legault explains, the exact definition of reinforced concrete and the proper principles for its deployment remained a matter of contention for decades following its invention.[4] A far-flung, ragtag set of amateur inventors, professional scientists, building contractors, civil engineers, and architects had contributed, each in distinct ways, to early uses of the new material.[5] Every group of professionals approached it with varying assumptions about what it was and how it might fit into their work. Individuals within each profession further argued amongst themselves about how reinforced concrete might be useful. Even the basic notion that it constituted a specific kind of

Exposed cast-in-place reinforced concrete on the east facade of Notre-Dame du Raincy, designed in 1922 by Auguste Perret. Photograph by Etien Santiago.

building material belonging to the same category as wood, iron, or brick—a notion we now take for granted—was vehemently debated toward the end of the 19th century and the start of the 20th.[6] Back then, competing ideas about reinforced concrete faced off in the specialized press as well as in the marketplace of construction.

Despite the wide range of positions and ideas that swirled around reinforced concrete before 1922, prior to that year all protagonists nevertheless agreed on one mostly unsaid premise: rough, unadorned concrete was not and could never be fit to replace the materials that clad the noble spaces in which civilized life took place.[7] In fact, the idea of using concrete in this manner seemed so aberrant at the time that it was only rarely articulated as such. Even the greatest champions of this new technology refused to contemplate a future in which concrete was not treated or clad in some way as to make it aesthetically acceptable in situations that called for a minimum of decorum.

Different designers upheld this premise in a variety of ways. In 1862, the architect Louis-Auguste Boileau broke new ground when he erected the neo-Gothic church of Sainte-Marguerite in Le Vésinet, just west of Paris, with outer walls made of reinforced concrete instead of stone or brick. Aiming to evoke the noble tradition of masonry construction, he incised the smooth coat of cement over the concrete walls with fake joints mimicking stacked blocks of stone. (This project became better known for its interior structure made of iron, which more explicitly advertised its material.[8]) Anatole de Baudot, an architect one generation younger than Boileau, designed Saint-Jean de Montmartre on the famous Parisian hill around 1894, causing quite a stir due to its extensive use of visible *ciment armé* (a variation of reinforced concrete with no rough aggregate, pioneered by the engineer Paul Cottancin).[9] In his contemporaneous writings and classes on French architectural history, Baudot correspondingly lambasted his peers' proclivity to hide concrete behind other materials or deceptively shape it in ways meant to mimic them.[10] Like Sainte-Marguerite, Saint-Jean also reinterpreted Gothic architectonic principles, but the latter blazed a new path in its use of concrete as an integral aesthetic constituent of the work. Its language of flat-faced pointed arches and intersecting curves results in a kind of abstracted structural tracery. Channeling the teachings of his mentor Eugène Viollet-le-Duc, Baudot manipulated and decorated the concrete surfaces in an attempt to render them aesthetically pleasing—analogous to how medieval masons once carved ornamentation into the visible faces of structural stones.[11] The concrete in Saint-Jean is therefore alternatively plastered, painted with flat geometrical patterns, or covered with small ceramic mosaics (manufactured by the ceramist Alexandre Bigot) that produce a glittering, embroidered effect.[12]

The same year that Saint-Jean was completed, in 1904, a 30-year-old Auguste Perret put the finishing touches on his offices and apartment building at 25 bis Rue Franklin in central Paris. For the structure of this innovative edifice, Perret and his architect brother Gustave employed a frame of concrete columns and beams—a highly unusual feature at the time for residential buildings. Yet, disregarding Baudot's plea for the honest exhibition of concrete, they clad this frame with lightly hued, glazed stoneware tiles that, like those adorning Saint-Jean, were also made by Bigot. Perret arranged two types of cladding tiles on the facade of the Rue Franklin building to create the appearance of a post-and-lintel frame protruding slightly in front of a leafy, flowery infill, but he did not put the actual structure on display. The architect explained the reasoning behind this strategy in an unpublished 1914 text cowritten with his brother-in-law Sébastien Voirol:

> . . . this material [reinforced concrete] permits the absorption of humidity and runs the risk, due to its color, of appearing sad. A facade of naked concrete thus only suits industrial buildings with a definite purpose. Concrete must be covered in stoneware or ceramics, for example, and, in the case of monumental building, with a richer material such as marble.[13]

Whether designers aimed to treat concrete such that it resembled another material, enlivened its surface, protected it from the weather, or hid its "sad" color, the consensus before 1922 affirmed that ordinary concrete was inappropriate for respectable architecture. Reinforced concrete construction underwent many transformations from the moment of its inception up to 1922, and many polemics raged during those years about how to best harness it, but the agreement about the need to mask or carefully treat it in some way for buildings of stature persisted throughout that entire stretch of time.[14]

We must put aside our own contemporary inoculation to the sight of cast concrete—placing ourselves in the shoes of men and women living prior to 1923—to imagine just how radical the sight of a raw concrete church must have been for them.[15] A 1924 article about the Notre-Dame du Raincy in *La Construction Moderne* tellingly gives voice to a common reaction: "Instinctively, our spirit rears back at the thought of using reinforced concrete to erect a church! All the poetry of the cut and sculpted stones that make up the multiple masterpieces of which religious architecture is most proud come to mind to justify our apprehension."[16] Another commentator, seduced by the overall forms of Raincy but disturbed by its material, urged his readers to behold the cantilevered organ tribune floating "amidst a marvelous assemblage of columns" so that they might "instantly forget the reinforced cement and certain defects."[17] Evidently, he did not regard the material as a positive feature. An article in a 1923 issue of *L'Illustration* dwelled more at length on negative reactions to the concrete at Raincy:

> Some of our correspondents, moreover, accept with great difficulty the idea of placing this solidified paste in the category of noble materials, [a paste] that they deem suitable only for making factories or hangars. For them, this byproduct of modern industry is unworthy of the honor of erecting a church.[18]

As we just noted, Perret himself had similarly insisted only eight years prior to designing Raincy that architects should always clothe reinforced concrete structures with some other material, especially in the case of "monumental" buildings such as churches.[19] Though he was highly aware of the risks involved in leaving concrete exposed to rain, and cognizant of its potentially unappealing looks, he flouted both of these concerns at Notre-Dame du Raincy.

For decades, historians have overlooked the importance of this dramatic move, both for Perret's career as well as for modernist architectural design more broadly. After Raincy, Perret went on to produce an idiosyncratic oeuvre comprising works proudly flaunting their naked concrete frames filled in with concrete block or another material. A number of younger French architects closely mimicked his style, but some European architects who did not nevertheless followed his lead by daring to employ exposed concrete in buildings with noble programs. Notable examples of such buildings include the second Goetheanum (1925), designed by Rudolf Steiner for Dornach, Switzerland, Christ-the-King Church (1926) in Bischofsheim,

Germany, by Dominikus Böhm, Karl Moser's church of Saint Antonius in Basel (1926–7), the Église du Saint Esprit in Paris (1928–35) by Paul Tournon, and of course the Unité d'Habitation in Marseille (1945) by Le Corbusier. Perret's Notre-Dame du Raincy constituted a first, loud volley in a series of works that, together, have branded rough-cast concrete surfaces as synonymous with a modern architectural aesthetic.

1   A plaque on the wall of the church baptistery reads: "L'édification de l'Église Notre-Dame du Raincy a été décidée, préparée, menée à bien par Monsieur le Chanoine NÈGRE, curé doyen avec le concours de Monsieur PHILIPPE et de tous les paroissiens qui en ont soldé seuls tous les frais. Monseigneur GIBIER Evêque de Versailles en a posé la première pierre le 30 avril 1922 et l'a bénite solennellement le 17 juin 1923. Architecte: Auguste PERRET. Vitraux: Maurice DENIS."
2   Karla Britton, *Auguste Perret* (London: Phaidon, 2001), 89. The following sources about Perret and Notre-Dame du Raincy may also be consulted: Simon Texier, "Église Notre-Dame-de-la-Consolation, Le Raincy," in *Les frères Perret: l'oeuvre complète*, ed. Maurice Culot et al. (Paris: Éditions Norma, 2000), 126. Jean-Louis Cohen, Joseph Abram, and Guy Lambert, eds., *Encyclopédie Perret* (Paris: Monum Éditions du Patrimoine, 2002). Roberto Gargiani, *Auguste Perret 1874–1954: Teoria e opere* (Milan: Electa, 1993).
3   Cyrille Simonnet, *Le Béton: histoire d'un matériau* (Marseille: Éditions Parenthèses, 2005); Gwenaël Delhumeau, *L'invention du béton armé: Hennebique 1890–1914* (Paris: Norma, 1999); Peter Collins, *Concrete: The Vision of a New Architecture* (London: Faber and Faber, 1959; repr., Montreal: McGill-Queen's University Press, 2004); and Aly Ahmed Raafat, *Reinforced Concrete and the Architecture It Creates* (PhD Diss., Columbia University, 1957).
4   See Chapter 1 of Réjean Legault, *L'appareil de l'architecture moderne: New Materials and Architectural Modernity in France, 1889–1934* (PhD Diss., Massachusetts Institute of Technology, 1997), 20–68.
5   Adrian Forty, *Concrete and Culture* (London: Reaktion Books, 2012), 16.
6   Legault, *L'appareil de l'architecture moderne*, 64. According to Legault, "By its very heterogeneity, reinforced concrete challenged architects' conceptions of building materials." Ibid., 68.
7   Ibid., 125.
8   Boileau's ideas about the use of iron in ecclesiastical buildings sparked a public controversy between him and the architect Eugène Viollet-le-Duc. Bernard Marrey, ed., *La querelle du fer: Eugène Viollet-le-Duc contre Louis Auguste Boileau* (Paris: Linteau, 2002).
9   Simonnet, Le Béton, 133.
10 Anatole de Baudot, *L'architecture: le passé, le présent* (Paris: H. Laurens, 1916), 2.
11 Many authors have underlined the influence of Viollet-le-Duc's ideas on de Baudot's and his followers' rationalist approaches to materials and ornamentation; e.g. Legault, *L'appareil de l'architecture moderne*, 10–11, 21–30.

12 Consider the precedent of Notre-Dame de l'Assomption in Rungis, designed by Édouard Bérard and built in 1909. The tectonics of this church unceremoniously expressed the frame-and-infill kit of concrete parts from which it was made, though the concrete was painted over. See Jean-Charles Cappronnier, Frédéric Fournis, Alexandra Gérard, and Pascale Touzet, "L'art sacré entre les deux guerres: aspects de la Première Reconstruction en Picardie," *In Situ* (Dec. 2009): 21, available online at http://insitu.revues.org/6151.
13 Auguste Perret and Sebastien Voirol, "Le style sans ornements," unpublished manuscript reprinted in Christophe Laurent, Guy Lambert, and Joseph Abram, eds., *Auguste Perret: Anthologie des écrits, conférences et entretiens* (Paris: Le Moniteur, 2006), 83. Also see the editorial note on this text, ibid., 75). As the editorial note explains, Voirol soon thereafter published a shortened version of the manuscript under his name only in the April-May-June 1914 issue of *Montjoie!* In it, he repeats the same argument as the one quoted above. Sebastien Voirol, "Où en sont les architectes?" *Montjoie!* 2, no. 4-5-6 (April-May-June 1914): 12.
14 From about 1900 to 1920, the challenge of how to mitigate the poor looks of concrete such that it could become a more palatable architectural material was addressed in construction publications on both sides of the Atlantic. An American advocate of concrete relayed the general sentiment of the industry in 1914, stating that "[a] frequent criticism is that concrete is monotonous in appearance and lacks beauty in itself." The author then outlined various possible treatments of the concrete surface intended to render it more acceptable: "The problem met with early in the modern use of concrete was to do away with the unpleasant effect of variation in color between different layers or courses, to remove blemishes from the face of the work, and to provide something which would offset that dull-colored monotony of surface which to many seems so objectionable." Paul Chesterton, "Decoration in Concrete Construction," *Cement World* 7 (February 1914): 33. Also see Simonnet, Le Béton, 179.
15 Upon seeing the raw concrete of Notre-Dame du Raincy, some contemporaneous critics erroneously thought that it was literally "unfinished," as in not yet complete. Simon Texier, "Les matériaux ou les parures du béton," in *Églises parisiennes du XXe siècle: architecture et décor* (Paris: Action Artistique de la Ville de Paris, 1996), 81.
16 "Une église en béton armé," *La Construction Moderne* 39, no. 254-256 (March 2, 1924): 185.
17 "La Nouvelle Église du Raincy," Bulletin de Gagny, reprinted in *Union Paroissiale du Raincy* II, no. 8 (September 1923): 12. A copy of this pamphlet

is conserved in the Auguste Perret archives, 535 AP 414/02, at the Cité de l'Architecture et du Patrimoine in Paris.

18 Le Semainier, "Courrier de Paris: Controverse," *L'Illustration* (July 28, 1923), a copy of which can be found in the Perret archives: 535 AP 550.

19 Perret covered the reinforced-concrete, post-and-lintel structure of the Théâtre des Champs Elysées with marble panels outside and painted plaster inside. While the pilasters and string courses of the marble facade loosely evoked the trabeated structure housed beneath them, its concrete was nowhere actually on view.

Formwork

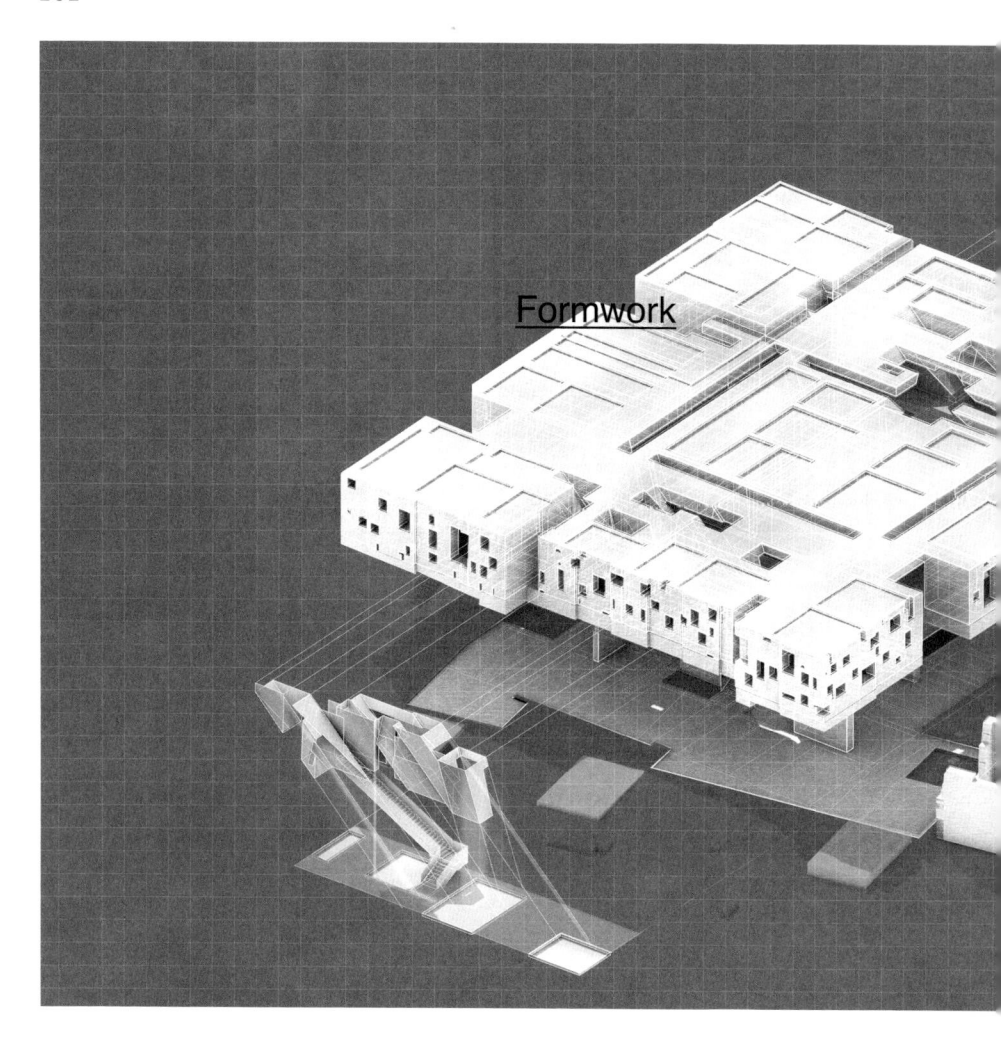

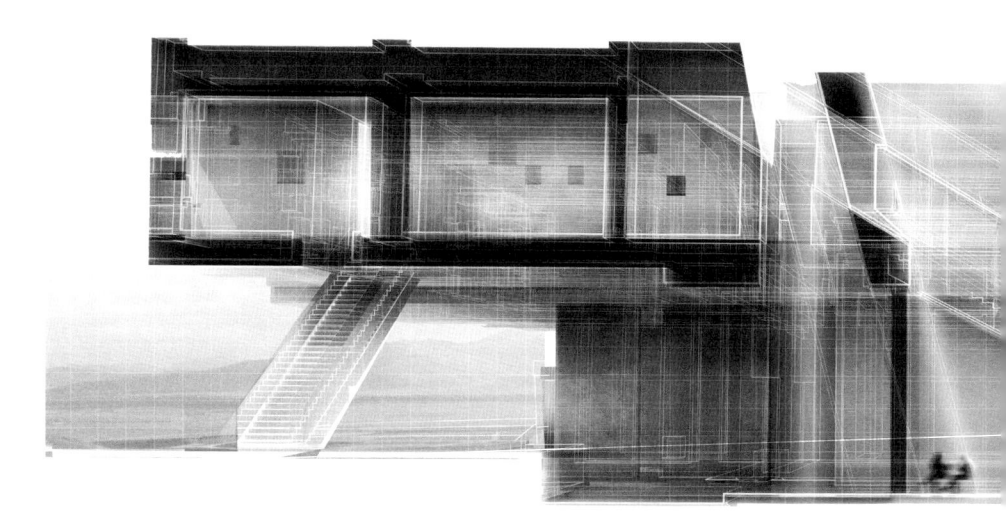

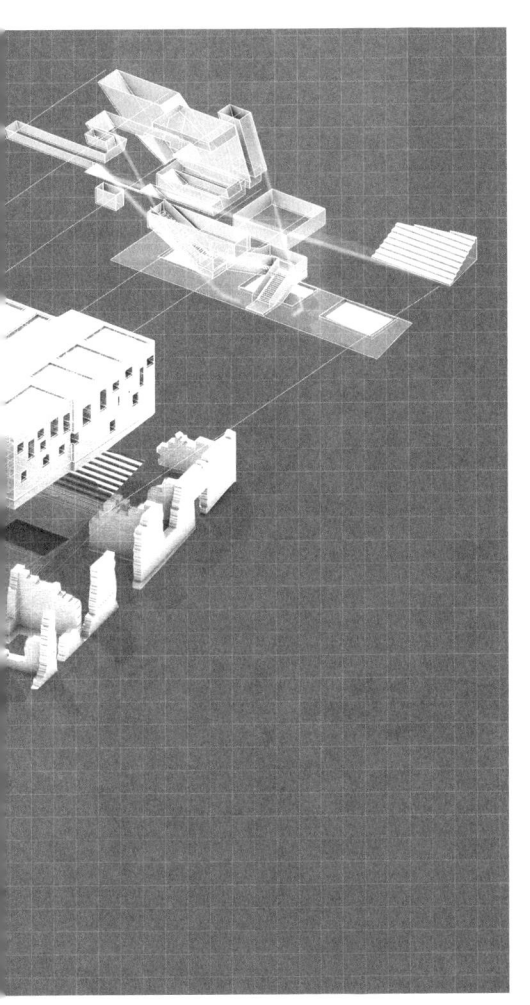

Collin Cobia
MArch I AP, 2017

Territorio Guaraní III

Instructor
Jorge Silvetti

This project, a design for a higher-education campus, explores construction technologies that intelligently address the extreme climatic and topographical challenges of Territorio Guaraní, a subtropical area, while also finding ways to integrate the historically and artistically important 17th-century Baroque ruins extant on the site.

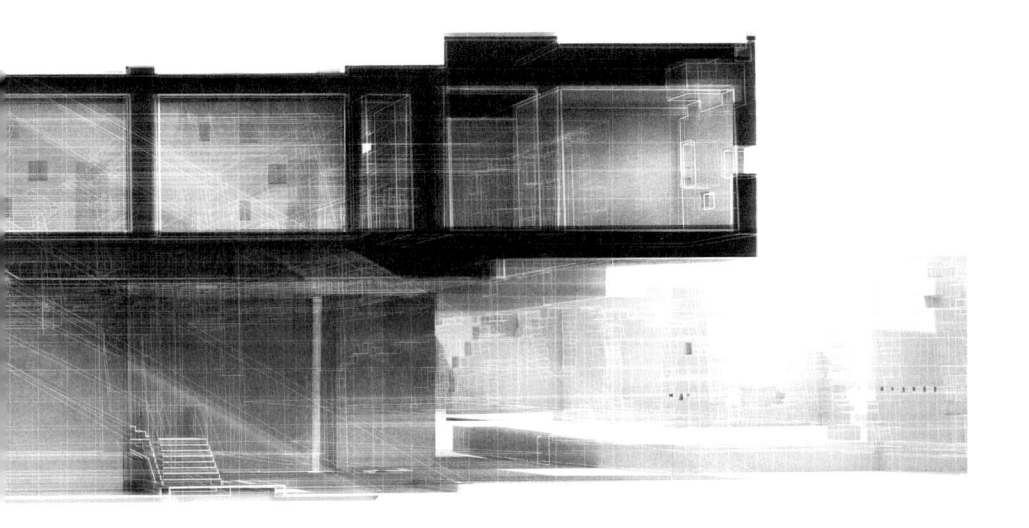

Nina Phinouwong
MLA I / MUP, 2016

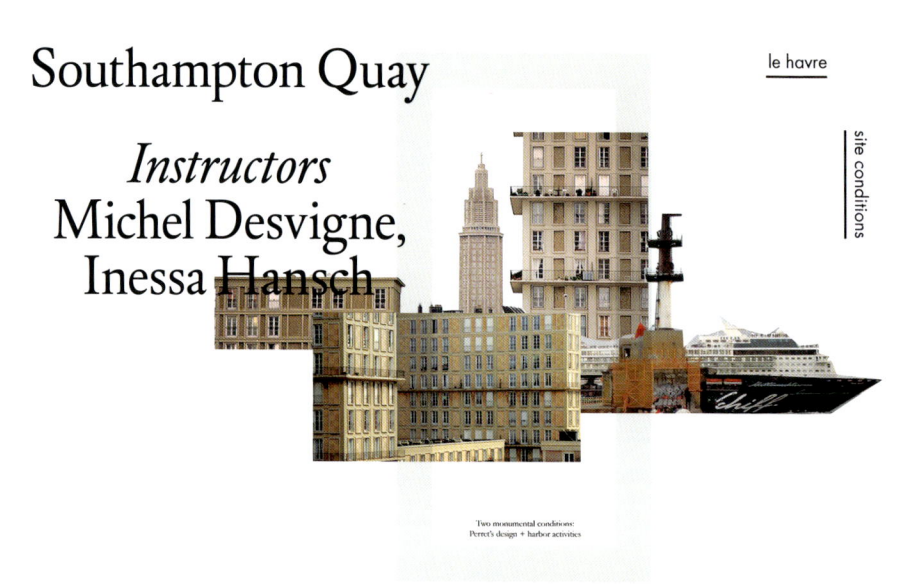

Southampton Quay

Instructors
Michel Desvigne, Inessa Hansch

le havre

site conditions

Two monumental conditions:
Perret's design + harbor activities

Le Havre is a major European port located in Upper Normandy at the mouth of the Seine. The Southampton Quay, once a prestigious point of departure, serves as the city's maritime facade as well as the entrance for the industrial port. The studio aimed to bring renewed vitality to the Southampton Quay, which has stood in disuse for more than 20 years, by converting it into a public space that links the city and port.

HEAVY MATTER — Option Studio — 285

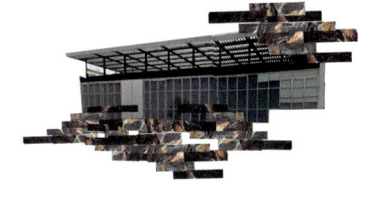

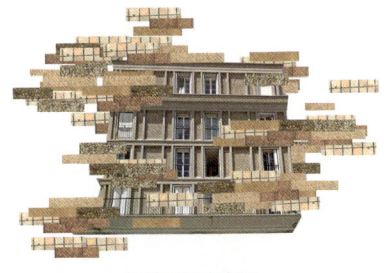

creating multiplicity of horizon line

allowing quality of light to come out in details of paving

Paving Joints

using water and drainage to create a 'facade' to atmosphere

manipulation of edges in texture

Overlaying textures and colors of Le Havre against the perimeter of facades on the harbor

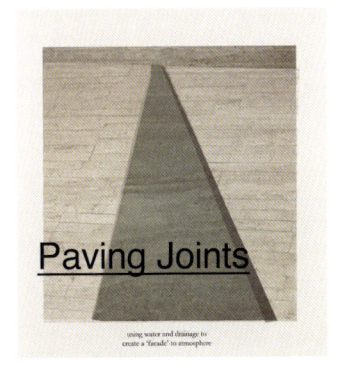

Taylor Baer, Andrew Madl, Izgi Uygur
MLA II, 2017

Mapping: Geographic Representation and Speculation

Instructor
Robert Pietrusko

Maps do not represent reality, they create it. As a fundamental part of the design process, the act of mapping results in highly authored views of a site. By choosing which features, forces, and flows to highlight—and implicitly, which to exclude—the designer first creates the reality into which their intervention will be situated and discussed. This seminar taught students how to embed these techniques within larger design workflows.

Crate

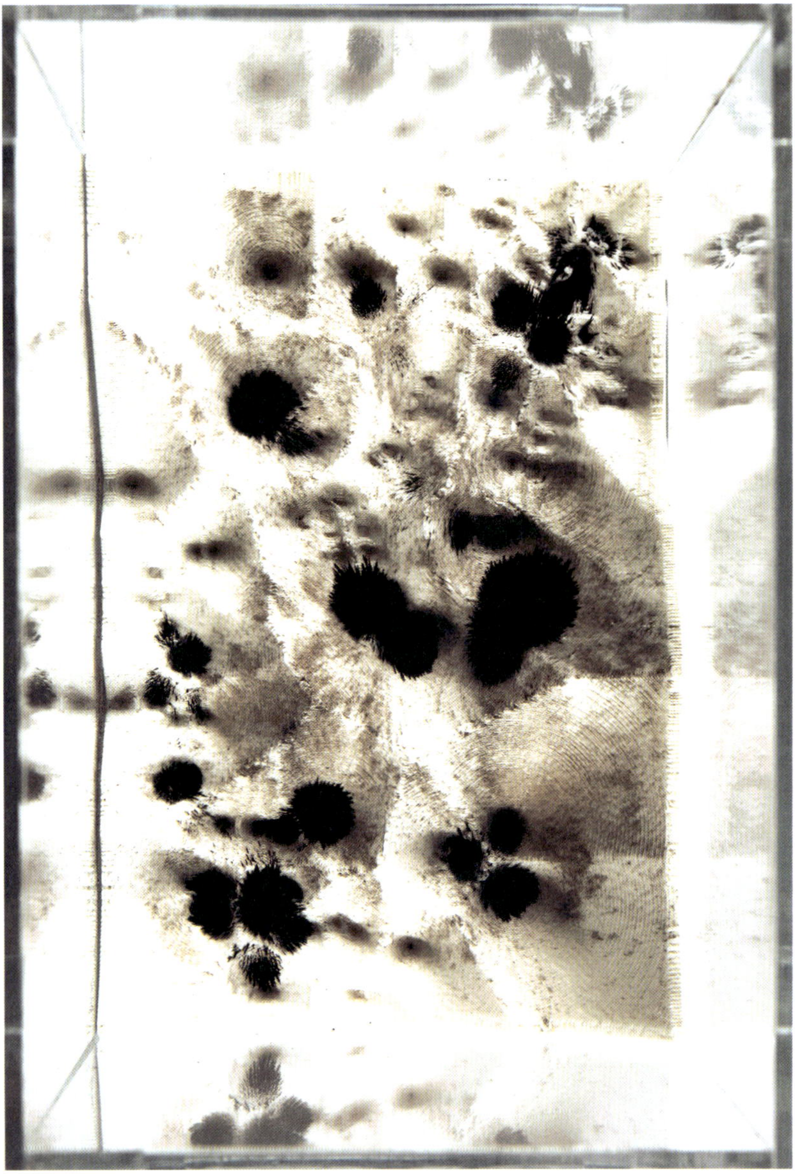

Leftovers

Don't get me wrong. I get it. That said, I simply don't get it—food as the organizing theme, substance, and sustaining principal of our current culture? Once, we read and reflected (sometimes even ruminatively), drew conclusions, and now we singly originate, locally source, and organically certify untasted morsels marinated or rubbed with the potent spice of race-, class-, and gender-consciousness. And those are just the entrées. It's what goes into the mouth that matters.

I'm looking at the portfolio of photographer Adam DeTour—his name inevitably makes me think of Henri Fantin-Latour, which brings us one step closer, in an imaginary but no longer visited gallery, to the softly luminous work of Jean-Baptise-Siméon Chardin, in which the thick impasto of oil paint veritably becomes the luscious mound of butter it represents. DeTour is the author of 16 still lifes commissioned for *Platform*, which I am meant to comment upon, provide a caption for, interpret. A master of focus, DeTour typically photographs canapés, cocktails, and microcreameries (in which microcream is produced? Is that like molecular gastronomy?). He also captures handsomely uninhabited hotel rooms, the trappings of room service expensively in evidence.

And then there's the student work stacked and arranged and bathed in syrupy light in the impromptu studio of Piper Auditorium. Since these *obiter dicta*, in terms of the space and time allotted them, befit the confined possibilities of the still life genre itself, I will pose a question rather than expand upon what I see in the photograph: What has the work of architecture (now) to do with what Norman Bryson has described as the "culture of artefacts," the bowls, jugs, pitchers, and vases that are the "permanent and inevitable background" of reality? The overlooked reward of still life, Bryson observes and writes, is that it captures inescapable "conditions of creaturality," of eating and drinking and domestic life.

Perhaps DeTour arrived on the scene too late, or was led into Piper when he was meant for Gund Hall's "trays." There, in the days leading up to the final public review, he would have seen the studio bays turned into an unwholesome larder of comfort foods and caffeinated decoctions, creaturely comforts for the ghastly charette. All is sleepless activity, giving rise to the monsters of reason (the best kind of theses). The leftovers, here pictured, tell the rest of the story.

Edward Eigen
Associate Professor of Architecture and Landscape Architecture

VARIATIONS ON THE DISPLAY

Flag, suitcase, balloon, cupboard, postcard, curtain, light box, disc, dollhouse, credenza, desk, lamp, view finder, paperweight, and cloche: This odd lot of objects represents a cross section of four disciplines, where experiments on display are taken seriously.

    A studio offered by the Department of Urban Planning and Design produced an MLK Street Atlas, analyzing streets across the US named after Martin Luther King, Jr., displaying the information inside a suitcase. Another studio, offered by the Department of Architecture, aimed to subvert banal public space by focusing on the "typological imaginations" of London. It generated new public artifacts, displayed here within a cloche and a cupboard. A project for an urban planning studio, presented here as a series of postcard-like images, visualizes a food-entrepreneurship district in an underserved Boston neighborhood. Here, in a display of displays, two flags borrowed from a thesis group titled Weak States are draped behind projects about rural Tokyo, medieval Lisbon, and Swedish waste-to-energy facilities. Other displays of architecture, planning, urban design, and landscape architecture reference an oversized lightbox, a dollhouse, and a Wunderkammer—the variations go on and on.

Variations on the Display

294

VARIATIONS ON THE DISPLAY

1 Neon Orange

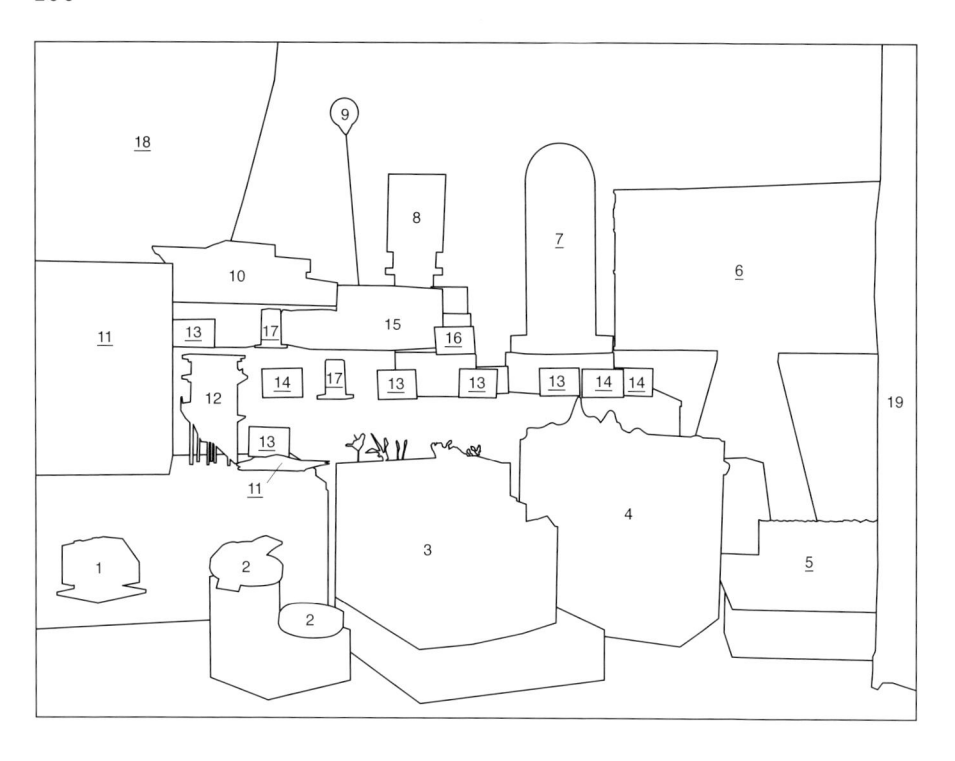

Humbi Song
MArch I, 2019
Architecture Core II: Situate
Instructor: Jeffry Burchard

2 Intersecting Circles

Steven Meyer, David Pilz
MArch I, 2018
Architecture Core IV: Relate
Instructor: Mariana Ibañez

3 Castle Stair

Niki Murata
MArch I, 2017
Lisbon Story—Architecture
  Between Atmosphere
  and Tectonics
Instructor: Ricardo
  Bak Gordon

4 Gradient

Collin Cobia
MArch I AP, 2017
Evan Farley, James Murray
MArch I, 2017
Mapping: Geographic
  Representation and
  Speculation
Instructor: Robert Pietrusko

5 Screen
p. 298

David Hamm,
  Yu Kun Snoweria Zhang
MArch I, 2017
(Re)planned Obsolescence . . .
  Rethinking the
  Architecture of Waste
Instructors: Hanif Kara, Leire
  Asensio Villoria

6 Cabinet
p. 300

Joseph Varholick
MArch II, 2017
Third Natures: London's
  Typological Imagination
Instructors: Cristina
  Díaz Moreno, Efrén
  García Grinda

7 Cloche
p. 302

Demir Purisic
MArch II, 2017
Third Natures: London's Typological Imagination
Instructors: Cristina Díaz Moreno, Efrén García Grinda

8 Wireframe

Aleksis Bertoni
MArch I AP, 2018
Architecture Core III: Integrate
Instructor: Elizabeth Whittaker

9 Tethered

Bruce Cannon Ivers
MLA II, 2016
Alimentary Design: The Final Course
Instructors: Shohei Shigematsu, Christine Cheng

10 Stacked

Ruoyun Xu
MAUD, 2016
Imprecise Tropics
Instructor: Camilo Restrepo Ochoa

11 Martin Luther King, Jr.
p. 304

Andrejs Rauchut
MArch II, 2017
The MLK Way: Building on Black America's Main Street
Instructor: Daniel D'Oca

12 Pilotis

Feijiao Huo
MArch II, 2017
Redesigning the Actor Network in Rural Areas around Tokyo
Instructors: Momoyo Kaijima, Yoshiharu Tsukamoto

13 Greetings
p. 306

Ximena de Villafranca
MArch II, 2017
The MLK Way: Building on Black America's Main Street
Instructor: Daniel D'Oca

14 Entrepreneurship
p. 308

Miriam Keller
MUP, 2017
Urban Planning Core I
Instructor: Ana Gelabert-Sanchez

15 Living

Naomi Levine, Farhad Mirza
MArch I, 2018
Yubai Zhou
MArch I AP, 2018
Architecture Core IV: Relate
Instructor: Jeannette Kuo

16 Hologram
p. 310

Matthew Allen
PhD Candidate
American Graph Fleeting Hologram
Advisor: Antoine Picon

17 +115 m
p. 312

Erin Cuevas
MArch II, 2016
Thesis: Kawaii-Kowai: Amplifying the Affective Loop
Advisors: Iñaki Ábalos, Christina Díaz Moreno, Efrén García Grinda, Alex Zahlten

18 Flags
p. 314

Pedro Aparicio, Boram Lee Jung, Mariana Llano, Namik Mackic, Olga Semenovych
MDes, 2016
Thesis: Weak States
Advisor: Pierre Bélanger

19 Gold

Inside Outside (Petra Blaisse, Rabia Zuberi, Peter Niessen)
Dividing Curtain, installed in Piper Auditorium in 2012

David Hamm, Yu Kun Snoweria Zhang
MArch I, 2017

(Re)planned Obsolescence... Rethinking the Architecture of Waste

Instructors
Hanif Kara, Leire Asensio Villoria

Through the study of built and proposed waste-to-energy facilities, this studio proposed novel and effective ways to rethink the relationship between architecture, waste, and energy production as they operate over a number of time scales—a (re)planned obsolescence.

VARIATIONS ON THE DISPLAY   Option Studio   299

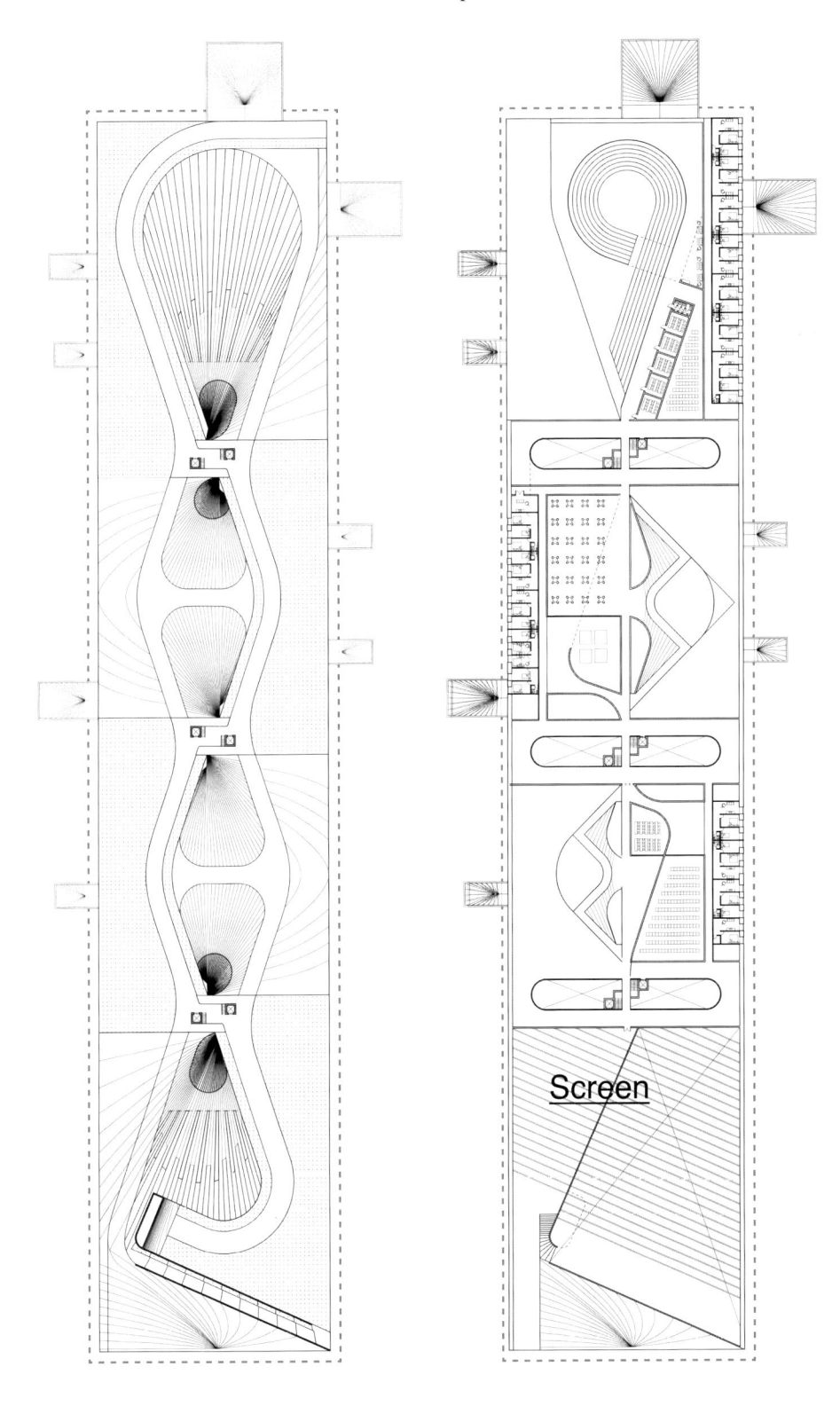

Screen

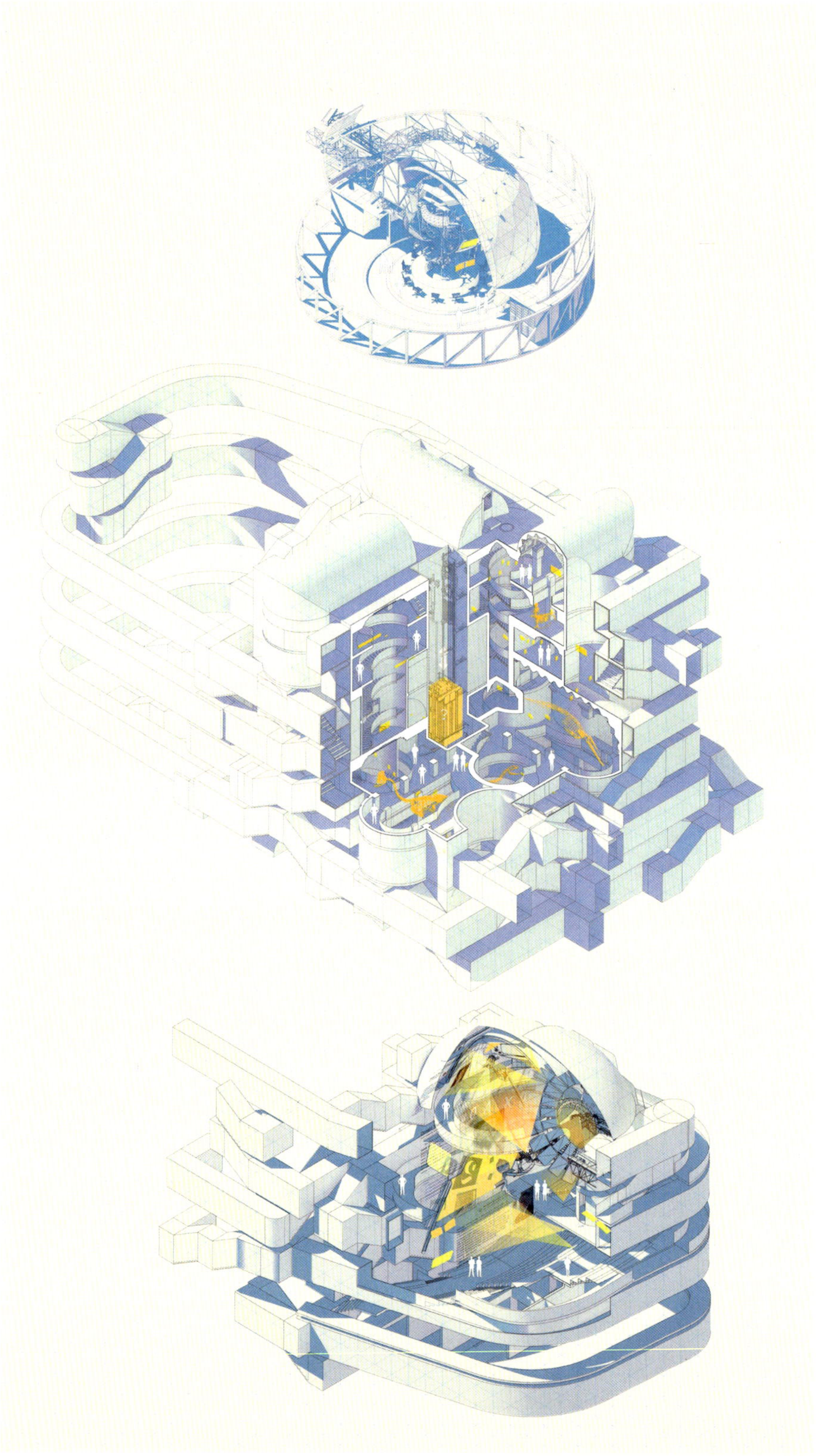

Cabinet

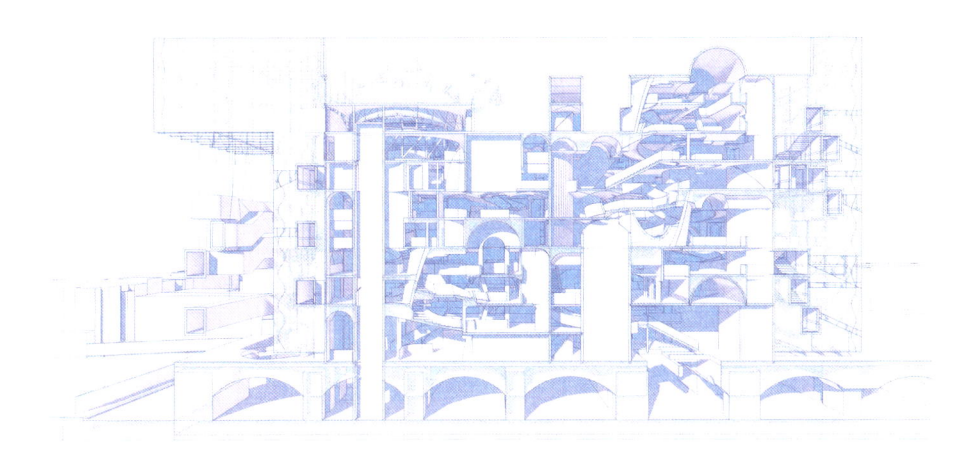

Joseph Varholick
MArch II, 2017

Third Natures: London's Typological Imagination

Instructors
Cristina Díaz Moreno, Efrén García Grinda

By revisiting genuine and extravagant "Londoners"—hot houses, gentleman clubs, banquet halls, square gardens, and public houses—this studio aimed to subvert recent spectacularly banal examples of public space in London. The result was a set of medium-scale interiorized public buildings, which tested the relevance of programs, typologies, languages, and spatial conditions to create a new species of public artifacts.

Demir Purisic
MArch II, 2017

Third Natures: London's Typological Imagination

Instructors
Cristina Díaz Moreno, Efrén García Grinda

This proposal, titled Digital Detox, aims to recreate atmospheres found in a typical detox retreat. Located on an abandoned-goods yard near a new, high-traffic train station, the proposal takes inspiration from the reuse of existing infrastructures and architectural elements.

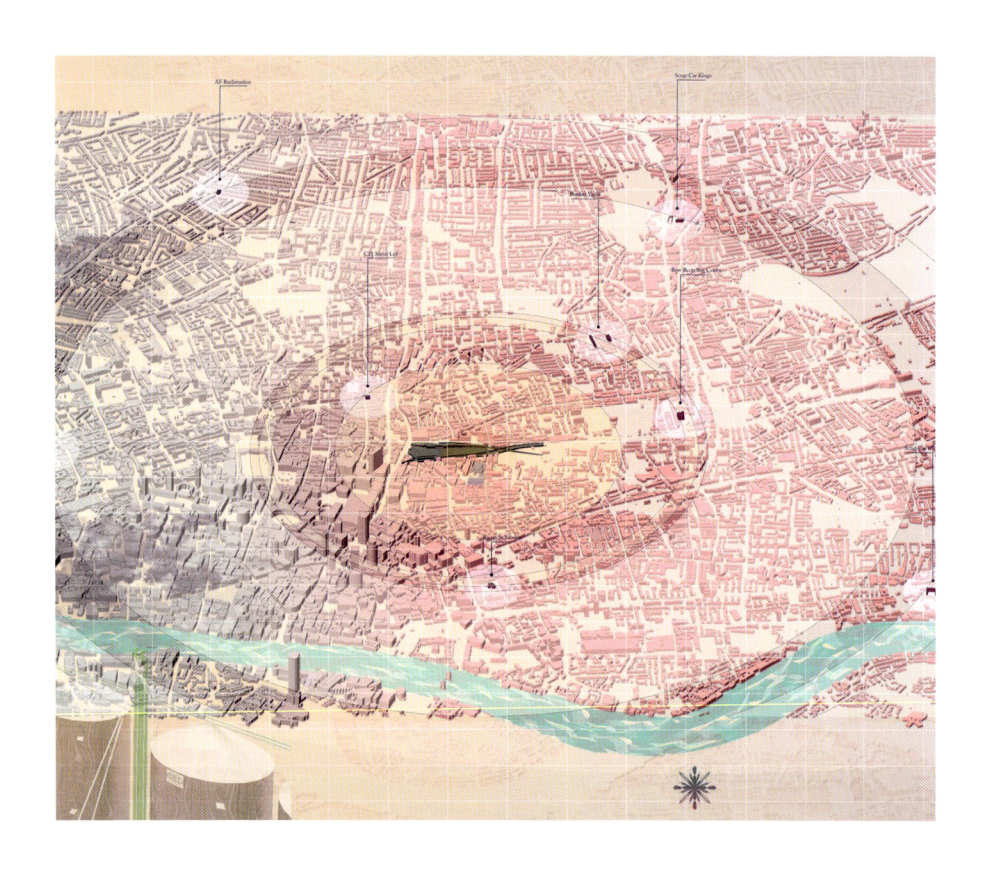

VARIATIONS ON THE DISPLAY   Option Studio   303

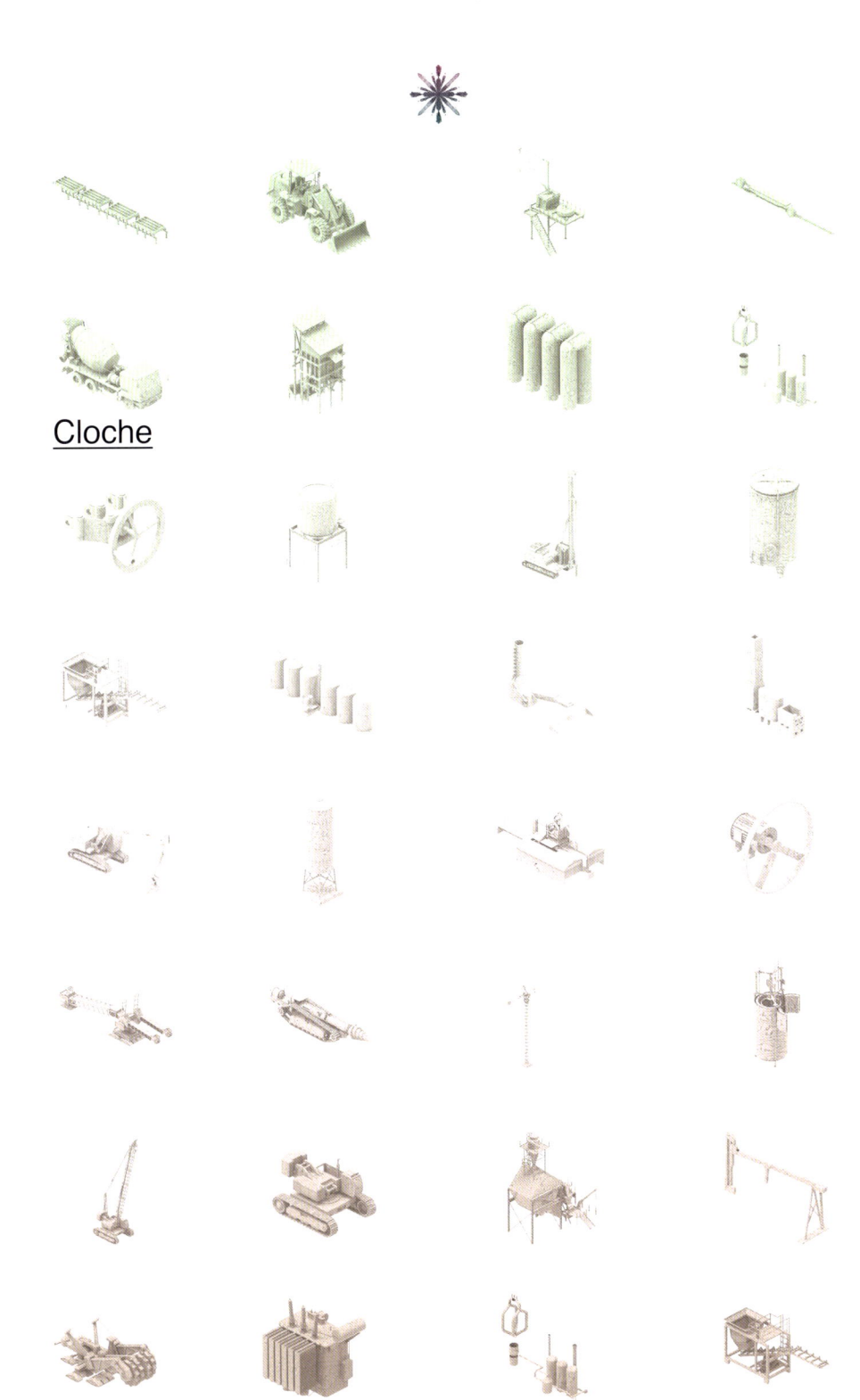

Cloche

Andrejs Rauchut
MArch II, 2017

The MLK Way: Building on Black America's Main Street

Instructor
Daniel D'Oca

Martin Luther King, Jr. is one of America's most revered historical figures. More than 100 streets are named for King, countless monuments and memorials have been built in his memory, and, perhaps most impressively, 893 communities in the US have named a street for him. This studio invited students to help shape the future of MLK streets in a way that neither ignores the structural racism that has led to segregation, poverty, and socioeconomic decay, nor overlooks the positive characteristics that make MLK streets King's "greatest living memorial."

VARIATIONS ON THE DISPLAY   Option Studio   305

Greetings

VARIATIONS ON THE DISPLAY   Option Studio   307

Ximena de Villafranca
MArch II, 2017

The MLK Way: Building on Black America's Main Street

Instructor
Daniel D'Oca

Business Taxonomy highlights the strengths of the community living along Martin Luther King Street in St. Louis. It looks to empower the surrounding community by designing a methodology of strategies for avoiding gentrification and for returning economic power to local business owners.

The first-semester Core Studio of Urban Planning introduces students to the fundamental knowledge and technical skills used by urban planners to research, analyze, and implement plans and projects for the built environment. This project attempts to find growth and expansion opportunities by enhancing community pride through diverse cultural identities.

Miriam Keller
MUP, 2017

Urban Planning Core I

Instructor
Ana Gelabert-Sanchez

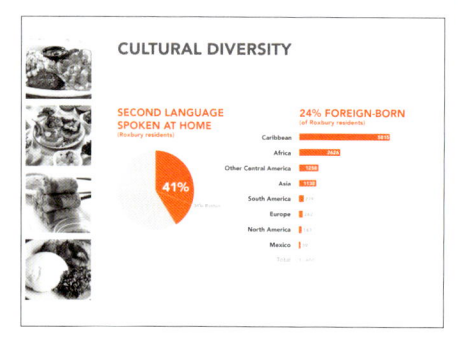

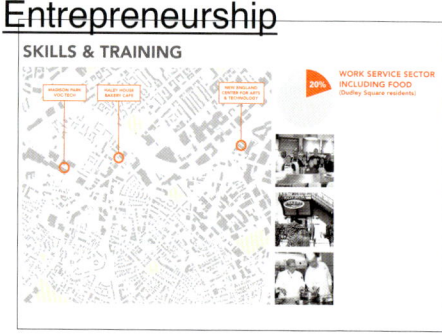

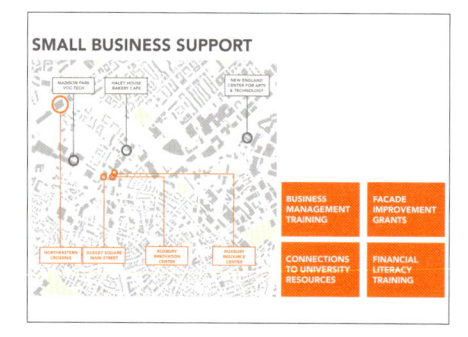

VARIATIONS ON THE DISPLAY — Core Studio — 309

5 INGREDIENTS FOR SUCCESS

BUILD A DENSER CLUSTER

CRITICAL MASS

17 DUDLEY SQUARE
52 CENTRAL SQUARE
50 SOUTH END

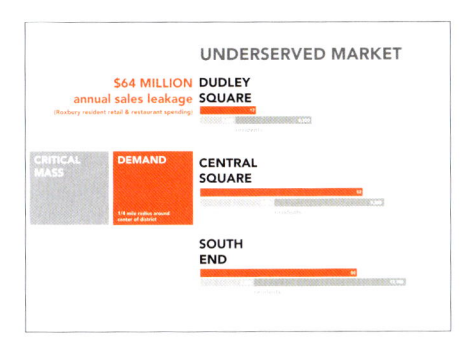

UNDERSERVED MARKET

CRITICAL MASS | DEMAND

$64 MILLION annual sales leakage (Roxbury resident retail & restaurant spending)

DUDLEY SQUARE
CENTRAL SQUARE (1/4 mile radius around center of district)
SOUTH END

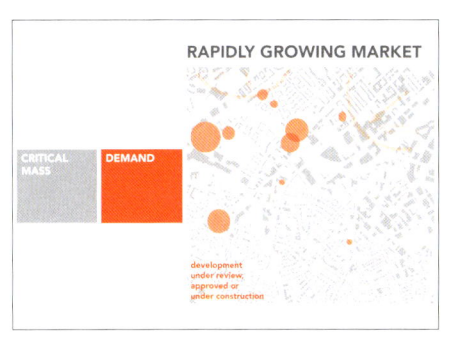

RAPIDLY GROWING MARKET

CRITICAL MASS | DEMAND

development under review, approved or under construction

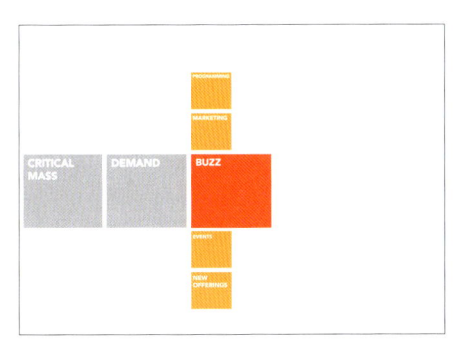

[BUZZ]

CRITICAL MASS | DEMAND | BUZZ

PROGRAMMING
MARKETING
EVENTS
NEW OFFERINGS

[LOWER BARRIERS TO ENTRY]

CRITICAL MASS | DEMAND | BUZZ | LOWER BARRIERS TO ENTRY

CHEAP SPACE
START SMALL
LEVERAGE PARTNERSHIPS
MORE SUPPORT

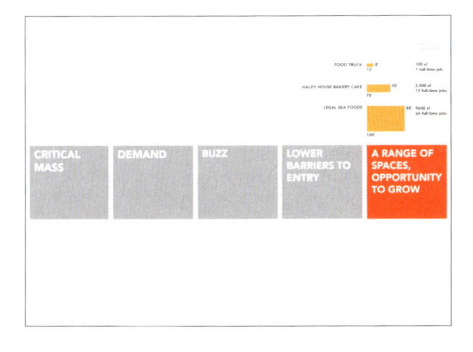

[A RANGE OF SPACES]

CRITICAL MASS | DEMAND | BUZZ | LOWER BARRIERS TO ENTRY | A RANGE OF SPACES, OPPORTUNITY TO GROW

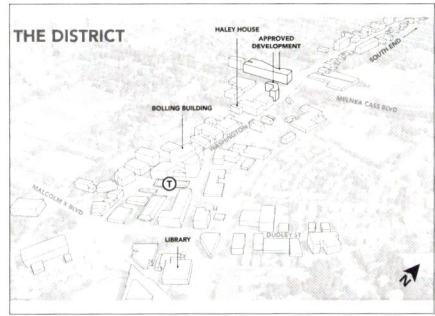

FOOD TRUCK
HALEY HOUSE BAKERY CAFE
LEGAL SEA FOODS

THE DISTRICT

HALEY HOUSE
APPROVED DEVELOPMENT
SOUTH END
BOLLING BUILDING
MELNEA CASS BLVD
MALCOLM X BLVD
LIBRARY
DUDLEY ST

Matthew Allen
PhD Candidate

American Graph Fleeting Hologram

Advisor
Antoine Picon

What is this strange contraption sitting in the Collection of Historical Scientific Instruments vault? Like a work of art, it has an author, a title, and a date: Geoffrey Dutton, *American Graph Fleeting*, 1979. It was not, however, produced as an aesthetic object, but as a technological demonstration, one of a series of experiments in visualization done in the 1970s by programmers working at the Harvard University Graduate School of Design's Laboratory for Computer Graphics and Spatial Analysis (which operated from 1965 to 1991).

The device combines off-the-shelf holographic display technology with brute-force plotting from the lab's own mapping software. Above the pedestal housing a lightbulb rotates a cylinder of holographic film that displays, over the course of 45 seconds, an animation of 1,000 frames.[1] Standing at a distance of about a foot, the viewer is treated to a God's-eye view of the United States. The animation begins in 1790, with tiny spikes in the east depicting the early postcolonial population. As time marches forward toward 1970, the population spikes in the northeast grow taller, and smaller but growing blips move steadily westward. These maps were produced as graphical support for a *National Geographic* article about manifest destiny on the occasion of the country's 200th birthday.[2] Each frame was output by the lab's software and plotted frame-by-painstaking-frame. The paper plots were then copied to 16-mm film by a company in Burlington, Massachusetts, and finally to holographic film by the Holographic Film Company in New York. The viewing apparatus was produced by the same company.[3] When it was put on display in 1979 at the Harvard Computer Graphics Week Conference, the slightly imperfect hologram must have looked like a ghostly apparition from a future of animated infographics (a future we now inhabit).[4]

Looking at the animation now, the information about population growth is less compelling than the implicit allegory about the rise of the computer (another instance of manifest destiny?). The allegory turns out to be ominous. For contrast, let's compare Dutton's animation to a much more famous spinning light contraption: Laszlo Moholy-Nagy's *Light-Space Modulator* (1922; on view over at the Harvard Art Museums). Moholy-Nagy's device projects light through a series

American Graph Fleeting (1979). Photograph courtesy of Geoffrey Dutton. This object is now preserved at the Collection of Historical Scientific Instruments, Harvard University.

of rotating screens, bars, and filters to replace the static white walls of the gallery with a dynamic, diverse, and ephemeral space. By so easily creating such a variety of immersive spatial effects, it offers a critique of architecture's fetish for solidity and permanence. The *American Graph Fleeting* hologram, in contrast, invites viewers to look at a small virtual space (the animated map) from a safe, objective distance. Technology is used to replace the outside world rather than to enhance it.

In retrospect, we can see that the lab's project was to gleefully dissolve architecture in an acid vat of data, returning it to its constituent molecules of space, topology, information, and so on. They seem to have imagined that architecture could be reconstructed from these elements with the help of computers, but it is probably fair to say that architecture simply eluded their grasp. This is not to say that the lab was a failure, however. In the place of architecture, the lab erected an equivalent disciplinary culture around computer graphics—a discipline every bit as alluring as architecture, but with its own distinct rituals and aesthetics.

This holographic contraption contains a lesson about architectural experimentation. Once something has become a consumer product, we ought to take a critical stance toward it. Architecture in the modernist mode depends on an element of shock or surprise.[5] This is hard to achieve with techniques that have been around for a long time, and even harder within the confines of a slickly packaged system. This is now the case with computer graphics: We can resist its alluring effects, interrogate its potentials, and twist it in unexpected ways—but simply having fun with Photoshop would be self-indulgent or worse. Better results are likely with a critical/analytical mindset.

But before something becomes a consumer product, it is inherently surprising. There is bound to be a brief productive period during which it exists as a subcultural phenomenon outside of established critical frameworks. This is the time to do the hard work of letting go and playing with something new. (So why not make some holograms!?)

1   Oliver Strimpel, "Computer and Image Exhibit Proposal and Panel Texts," draft of exhibition text for the Computer Museum, Boston, September 5, 1984, http://tcm.computerhistory.org/CHMfiles/Exhibit%20Text%201984.pdf, 53.
2   Peter T. White and Emory Kristof, "This Land of Ours—How Are We Using It?" *National Geographic* 150, no. 1 (July 1976): 20–67. Nick Chrisman, *Charting the Unknown: How Computer Mapping at Harvard Became GIS* (Redlands, CA: ESRI Press, 2006), 147–149.
3   Ibid.
4   Geoffrey Dutton, "Project Descriptions," Spatial Effects, accessed June 17, 2016, http://www.spatial-effects.com/SE-past-projects1.html.
5   Fredric Jameson, *The Prison-House of Language: A Critical Account of Structuralism and Russian Formalism* (Princeton, NJ: Princeton University Press, 1972).

+115 m

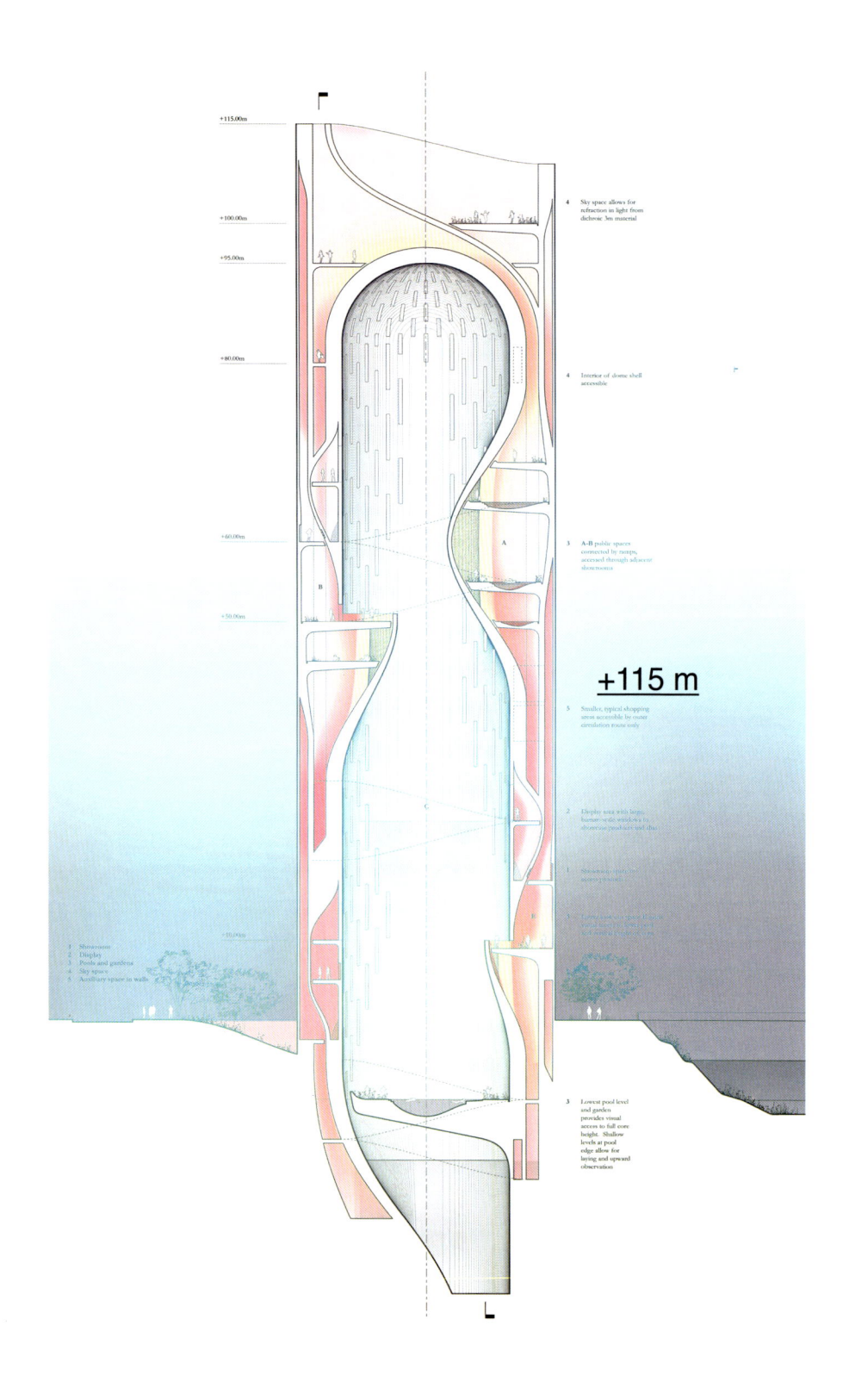

Erin Cuevas
MArch II, 2016

Thesis
Kawaii-Kowai: Amplifying the Affective Loop

Advisors
Iñaki Ábalos, Cristina Díaz Moreno, Efrén García Grinda, Alex Zahlten

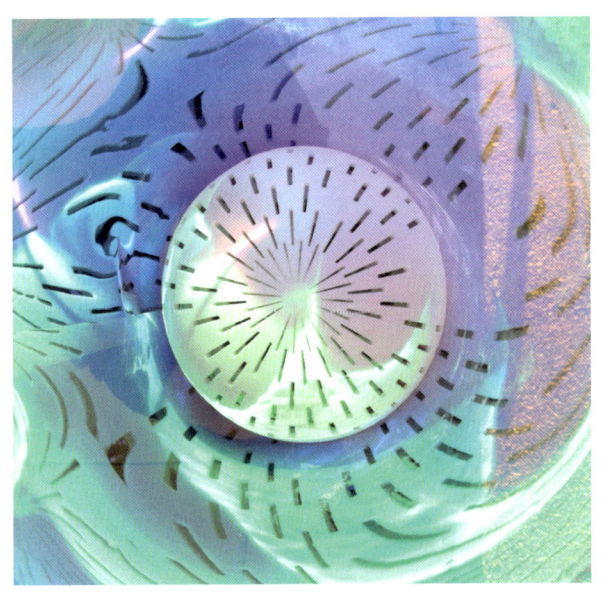

This thesis addresses the duality between *kawaii* and *kowai*, two Japanese words with similar phonetics, but opposing meanings. *Kawaii* denotes purity, innocence, and femininity, while *kowai*, on the other hand, denotes fear, danger, and perversity. The architecture provokes the overlapping of *kawaii* and *kowai* in terms of social interaction and subjective perceptual experience.

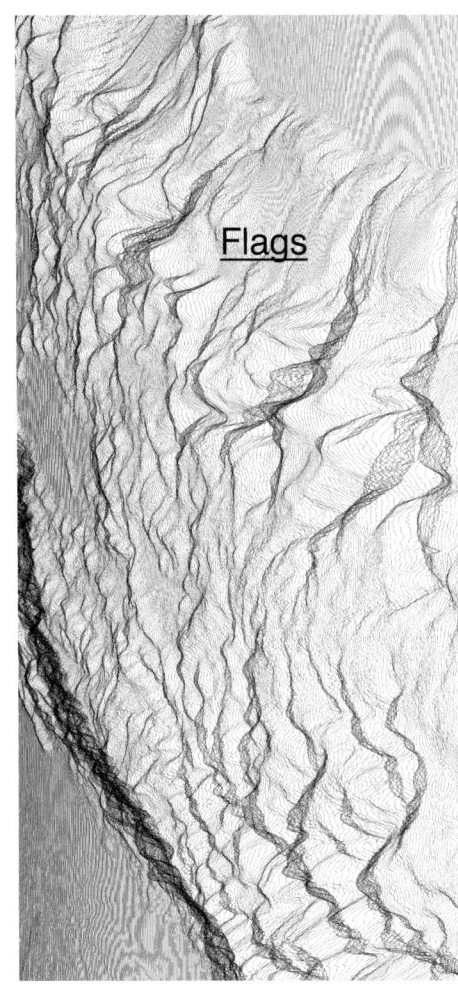

Pedro Aparicio,
Boram Lee Jung,
Mariana Llano,
Namik Mackic,
Olga Semenovych
MDes, 2016

Flags

Thesis
Weak States

Advisor
Pierre Bélanger

Weak States is a group of four thesis projects directed by Pierre Bélanger that investigate the emergence of weak states and the generative capacities they carry in lieu of currently perceived crises and catastrophes. By prepositioning territorial politics, this approach is preconditioned by alternative ways of seeing, reading, and sensing conditions of the state.

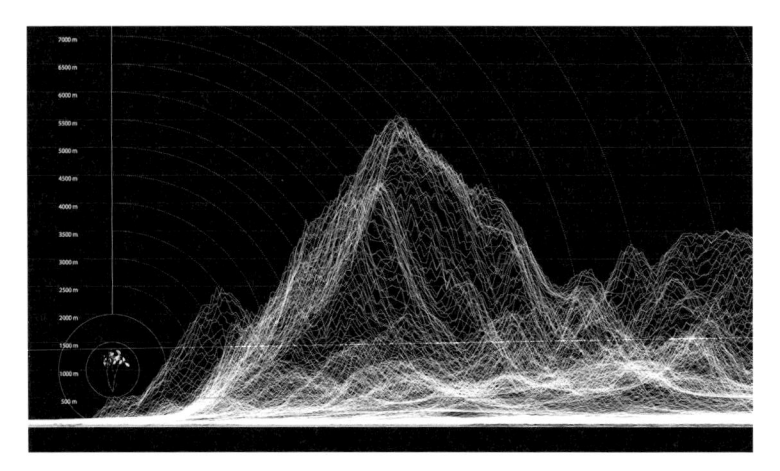

VARIATIONS ON THE DISPLAY Thesis Project 315

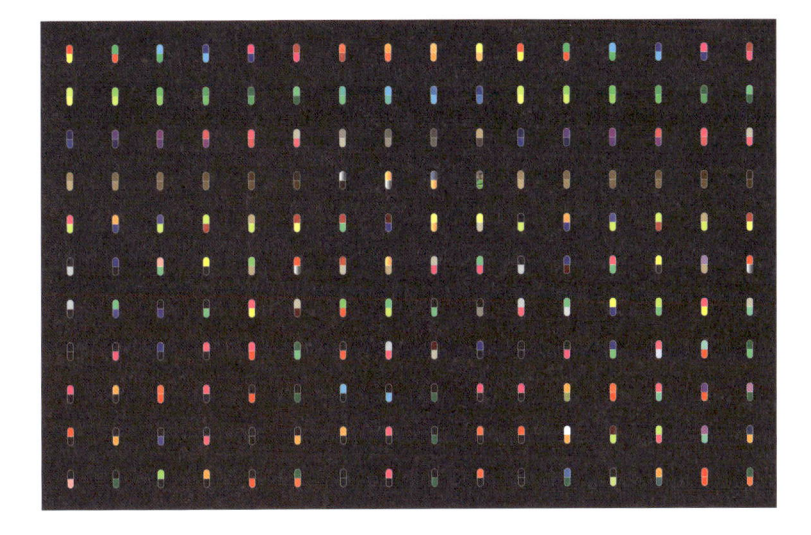

These drawings and models—methodically displayed to reveal the intense labor that goes into producing architecture—are composed primarily in black and white. Muted in terms of color, these constraints turn up the volume on output. One architecture thesis student produced eight sets of images, resulting in 563 individual works (96 are displayed here) while another architecture student printed six Z-corp models (four are displayed here). A seminar on design writing, which emphasized the endless editing and revisions that go into making a strong text, yields a text on an endless loop of another sort, the Interstate 610, "the loop," in Houston. Is there concern for the discipline when production happens at such a rapid pace? Does the author's individual voice get lost? Or, when everything is beautiful, is selecting the "best" work near impossible?

    The editors took a quick survey, and the results are in: the authorial voice is not diluted when working with seriality in design. It only gets louder. And it can happen without color.

Hold the Color

318

HOLD THE COLOR

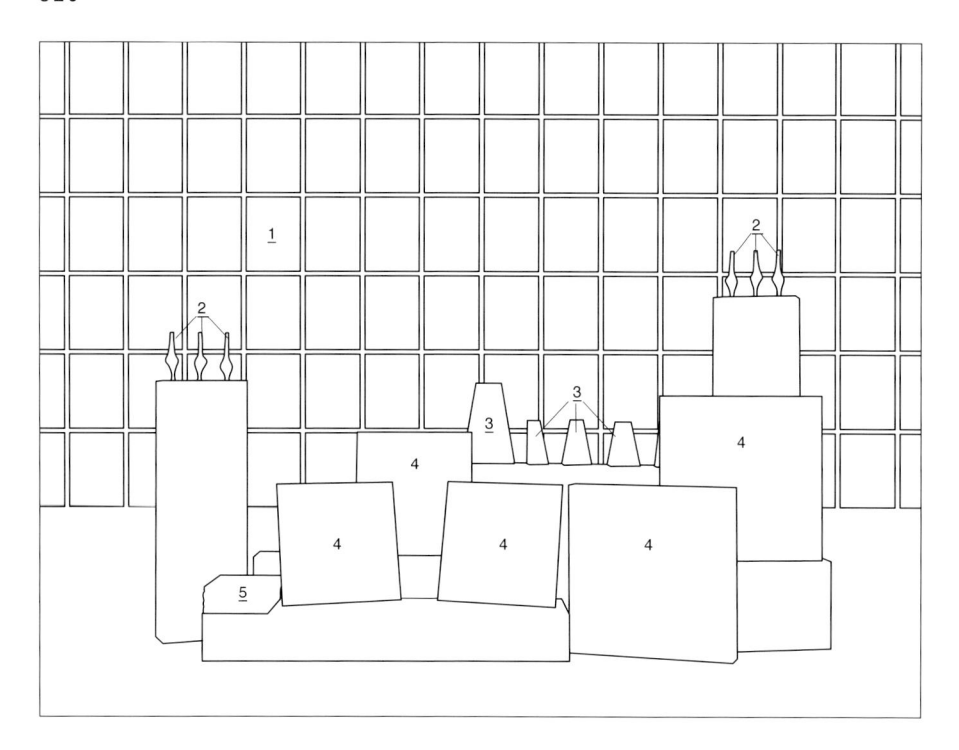

1   Ostranenie
   p. 322

Patrick Herron
MArch I, 2016
Thesis: The
   Familiar Uncommon
Advisor: Mack Scogin

2   Bulbous
   p. 324

Yousef Hussein
MArch I, 2018
Architecture Core III: Integrate
Instructor: Jeffry Burchard

3   Twist
   p. 326

Isabelle Verwaay
MArch I, 2018
Architecture Core III: Integrate
Instructor: John May

4   Signifiers

Georgia Williams
MArch I, 2016
Thesis: Portraits in
   Architecture
Advisor: Mack Scogin

5   Houston
   p. 328

Georgia Williams
MArch I, 2016
On the Loop
The Poetics of Place: Critical
   Writing for Designers
Instructor: Alastair Gordon

Ostranenie

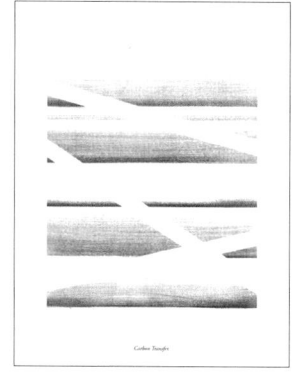

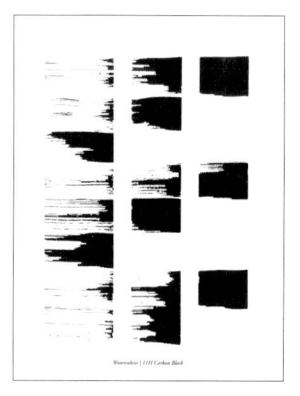

Patrick Herron
MArch I, 2016

Thesis
The Familiar Uncommon

Advisor
Mack Scogin

HOLD THE COLOR — Thesis Project — 323

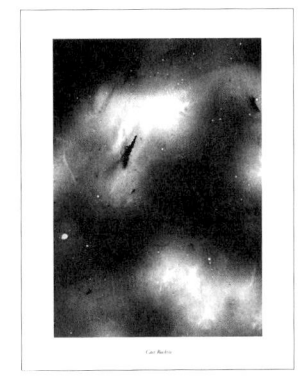

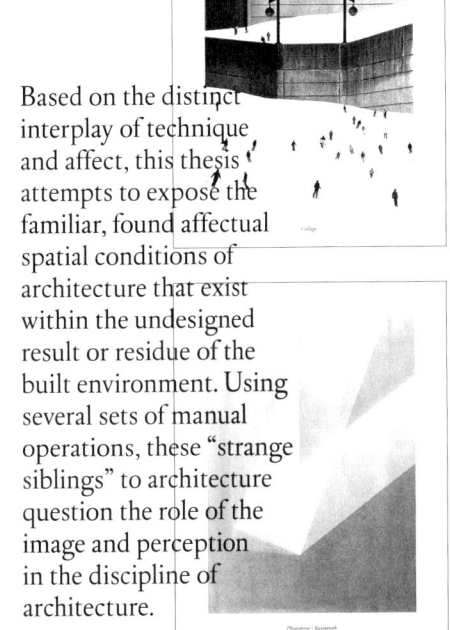

Photogram | Rayograph

620 Film | Kodak Duaflex

Cao Backer

Based on the distinct interplay of technique and affect, this thesis attempts to expose the familiar, found affectual spatial conditions of architecture that exist within the undesigned result or residue of the built environment. Using several sets of manual operations, these "strange siblings" to architecture question the role of the image and perception in the discipline of architecture.

Collage

Photogram | Rayograph

Collage

Yousef Hussein
MArch I, 2018

Architecture Core III: Integrate

Instructor
Jeffry Burchard

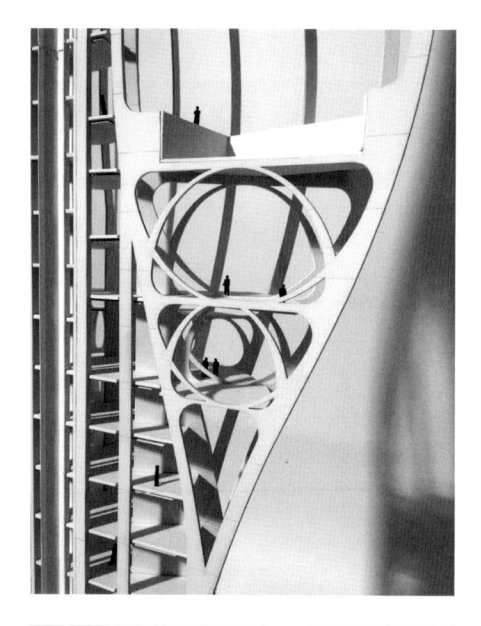

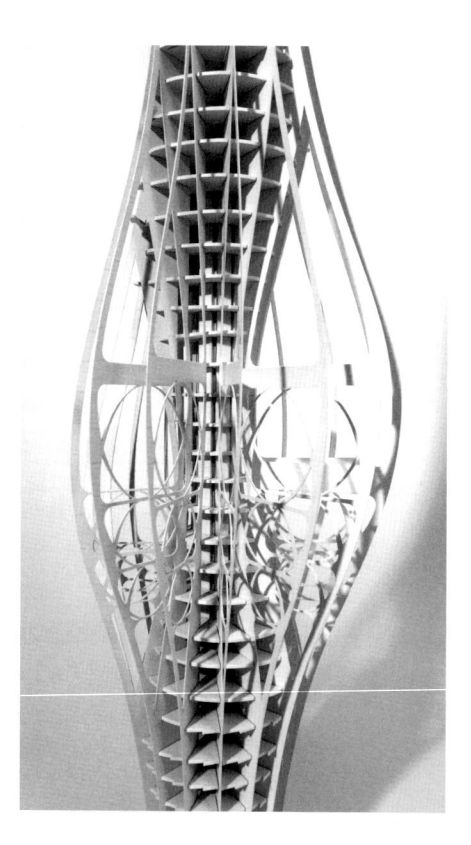

Singapore's relatively new business district has a culture of austerity. This building aims to juxtapose the diverse worlds of Singapore within one holistic, singular form. The building can be read in successive layers, similar to layers of skin, which fatten, swell, and deform to accommodate program volumes as well as choreography of user sequences, approaches, moments, and views.

Bulbous

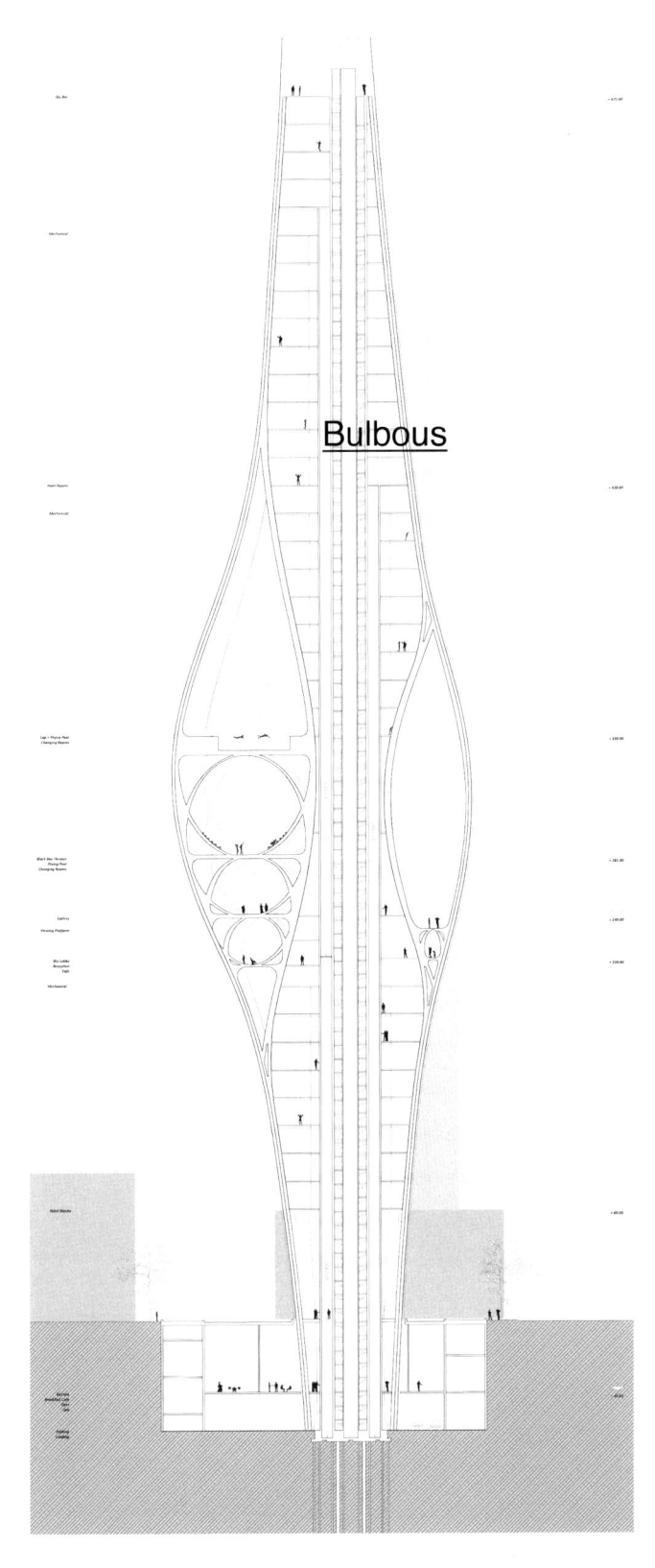

326

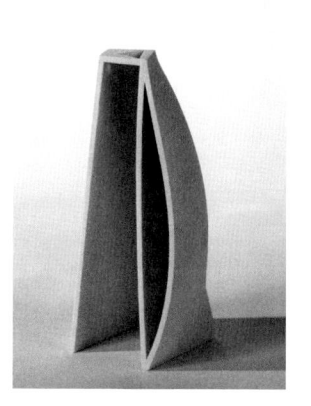

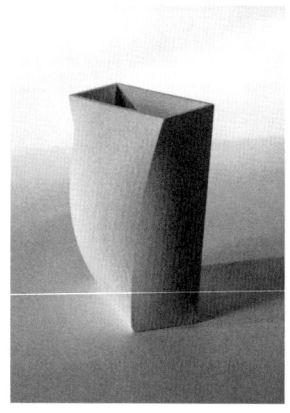

HOLD THE COLOR			Core Studio			327

Structural systems, envelope design, and environmental and thermodynamic processes are systematically addressed in the development of a single project over the course of the whole semester in Architecture Core III: Integrate. Using specific mapping strategies, this project seeks to carve out space from the deep poché of a twisted form.

Twist

Isabelle Verwaay
MArch I, 2018

Architecture Core III: Integrate

Instructor
John May

Georgia Williams
MArch I, 2016

On the Loop

The Poetics of Place: Critical Writing for Designers

Instructor
Alastair Gordon

Houston is where the gas is cheap and the drivers speed, always flirting with the potential of a pile-up. Particularly along the 610 loop. To take the loop is to embrace the intrepid part of myself. The joke goes that, on the loop, you drive 90 miles per hour until you hear glass.

    I take the 610 loop when I go farther than my neighborhood. It is a central artery stretching 38 miles, circling the city's original neighborhoods. Though it connects drivers to almost every freeway in Houston, the loop also divides. It is a physical partition, separating the inner and outer loop, but it is also a social marker. You are either an *outer looper* who lives outside the loop, or an *inner looper* who lives inside. You either own two purebred golden retrievers or reluctantly foster 13 diseased cats who call your porch home.

    I'm an inner looper and I take the dividing line at every opportunity. Taking the loop is proof of your impudence.

    On the road, we are players in a driving drama. Within our cars, we construct moral dramas and heroic traffic poems in which we are the wronged victims. We try to catch sight of the driver who wronged us and invoke their identity as a reason for blame: men, women, young, old, texters, talkers, distracted idiots on cell phones.

    On the 610 loop you play out this epic of human relations. Your power is in going eight or ten miles per hour over the speed limit, and your unwillingness to heed to the movements of surrounding cars. You will witness an accident—or be a part of one.

    Late at night, when the traffic along the loop has thinned and I can choose any lane, I consider the damage of my car hitting a concrete barrier at 90 miles per hour. The organs of my car shaken, smashed together. How far would the sound travel? My whole body shudders at how easy it is to accidentally or intentionally veer left and aim for a median. It will happen to someone else on the 610 loop.

<u>Houston</u>

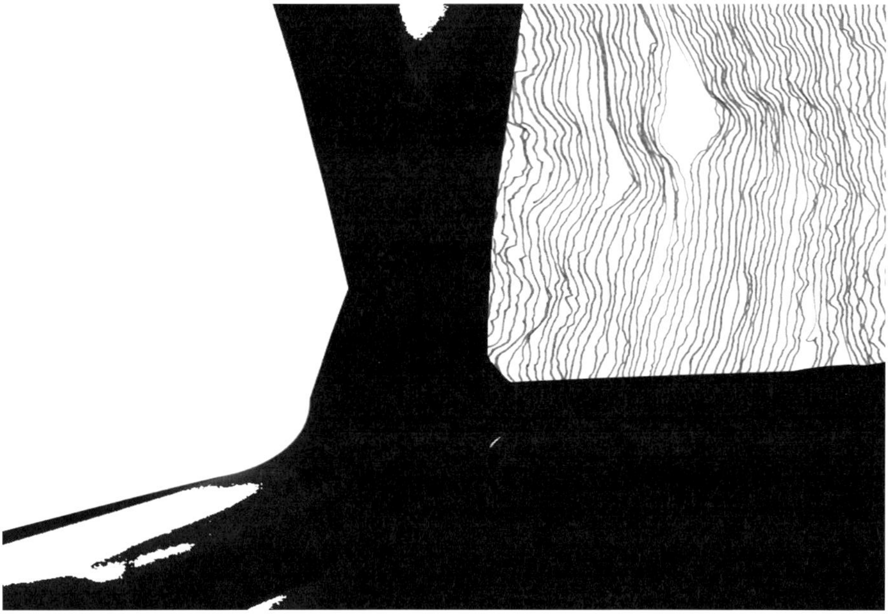

Second guesses, double-takes, closer looks, and productive misreading provide a way to read this body of work. Are these works crafted in the tradition of bas-relief (carved from a single material as in a sunken relief) or trompe l'oeil (deceiving the eye, as in forced perspective)? Regardless, they require a closer look. A landscape architecture studio uses multiple materials for rendering similarly scaled landscapes. A transparent block reminds us of an abstracted ground but, on a second look, may actually be a facade study. Doubling as a series of shallow ditches—or is it a deep ravine?— a dark brown landscape requires scrutiny. An urban design thesis project, titled City Hallucinations, challenges the purpose of Boston City Hall while doubling as an urban proposal for the 21st century. Lastly, an architecture thesis project productively misreads decline and anonymity in the city. In the designer's own words, "An inauthentic actor on an open set, Cleveland begins a portrayal of a city and winds up playing itself."

Double-Takes

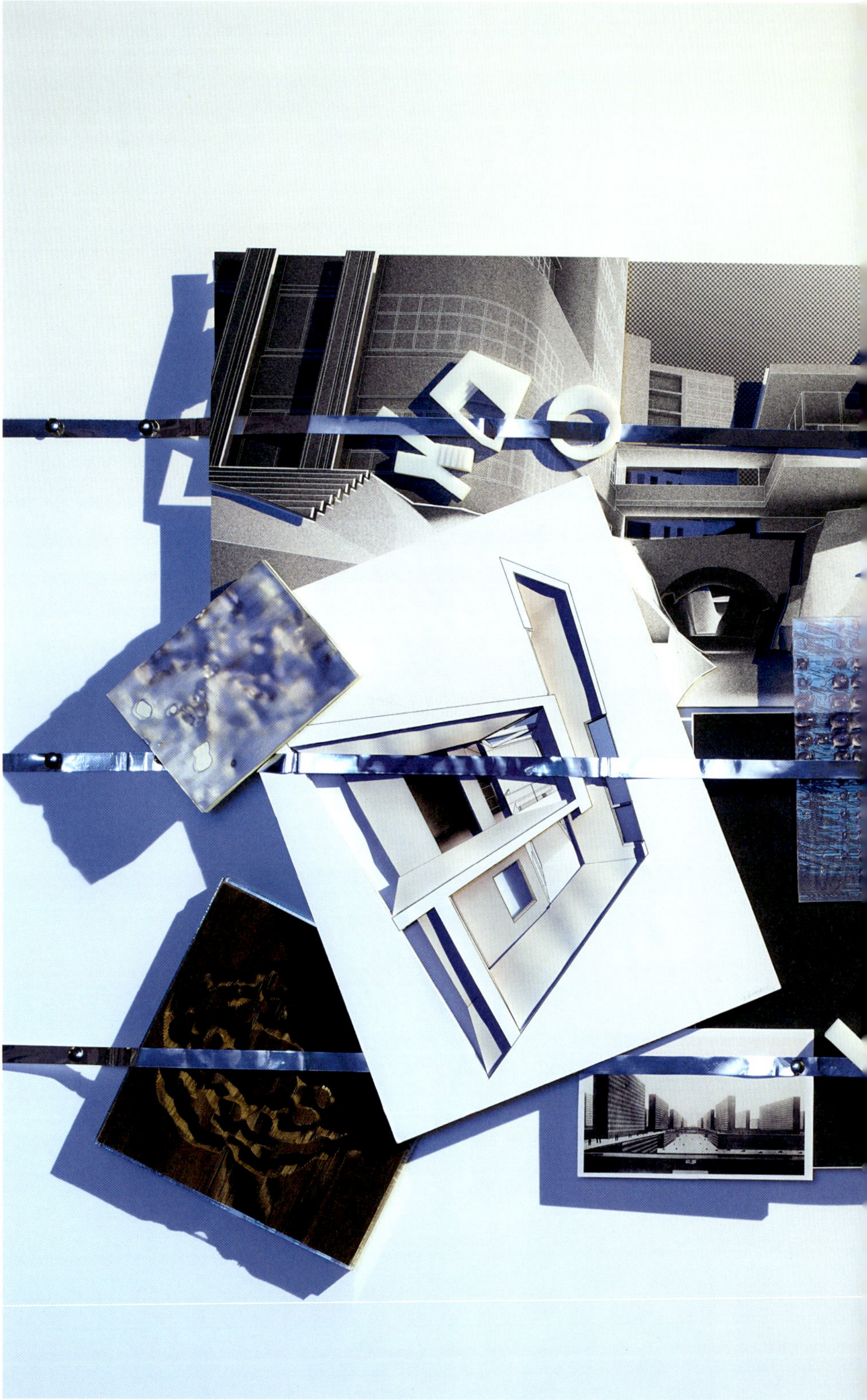

DOUBLE-TAKES 333

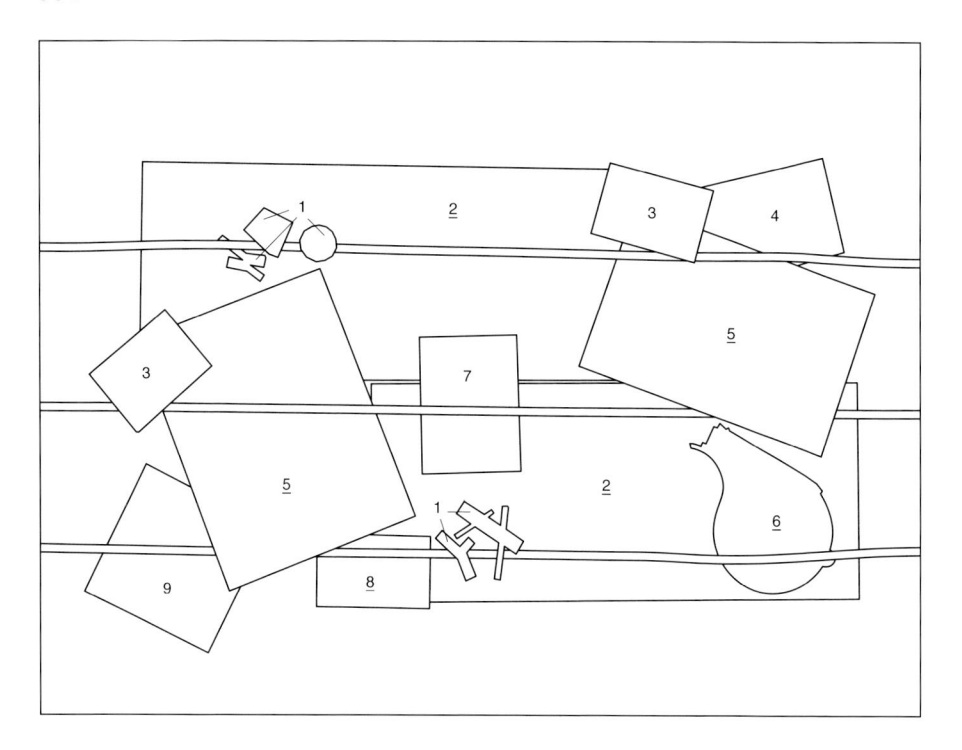

1 Latour

Yutian Wang
MAUD, 2016
Redesigning the Actor Network in Rural Areas around Tokyo
Instructors: Momoyo Kaijima, Yoshiharu Tsukamoto

2 [Stage Set p. 336](#)

Julian Funk
MArch I, 2016
Thesis: Cleveland Plays Itself
Advisor: Eric Höweler

3 Registered Forces

Tiffany Dang, Rebecca Liggins
MLA I, 2017
Wenyi Pan
MLA I AP, 2017
Landscape Core IV
Instructor: Nicholas Pevzner

4 National Mall

Yujia Wang
MLA I AP, 2017
Landscape Core IV
Instructor: Sergio Lopez-Pineiro

5 [Deep Space p. 338](#)

Julia Roberts
MArch I, 2016
Architecture Core I: Project
Instructor: Megan Panzano

6 [Urban Node p. 340](#)

Yinan Wang
MAUD, 2016
Thesis: City Hallucination
Advisor: Felipe Correa

7 Glaciology

Gary Hon
MLA I AP, 2017
Maria Robalino
MLA I, 2017
Xin Zhao
MDes / MLA I, 2017
Landscape Core IV
Instructor: Robert Pietrusko

8 [Hilberseimer p. 342](#)

Miguel Lopez Melendez
DDes, 2018
Perfect Horror: A Poetic Reflection on Ludwig Hilberseimer's *Hochhausstadt* (1924)
Advisor: Charles Waldheim

9 Radio Waves

Yuxi Qin
MLA I, 2017
Landscape Core IV
Instructor: Sergio Lopez-Pineiro

Stage Set

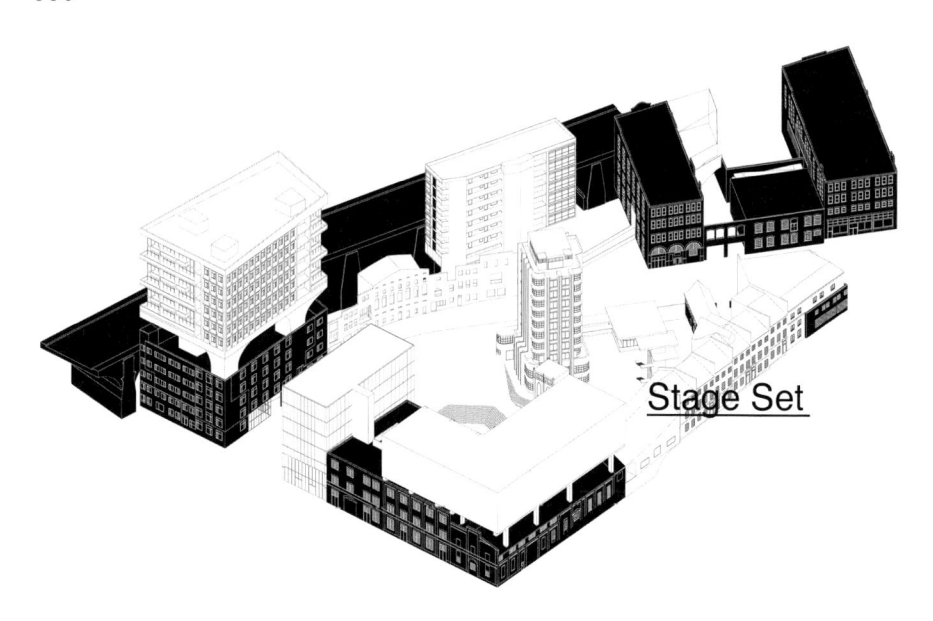

In the theater of the city, historic preservation is now the most relevant forum for the discussion of identity. Cleveland wants to be New York *and* Stuttgart. For this thesis the cinematic becomes a way of framing the relationship between the identity of a city and its physical reality. In Cleveland, the architectural interrogation of the city's historic fabric constitutes the cinematic through other means.

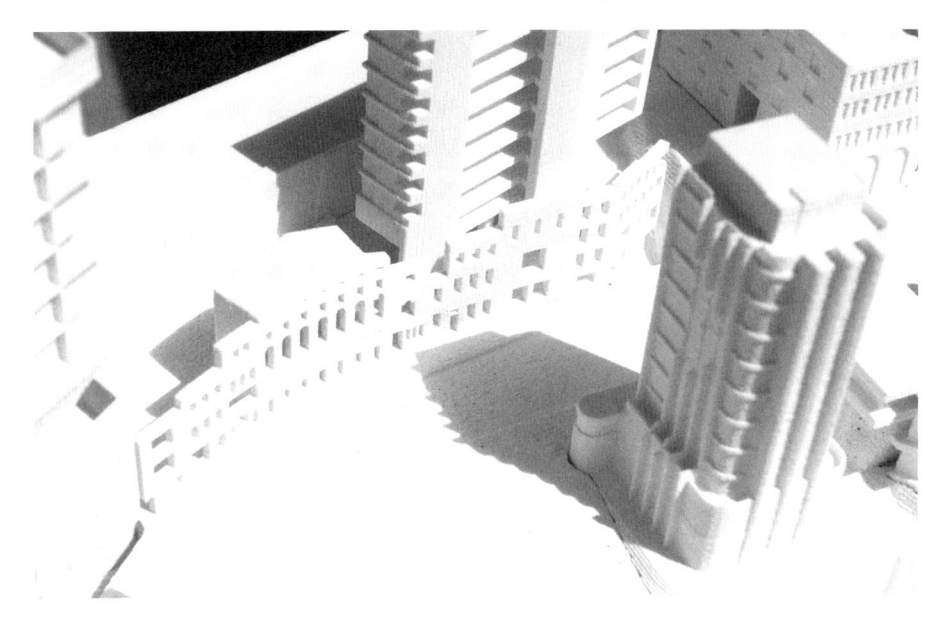

Julian Funk
MArch I, 2016

Thesis
Cleveland Plays Itself

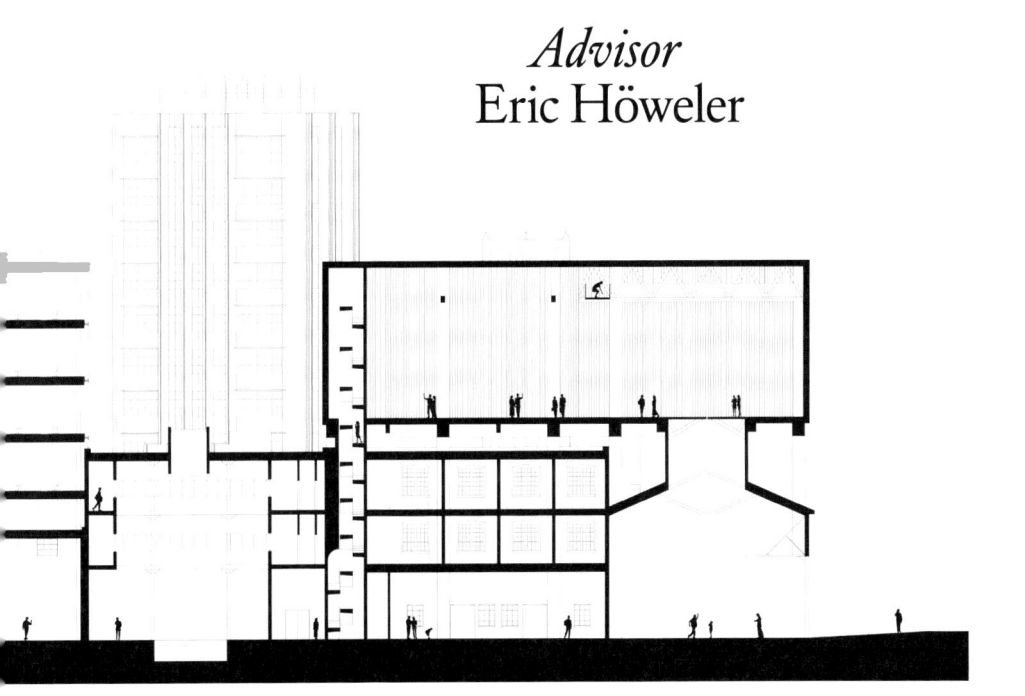

Advisor
Eric Höweler

In the first semester of Architecture Core, students are encouraged to leverage their varied expertise in the sciences, humanities, and other disciplines to find provocative and perhaps unexpected motivations of architectural form. Here, the "perimeter plan" project operates at the efficiency of a tightly wrapped facade.

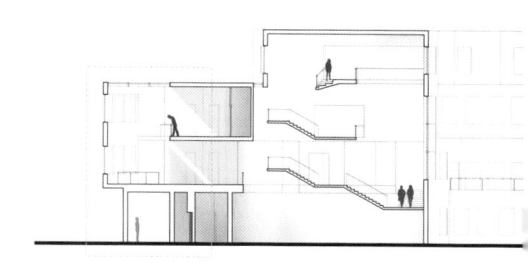

Julia Roberts
MArch I, 2019

Architecture Core I: Project

Instructor
Megan Panzano

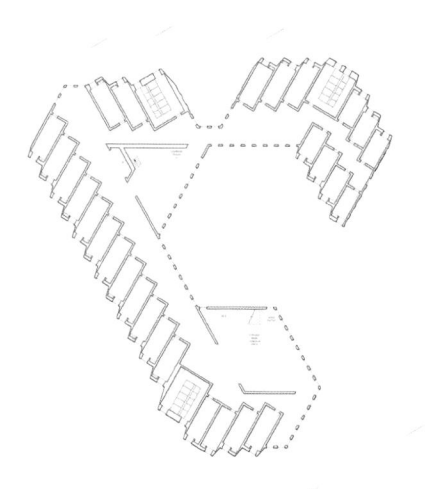

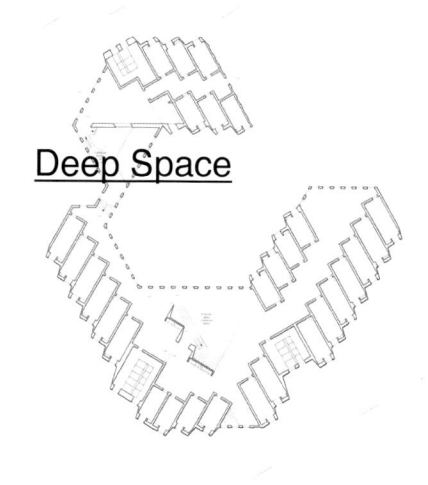

Deep Space

DOUBLE-TAKES   Core Studio   339

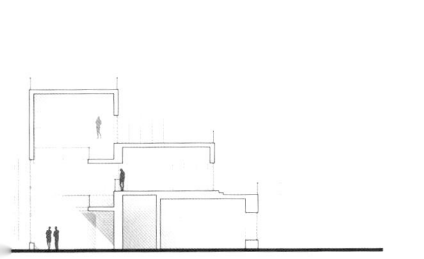

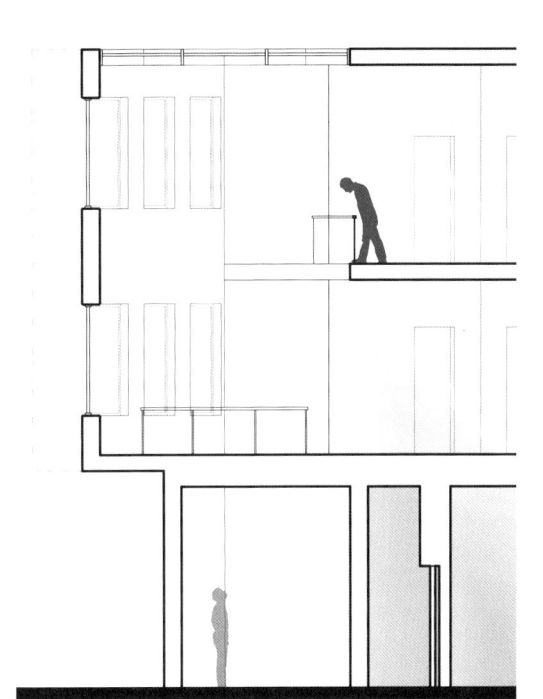

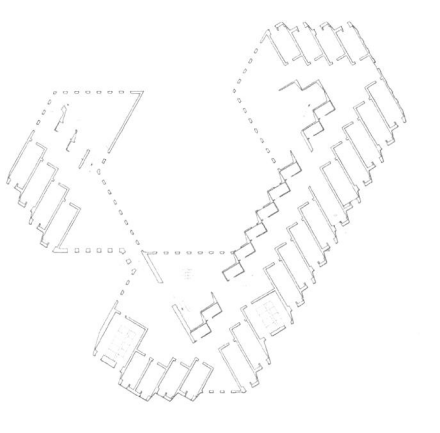

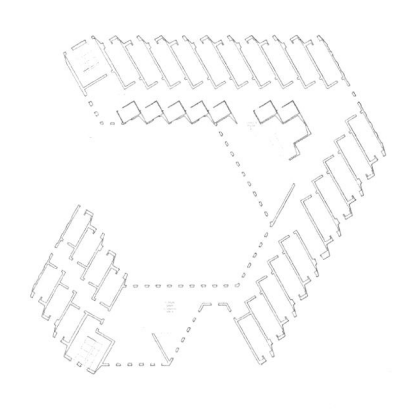

Yinan Wang
MAUD, 2016

Thesis
City Hallucination

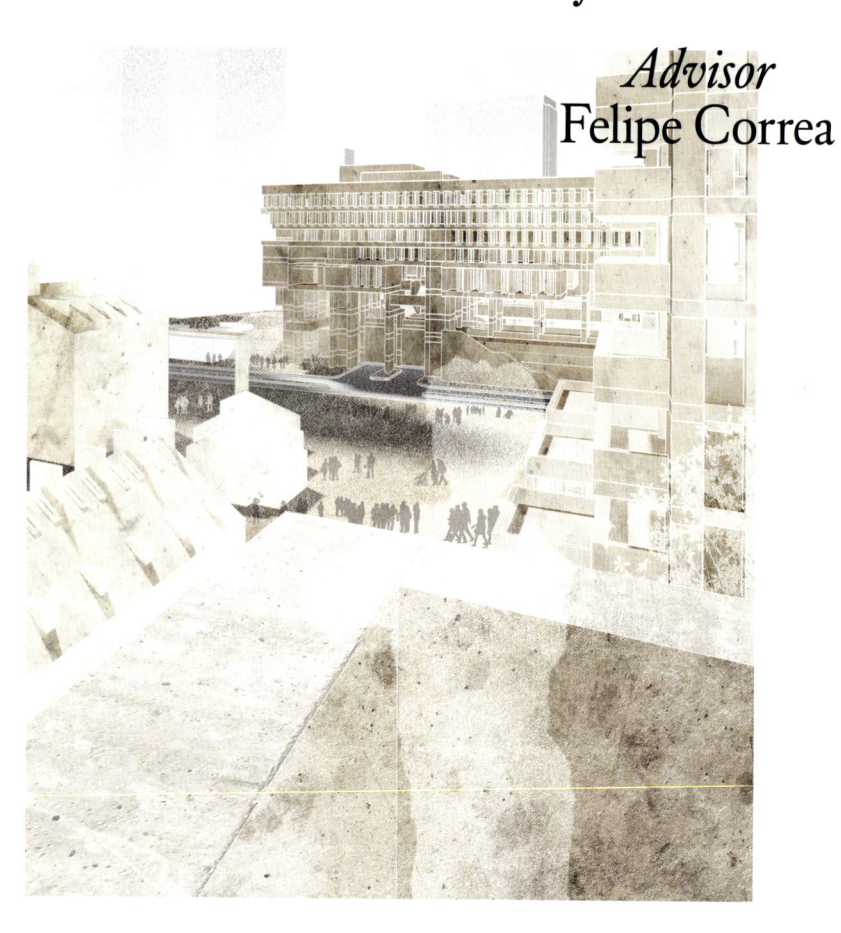

Advisor
Felipe Correa

DOUBLE-TAKES Thesis Project 341

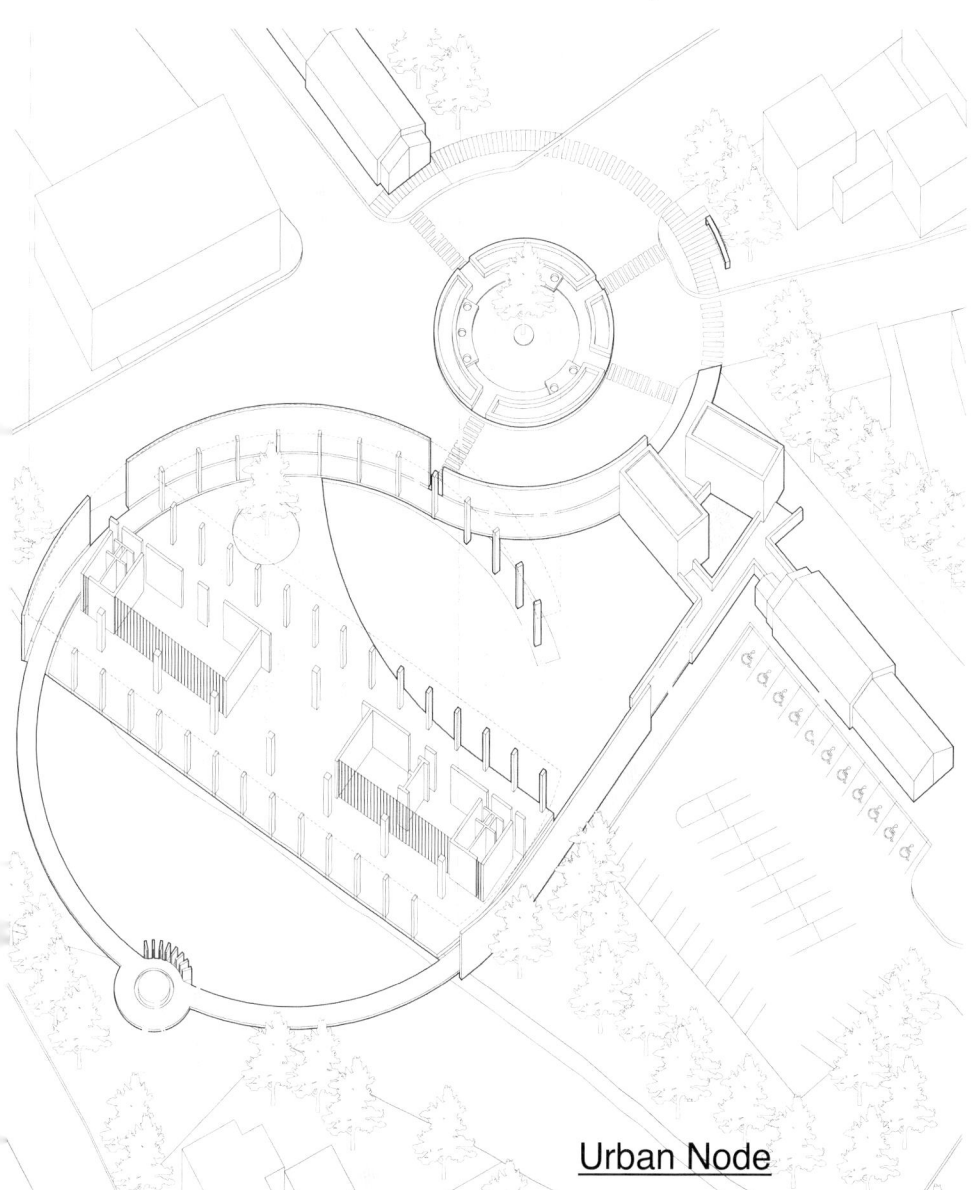

Urban Node

Using Boston City Hall as a generator for new urban typologies and centers for housing and program, this project reimagines the city through three distinct sites in Paducah, Kentucky; Jaffrey, New Hampshire; and Boston, Massachusetts. This thesis was awarded the Department of Urban Planning and Design Thesis Prize in Urban Design.

Miguel Lopez Melendez DDes, 2018

Perfect Horror: A Poetic Reflection on Ludwig Hilberseimer's *Hochhausstadt* (1924)

Advisor
Charles Waldheim

Ludwig Hilberseimer's *Hochhausstadt* is a theoretical urban scheme with architectonic character. Reality was assumed as what it is, to provide an alternative to the chaos of the metropolis. The "Real" was understood as a defeat, while the urban project was presented as a potential remedy for our ills. What if we just simply assume failure as fate? Look around. "Perfect Horror" is a provocation, a reflection on the implicit success of failure and the tacit failure of success.

What do you prefer: reality (no lies, no truths) or idealism (lies and truths)?

The dehumanized urban landscape of the *Hochhausstadt* casts a shadow on a coherent urban proposal to reorder the chaos of the metropolis.
A chaos provoked, according to architect Ludwig Hilberseimer, by industrialization and speculation as economic and aesthetic category.[1]
The overwhelming reality eclipses any urban project.

The radicalism of Ludwig Hilberseimer relies on his lucid and realist analysis of the capitalist city, according to Pier Vittorio Aureli.[2]
Reality is radical.

The Real is what it is, no imagination, no symbolism, no humans.
There is no idealism.
The *Hochhausstadt* is a framework, not a messianic solution, which emerged from and for the Real.
A Real that is impossible, according to Jacques Lacan, because it doesn't have fissures.[3]
The fissures proposed by the dialectic of symbolism, therefore reality is radical.
You can't hide your miseries anymore.
Perfection is impossible.
Is reality perfect?

The paradoxical "radicalism" of reality emerges within a territory of fairy tales with happy endings.
Utopias lie when they promise better futures.
The dream will vanish sooner or later.

Hilberseimer echoed the ambitions of the Modern Movement and aspired to provide order to disorder,
a perfectible architecture for a perfectible world.
In 1963, he would write: "The repetition of the blocks resulted in too much uniformity. Every natural thing was excluded: no tree or grassy area broke the monotony ... the result was more a necropolis than a metropolis, a sterile landscape of asphalt and cement, inhuman in every aspect."[4]
The latter describes the apocalyptic reality depicted in the *Hochhausstadt* from which humans have been obliterated.
Hilberseimer seeks redemption.
Don't do good things that may seem bad.[5]

The apocalyptic reality acquires a positive connotation when it becomes a means to an end, when it is not diminished by perfect futures.
The apocalyptic reality becomes part of the process of designing an alternative urban landscape.
An alternative urban landscape that emerges not to confront, but as a consequence of reality and its horrors. "Against from within" as a method in which the critique comes from inside, when we don't escape, when we challenge the reflected image in the mirror.[6]

Different interpretations present reality as:
what appears to us,
what appears to most people,
what we don't make up,
where the buck stops, and
what is there anyway.[7]
If reality is what it is, then we have to go through it in order to arrive to a coherent urban proposal.
An urban proposal that embraces the real rather than rejects it with the aspirations of idealism.
Idealism follows reality?

Since the world is a world we have been waiting for,
a better future that is yet to come.
During the history of architecture, we have witnessed several frustrated promises supported by the flexibility of idealism, which changes according to the Monday morning mood.
Idealism as intangible horror, with a messianic tone.
Reality as tangible horror without the mediation of idealism between us and the mirror.
Reality is radical.

Don't turn away from the painful.
Don't turn away from your own image.
Reality as shock therapy.
Reality as design process, as a means to an imperfect end.
The horror is not expensive, it is at hand.
Choose your own horror.
What do you prefer: reality (no lies, no truths) or idealism (lies and truths)?
Liquid or material horror?
Messianic or apocalyptic horror?
Go and embrace it, don't be shy.
Don't be afraid, it is harmless.

The future won't be perfect.
Lacanian Reality is impossible.
Perfection is impossible.
Look around!
The horror is pervasive.
Let's give it a chance.
The horror might be perfect ...

1. Ludwig Hilberseimer, Richard Anderson, and Pier Vittorio Aureli, *Metropolisarchitecture and Selected Essays* (New York: GSAPP Books, 2012), 269.
2. Ibid., 335.
3. Jacques Lacan, *Seminar II*, trans. Sylvanna Tomaselli (Cambridge: Cambridge University Press, 1988), 98.
4. Ludwig Hilberseimer, *Entfaltung einer Planungsidee* (Berlin: Verlag Ullstein, 1963), 22.
5. My mom told me...
6. Pier Vittorio Aureli, *The Project of Autonomy: Politics and Architecture within and against Capitalism*, Buell Center/FORuM Project Publication 4 (New York: Temple Hoyne Buell Center for the Study of American Architecture/Princeton Architectural Press, 2008), 19.
7. Jan Westerhoff, *Reality: A Very Short Introduction* (Oxford: Oxford University Press, 2011), 31.

Ludwig Karl Hilberseimer, *Highrise City (Hochhausstadt): Perspective View: North-South Street*, 1924. Ink and watercolor on paper. 97.3 × 140 cm. Courtesy of the Art Institute of Chicago.

Printed on the backs of shampoo bottles, the generic instructions to "lather, rinse, repeat" could thrust the obedient user into an endless loop of hair washing. In the computer sciences, these step-by-step operations, referred to as the "shampoo algorithm," are often used in introductory coursework, with parallels to digital modeling in design studies. A similar algorithm was found in the work of a collaborative seminar project, as three students delivered an experimental live performance at their final review, on the mundane act of making a sandwich. The project included an eight-step instruction pamphlet on the construction of a ham sandwich. If the method of sandwich fabrication is still unclear—and that's partly the point—just "follow the directions."

Working toward greater densities in urban housing, an urban design studio used the Manhattan block to test, model, print, mount, and present the many options displayed here. Similarly, a landscape architecture studio worked through several procedural form proposals by holding a constant dimension and limiting variables for manipulation. Regardless of how best to interpret "lather, rinse, repeat," repeated trials are necessary when working on design fundamentals, and the formal results are astonishing.

Lather, Rinse, Repeat

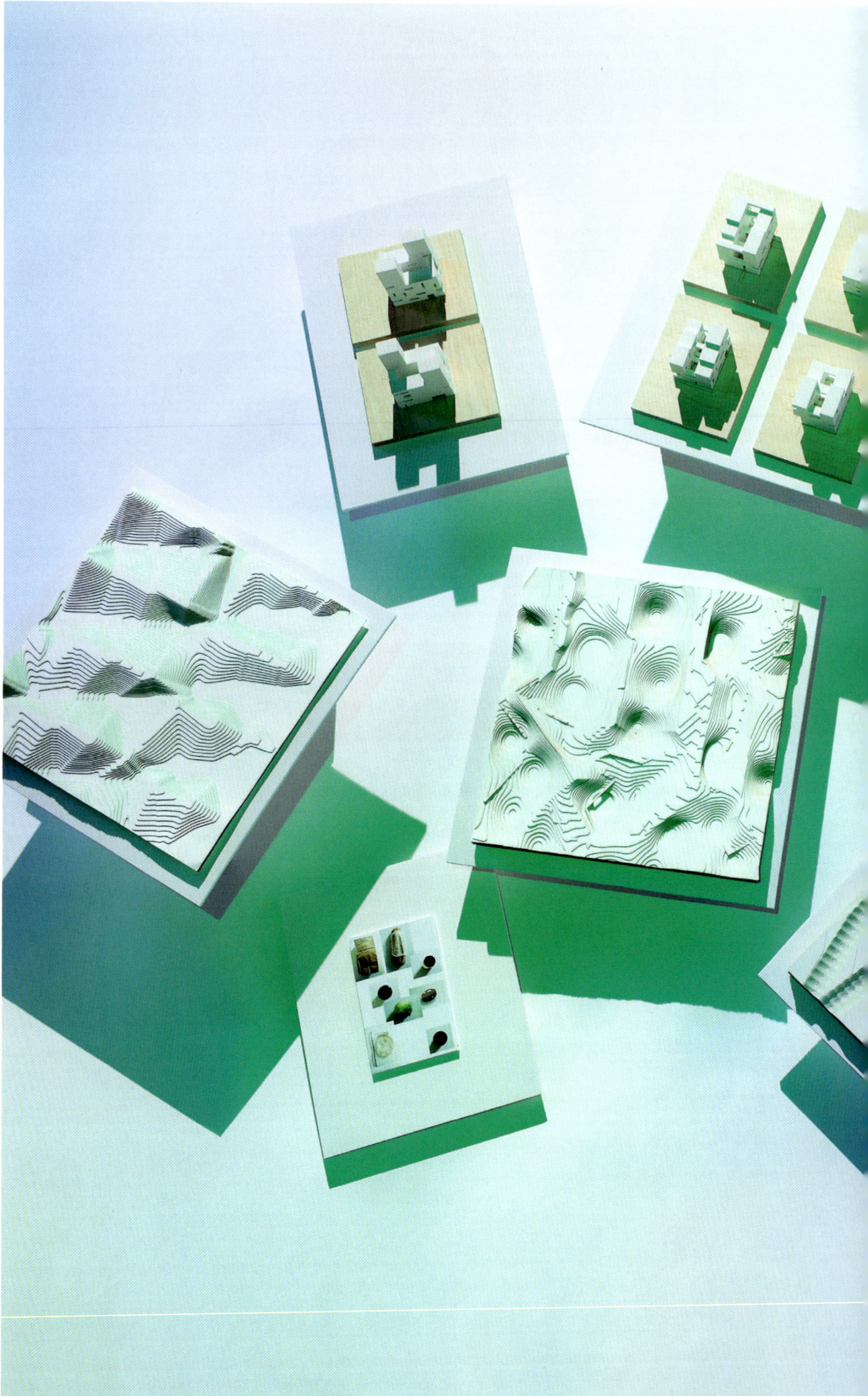

LATHER, RINSE, REPEAT

350

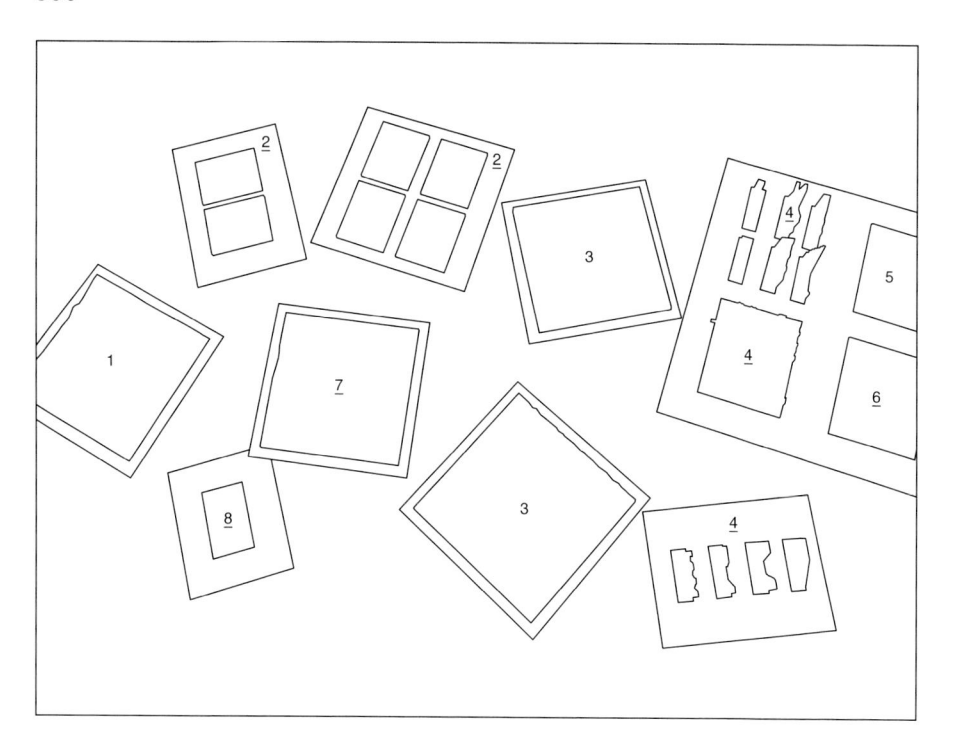

1 Inlet

Robert Hipp
MLA II, 2017
Carlo Urmy
MLA I, 2017
Landscape Core III
Instructor: David Mah

2 57%
p. 352

Kyriaki Kasabalis
MAUD, 2016
Extreme Urbanism IV:
 Looking at Hyper Density—
 Dongri, Mumbai
Instructor: Rahul Mehrotra

3 Switchback

Jonah Susskind, Lu Wang
MLA I, 2017
Landscape Core III
Instructor: Bradley Cantrell

4 5 Piers
p. 354

Difei Chen, Jianwei Shi
MAUD, 2017
Elements of Urban Design
Instructors: Anita Berrizbeitia,
 Carlos Garciavelez Alfaro

5 Plinth

Liang Wang, Lu Zhang
MAUD, 2017
Elements of Urban Design
Instructor: Felipe Correa

6 Manhattan Block
p. 356

Adam Himes, Jessy Yang
MAUD, 2017
Elements of Urban Design
Instructor: Felipe Correa

7 Drainage
p. 358

Yun Shi
MLA I, 2017
Yujia Wang
MLA I AP, 2017
Landscape Core III
Instructor: Chris Reed

8 Chauhaus
p. 360

Andrea Carrillo Iglesias,
 Marielsa Castro, Jolene
 Wen Hui Lee
MDes, 2017
Interdisciplinary Art Practices
Instructor: Silvia Benedito

57%

HOUSING MUMBAI the public, the private and the sacred

Kyriaki Kasabalis
MAUD, 2016

Extreme Urbanism IV: Looking at Hyper Density—Dongri, Mumbai

Instructor
Rahul Mehrotra

As its overarching premise this project contemplates the relationship among the public, the private, and the sacred. It is situated in the heart of Mumbai, where housing that enables different forms of collective living is crucial. Under this framework, the project first engaged in a detailed mapping of existing ecologies as well as schools, health clinics, heritage buildings, and religious institutions in order to create an alternative mapping of the site.

Difei Chen, Jianwei Shi
MAUD, 2017

Elements of Urban Design

Instructors
Anita Berrizbeitia, Carlos Garciavelez Alfaro

This studio introduces critical concepts, strategies, and technical skills associated with current thinking on urbanism, and speculates on the designer's role in analyzing and shaping complex metropolitan systems. This project explores the opportunity for an expanded threshold between New York City's Stuyvesant Town and the East River.

5 Piers

Adam Himes,
Jessy Yang
MAUD, 2017

Elements of Urban Design

Instructor
Felipe Correa

LATHER, RINSE, REPEAT   Core Studio   357

This Urban Design studio focuses on how an expanded notion of housing and domestic space in the city can serve as the backbone of a much more integral urban project. It tests the capacities of the Manhattan block to accommodate greater densities with experimental typologies that can reshape conventions of urban life.

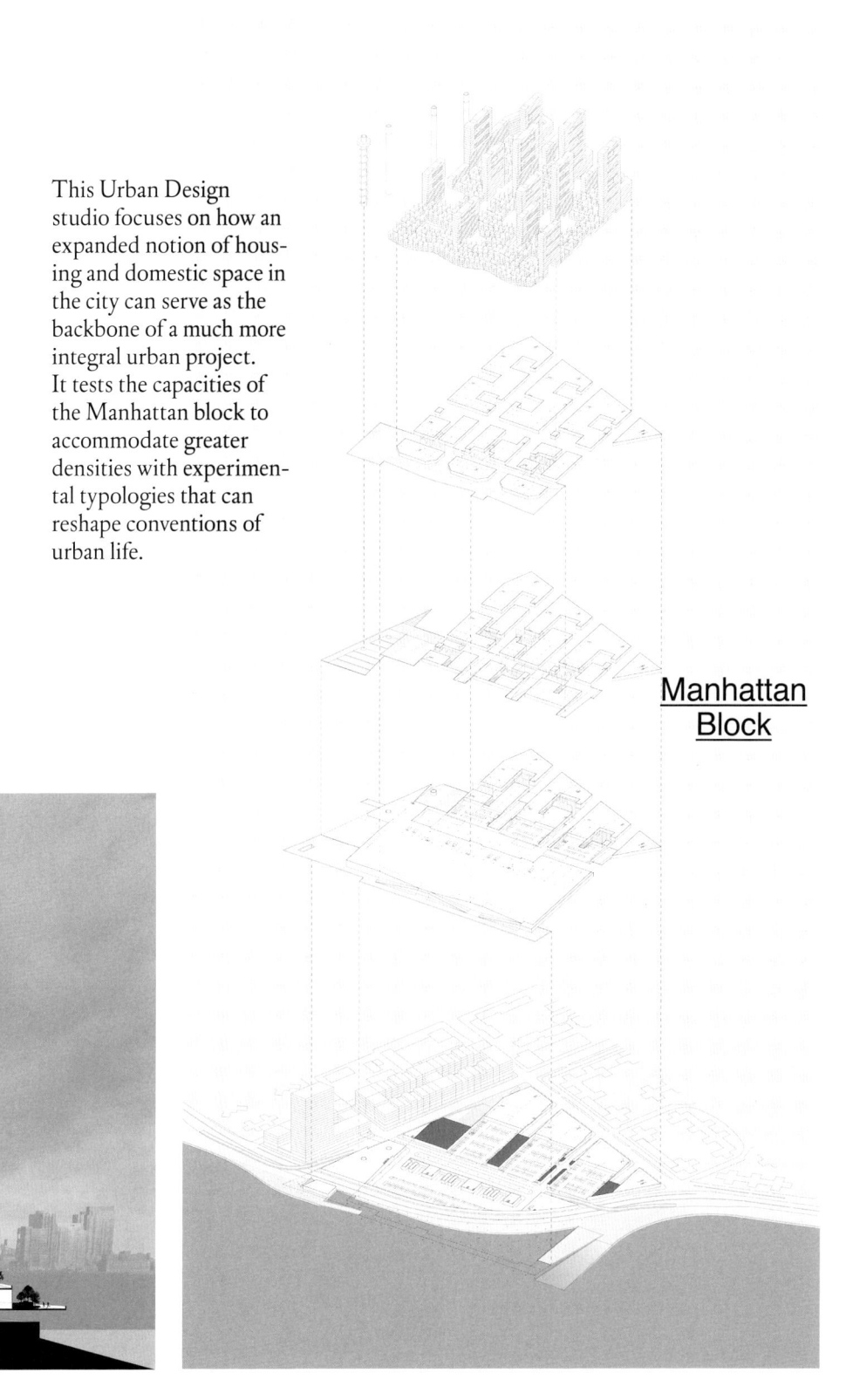

Manhattan
Block

Drainage

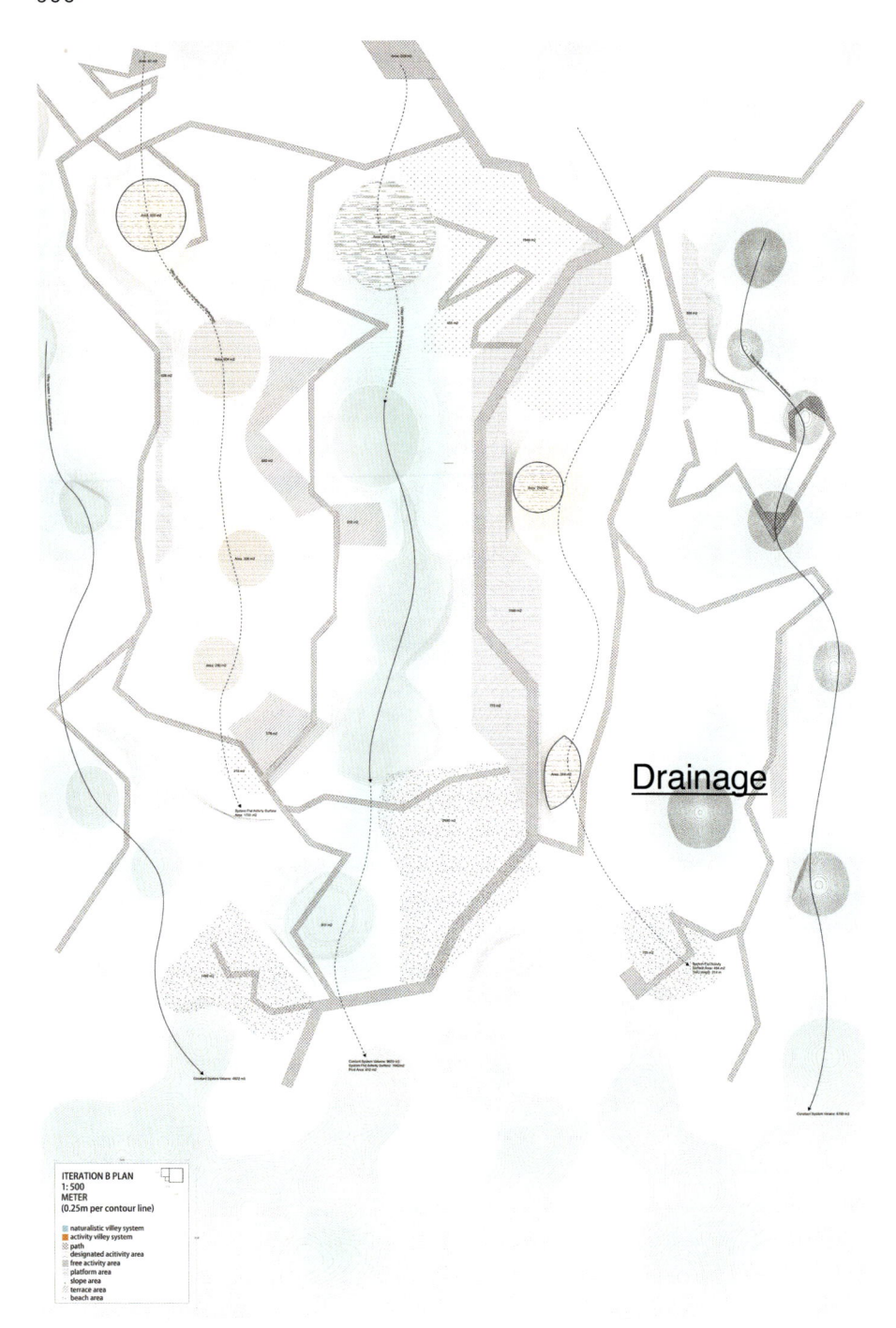

Yun Shi
MLA I, 2017
Yujia Wang
MLA I AP, 2017

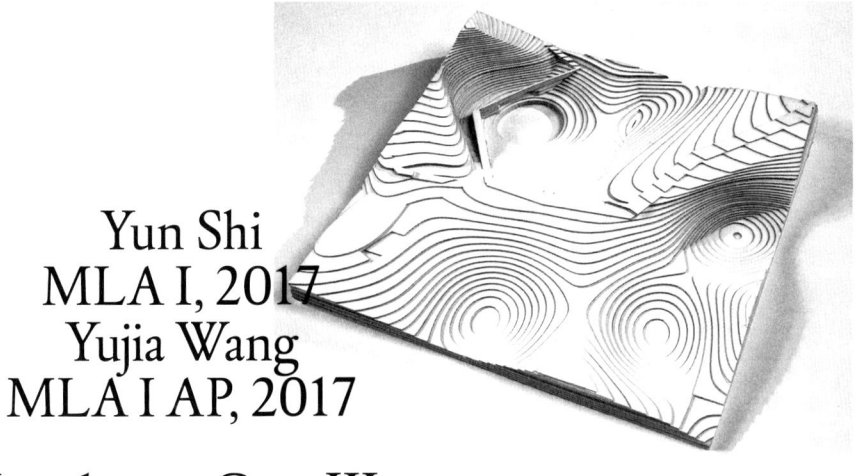

Landscape Core III

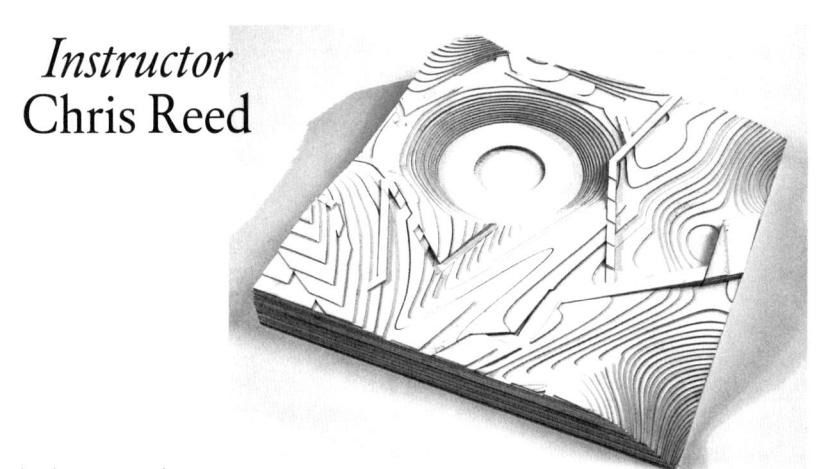

Instructor
Chris Reed

This studio begins with mapping and diagramming larger ecological processes and dynamics on an urban brownfield site, and then focuses on the description of built form, urban infrastructure, and the relationships between the city and its reconstituted riverine setting. Two separate studies from a series of studio workshops are featured here.

time expanded　　　pamphlet #4

1

Reach into the paper bag with one hand, grab onto the baguette with your fist. Place the other hand on the paper bag, holding it securely.
Remove the baguette from the bag one inch at a time until the baguette is free from the paper bag.
Place the paper bag aside.
Gently place the baguette on the surface of the table. With your free hand, grab a knife. Switch hands if necessary so that your dominant hand holds the knife.
Use your other hand to hold on to the baguette securely.
Place the knife about three fingers length away from the edge of the baguette.
Apply pressure in a forward motion, moving the knife back and forth to slice the baguette.
Repeat.
Place the knife about three fingers length away from the edge of the baguette.
Apply pressure in a forward motion, moving the knife back and forth to slice the baguette.
Place the knife down.
You now have two slices of baguette.

2

Place the two slices of baguette next to each other.
Grab the bottle of mayonnaise with your right hand and apply pressure with your palm and thumb.
Squeeze the bottle and apply three streaks of mayonnaise on each slice of baguette.
Place the bottle aside.
Grab a knife with your right hand and a slice of baguette with your left hand.
Press the flat face of the knife against the slice of baguette and mayonnaise and in three swiping motions, spread the mayonnaise evenly on the slice of baguette.
Place the slice of baguette down.
Repeat.
Pick up the other slice of baguette with your left hand.
Press the flat face of the knife against the bread and mayonnaise and in three swiping motions, spread the mayonnaise evenly on the bread.
Place the knife down.
You now have two slices of baguette with mayonnaise sauce.

3

Place the two slices of baguette with mayonnaise sauce next to each other.
Grab a bottle of dijon sauce with your left hand.
Use your right hand to twist open the cap of the bottle.
Place the cap of the bottle aside.
Pick up the knife with your right hand and dip it into the bottle.
Pick up a dollop of sauce the size of your thumb and lift the knife from the bottle.
Place the bottle down and pick up one slice of baguette with your free hand.
Apply the sauce to the surface of the slice of baguette with two swipes of the knife.
Place the slice of baguette down.
Repeat.
Dip the knife into the bottle.
Pick up a dollop of sauce the size of your thumb and lift the knife from the bottle.
Place the bottle down and pick up one slice of baguette with your free hand.
Apply the sauce to the surface of the slice of baguette with two swipes of the knife.
Place the slice of baguette down.
Place the knife down.
You now have two slices of baguette with mayonnaise and dijon sauce.

4

Pick up the head of lettuce wrapped in plastic and remove it from the plastic.
Put aside the plastic.
With your left hand holding the head of lettuce, use your right hand to peel two leaves of lettuce and place them on the table.
Pick up one piece of lettuce and tear it into three pieces.
Place it on the slice of bread to your left.
Repeat.
Pick up one piece of lettuce and tear it into three pieces.
Place it on the slice of bread to your left.
You now have two slices of baguette with mayonnaise and dijon sauce and one slice has six pieces of lettuce on it.

5

Pick up the tomato with your left hand and place it in front of you.
Pick up the knife with your right hand and hold the tomato with your left hand.
Place the knife in the middle of the tomato and apply pressure in a forward motion.
Slice the tomato into half.
Put aside one half of the tomato with your left hand.
Return your left hand to the other piece of tomato, holding it securely.
Place the knife slightly away from the edge and apply pressure in a forward motion.
Slice a thin slice of tomato.
Repeat.
Place the knife slightly away from the edge and apply pressure in a forward motion.
Slice a thin slice of tomato.
Repeat.
Place the knife slightly away from the edge and apply pressure in a forward motion.
Slice a thin slice of tomato.

Place the knife down.
Pick up the three slices of tomatoes with your right hand.
Place the tomatoes on top of the lettuce.
You now have two slices of baguette with mayonnaise and dijon sauce and one slice has six pieces of lettuce and three slices of tomatoes on it.

6

Pick up the packet of ham.
Open up the packet of ham with both hands.
With your left hand holding the packet, use your right hand to remove one slice of ham
Place the ham squarely on top of the slices of tomato.
Place the packet of ham aside.
You now have two slices of baguette with mayonnaise and dijon sauce and one slice has six pieces of lettuce, three slices of tomatoes and one piece of ham on it.

7

Pick up the bottle of pepper with your left hand
Turn the bottle upside down and place it over the slice of baguette with only mayonnaise and dijon sauce.
Grabbing the cap of the bottle with your right hand rotate it left and right quickly three times each.
Remove your right hand from the bottle.
Turn the bottle right side up.
Place the bottle of pepper aside.
You now have two slices of baguette. One slice with mayonnaise, dijon sauce and lightly peppered. One slice with mayonnaise, dijon sauce, six pieces of lettuce, three slices of tomatoes and one piece of ham on it.

8

Pick up the slice of baguette with only the mayonnaise, dijon sauce and pepper with your right hand.
Flip this slice upside down so that the side with sauce faces downwards.
Place this slice ontop the slice with ham, tomato and lettuce.
Apply pressure with your right palm and press gently into the slice of baguette until sandwich is compressed by one-third of an inch.
You now have a sandwich with two slices of baguette, with mayonnaise, dijon sauce, pepper, lettuce, tomatoes and ham.

Pick up the sandwich with both hands, compressing gently with your fingers.
Raise the sandwich to your mouth.
Rotate the sandwich by ninety degrees.
Open your mouth.
Place the sandwich in your mouth.
Take a bite.
You now have a sandwich with two slices of baguette, with mayonnaise, dijon sauce, pepper, lettuce, tomatoes and ham, with one bite removed.

Chauhaus

This seminar leveraged the exploratory nature of art and design work to discover the interdisciplinary modalities of contemporary culture. The text and objects pictured here were taken from an experimental performance in which a simple activity was expanded and extrapolated through three different mediums: action, sound, and text. Extending the activity of making a sandwich into sometimes excruciatingly mundane detail through these mediums amplifies the experience and encourages viewers to reconsider their habits and assumptions.

LATHER, RINSE, REPEAT Seminar 361

Andrea Carrillo
Iglesias,
Marielsa Castro,
Jolene Wen Hui Lee
MDes, 2017

Interdisciplinary Art
Practices

Instructor
Silvia Benedito

Students and faculty often use the steps of Piper Auditorium as a prep space—an area to set up materials before or after the final review—but the editors of *Platform* noticed a landscape architecture studio bold enough to use the steps more formally, as a stage for presentations, during one final review this year. The original placement of a series of vivid, NASA-blue (or are they International Klein Blue?) drawings has been carefully reconstructed here. We added drawings from an architecture studio, and, taken together, these 46 drawings illustrate a wide range of techniques. Bound blueprints, watercolor drawings, mounted renderings—the representation and delivery elevate the typical digital work beyond the screen. Drawings are the support documents that prop up any project. The designers "deserve props" for delivering such compelling materials on the topics of conservation in a rare books library and ecology in public infrastructures.

Drawing Props

364

DRAWING PROPS

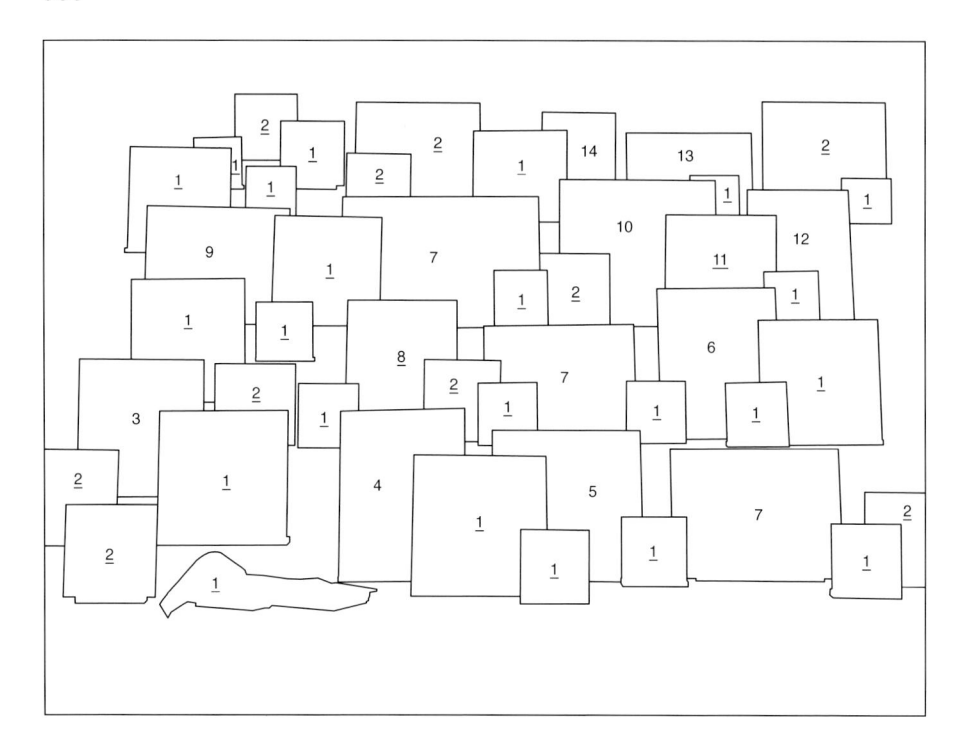

DRAWING PROPS

1 NASA
p. 368

Emily Blair, Timothy Clark, Emma Goode, Rayana Hossain, Qi Xuan Li, Kira Sargent, Carlo Urmy, Yuan Xue
MLA I, 2017
Mengqing Chen, Yuqing Nie, Soo Ran Shin, Andrew Younker
MLA I AP, 2017
Landscape Core IV
Instructor: Pierre Bélanger

2 Arctic
p. 370

Lanisha Blount, Tiffany Dang, Jeremy Hartley, Rebecca Liggins, Keith Scott, James Watters
MLA I, 2017
Yijia Chen, Yifei Li, Andrea Soto Morfin, Wenyi Pan, Dandi Zhang
MLA I AP, 2017
Xi Zhang
MArch II / MLA I AP, 2018
Landscape Core IV
Instructor: Nicholas Pevzner

3 Floor Plan

Mahfuz Sultan
MArch I, 2019
Architecture Core II: Situate
Instructor: Jennifer Bonner

4 Big Footings

Radu-Remus Macovei
MArch I, 2019
Architecture Core II: Situate
Instructor: Grace La

5 Chair Club

Daniel Kwon
MArch I, 2019
Architecture Core II: Situate
Instructor: Jennifer Bonner

6 Meditation

Khoa Vu
MArch I, 2019
Architecture Core II: Situate
Instructor: Jeffry Burchard

7 Bay Village

Ahmad Altahhan
MArch I, 2019
Architecture Core II: Situate
Instructor: Max Kuo

8 Copy, Paste
p. 372

Kai-hong Chu
MArch I, 2019
Architecture Core II: Situate
Instructor: Grace La

9 Overlap

Emily Ashby
MArch I, 2019
Architecture Core II: Situate
Instructor: Jeffry Burchard

10 Rhizome

Julia Roberts
MArch I, 2019
Architecture Core II: Situate
Instructor: Grace La

11 Section A
p. 374

Lindsey Krug
MArch I, 2019
Architecture Core II: Situate
Instructor: Tomás dePaor

12 Membership

Paris Nelson
MArch I, 2019
Architecture Core II: Situate
Instructor: Grace La

13 Hoarding

Martin Fernandez
MArch I, 2019
Architecture Core II: Situate
Instructor: Tomás dePaor

14 Fight Club

Khorshid Naderi-Azad
MArch I, 2019
Architecture Core II: Situate
Instructor: Max Kuo

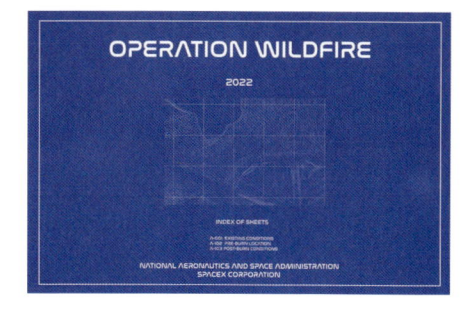

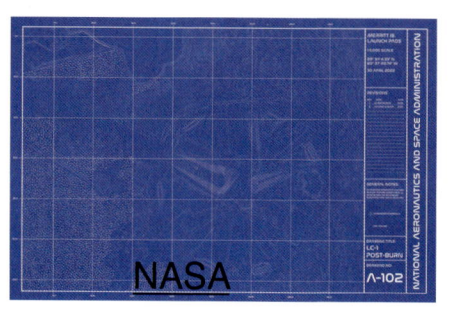

Emily Blair,
Timothy Clark,
Emma Goode,
Rayana Hossain,
Qi Xuan Li,
Kira Sargent,
Carlo Urmy,
Yuan Xue
MLA I, 2017

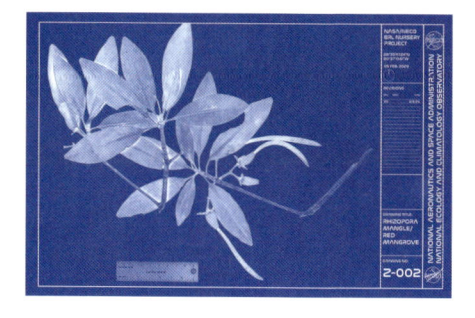

Mengqing Chen,
Yuqing Nie,
Soo Ran Shin,
Andrew Younker
MLA I AP, 2017

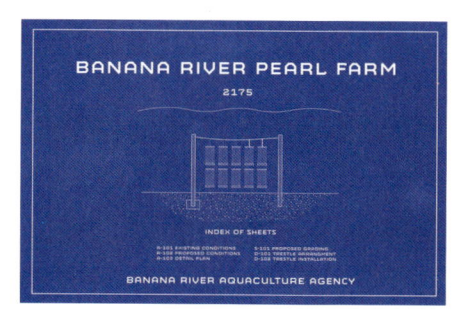

Landscape Core IV

Instructor
Pierre Bélanger

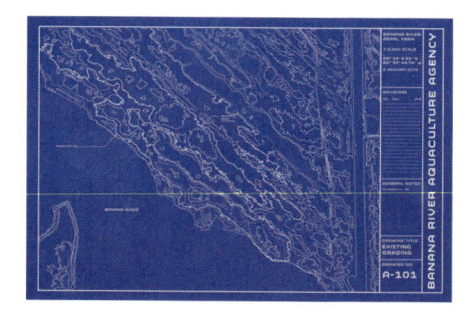

DRAWING PROPS   Core Studio   369

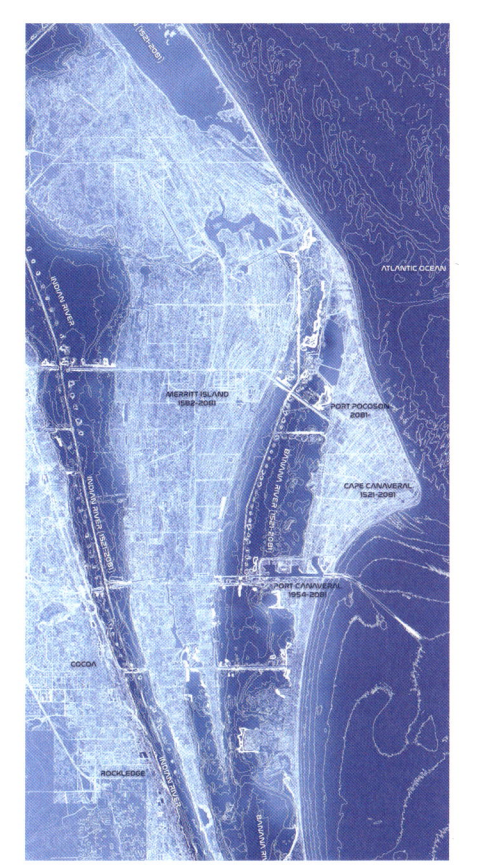

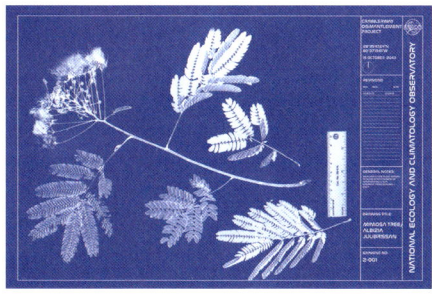

Employing the agency of regional ecology and landscape infrastructure as the dominant drivers of design, this studio involves the development of biodynamic and biophysical systems that provide flexible yet directive patterns for future urbanization. The large-scale project pictured here combines NASA-style blueprints with contemporary mapping methods.

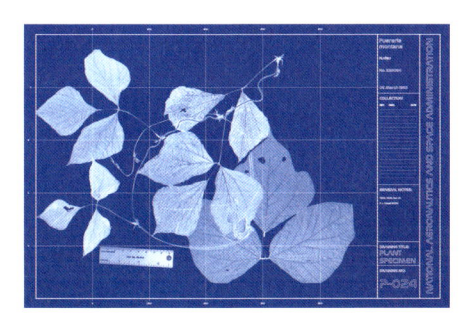

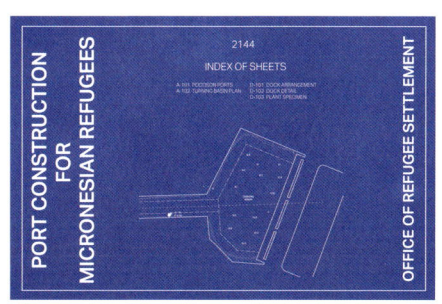

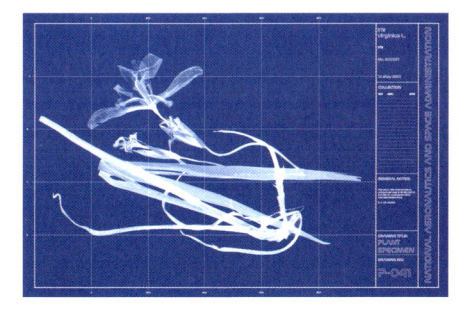

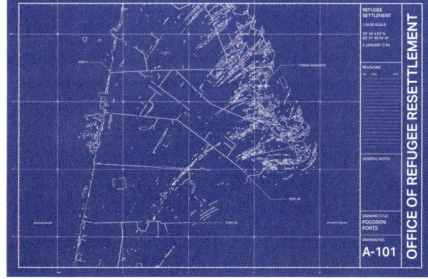

Arctic

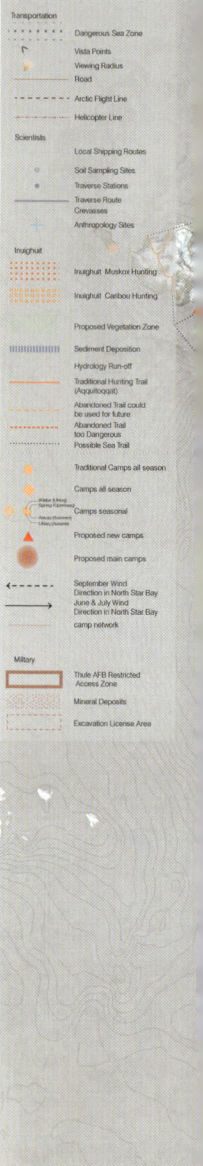

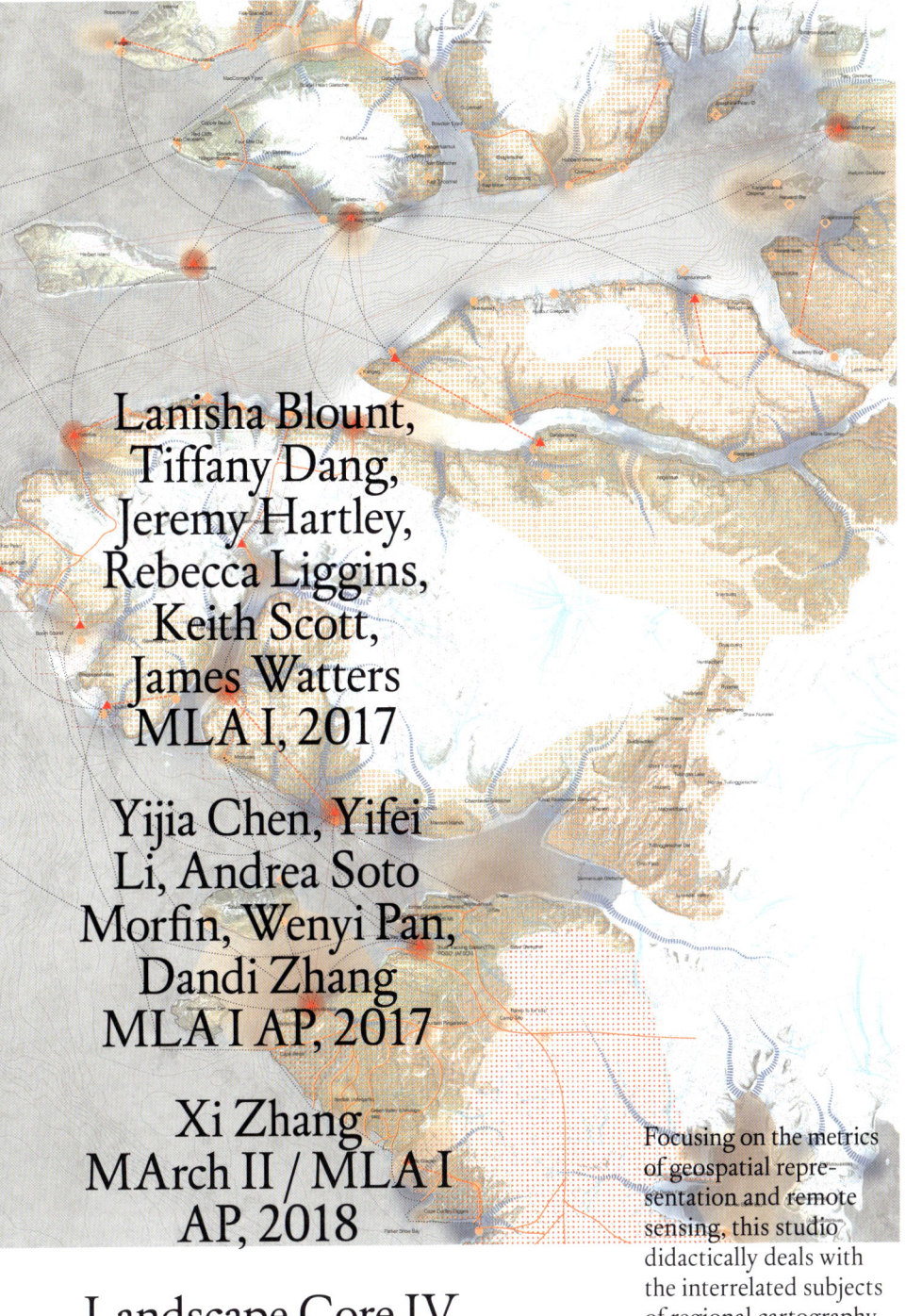

Lanisha Blount,
Tiffany Dang,
Jeremy Hartley,
Rebecca Liggins,
Keith Scott,
James Watters
MLA I, 2017

Yijia Chen, Yifei
Li, Andrea Soto
Morfin, Wenyi Pan,
Dandi Zhang
MLA I AP, 2017

Xi Zhang
MArch II / MLA I
AP, 2018

Landscape Core IV

Instructor
Nicholas Pevzner

Focusing on the metrics of geospatial representation and remote sensing, this studio didactically deals with the interrelated subjects of regional cartography and site topography as operative and telescopic instruments of design across scales.

Copy, Paste

Kai-hong Chu
MArch I, 2019

Architecture Core II: Situate

Instructor
Grace La

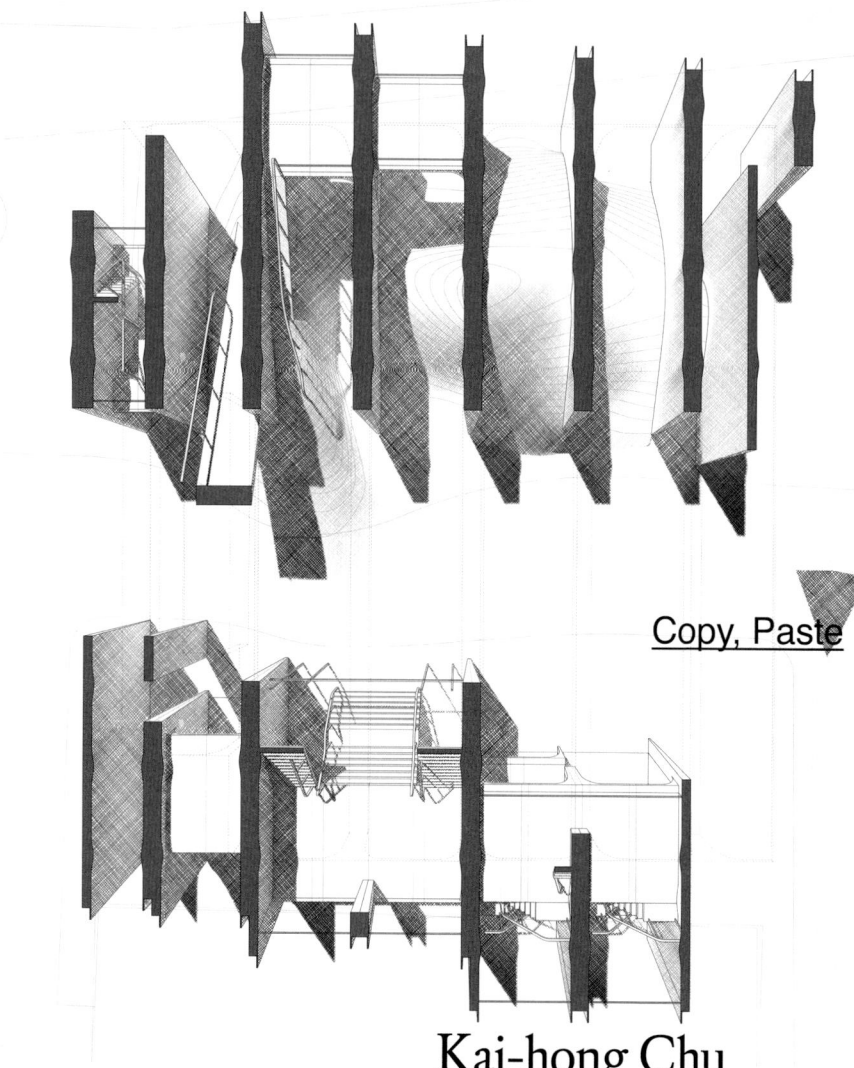

The overarching pedagogical agenda for second-semester Architecture Core is to expand upon the design methodologies developed in the first semester, furthering understanding of the interwoven relationships among form, space, structure, and materiality. This project explores the proliferation of a simple manipulation of an indented arched member in order to create a new organization for a club program.

DRAWING PROPS Core Studio 373

Lindsey Krug
MArch I, 2019

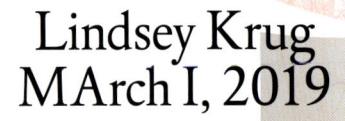

Architecture Core II: Situate

Instructor
Tomás dePaor

This studio, the second in the Architecture Core sequence, expands upon the design methodologies of form, space, structure, and materiality to include the fundamental parameters of site and program, which are considered foundational to the discipline of architecture. Sited in Boston's Back Bay Fens, a proposal for a rare books library engages the ground.

Section A

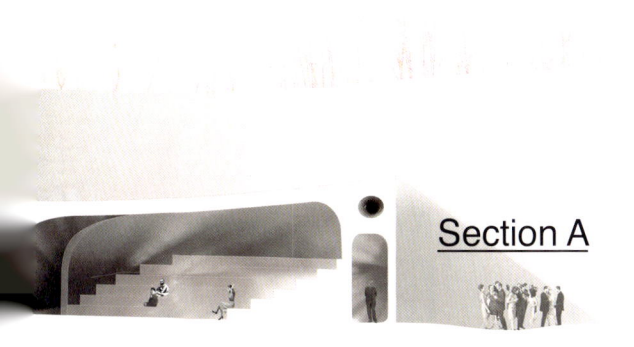

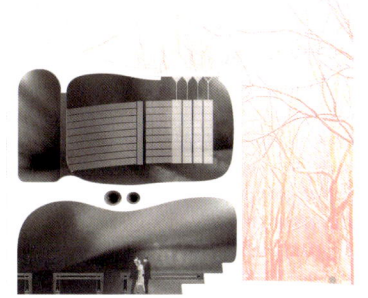

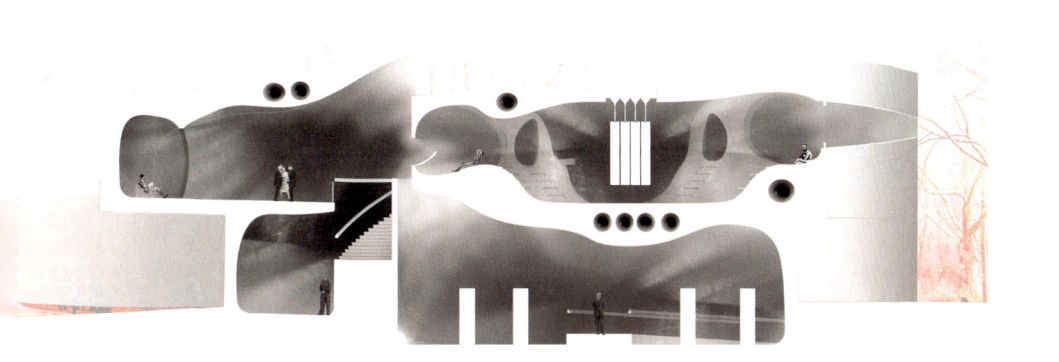

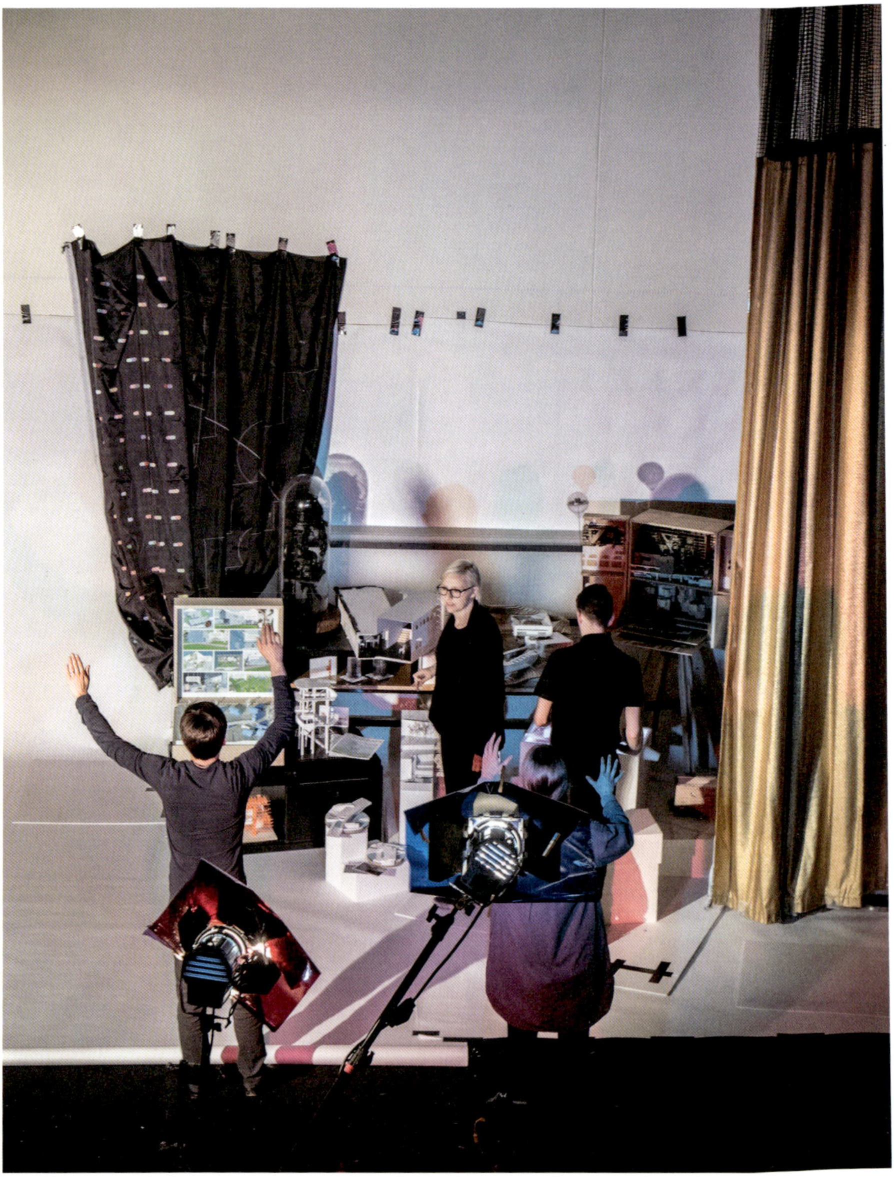